The Ten Commandments

INTERPRETATION
Resources for the Use of Scripture in the Church

INTERPRETATION

RESOURCES FOR THE USE OF SCRIPTURE IN THE CHURCH

PATRICK D. MILLER

The Ten Commandments

INTERPRETATION *Resources for the Use of Scripture in the Church*

WESTMINSTER
JOHN KNOX PRESS
LOUISVILLE · KENTUCKY

First edition
Westminster John Knox Press
Louisville, Kentucky

09 10 11 12 13 14 15 16 17 18—10 9 8 7 6 5 4 3 2 1

Book design by Drew Stevens
Cover design by designpointinc.com

Library of Congress Cataloging-in-Publication Data

Miller, Patrick D.
 The Ten commandments / Patrick D. Miller.
   p. cm.—(Interpretation)
 Includes bibliographical references and indexes.
 ISBN 978-0-664-23055-5 (alk. paper)
 1. Ten commandments—Criticism, interpretation, etc. I. Title.
 BS1285.52.M55 2009
 222'.16077—dc22

                                         2009001918

PRINTED IN THE UNITED STATES OF AMERICA

♾ The paper used in this publication meets the minimum requirements of the American National Standard for Information Sciences—Permanence of Paper for Printed Library Materials, ANSI Z39.48-1992.

Westminster John Knox Press advocates the responsible use of our natural resources. The text paper of this book is made from at least 30% postconsumer waste.

CONTENTS

SERIES FOREWORD

This series of volumes supplements Interpretation: A Bible Commentary for Teaching and Preaching. The commentary series offers an exposition of the books of the Bible written for those who teach, preach, and study the Bible in the community of faith. This new series is addressed to the same audience and serves a similar purpose, providing additional resources for the interpretation of Scripture, but now dealing with features, themes, and issues significant for the whole rather than with individual books.

The Bible is composed of separate books. Its composition naturally has led its interpreters to address particular books. But there are other ways to approach the interpretation of the Bible that respond to other characteristics and features of the Scriptures. These other entries to the task of interpretation provide contexts, overviews, and perspectives that complement the book-by-book approach and discern dimensions of the Scriptures that the commentary design may not adequately explore.

The Bible as used in the Christian community is not only a collection of books but also itself a book that has a unity and coherence important to its meaning. Some volumes in this new series will deal with this canonical wholeness and seek to provide a wider context for the interpretation of individual books as well as a comprehensive theological perspective that reading single books does not provide.

Other volumes in the series will examine particular texts, like the Ten Commandments, the Lord's Prayer, and the Sermon on the Mount, texts that have played such an important role in the faith and life of the Christian community that they constitute orienting foci for the understanding and use of Scripture.

A further concern of the series will be to consider important and often difficult topics, addressed at many different places in the books of the canon, that are of recurrent interest and concern to the church in its dependence on Scripture for faith and life. So the series will include volumes dealing with such topics as eschatology, women, wealth, and violence.

The books of the Bible are constituted from a variety of kinds of literature such as narrative, laws, hymns and prayers, letters, parables, miracle stories, and the like. To recognize and discern the contribution and importance of all these different kinds of material enriches and enlightens the use of Scripture. Volumes in the series will provide help in the interpretation of Scripture's literary forms and genres.

The liturgy and practices of the gathered church are anchored in Scripture, as with the sacraments observed and the creeds recited. So another entry to the task of discerning the meaning and significance of biblical texts explored in this series is the relation between the liturgy of the church and the Scriptures.

Finally, there is certain ancient literature, such as the Apocrypha and the noncanonical gospels, that constitutes an important context to the interpretation of Scripture itself. Consequently, this series will provide volumes that offer guidance in understanding such writings and explore their significance for the interpretation of the Protestant canon.

The volumes in this second series of Interpretation deal with these important entries into the interpretation of the Bible. Together with the commentaries, they compose a library of resources for those who interpret Scripture as members of the community of faith. Each of them can be used independently for its own significant addition to the resources for the study of Scripture. But all of them intersect the commentaries in various ways and provide an important context for their use. The authors of these volumes are biblical scholars and theologians who are committed to the service of interpreting the Scriptures in and for the church. The editors and authors hope that the addition of this series to the commentaries will provide a major contribution to the vitality and richness of biblical interpretation in the church.

The Editors

PREFACE

For a number of years I taught a seminary course on Old Testament ethics. My regular routine was to begin with some general attention to the place and character of the law, followed by two weeks or so on the Ten Commandments before going on to look at various ethical and moral issues as they arise and are addressed in the Old Testament, topics such as the administration of justice, land and property, war and violence, man and woman, and marriage and family. After teaching the course several times, I realized that I had gradually shifted its plan and character. What had been a couple of weeks on the Commandments had gradually come to consume about two-thirds of the course. Originally discrete subjects of discussion had slowly been drawn into the treatment of the Commandments. The Commandments began to take over the course, largely because they seemed again and again to lead into the moral issues or concerns that I had formerly treated as separate topics. That discovery provoked me to begin asking to what extent the Commandments do indeed serve as a comprehensive framework and ground for the ethics of the Old Testament or indeed of the Bible as a whole. The process had two results. One was a shift to teaching my subject as a course on the Ten Commandments together with my colleague in ethics, Nancy Duff. The other result is the book that follows here.

The above sequence of events should not mislead the reader. What is before you is not a treatment of Old Testament ethics. It is rather an exposition of the Commandments in depth, seeking to give not only a reading of each commandment in its context but also to lay out the trajectory of its movement and place in Scripture. In the process, the interplay and resonance of the Commandments with many other texts is uncovered, and the outcome is a thick description of the Commandments resulting in various theological and moral issues coming to the fore and receiving some illumination. The treatment takes seriously the long-standing high status of the Commandments and seeks to show how various aspects of the presentation of the Commandments attest to their centrality and importance.

I hope that this reading of the Commandments can be of use to persons in several ways:

1. One may approach the text to get at the Decalogue *as a whole* and work through each one of the commandments as they are presented here, or one may choose to focus on a single commandment and the moral or theological issues that unfold from it. It is hoped that along with surveying the Commandments comprehensively via this presentation, readers will also want to turn to it when treating *particular commandments* or *topics* on their own, such as marriage and divorce, lying, theft, idolatry, and the like. The chapters share a common approach to the Commandments, but each is a discrete treatment of the subject of the commandment even as there are frequent references to other commandments in the discussion.

2. For each commandment, there is an effort to get at the *fundamental meaning* of the commandment, what it is about in its basic form. In most cases, that is an explicit part of the chapter on the commandment, as in the interpretation of the commandments about the name, the Sabbath, and killing. In some instances, discussion of the basic or essential meaning is part of the broader treatment of the commandment, as in the discussion of honoring parents. If one chooses, one may therefore confine oneself to a close look at the meaning of the commandment, to gather a basic sense of what it is after, without then pursuing its development, illustration, and elaboration in the rest of Scripture, a part of what each chapter also tries to accomplish.

3. Where it is important for either the interpretation of the whole or of a particular commandment, some attention is given to the *context* of the commandment: where it is in the Decalogue and how it is related to other commandments.

4. One of the main features of this book is the effort to move beyond the places where the Commandments are set forth, Exodus 20 and Deuteronomy 5, to explore their *resonances and reflections in the rest of Scripture:* more particularly, how each commandment is picked up in other contexts, for example, how it is illustrated in the legal texts or spelled out in relation to particular cases; what stories of the Bible reflect the teaching of the commandment; where and how it becomes a part of the prophetic teaching, the Psalms, and other parts of Scripture. The Commandments are not simply a text that is given once and for all. They have ongoing implications, and they are reflected in many texts. So in teaching about the Commandments, one will have resources available that illustrate the force or particularity of each commandment and stories that

vividly portray the impact of the Commandments. The legal texts especially, but also the stories in which the Commandments come to play, help uncover the appropriate complexity and fullness of the Commandments. For example, as one delves into some of the texts of Numbers and Deuteronomy, one begins to see ways the command "You shall not kill" (RSV) has to do with manslaughter, murder, execution, and war. The legal texts of Exodus, Leviticus, and Numbers spell out in some detail how it is that the property of a neighbor is to be guarded from theft and the positive and prohibitive dimensions of not stealing. Stories and prophetic texts uncover the negative outcomes of coveting what belongs to another. The story of Ruth may be read as a kind of commentary on how one honors father and mother. And on turning to the legal texts, one discovers that commandment has to do with the way persons are to respond to and treat authority figures in general, not only parents.

5. For each commandment, there is some discussion of the way it comes to play in *the New Testament*. Where there are explicit quotations of the Commandments, that is obvious, but I have sought to go beyond those to see how the subject matter of particular commandments is reflected in and dealt with in the New Testament as well as the Old.

6. In the introduction to this volume, I note the way in which use of the *lectionary* to determine preaching texts has tended to reduce the once-common practice of preaching series of sermons on topics such as the Ten Commandments. That does not mean, however, that the Commandments cannot come into our preaching in other ways. In the pages that follow, many texts of Scripture are taken up because they deal with one or more of the Commandments in some fashion. That means one may come at the subject matter of a commandment from texts other than just the Decalogue texts themselves. I hope that as preachers take up their lectionary texts, they may turn to the textual index of this volume to see if, where, and how the Commandments belong to the interpretation and proclamation of the lectionary text.

7. While the *main goal* of the book is to probe deeply into the meaning and complexity of the Commandments and the way they are developed, elaborated, and specified in the whole of Scripture, I have included an appendix that seeks to look more systematically at the ethics of the Commandments. For further attempts in that direction, the reader may consult the following essays by the author

listed in the bibliography: "The Good Neighborhood: Identity and Community through the Commandments," and "'That It May Go Well with You': The Commandments and the Common Good."

My work on the Commandments has benefited from many conversations with colleagues at Princeton Theological Seminary and the Center of Theological Inquiry as well as from those who have listened to lectures and been willing to engage me in thinking about this significant text and what it means for faith and life. I will mention three persons in particular whose assistance has been invaluable. Nancy Duff taught me as well as our students as we shared a course on the Commandments over several years. Ellen Davis of Duke Divinity School did substantive editing of the manuscript to improve its quality and its communication. Finally, my wife, Mary Ann, has not only supported me through the many years of working on this topic; she has also talked with me about the issues of the book and carefully edited the whole manuscript.

ABBREVIATIONS
FOR SCRIPTURE VERSIONS

E	English versions
Heb.	Hebrew Scripture
NJPS	New Jewish Publication Society version, Tanakh
NRSV	New Revised Standard Version
RSV	Revised Standard Version

Introduction

The Significance of the Commandments

There are few biblical texts that have played as large a role in church and public life as the Ten Commandments. From their setting in Scripture to the contemporary debate about their public display, the Commandments have seemed to embody God's will for human life as fully as any particular body of teaching or Scripture. Martin Luther famously said: "This much is certain: those who know the Ten Commandments perfectly know the entire Scriptures and in all affairs and circumstances are able to counsel, help, comfort, judge, and make decisions in both spiritual and temporal matters" (Large Catechism, in Kolb and Wengert, *Book of Concord*, 382). The Commandments—also known as the Decalogue ("the Ten Words"; see discussion of the Prologue, below)—probably rank with the Twenty-third Psalm and the Lord's Prayer as the best-known and most memorized texts from the Bible.

From early in the church's history, the Commandments have had a place in the confessions of the church and its catechetical processes. The catechetical tradition seems to have begun with Augustine but continued and grew through the centuries. The Commandments have been taught in many if not most of the catechisms of the Catholic Church as well as in the Lutheran and Reformed catechisms and those of other denominations. Focus on the Commandments, however, has not been confined to strictly catechetical genres. Thomas Aquinas, Martin Luther, and John Calvin, for examples, all recognized the significance of the Decalogue and took it up in various contexts such as the *Summa theologiae* (Thomas), *Treatise on Good Works* (Luther), and the *Institutes of the Christian Religion* (Calvin) as well as in commentaries and sermons.

The Commandments have had their play as well in larger contexts. From the church fathers onward, they have been associated with or seen as a kind of natural law. Among the Reformers, both Calvin and Luther perceived the Decalogue as having "summarized and sharpened natural law for special purposes" (Dowey, "Law in Luther and Calvin," 149). Central to those purposes are both the accusation of the conscience—the theological use of the law—and the provision of a civil order by restraining transgressions—the civil use of the law. For both Luther and Calvin, the Decalogue especially shows the law moving beyond these functions and serving as a kind of universal, eternal law to provide instruction for the life of faith, though for Luther it was important that such instruction be understood as doctrine and not law (Miller, "Commandments in Reformed Perspective").

The equation of the Commandments with some kind of natural law or moral law available to humankind, even if perceived as part of the divine law, has led to a focus on them beyond their function within the community of faith, whether Jewish or Christian. They thus have been seen as instructive in ways that have influenced the civil and political order. So Alfred the Great prefaced his code of Saxon law with the Ten Commandments, and Thomas Hobbes found in the Decalogue grounding for his understanding of sovereignty. It is widely recognized that the Commandments have had "a significant impact on the development of the secular legal codes of the Western World" (Carter, *Culture of Disbelief*, 208). The specific impact of the Decalogue on American constitutionalism is a subject of debate (Green, "Fount of Everything Just and Right?"), but it is clear that it has had and continues to have a formative and normative role in much discussion of judicial and political matters in the United States.

In contemporary American life, the Commandments have become a kind of cultural code, as evidenced by the wide interest in their public display in public settings. As such, they have become a symbol and an icon as much as a text for learning, interpretation, and moral and religious guidance. The Commandments have long been on display, but that has characteristically been on the walls and windows of churches, as was required, for example, by the Anglican Canons of 1604. The movement of the Commandments into the more public sphere and into judicial and political contexts comes at a time when there appears to be less focus and emphasis on them in church life, as reflected in the decline of catechetical instruction on the one hand and the dominance of preaching by the lectionary on the other. The large place the Commandments have in the tradition, however, joins with the broader public discussion to provide an opportunity for more careful attention to the Commandments and their meaning and significance for our life with God and with each other.

That attention should start with the recognition that, whatever the ebb and flow of interest in the Commandments, the heavy focus on them in the history of Christianity is not misplaced. The way they are communicated in Scripture tells us that these Commandments matter very much and are the basic guidelines for our life. Among the scriptural indicators of their weight and importance are the following:

- Unlike any other body of instruction in the Old Testament, the Ten Commandments are given *twice*, once in the narrative of the events at Sinai (Exod. 20) and again when Moses recalls those events as the people prepare to go into the land (Deut. 5).
- The Commandments are given by the Lord *directly* to the people ("face to face," Deut. 5:4), and this is the only time such direct speech to the whole people takes place. The rest of the statutes and ordinances are given to Moses to be taught to the people, differentiating them from the Commandments.
- They are the *first* piece of legal material and *separated* from the statutes and ordinances that follow in the rest of Exodus and Deuteronomy as well as in Leviticus and Numbers. Those statutes and ordinances function as interpretative specification of the Commandments (see below).
- The Commandments are written by the *finger of God* on *stone*, to make clear their source and endurance (Exod. 31:18; Deut. 4:13; 5:22; 9:10).
- They are placed in the ark of the covenant, the Lord's dwelling place in the midst of the people (Deut. 10:5), while the other legislation/instruction is written on a scroll and put beside the ark not in it (Deut. 31:24–26).

3

All these features of the Commandments and their place in the biblical story suggest that here indeed is something of primary importance. Repetition, placement, highlighting, divine authorship—all serve to tell the community of faith that here is the foundational word for your life as God's people. All you need to know is given to you in these Ten Words. They may be summed up succinctly (as in the Great Commandment) and elaborated in great detail (as in the legal codes; see below), but they are a sufficient guide for one's life with God and neighbor.

How to Think about the Commandments

Since the Ten Commandments have such a central role in the teaching of Scripture and the church as well as in the public sphere, they merit serious attention. In the pages that follow, several assumptions guide the treatment of the Commandments presented therein:

1. *There is a continuing tension between the universality and the particularity of the Commandments* and their simplicity and complexity. There are clearly ways in which they require modes of conduct or prohibit certain actions that are universally required or prohibited. Some of the Commandments, especially the second table—the Commandments dealing with the neighbor—are present in various ancient Near Eastern legal codes and widely assumed as normative in all societies. The fact that this is largely true of the second table, however, is indicative of the particularity of the Commandments, manifest especially in the first table, dealing with the relationship between Israel and its God. "The Commandments depend from the start on a particular story and communal memory of that story as the ground for obedience" (Miller, "Is There a Place for the Ten Commandments?" 1). One of the oft-neglected but implicit assumptions of the Decalogue is that it is a whole and one cannot take part of it without the whole. Especially one cannot claim authority for the second table apart from the first.

The tension between the simplicity and complexity of the Commandments is just as important. The Commandments' simplicity—ten short rules—is one of the primary characteristics that have nourished their learning and keeping. They are easily learned and remembered and kept in mind. Indeed, the rubric "Ten Commandments" has come to apply to almost any set of simple rules for

4

subjects from business to golf. Nothing should diminish that aspect of the Commandments. At the same time, what is often missed is that these simple rules affect all sorts of circumstances in human life. An account of that complexity is necessary for proper attention to them in our lives. The presence of much longer and quite particular legal statutes following the Commandments and clearly having to do with matters handled briefly in the Commandments makes that clear. The catechisms that take up the Commandments regularly have the students learn not only the commandment but also what it means.

2. *The Commandments, therefore, need to be interpreted.* The story itself makes that clear as Moses is sent to get the rest of the teaching from the Lord (Exod. 20:18–20; Deut. 5:22–33). The issue is not the obscurity of the Commandments but their breadth and the need to fill out the particulars of what all this way of acting means. What follows the Commandments in Scripture is an extended process of interpreting the Commandments, often in an explicit way as they are related to other statutes and ordinances in the legal texts of the Torah or Pentateuch. Frequently there are obvious connections between the subject matter of particular statutes and a commandment, as for example, in the statutes of Exodus 22:1–15, which deal at some points specifically with stealing but throughout with issues of property and its endangerment (see chap. 7, below). The connections between the Decalogue in Deuteronomy and the statutes of the Deuteronomic Code in Deuteronomy 12–26 are especially close. As Stephen Kaufman has put it, the statutes and ordinances of the Code are brought together "in a highly structured composition whose major topical units are arranged according to the laws of the Decalogue" ("Structure," 108–9). The very specific and varied legal cases and statutes of the Code are thus in sequence according to the Commandments of Deuteronomy 5. They are not the same as the statutes in the Book of the Covenant (Exod. 20:22–23:33) because they represent different times and circumstances, yet the Commandments, which are essentially the same in both Exodus and Deuteronomy, provide a perduring and essentially unchanging foundation of basic principles.

This understanding of the relation of the statutes and ordinances to the Ten Commandments has been recognized from earliest times. One can see it in the Jewish tradition in Philo of Alexandria, who claimed that the "Decalogue encompasses the whole of the Torah, for all of the [laws] simply elaborate in detail what the Ten Commandments say in compressed form" (Amir, "Decalogue according to Philo," 126). In the Christian tradition, Aquinas argued that "all the precepts of the Law are so many parts of those of the decalogue" (*Summa theologiae*, vol. 29). Martin Luther began each chapter of his Deuteronomy commentary by identifying which commandment that chapter develops, and Calvin developed most of his *Harmony of the Pentateuch* largely around the Commandments.

3. *The Commandments are thus the starting point of a rich trajectory of meaning and effects, principles and actions, that tell the community of faith how to live its life in relation to God and neighbor.* To comprehend and act upon the instruction of the Commandments fully involves a look at the trajectory they create. It begins with the Commandments and continues through Scripture and the church's teaching and history on down to the present. This is in marked contrast to what is often a misunderstanding of the simplicity of the Commandments, reflected, for example, in a comment in an issue of *Newsweek*: "The Ten Commandments are generally cut and dried, but—let's face it—other religious rules and customs can be hard to grasp" (Sheahen, "Beliefwatch Thou Shalt"). A more accurate picture of the way the Commandments function is as follows:

> Rather than being rigid, fixed, archaic, and obvious, the Commandments open up a moral and theological arc or movement that began long ago and is still going on. They are dynamic, open in meaning and effect, and uncovering many dimensions subtle and obvious of the moral life for the community that lives in covenant with the Lord of Israel who is known to us in Jesus Christ. . . . The result of perceiving, tracing, and appropriating such a trajectory or arc of moral understanding flowing out of the Commandments is, in effect, a "thick description" of the morality or ethics of the Commandments. (Miller, "Metaphors for the Moral," 39)

One can compare the relation between the Commandments and the various statutes and ordinances that follow them in the books of the Torah or Pentateuch with the relation of the United States Constitution to the extensive cases or case laws that have developed out of the Constitution in seeking to work out its implications in particular situations. The Commandments serve as a kind of constitution for the covenanted community; they stand in relation to all further direction for life, more specific and contextual, in the Mosaic teaching, roughly as the Constitution stands in relation to the later legal and judicial issues and cases that have come up in the history of this nation. Here story is also important, for many persons know and hold to the Constitution as much because of their knowledge of the story of its creation and preservation as for their knowledge of the details of the Constitution itself.

In this book, the focus is on the way in which the whole of Scripture—New Testament as well as Old—opens up the meaning of the Commandments and informs us how to live and act—and think—in the light of them. Particular attention is given to the legal codes that are presented as a continuation of the teaching of the Commandments, yet prophets, sages, and psalmists come into view as well. Not least of all, one must listen to the stories of Scripture as they tell about the meaning of the Commandments in the life of the people of God. Specific cases and illustrative stories help us understand what the Commandments mean, how they work out in specific concrete situations, what actions are involved or excluded, what effects come from obedience or disobedience.

4. *All the Commandments, either explicitly or implicitly, have both a positive and a negative meaning.* They tell us what we are not to do and what we are to do. Though the Commandments are largely prohibitive in form, it is important that two of the Commandments—Sabbath observance and honoring parents—are in positive form. In the case of the Sabbath Commandment, we have it in both positive form—"Remember the sabbath day, and keep it holy"—and negative—"You shall not do any work." Calvin has argued that this assumption is one of the critical interpretive principles in understanding the Commandments. In his view "a sober interpretation goes beyond the words," and the best rule is "attention . . . is directed to the reason of the commandment" (*Institutes* 2.8.8). This means an interpretive process is necessary for finding out the fullness of the Commandment.

> Thus in each commandment we must investigate what it is concerned with; then we must seek out its purpose, until we find what the Lawgiver testifies there to be pleasing or displeasing to himself. Finally, from this same thing we must derive an argument on the other side, in this manner: if this pleases God, the opposite displeases him; if this displeases, the opposite pleases

7

him; if he commands this, he forbids the opposite; if he forbids this, he enjoins the opposite. (*Institutes* 2.8.8).

Calvin then goes on to be more explicit and illustrative:

> For by the virtue contrary to the vice, men [e.g., Aquinas] usually mean abstinence from that vice. We say that the virtue goes beyond this to contrary duties and deeds. Therefore in this commandment, "You shall not kill," men's common sense will see only that we must abstain from wronging anyone or desiring to do so. Besides this, it contains, I say, the requirement that we give our neighbor's life all the help we can. To prove that I am not speaking unjustly: God forbids us to hurt or harm a brother unjustly because he wills that the brother's life be dear and precious to us. So at the same time he requires those duties of love which can apply to its preservation. And thus we see how the purpose of the commandment always discloses to us whatever it there enjoins or forbids us to do.

While Luther does not seem to articulate this point so much as an interpretive principle, he does operate in much the same manner in his comment on the Commandments. Thus the commandment against false witness means not only "No one shall use the tongue to harm a neighbor." It also means: "Rather we should use our tongue to speak only the best about all people, to cover the sins and infirmities of our neighbors, to justify their actions, and to cloak and veil them with our own honor" (Large Catechism, in Kolb and Wengert, *Book of Concord*, 424). One may see Calvin's point about uncovering both what each commandment enjoins and what it prohibits illustrated well in the Westminster Larger Catechism, where there are three questions about each commandment: What is the commandment? What are the duties required in the commandment? and What are the sins forbidden in the commandment?

5. *There are different ways of numbering the Commandments, followed by different traditions.* Each of these ways has some justification on the basis of the text of the Commandments, and each numeration presents a particular angle on the Commandments as a whole, what is emphasized, and how they are related to each other. The different numerations, their rationales and their implications, are discussed in the chapters that follow, especially in the first and last, and along the way some attention is given to the ordering and

sequence of the Commandments, variations in the order, and what that may tell us. In this book, the numbering associated with the Reformed tradition is followed. The prohibition of other gods and the prohibition of making images are the First and Second Commandments, and the two sentences about coveting at the end are read as a single commandment, the Tenth Commandment. The fact that the chapter numbers of the book do not agree with this numbering—the First and Second Commandments and the Prologue are treated in a single chapter—is an implicit indication that other ways of associating the Commandments are acknowledged and given credence.

6. *While in some sense each commandment takes up a particular topic, there is also much overlap and interplay between the commandments.* The variations in numbering reflect that overlap, since they have to do in part with whether a particular sentence is a separate commandment or an aspect of another commandment. Whatever numbering is followed, one must still take account of the resonances and connections between or among the individual commandments.

The Place of the Commandments in the Christian Life

Reflection on the Commandments inevitably raises the question of the role they play in the life of individual Christians and the church. In some ways that is the subject of the whole book that follows, but a particular facet of that is the matter of what place the Ten Commandments as a whole have in our life. What do we do with them? Where do they belong? Several answers may be given to those questions.

The Commandments cannot play a role in the lives of Christians unless they are learned and taken to heart. That means then that the long-standing association of the Commandments with the teaching and catechetical traditions of the church needs to be maintained. They can play no role if they are not first memorized and learned, so that they are held in the mind and memory of individuals from an early age onward. Here is where the brevity and simplicity of the Commandments—at least most of them—is a clue to what we are to do with them. Take them to heart and learn them so that they are

9

implanted in the mind and available for guidance. This may happen through learning one of the catechisms, but that is not the only avenue. Catechisms are less in vogue, so the church needs to find places for learning the Commandments in the educational events that it carries on, whether in church school classes or in confirmation classes. Also the family, which was the original context in which the Commandments were learned and appropriated, is still a locus for learning the Commandments. Memorization of biblical texts is a disappearing practice, but there are some texts, such as the Lord's Prayer and the Twenty-third Psalm, that are still assumed to be held in the minds of most Christians. If one attends to the central place of the Commandments in Scripture and the place they have had in the church's teaching, then they also belong to the enterprise of memorizing and holding texts in one's mind and heart.

Teaching the Commandments, however, involves more than simply memorizing them, which is the point of the chapters that follow. They need to be interpreted and discussed so that the community learns what they mean and what is expected of us if we are to live by these foundational principles. If the Commandments are as important as seems to be suggested by the tradition and the culture, they should have a place in the teaching and preaching of the church. Recovery of the Commandments as a subject of preaching is especially important because the gradual rise of the lectionary as a guide to the subject matter of contemporary preaching has meant a significant decrease of sermons on series of biblical texts, such as the Commandments or the Lord's Prayer or the Apostles' Creed. Such series have not disappeared, however, and they need to be reclaimed, especially for the Commandments, precisely because the congregation assumes their normative place but often does not know what all that means. The simplicity of the Commandments, which makes them available for learning and comprehending in their essence, needs to be supplemented by opening up their complexity and fullness, illustrating and developing ways they touch base with contemporary issues.

What place do the Commandments have in the liturgy? Historically, they have been a part of the service in Anglican, Lutheran, and Reformed worship from the beginning, but that is rarely the case now. In Protestant and Catholic liturgy, the Commandments have largely disappeared. As Reinhard Hütter observes, "It is a matter of fact that in mainline liturgies across the board ecumenically, the Ten Commandments have ceased to be a regular component of Christian worship on the Lord's day" ("The Ten Commandments as a Mirror of Sin(s)," 55). If, however, the Commandments belong with the Lord's Prayer and the Creed as the central texts of the church's tradition, something suggested by the attention they receive in the catechetical and confessional history of the church, then it is desirable that they be before the congregation in order that the people may learn and remember them, being reminded each Sunday of God's way for God's people. The Commandments also have a function in the movement of the liturgy, though that can vary depending upon their location in the sequence and order of the service. In the Lutheran context, the Commandments were usually read as preparation for the confession of sin, thus serving one of the functions of the law: to convict us of our sins so as to open our hearts to confession and God's forgiveness. Similarly, up to the modern era the Anglican Book of Common Prayer has called for the repetition of the Commandments by the priest while the people would respond to each commandment with "Lord, have mercy." While the Reformed tradition did not worry too much at first about where the Commandments belonged in the liturgy, because they were understood to function primarily catechetically, Calvin and other Reformed leaders came to have the Commandments sung or read after the confession of sin and the words of absolution, as a guide to living according to God's instruction.

While consistent with the general view of the law in the respective traditions, these different placings of the Commandments were not and should not be regarded as fixed. Reformed worshipers have also read or said the Commandments before the confession of sin as a way of the people acknowledging their failure to live by God's commands. Nor should one assume only one place for the Commandments. It certainly would be appropriate in the Reformed tradition, for example, to have a recitation of the Commandments following the preaching of the Word, reminding the congregation of how one is to live after hearing and receiving the gospel. The issue finally is not so much the necessity to fix a single place for reading or saying the Commandments as it is the matter of whether they shall have any place in the regular worship of the people of God.

Finally, what then about the physical location of the Commandments? That may not be a large question, but it is worth consideration both because the physical location of the Commandments has

11

been a matter of serious concern from their initial promulgation in Scripture, when Moses was instructed to place the tablets with the Commandments in the ark of the covenant and because the physical placement of the Commandments has come to be a large political and judicial issue in American life. The decline of the use of the Commandments in catechesis and worship suggests that we may need to think afresh about how to post the Commandments so that they do not disappear from our common life. We may need to write them on the walls and build stone monuments with the Commandments inscribed on them so that they are regularly seen and read and not forgotten. The best place for doing that, however, is where Christians receive and learn them in the context of the life of faith, in the sacred spaces of church and synagogue, where parents and children learn together how to serve the Lord our God and how the Commandments can help us with critical issues of faith and morals. Perhaps we should go back to the early Anglican tradition in this country, following the Canons of 1604, according to which the Ten Commandments were to be "set up on the East end of every Church and Chapel, where the people may best see and read the same." No pattern of church architecture can be exclusive any more, but there may be new ways of "posting" the Commandments visibly in the sanctuaries or classrooms of the church" (Miller, "Is There a Place for the Ten Commandments?").

CHAPTER 1

The Lord Alone

²I am the LORD your God, who brought you out of the land of Egypt, out of the house of slavery; ³you shall have no other gods before me. ⁴You shall not make for yourself an idol, whether in the form of anything that is in heaven above, or that is on the earth beneath, or that is in the water under the earth. ⁵You shall not bow down to them or worship them; for I the LORD your God am a jealous God, punishing children for the iniquity of parents, to the third and fourth generation of those who reject me, ⁶but showing steadfast love to the thousandth generation of those who love me and keep my commandments.

Exodus 20:2–6//Deuteronomy 5:6–10

The beginning of the Commandments is in a strict sense their foundation. Everything depends upon and flows from this starting point. That beginning, however, is not simply the First Commandment. In fact, it is a whole that is comprised of three parts so integrally related they may be seen as involving only two parts, and different readers will view the two parts differently. In what follows, this section of the Decalogue will be treated as having three parts, while we recognize that they are profoundly connected and that other numerations are also justified by what the text presents. Those three parts are the Prologue (Exod. 20:2//Deut. 5:6); the First Commandment (Exod. 20:3//Deut. 5:7); and the Second Commandment (Exod. 20:4–6//Deut. 5:8–10). Before dealing separately with these different pieces, therefore, it is necessary to look at what holds them together and produces different ways of numbering the Commandments:

A. *Person and speaker.* In these verses the Lord speaks in the first person. The rest of the Decalogue will speak of the Lord in the third person. The change in voice beginning with the Name Commandment invites the hearer to see the preceding verses as some kind of unity.

B. *The Masoretic Hebrew text.* In both versions of the Hebrew text of the Decalogue, these verses are held together as a single paragraph.

13

C. *Grammar and syntax*. The sentence "You shall not bow down to them or worship them" in what is here called the Second Commandment (Exod. 20:4–6//Deut. 5:8–10) is connected to the First Commandment by its content and its object. The expression "bow down to them or worship them" is characteristic language for the worship of "other gods," not specifically for bowing down before idols or images (e.g., Exod. 23:24; Deut. 28:14). The plural object "them" refers back to the "other gods" of the First Commandment because the word for "idol" in the Second Commandment is singular and not plural. In the present form of the text, therefore, the Second Commandment has been incorporated within the framework of the First Commandment (Childs, *Exodus*, 405).

D. *Substance and logic*. The First Commandment is the corollary of the Prologue. That is, *because* "I am the LORD your God who brought you out of the land of Egypt, . . . you shall have no other gods before me." This connection, this logic, is not confined to the Decalogue. In what some would see as one of the earliest references to the First Commandment, Hosea 13:4 says: "Yet I have been the LORD your God ever since the land of Egypt; you know no God but me, and besides me there is no savior" (cf. Lev. 25:38; Josh. 24:16–19; Judg. 6:7–10; Jer. 11:6–13; Ps. 81:9–10). In other words the exclusive devotion to the Lord begins with the reality, the experience, of delivery from bondage. The two go together inextricably. The logic has been articulated by James Mays as follows:

> By his salvation the LORD claimed and took Israel as his people and revealed himself as "the LORD your God." . . . Henceforth all other gods should be strange and foreign to Israel. The first commandment is the true meaning of the exodus. (*Psalms*, 267)

To be set free is to be set on a journey to the mountain where the full implications of the act are set forth in the Commandments and joyfully accepted.

As the First Commandment is connected to the Prologue, so also is it connected substantively to the Second Commandment because the other gods and the idols are often one and the same thing (e.g., Exod. 32:4, 8; Deut. 4:28; 28:36, 64; 32:16–21). This means that although the long motivational clause of Exodus 20:5b–6 and Deuteronomy 5:9b–10—"for I the LORD your God am a jealous God . . ."—will be discussed below as part of the Second Commandment, it is both a continuation of the self-presentation of

14

the deity in the Prologue and the motivating ground for the First Commandment as well as the Second.

The features of the text described above make it unsurprising that there are different numerations of the Ten Commandments. Orthodox Jewish numbering takes very seriously the role of the Prologue by interpreting it as the First Commandment. That would seem to be anomalous since the sentence is not in command form as is the case with the rest of the Commandments. One must remember, however, that when the Decalogue is specifically named with the number "ten," it is always "the Ten *Words*" (in Heb.: Exod. 34:28; Deut. 4:13; 10:4). So it is quite sensible to see in the Prologue the "first" of those words. The intricate connection between prohibiting other gods and prohibiting idol making, together with the way that bowing down to them and serving them (RSV) can be connected to both other gods and idols, leads some, specifically Jewish as well as Catholic and Lutheran traditions, to see a single commandment in the double prohibition of having other gods and making an idol of anything. Still others, for example, the Reformed tradition, have numbered as is being done in this book: marking the first actual command, not to have other gods, as the First Commandment and the prohibition of image making as the Second Commandment. As close as they are in meaning and effect, there is still some particularity to each of them that merits receiving each one as a pointed word from the Lord.

The Prologue

The Prologue to the Commandments can be translated either as "I, the LORD, am your God who brought you out . . ." (e.g., NJPS) or "I am the LORD your God, who brought you out . . . (e.g., NRSV). The force of the two alternatives is not sharply different. Both serve to present and identify the one who now sets before the people the covenantal obligations. As the starting point of the Decalogue, this self-presentation by the deity does several things:

The Prologue gives the name, and thus the identity, of the one who places these obligations upon the people. It is "YHWH," "Adonai," "the LORD." What follows cannot be separated from this identity. It may be that there are rules, or principles, here that can be found in other contexts, but those who consent to these obligations—by their own actions or through the assent of their forebears—do so in response to the one with this name, the God whose deeds and words are recounted in the Bible. Living this way, according to these guidelines, is always both a response to the one whose name is the Lord and a reflection of the character and way of the God who so commands.

The Prologue establishes a relationship as the context in which the Commandments are to be lived out. The identity of this deity is also relational: "I am the LORD *your God.*" The directives that follow the Prologue are what characterize the relationship. Obligation arises out of the covenantal relationship: "I will take you as my people, and I will be your God" (Exod. 6:7). The phrase "your God" is reiterated so much in the Commandments that it almost becomes a part of the name and is clearly a part of the identity. The close connection to the First Commandment is evident: I am the Lord your God, so you shall not have other gods.

In its final clause the Prologue makes clear that the relationship is neither nebulous nor insubstantial. It is rooted in the experience of delivery out of slavery. The ethic of the Commandments is not a general ethic. Worship by this community is not a general requirement. It is in response to the one who has saved the community from bondage (cf. Exod. 3:17; Isa. 58:6). Even the language "brought you out of Egypt" is juridical language for release of slaves or land (e.g., Lev. 25:41–42). A slave goes out or is set free according to the statutes or is "brought out/led out" by another party by a price of redemption or by force (Lohfink, *Great Themes*, 45). Again and again in the statutes and ordinances that spell out the specifics of living by the Commandments, one encounters a recollection or a call to remember how the Lord led them out of Egypt, out of the house of slavery (Lev. 25:42; Deut. 13:5; 15:15; 20:1; 24:18, 22; et al.). All this means that the way of the Commandments is the way to live in both freedom and subjection. That freedom is not a kind of implicit or natural freedom as human beings. Those who live this way are not a free people but a *freed* people. That freedom is not inherent: it is a gift and it shapes everything that follows. The ethic of the Commandments is as much an ethic of gratitude and response as it is an ethic of obligation and duty (cf. the appendix below).

16 In sum, by the self-presentation formula in the Prologue, both the Lord of Israel and the people of Israel are given primary identities. There is no more specific way of identifying this God, who is

named the Lord, than as the one who has set free a people upon whom an oppressive slavery had been inflicted. And the people who live by this constitutional law identify themselves as a community of persons redeemed from bondage. Two things happen when slaves are set free, according to the paradigm of Exodus. They sing praises to the liberating God (Exod. 15), and they learn what it means to be free (Exod. 20). That is why Paul Lehmann says that "the two tablets of Moses' are a primer for learning to spell and to spell out freedom" (*The Decalogue*, 95). If we ever find these commands too "binding," it may be because we do not really know what it means to be slaves who have been liberated from terrible slavery into a new service. In the statutes for the jubilee year of release, Leviticus 25:42 puts it this way: "For they are my servants, whom I brought out of the land of Egypt; they shall not be sold as slaves are sold." There is a powerful irony, a paradox, a dialectic at work here that is central to the being and doing of this people and any people who follow in their train. It is probably best expressed in the claim, embodied in these commandments, that in the service of this God is perfect freedom (Collect for Peace, Morning Prayer 1, Book of Common Prayer). Or as 1 Peter puts it, "As servants [slaves] of God, live as free people" (2:16).

The foundational character of the Prologue is further evidenced in the way in which the story of God's redemption of the Israelites from Egypt in Exodus 1–15 is told in terms of the two parts of the Prologue: the identification or self-presentation of the deity and the characterization of the Lord as the one who redeemed Israel from slavery. The two main foci of the Exodus narrative in Exodus 1–15 are exactly those two matters. In Exodus 3–4, the account of the call of Moses, the critical moment is the revelation of the name of the God (3:13–14): "[When] they ask me, 'What is his name?' what shall I say to them?" "I AM WHO I AM, . . . the LORD," is the response. In Exodus 5–15, one hears the detailed and long story of the Lord's bringing the people out of the land of Egypt and the house of bondage. Already in the call account, however, it is clear that the words and deeds that follow shall give the identity to the God who speaks. Again and again one hears, "that you may know that I am the LORD." And when the Exodus is completed, it culminates in a song of praise: "I will sing to the LORD, for he has triumphed gloriously. . . . This is my God, and I will praise him. . . . The LORD is his name" (Exod. 15:1–3). One can read Exodus 1–15

17

as entirely and solely an interpretive account of the meaning of the Prologue to the Commandments and the narrative ground for the First Commandment.

The story of identity and relationship that begins in the exodus event is paradigmatic. Its trajectory continues throughout the whole of Scripture. We shall mention only two critical expressions of it in the New Testament. In Luke 4, Jesus describes the ministry that lies before him as he reads two texts from Isaiah 61:1–2 and 58:6:

> The Spirit of the Lord is upon me,
>   because he has anointed me
>   to bring good news to the poor.
> He has sent me to proclaim release to the captives
>   and recovery of sight to the blind,
>   to let the oppressed go free.
>
> (Luke 4:18)

The texts are joined by a single Greek catchword, *aphesis*, "release" to the captives, "let go free" the oppressed, a word that in the New Testament is also the word for *forgiveness*. When Jesus says, as he closes the book of Isaiah, that "today this scripture has been fulfilled in your hearing" (4:21), he makes a total identification of his ministry and mission with the character of the God who brought Israel out of the house of slavery. So the New Testament sees in Jesus an active participation in the identity and character of the God who sent him.

The arc of identity and relationship that begins in the Prologue to the Commandments has its zenith in God's raising Jesus from the dead. The bonds of sin and death are broken; the redemptive work of God begun in Egypt reaches its climax at the empty tomb. This has been expressed well by Robert Jenson, precisely in relation to the self-presentation formulation of the Prologue to the Commandments:

> To the question "Who is God?" the New Testament has one new descriptively identifying answer: "Whoever raised Jesus from the dead." Identification by the Resurrection neither replaces nor is simply added to identification by the Exodus; the new identifying description *verifies* its paradigmatic predecessor. For at the outcome of the Old Testament it is seen that Israel's hope in her God cannot be sustained if it is not verified by victory also over death. . . . Thus "the one who rescued Israel from Egypt" is confirmed as an identification of *God* in that it is continued "as he

18

thereupon rescued the Israelite Jesus from the dead." (Jenson, *Systematic Theology*, 1:44)

The resurrection also verifies the way the church is to live its life in relation to the one who "rescued" Israel and Jesus. In nuce and in full, that is the way of the commandments that follow.

The First Commandment: No Other Gods

The Meaning of the Commandment

Like several other commandments, the first one has a simplicity that turns out to be more complex but not more difficult to understand. That simple sentence invites reflection on what is meant by "having a god" and on the force of the prepositional phrase at the end of the sentence. There may be no better interpretation of what it means "to have a god" than what Martin Luther says at the beginning of his treatment of this commandment in his Large Catechism:

> To have a god is nothing else than to trust and believe in that one with your whole heart. . . . To have a God, as you can well imagine, does not mean to grasp him with your fingers, or to put him into a purse, or to shut him up in a box. Rather, you lay hold of God when your heart grasps him and clings to him. (in Kolb and Wengert, *Book of Concord*, 386, 388)

In a real sense, Luther's interpretation precludes the possibility of other gods because to have a God in this way is a total and complete trust and commitment. Yet it is clear from the beginning of the biblical story—check what happens in the garden of Eden—that it is possible to have divided loyalties, to obey some of the time, to turn away from the object of one's devotion. Yet everything depends upon holding fast and complete trust. So the commandment protecting that trust and safeguarding the complete devotion is the starting point of everything else.

The small phrase at the end of the First Commandment, ʿal pānāy, is quite, and importantly, ambiguous or multivalent in its meaning. A close look at the usage of that phrase elsewhere indicates several possible meanings, each of which may be found in one or another translation of this commandment:

1. "before me," that is, "in front of me"
2. "beside me," that is, "alongside me"
3. "besides me," that is, "in my place," or "instead of me"
4. "over against me," that is, "in hostile confrontation with me," "against my face"

Scholars debate which is the particular force of this phrase inasmuch as all of these meanings are possible. Indeed they are, and all of them are present in this command: (1) For you, no other god goes *in front of* this deity or can take a place prior to the Lord of Israel. But also, (2) no other god may be placed in a pantheon *alongside* this deity for you. Further, (3) no other god may *take the place* of the Lord for you. And finally, (4) for you, no other god *may be set over against* the Lord. The force of the phrase is only fully realized in the awareness of all these readings being possible. While there may have been a cultic context assumed at one time, such as divine representations next to or over against each other in a sanctuary, that is now too narrow for what is implied in this sentence. The phrase ʿal pānāy eliminates any other deity in any place for those whose God is the Lord.

The plural "other *gods*" should not be ignored. It is not simply the danger of replacing the God we have with another god. The possibilities of being lured away to other centers of meaning and value are multiple. Though the conflict is often between the God you have and some other god who lures you away, there may be many objects of possible devotion out there. "The issue is not simply replacing the God you have with another one but being attracted by and succumbing to multiple claims on your obedience" (Miller, *The God You Have*, 21). Those other realities, single or multiple, may not take the place of the Lord, may not come before the Lord, may not be set alongside the Lord as objects of equal devotion, may not be placed in conflict with our devotion to the Lord.

In Deuteronomic literature especially, what is prohibited by the First Commandment is often spoken of as "following" or "going after" other gods (e.g., Deut. 6:14; 8:19; 11:28; 13:2). So also, proper obedience to the First Commandment is expressed as "following the LORD" (e.g., Deut. 7:4; 1 Kgs. 9:6). When Elijah confronts the people of Israel about their worship of the god Baal, he puts the issue of the First Commandment in sharp and unequivocal terms: "If the LORD is God, follow him; but if Baal, then follow him" (1 Kgs.

18:21). It is a clear either/or. One of the strongest positive formulations of the First Commandment occurs in Deuteronomy 13:4:

> The LORD your God you shall follow, him alone you shall fear, his commandments you shall keep, his voice you shall obey, him you shall serve, and to him you shall hold fast.

Every sentence of the verse is an emphatic articulation of the First Commandment, and the lead sentence shapes the whole. To obey/keep the First Commandment is to follow the Lord. And here is where Scripture first speaks about discipleship, for this is the language that Jesus uses when he calls on his disciples and others to give themselves completely to him and his way. The Commandments remind us of the negative meaning of that discipleship, the exclusive loyalty and setting aside of any other claims on our "following after" than the *kyrios*, the Lord of Israel and the church.

The verse just quoted in Deuteronomy 13:4, however, makes one aware also of how thoroughly the First Commandment is expressed and elaborated in positive language. Indeed, it cannot be perceived and appropriated fully without the positive formulations complementing the negative and demonstrating how expansive and total and full the response to this directive is. Each clause offers a way of understanding the call of the First Commandment: to follow the Lord your God, to fear the Lord, to keep the commandments, to obey the Lord, to serve the Lord, and to cling to the Lord. All through Scripture, such expressions mark what is expected of those whose God is the Lord, those who have been redeemed by this God.

Immediately before this verse in Deuteronomy 13, Moses tells the people that if a prophet appears in their midst, telling them, "'Let us follow other gods' (whom you have not known) and '. . . serve them,'" this is God's testing the people "to know whether you indeed love the LORD your God with all your heart and soul" (Deut. 13:3). Such language is a reflection of the primary positive form of the First Commandment, that is, the Shema, as it is called, which Jesus cites when asked what is the first, or foremost, commandment (Mark 12:28–29): "Hear, O Israel: The LORD is our God, the LORD alone. You shall love the LORD your God with all your heart, and with all your soul, and with all your might" (Deut. 6:4–5). The first sentence is capable of varying translations, either emphasizing that the Lord is our God, as in the NRSV translation quoted above, or emphasizing that the Lord is one: "The LORD [is] our God, the

21

LORD is one." The likely translation is the former, especially since it best conveys the thrust of the Great Commandment, that the Lord alone is our God. The second translation, however, is not to be ruled out, for there were possibilities of understanding the Lord of Israel as having multiple representations, associated especially with local cults, and thus the possibility of divided character and purpose, marring the Lord's "integrity or moral unity" (Janzen, "Most Important Word in the Shema"). There are even ancient Hebrew inscriptions that speak of "YHWH of Samaria" and "YHWH of Teman." The unity of God is central to the undivided character of our human obedience, and in the Septuagint the Greek translation of the Hebrew is "the Lord is one" (cf. Zech. 14:9b). Nevertheless, the translation of the Shema as "the LORD alone" most clearly represents the force of the First Commandment, which is its foundation and counterpart. From this point onward, loving the Lord is the primary but not the only way of expressing the fullness of devotion conveyed by the First Commandment in its prohibitive form.

That "fullness" is represented in the extended amplification of the love of God: "with all your heart, and with all your soul, and with all your might." In one sense, it is possible to see the heaping up of these phrases as simply expressing totality: every part of you, everything you have and are. That certainly is the ultimate outcome. The repeated "all" is as important as the different phrases. Nothing is held back from this total commitment. The tradition, however, has also seen in the three expressions different aspects of that commitment. That is especially the case with Jewish exegesis since it has at times interpreted these phrases as follows: "with all your heart," meaning with an undivided loyalty, both good and bad inclinations; "with all your soul," suggesting a loyalty even unto death and martyrdom, since the Hebrew term *nepeš* can mean life—as one interpreter says, "Love him until the last drop of life is wrung out of you"; and "with all your might," pointing to the commitment of all that one has—possessions, wealth, everything given over to God (see Hammer, *Sifre*, 62–64; Tigay, *Deuteronomy*, 77). Something akin to this way of interpreting the three phrases modifying "You shall love the LORD your God" is found also in John Calvin's interpretation in one of his sermons:

22

> Thou shalt love God with all thy soul, is as much as to say thou
> shalt not spare thy life for the love of thy God. . . .Thou shalt love

thy God with all thy mind or heart, betokeneth with them but as it were a comparison, so as a man should prefer God above all other things, . . . and finally thou shalt love God with all thy strength, imparted among them, that thou must love him with all thy substance and with all thy goods, as if the case required that thou shouldst be impoverished. (Calvin, *Sermons Upon Deuteronomy*, 272)

Elsewhere I have suggested that there is an important theological and pastoral implication in the First Commandment in both its positive and negative forms:

The oneness of the reality that grounds existence, God, is what keeps life from being chaotic and divided beyond the limits of human management. In the face of the multiple pulls and dimensions of human life and experience, human existence is held together and in order by that one and absolute object of our allegiance and loyalty. We do not find conflicting claims on our ultimate allegiance, only on secondary interests and loyalties. It is possible to deal with these secondary claims if we have a sense that our ultimate and full allegiance is directed toward one alone. The demand of the Shema [and of the First Commandment] is, therefore, finally not just a demand. It is also what makes human life possible. All claims on human life are relativized and subsumed within the one total claim of God so that the demand is ultimately the gift of grace. (Miller, *Deuteronomy*, 104)

What follows the Shema in Deuteronomy 6–11 is in effect a long sermon by Moses on the First Commandment in both its prohibitive and commanding forms. It also shows how closely that commandment is linked with what comes before it, the Prologue, and what comes after, the prohibition of making and worshiping images. A good example of this homiletic commentary on the principal command of the Decalogue is evident in Deuteronomy 6:10–16, the first part of Moses' sermonic elaboration:

[10]When the LORD your God has brought you into the land that he swore to your ancestors, to Abraham, to Isaac, and to Jacob, to give you—a land with fine, large cities that you did not build, [11]houses filled with all sorts of goods that you did not fill, hewn cisterns that you did not hew, vineyards and olive groves that you did not plant—and when you have eaten your fill, [12]take care that you do not forget the LORD, who brought you out of the land of Egypt, out of the house of slavery. [13]The LORD your God you shall

fear; him you shall serve, and by his name alone you shall swear.
[14]Do not follow other gods, any of the gods of the peoples who
are all around you, [15]because the LORD your God, who is present with you, is a jealous God. The anger of the LORD your God
would be kindled against you and he would destroy you from the
face of the earth.[16]Do not put the LORD your God to the test, as
you tested him at Massah.

Verses 10–12 function in the same way as the Prologue and indeed
repeat the Prologue in verse 12. Here that reminder of what the
Lord has done for those now called to the Lord's service includes
also an anticipation of all the benefits that will come from finding
a home in the promised land, goods and well-being that are not
the result of the people's actions but are the gift of God, a point
elaborated at length in Deuteronomy 8. The First Commandment
is explicit in the commands to fear the Lord your God and not to
follow other gods. The First, Second, and Third Commandments
are present in positive form in 6:13, and the First and Second are
in view in the reference to "a jealous God" (v. 15). A new way of
violating the First Commandment is identified in verse 12, where
the people are told "take care that you do not *forget* the LORD."
Forgetting the Lord is a form of disobeying the commandment that
arises especially when the people are prospering and things are
going well. There are two dangers in that context.

One is the point of Deuteronomy 8, where the people are
warned not to forget the Lord when they come into the rich and
fertile land and have eaten their fill and built fine houses and multiplied their riches. Moses says: "Do not say to yourself, 'My power
and the might of my own hand have gotten me this wealth.' But
remember the LORD your God, for it is he who gives you power to
get wealth" (8:17). In prosperity, the people may think that what
they have is simply the result of their own endeavors and forget that
it is the Lord who has brought them to this place and provided the
good. Such forgetfulness is manifest in not keeping the commandments (8:11), and it has potentially dire consequences (8:19–20).
At bottom, it is the sin of assuming self-sufficiency in a world created by God and sustained by God's good care. Once again we are
reminded of why the Prologue is so important. It is the reminder of
who is God for us and why we keep the Commandments, a reminder
that we love because we have first been loved (cf. Deut. 7:7–8).

The other danger when all is going well is intimated in Deuteronomy 6:14. It is the tendency to think that one's prosperity comes from the gods of the area, especially those associated with food and goods and prosperity. The prophets often encountered this. The Lord speaks through the prophet Hosea to say: "She [Israel] did not know that it was I who gave her the grain, the wine, and the oil" (Hos. 2:8); she thought it was Baal. A cogent and blatant instance of this is in Jeremiah 44, where the women among the Jewish refugees in Egypt insist on making offerings to the Queen of Heaven, the goddess Ishtar, because they had plenty of food when they made offerings to her but not since they have stopped, unaware that their present sufferings are divine punishment for their evil doings (cf. Jer. 7:18).

Jesus nailed this down explicitly: "You cannot serve God and mammon [wealth]" (Matt. 6:24//Luke 16:13 RSV). The use of the proper name "Mammon" is a reminder that in wealth, money, goods, and possessions, there really is another god before or beside the God who has called us and redeemed us. One should recognize that here in Jesus' words and certainly in the Jeremiah incident above, it is not only a matter of personal or individualized acquisitions but also of devotion to systems of productivity that create wealth and provision. Much of the worship of other gods in Scripture is a communal enterprise having to do with the systems of getting and having, making and spending. "The god is the symbol, often highly visible, of the productivity and consumption that has erected it" (Miller, *The God You Have*, 26–27). Because Jesus' statement "You cannot serve God and wealth" (Matt. 6:24b) is an example of the principle of not serving two masters (6:24a), it is easy to see this as simply illustrative without realizing that it is also foundational. One may read Jesus' saying as either illustration (6:24b) of a principle (6:24a) or as elaboration (6:24a) of a fundamental claim (6:24b). Jesus' "example" of the other master is a recognition of who is first in line for our affections.

All these passages and their different ways of connecting to the First Commandment are implicit reminders of why thanksgiving is one of the primary positive ways of keeping the First Commandment. It is a constant reminder of who is God and who has provided. It is a guard against thinking that "my own hand" has produced the good that one has, and it orients one's being toward the Lord and away from other objects of idolization, starting with

25

oneself. Thanksgiving by definition orients one toward the object of thanks and away from oneself. One may mistake the giver, as Israel often did—but not when they sang its psalms and songs of thanksgiving. Then they lived and acted out the proper obedience of the First Commandment (see below on the Psalms).

Is This Monotheism?

The First Commandment has often been characterized as a form of monotheism; just as often, however, it has been seen as indicating that monotheism was not characteristic of Israel's faith when it received this commandment. The argument for monotheism is in the claim that the point of the First Commandment is to reject all other gods, leaving only the Lord of Israel as God. The problem with that is identified by those who note that the very expression "other gods" presumes there were other gods in the mind-set and understanding, the conceptual world, of ancient Israel. Thus the First Commandment may be seen as a clear indication of some sort of polytheism in ancient Israel or at best a henotheism or monolatry, acknowledging other deities but precluding worship of any of the other gods that were clearly around, the gods of the other nations. Israel's worship was to be confined to its own national god.

Dean McBride has aptly identified the problem with seeking to identify the First Commandment with monotheism, which is not so much that such a view ignores the "other gods" of the commandment but that it lets these abstract categories serve to define and interpret what is going on in the commandment:

> The trouble with monotheism as a theological home is that it values abstraction over particularities, pure being over doing, inclusiveness over integrity. . . . [T]he trouble with polytheism is that it assigns independent divinity to powers and attributes that belong exclusively to the LORD and it deifies entities that the LORD created (e.g., Deut 4:19; Isa 40:25–26; cf. Ps 96:4–5) or worse, confuses deity with things that are merely creations of human imagination and industry. ("Essence of Orthodoxy," 148–49)

The radical form of this commandment renders such categories moot and of little significance. They fail to show that the reference to the other gods is a reality just as present for the contemporary community as for the ancient Israelite community. The stories of

26

the conflicts among the gods and the very language of polytheism suggest a premodern, prerational time, with its myths not applicable to our own time because we have gotten past that. For us, the battle has been won and the issue no longer relevant in a philosophically monotheistic world.

> We would do well to discern in this dimension of Scripture some indication of the reality of other powers at work in the world whose ultimate conquest by the Lord of history is sure but whose power to entice and appeal, to exercise control over our lives, and thus to affect and effect history in other ways than those intended by the Lord your God is real and constantly present. (Miller, *The God You Have*, 22)

The First Commandment is a tacit acknowledgment that there are always claims of an ultimate sort confronting us, "other gods." While Scripture reformulates this command in positive forms that are helpful and crucial for full comprehension of what is involved in this commitment, the positive form alone does not remind us as sharply of the temptation to turn to other gods, to make other realities ultimate, the center of meaning and value in our lives.

Stories of the First Commandment

The story of the First Commandment, that is, the stories having to do with its obedience or disobedience, are too numerous in Scripture to begin to cover in a single chapter. One might say that the whole of Scripture is in some sense commentary on and story of the First Commandment. A few of the particular stories, however, may be lifted up to help characterize the issues at stake and operative in the commandment.

Exodus 1–15. The story of the prohibition of "serving" or worshiping other gods begins in the account of Egyptian bondage and God's deliverance of the Israelites from slavery. The issue there was whether this people would be free to go and "serve"—worship—the Lord, or whether they would be forced to "serve"—carry out hard labor—for the Egyptian pharaoh. The story thus equates the forced service of human tyrants with the service of other gods. Resistance to oppressive tyranny is part of the covenant community's obedience of the First Commandment. As Karl Barth said in the face of the rise of National Socialism in Germany: "Today the conflict in

27

the Church is not over the Lord's Supper but over the First Commandment, and we have to confess" (Cochrane, *Church's Confession under Hitler*, 135).

Exodus 17, Testing the Lord at Massah and Meribah. Among the stories of Israel complaining in the wilderness is the account of Moses striking the rock at Massah in order to get water for the Israelites after they quarreled with him about their lack of water to drink. There is no explicit connection to the First Commandment, but Deuteronomy 6:10–16 makes clear that full commitment to "the LORD your God" is what was at stake in that episode. The first three commandments are set forth in positive form in verse 13: "The LORD your God you shall fear; him you shall serve, and by his name alone you shall swear." Two prohibitions follow this, the first one of which is clearly a rearticulation of the First and Second Commandments:

> [14]Do not follow other gods, any of the gods of the peoples who are all around you, [15]because the LORD your God, who is present with you, is a jealous God.

Note the addition of the phrase "who is present with you," which clearly anticipates what is at stake in the next verse. That verse is a further prohibition, one that does not seem at first glance to have to do with the Commandments: "Do not put the LORD your God to the test as you tested him at Massah" (v. 16). From the story in Exodus 17, however, it is clear that obedience to the First Commandment is the issue, especially when one is conscious of its positive forms as indicated in verse 13 and elsewhere. What the First Commandment calls for is a commitment of trust in the Lord your God, a trust that does not waver whatever the circumstances. That is what was missing at Massah when the people quarreled with Moses and "tested" the Lord, asking Moses, "Why did you bring us out of Egypt, to kill us and our children and livestock with thirst" (Exod. 17:3). The names Meribah ("quarreling place") and Massah ("testing place") are given to the place "because the Israelites quarreled and tested the LORD, saying, 'Is the LORD among us or not?'" (v. 7; cf. Deut. 6:15 above and Ps. 95:9).

The story is a vivid confirmation of Martin Luther's interpretation of the First Commandment in his Large Catechism: "A 'god' is the term for that to which we are to look for all good and in which we are to *find refuge in all need*. Therefore, to have a god is nothing

28

else than to *trust and believe in that one with your whole heart*" (in Kolb and Wengert, *Book of Concord,* 386; emphasis added). The issue is not only *where* we put our ultimate trust but also whether we truly believe that the God who has delivered us from bondage can be counted upon in all circumstances. This was the issue as well in that first action on the part of the Israelites after the Commandments had been given. Making the golden calf was an act of idolatry, but it was triggered by the anxiety of the people in the wilderness when Moses disappeared up the mountain and did not return. So they said to his brother Aaron: "Come, make gods for us, who shall go before us" (Exod. 32:1). The explicit question of Exodus 17, "Is the LORD among us or not?" (v. 7), is there implicitly in the wilderness when Aaron and the people build the golden calf and Aaron announces: "These are your gods, O Israel" (32:4). The point is then made explicit once more in Deuteronomy 9, when Moses recalls the disobedience of the people in making the golden calf as well as other places where the people rebelled and provoked the Lord to wrath, including Massah. With reference to the fearfulness of the people about going up into the land at the Lord's command, Moses says: "You rebelled against the command of the LORD your God, *neither trusting him nor obeying him*" (Deut. 9:23; emphasis added). The principal commandment of the Decalogue, therefore, is not simply a rejection of all other claims on our ultimate devotion. It is also a call to say *and believe*: "God is our refuge and strength, a very present help in time of trouble. Therefore we will not fear" (Ps. 46:1–2).

Numbers 25. As the narrative of Israel's journey through the wilderness comes to an end, we are told of another instance of the people's being lured away to the worship of another god, the Baal (or "lord") of Peor. The later use of the language of fornication and adultery for speaking about disobedience of the First Commandment (see below and chap. 6) resonates with this text as the people having had sexual relations with the Moabite women are then invited by these women to join them in the sacrifices of their gods, which they do, eating and bowing down to them (vv. 1–2). The text speaks of this as Israel "yoking itself" to the Baal of Peor, the deity of that place (vv. 3, 5). This infrequent verb, connoting the joining of animals, like a team of oxen, becomes the identifying term for Israel's worship of the Moabite god (Ps. 106:28). It points to the choice that is always before the community that lives by the First

Commandment. It is never "the Lord and . . ." as recipients of the people's worship. To serve another deity, whether in worship, sacrifice, meals, or anything is to cut yourself off from the "LORD your God," who has redeemed you and provides for your good, and to join yourself inextricably to another center of meaning and value. To serve other gods is to join another team. Walter Brueggemann has suggested that "the issue for God's people is characteristically *wrong* God and not *no* God" (Brueggemann, "Foreword," 1). However common atheism may be in our time, such was clearly not the issue for ancient Israel.

Joshua 2. The story of Rahab's encounter with the Israelite spies is a particular manifestation of obedience to the First Commandment, in this instance on the part of someone outside the community that has received the Commandments. The encounter between the spies and Rahab, and indeed the whole rest of the story of conquest of the land of Canaan by the Israelites, centers on Rahab's confession. She tells the spies that word of the victories of the Israelites has come into the land, and the hearts of the Canaanite inhabitants have melted (v. 11a). There is a difference, however, between the further response of Rahab and the king as representative of the people. Rahab's response is a confession of faith and an act of obedience. She declares: "The LORD your God is indeed God in heaven above and on earth below" (v. 11b). This confession is a genuine act of conversion: while the king of Jericho and his men seek to find the spies, Rahab engages in an act of treason by hiding the spies and sending the king's men on a false search. Rahab's obedience to the First Commandment is not only a *confession of faith* in the God of Israel. It is also an *act of faithfulness* that totally changes the situation, one requiring her to abandon loyalties and commitments that had seemed secure (Miller, "Story of the First Commandment: Joshua").

Joshua 23–24. The book of Joshua concludes with two extended speeches by Joshua to the people, the second in the context of a covenant-renewal ceremony. In both instances the heart of the matter is the challenge to the people to "love the LORD your God" (23:11) and not to "go and serve other gods and bow down to them" (23:16; cf. v. 8). The positive form of the First Commandment is set alongside the negative: "But to the LORD your God you shall cling" (Josh. 23:8, my trans.). Luther's implicit commentary on these injunctions is in his catechetical interpretation of the First Commandment:

30

> You lay hold of God when your heart grasps him and clings to him completely. To cling to him with your heart is nothing else than to entrust yourself to him completely. He wishes to turn us away from everything else apart from him, and to draw us to himself, because he is the one, eternal good. (in Kolb and Wengert, *Book of Concord*, 388)

In chapter 24, Joshua speaks with the voice of the Lord at length about all that the Lord has done to deliver and take care of this people. Like the Prologue to the Commandments, the issue is how the people will respond to the good deeds of the Lord; like the Commandments, that response has to do with one thing alone. Thus the people say: "It is the LORD our God who brought us and our ancestors up from the land of Egypt, out of the house of slavery. . . . Therefore we also will serve the LORD, for he is our God" (24:17–18).

That will not be easy, as Joshua says, "for he is a holy God. He is a jealous God; he will not forgive your transgressions" (24:19), to which the people respond once more: "No, we will serve the LORD!" (24:21). The stage is thus set for the rest of the story, which is always about whether and how this people will serve the Lord their God. From Joshua through Chronicles and beyond, this is the issue: Will the people hold firm to the vow of obedience made in the face of Joshua's skepticism, or will they succumb to the enticements of the surrounding culture, no longer able to distinguish between the attractiveness of other religious voices and claims and full loyalty to the God whose action in their behalf has been manifest in all the events of deliverance and conquest?

Judges 6–9. Joshua's skepticism turns out to be well founded. The failure of the people to live by their commitment to the Lord is told again and again in the book of Judges. Chapter 2 summarizes the steady disintegration of Israel's loyalty as "they lusted after other gods and bowed down to them" (2:17). When the people cry out to the Lord under the oppression of the Midianites, the Lord sends a prophet who reminds them who it was that led them out of Egypt and out of the house of slavery (6:9), telling them: "I am the LORD your God; you shall not fear the gods of the Amorites" (6:10, my trans.). But they would not listen. Symptomatic of the situation is the story of Gideon, who is told by the Lord to pull down the altar of Baal built by his father and the asherah or sacred pole alongside it. When confronted by the townspeople who want to kill him for

31

this act, Gideon's father, now abandoning his idolatrous actions for the sake of his son, says to the people: "Will you contend for Baal? Or will you defend his cause? Whoever contends for him shall be put to death by morning. If he is a god, let him contend for himself, because his altar has been pulled down" (6:31). Like the story of Elijah and the prophets of Baal (see below), the issue is who is active and powerful to do anything. Here as there, the people are faced with a life-or-death challenge, and the ineffectiveness of the false god they would worship is made clear even if they are not permanently convinced (see 8:22–35). The people do not "*remember* the LORD their God, who had rescued them from the hand of all their enemies on every side" (8:34). As is evident from the first word of the Decalogue, memory of the Lord's redemptive acts is the foundation of moral behavior. It is why the community of faith "remembers" the Sabbath Day and at the table remembers afresh what God has done in Jesus Christ. It must never forget lest it lose its Lord.

First Samuel 4–6. The Ark Narrative in 1 Samuel 4–6, and particularly the account of the Philistines carrying the captured ark of the covenant into the temple of Dagon (5:1–5) is a story of the First Commandment. The victorious Philistines place the ark, the throne of the Lord, alongside the statue of the Philistine god Dagon. It is found the next morning fallen on its face before the ark. Replaced by the priests, the statue is found the following morning fallen over with its head and hands cut off. No deity may stand alongside or in hostile confrontation with this God. If it is alongside, it will be knocked down. If it is in hostile confrontation, it will have its hands and head cut off. And the only way for any divine or human being to come before this deity is prostrate in awe and worship.

What is particularly interesting about this story is that the meaning of the First Commandment is worked out not in this instance among the Israelites but among the Philistines; one thus begins to see the address of the commandment breaking out of the covenant community to make an increasingly universal claim. In this connection, one is led to recall some other texts. In the prophecy of Amos the Lord says, "Did I not bring . . . up . . . the Philistines from Caphtor?" (Amos 9:7), claiming an exodus relation to the Philistines similar to that with the Israelites! And the psalms regularly call for the nations of the earth to bow down and praise the Lord of Israel. The "you" of the First Commandment begins to be stretched.

First Kings 18. The account of Elijah's encounter with the prophets of Baal at Mount Carmel is a paradigmatic story of the disobedience of the First Commandment, placing another god alongside, in front of, and over against the Lord. Like the story of Gideon and the destruction of the Baal altar, this other "god" is proved to be ineffective and powerless before the Lord. The wholeness of the Decalogue, the interrelationship of the various commandments, is dramatically illustrated as the violation of the First Commandment and the first table of the Decalogue under the aegis and leadership of King Ahab and his wife Jezebel (1 Kgs. 18:17; 19:1–3) culminates in their violation of the second table of the Decalogue in the Naboth incident: the king covets the vineyard of Naboth, and his wife Jezebel arranges a kangaroo trial with false witnesses in order to effect a judicial murder of Naboth and thus steal his vineyard (1 Kgs. 21; cf. chaps. 6, 8–10 below). Only adultery is missing from their violations of the commandments of the second table.

The First Commandment in the Law and the Prophets

Allusions, implicit and explicit, to the First Commandment reverberate throughout the Law and the Prophets. Though it is not necessary to allude to every single instance, it is helpful to see what some of the particular concerns are about the worship of other gods. Making and worshiping images of the Lord or other deities is obviously a central concern, but that will be taken up below in discussion of the Second Commandment.

The Book of the Covenant (Exod. 20:22–23:33). We have already noted how the first fifteen chapters of Exodus are structured around the form and content of the Prologue and how in various episodes of the wilderness journey, as recounted in the book of Exodus, there are disturbing stories of Israel's violation of the First Commandment. As Moses spells out the law in more detail in the Book of the Covenant, he begins, not surprisingly, with the first three commandments (Exod. 20:22–26). Much of this we will examine in relation to the Second and Third Commandments, but it is appropriate to call attention to the central concern at the beginning of the Book of the Covenant for preserving the pure and proper worship of the Lord of Israel. The First Commandment is in play when the Lord tells Moses: "You shall not make gods of silver *alongside*

33

me" (20:23; emphasis added). While the language is different, one hears echoes of the First Commandment's prohibition of having other gods "beside(s) me" or "alongside me" or "over against me." Whether in idol form or not, there is no "God and . . . ," only the Lord. In place of the image—of any god—one is to hear and know the *name* of God (20:24), that which God has revealed and given to the people as a mode of access to the creator of all.

The significance of the name is discussed in the treatment of the Third Commandment (chap. 2). The function of a name to represent and identify is clear on the human level. It is just as evident for the representation of deity in the fact that in Deuteronomic theology it was the *name* of God that dwelled in the sanctuary. The name "protected, assured the reality of God's dynamic immanence at the chosen shrine without localizing him there" (McBride, "Deuteronomic Name Theology," 209). By implication, obedience to the First Commandment means that the names of other gods may not be invoked, an implication that becomes explicit in Exodus 23:13: "Do not invoke the names of other gods; do not let them be heard on your lips."

Analogously, the paraphernalia associated with the worship of other gods are to be avoided and actually destroyed so that they may not draw persons away from the true worship of the Lord of Israel. At the conclusion of the Book of the Covenant, this point is made in direct connection to the First Commandment:

> [24]You shall not bow down to their gods, or worship them, or follow their practices, but you shall utterly demolish them and break their pillars in pieces. [25]You shall worship the LORD your God. (Exod. 23:24–25)

Moses reiterates this need to remove all the vehicles of ritual and worship of the other gods, again in the context of the demands of the First Commandment (Exod. 34:13; Deut. 7:5). Particularly important, then, is the restriction against sacrifices to any other god than the Lord (Exod. 22:20; cf. 2 Kgs. 17:35; 2 Chr. 28:25; Jer. 7:18; 19:13; 44:2–8). No act so signaled devotion to a deity as did sacrifice, as witnessed in the careful legislation about sacrifice so widespread in the Pentateuch. The first act of the Israelites after making the golden calf was to offer burnt offerings and sacrifices (Exod. 32:6), but that was not the last such occasion by any means (e.g., Jer. 19:4; 44:2–8).

The Deuteronomic Code (Deut. 12–26). Within the statutes and ordinances that make up the Deuteronomic elaboration of the Ten Commandments, the first two chapters (Deut. 12–13) are the primary place where the First Commandment is developed in particular cases. *Deuteronomy 12* focuses on the proper worship of the Lord. At the beginning of the chapter (vv. 2–4) and at the end (vv. 29–31), the people are warned against any appropriation of the ways of worship and veneration of the gods of the nations they have encountered. Syncretism in any form, whether it arises out of political alliances (7:1–5) or simply the attraction of novel and different forms of religious ritual and practice (12: 29–31), is a violation of the First Commandment. The exclusivity of the Lord's claim on the people who have been delivered and blessed by the Lord's hand brooks no modification. The attractiveness of different modes of worship is obvious: "Look at their temples, their altars, their liturgies!" There are proper ways to worship the Lord; such worship is not devoid of place and offering, song and dance, joy and good times (cf. Ps. 150). That is indicated in some detail in the rest of Deuteronomy 12, which serves to prescribe modes of sacrifice and worship in the house of the Lord. But "you," the people, do not determine that; "you" do not pick and choose from what everybody else is doing.

Moses' teaching here has two dimensions. One is recognition of the temptation and allure of different religious practices and the fact that to turn toward them inevitably compromises the sole devotion "with all your heart and all your soul" to the Lord. That means—and this is the other lesson of this chapter, the flip side of the coin, so to speak—the "Lord your God" alone shall determine the way you worship the Lord. The heart of the matter is *the place of worship* and how that is determined. Immediately after the words "You shall not worship the Lord your God in such ways" (Deut. 12:4)—by the religious practices of these other nations and their gods—Moses says: "But you shall seek the place that the Lord your God will choose out of all your tribes as his habitation to put his name there. You shall go there" (12:5). Where God's name is present, God is there, and there you shall go to worship. Although that place came to be Jerusalem, that is not the point of this chapter. No particular place is identified here. It is the place *the Lord chooses.* Divine presence, the object and locus of our worship, is not something we human beings determine. The church has heard this once again, and in an ultimate sense, as it found—to its surprise—the

35

presence of God in Jesus Christ. In its early confession that "Jesus Christ is Lord," it affirmed that in him God is present, and this one shall be where and whom we worship. In such a claim and in such a manner of worship is to be found the church's faithfulness to the First Commandment.

Deuteronomy 13 warns against listening to the voice of those who seek to entice the community away from the worship of the Lord to follow after other gods. These may be prophets whose authority seems to be guaranteed by the way their omens and portents come to pass (vv. 1–5); or they may be close and dear members of the family (vv. 6–11). They may even be a whole town or community (vv. 12–17). Whatever the case, those voices are to be resisted and punished. The Lord's voice alone is to be heard and obeyed (13:4, 18). The point is clear and perhaps a little too obvious. If each of these voices says, "Let us go and worship other gods," there should be little problem with resistance. That assumes, however, that all is well in the community, that there is plenty of food and harvest, or that the other gods are obvious. But such is not always the case. The other gods of power and wealth, for example, are always making their appeal through various voices and spokespersons. As Jesus recognized so directly, these other gods may have names like Baal (lord) and Mammon (wealth), but their allure is not simply a matter of going to another church. It is finding another center of ultimate meaning and obedience in one's life. "Let us follow other gods."

The Prophets. Concern for proper obedience to the First Commandment so permeates the prophetic message that one cannot begin to cover all the texts and prophetic sayings that raise the issue. Much of what they have to say is reflective of what one encounters in the legal texts. Yet even if one must be selective, there are some prophetic claims about the First Commandment that continue to illumine our understanding of what is at stake.

Hosea 13 is part of the prophet's announcement of judgment against Israel for its unfaithfulness to the Lord. The heart of the matter is found in verses 4–6:

> [4]Yet I have been the Lord your God
> ever since the land of Egypt;
> you know no God but me,
> and besides me there is no savior.
> [5]It was I who fed you in the wilderness,
> in the land of drought.

⁶When I fed them, they were satisfied;
>they were satisfied, and their heart was proud;
>therefore they forgot me.

As one interpreter has put it, we have in verse 4b "a narrative form of the first commandment" (Mays, *Hosea*, 174). One may go further than that. The verse as a whole is a form of the connected Prologue and First Commandment. The point of the Prologue is underscored as reference is made not only to the deliverance from Egyptian slavery but also to God's providential care during the hard journey through the wilderness. Once more the First Commandment is understood at base as response to God's gifts, and obedience is the form of gratitude. Israel has no other savior or helper, as one hears in verse 9b: "Who can help you?" Israel "knows" no other God, both in the sense of acknowledgment and experience. The result of God's help and care, however, has not been gratitude/obedience. On the contrary, Israel has "forgotten" the source of all its blessing. The problem—better, the *sin*—is twofold. One mode of forgetting the source of all one's good is found in the arrogant assumption that that good is one's own doing. The text is reminiscent of Deuteronomy 8, where Moses reminds the people of God's care in the wilderness and warns them against assuming that once they are in the land and have eaten their fill, built fine houses, and multiplied their flocks, they can say to themselves, "My power and the might of my own hand have gotten me this wealth" (v. 17).

There is another facet to Israel's disobedience. James Mays puts it this way:

>This assertion that Israel is completely dependent on Yahweh is in Hosea's situation a polemic against all other forces to which Israel looked for deliverance: the king and his princes (13:10; cf. 1 Sam 10:18f.), military power (14:3), and idols (14:3; 13:2). (*Hosea*, 174–75)

The people assume that there are other powers in whom they can trust, who will come to their aid. But there is no other helper, no king, no other nation, and certainly not the things they have made with their own hands and call "our God" (Hos. 14:3). "You know no God but me, and besides me there is no savior." Obedience to the First Commandment is to live and act under that assumption

37

because the claim is true, a fact made evident when one assumes there are other possibilities.

Jeremiah makes the same point in one of his oracles (Jer. 2:26–28). With reference to the people of Judah, the prophet speaks the divine word with force and sarcasm (vv. 27–28):

> ²⁷But in the time of their trouble they say,
>   "Come and save us!"
> ²⁸But where are your gods
>   that you made for yourself?
> Let them come, if they can save you,
>   in your time of trouble;
> for you have as many gods
>   as you have towns, O Judah.

Here and elsewhere (e.g., 11:13), the prophet mocks the people's reliance on other forces to help them, forces that are powerless. Faithfulness to the commandment's prohibition of other gods is as sensible as it is logical and rewarding. The hope that other powers and forces can help is a mistake. If the songs of thanksgiving are a form of obedience to the First Commandment, acknowledging that our help is in the name of the Lord, then so also are the many cries of lament and complaint, petitions that by their very character as cries to the Lord, acknowledge that the Lord is the only one who can help.

Jeremiah makes this same point in another way, one that other prophets echo. Several times he denounces the people for turning to other gods (or idols) that do not "profit." The covenant lawsuit God brings against the people of Judah in Jeremiah 2:4–13 is a particular instance in which the whole accusation revolves around apostasy as a failed turning to other gods for profit. He begins by accusing the ancestors of going after "worthless things, and [becoming] . . . worthless themselves" (v. 5); "worthless" is the same term more familiarly known from Ecclesiastes and often translated as "vanity," what is empty, no more useful or substantive than a puff of air. Then in a dramatic wordplay, the Lord says, "The prophets prophesied by Baal [*ba‘al*], and went after things that do not profit [*yā‘al*]" (v. 8b), and elaborates further with a claim (v. 11):

> Has a nation changed its gods,
>   even though they are no gods?
> But my people have changed their glory
>   for something that does not profit.

What binds these verses together is the abandonment of the Lord for what does not work and bring benefit. "The search for God becomes a search for whatever enhances my (or our) well-being, makes my land more productive, increases my wealth and my place and my status" (Miller, "Jeremiah," 599). Such, however, is not to be found in turning to Baal, or Mammon, or one's own constructed gods/idols (cf. Isa. 44:9–10; 57:12). The source of good, of what profits and helps one, is already known and has claimed their lives with the promise and the actuality of blessing:

> ¹⁷I am the LORD your God,
>> who teaches you for your own good [or "profit"],
>> who leads you in the way you should go.
> ¹⁸O that you had paid attention to my commandments!
>> Then your prosperity would have been like a river,
>> and your success like the waves of the sea.
>> (Isa. 48:17–18)

Prosperity, success, and profit come only from the Lord and the Lord's way. Once again failure to serve and worship the Lord alone is not only disobedience; it is also stupid and gains nothing. (For discussion of the reverse situation, when the people believe they have profited from other gods, see above under "The Meaning of the Commandment.")

Amos does not seem to be one of the prophets for whom obedience to the First Commandment is a critical issue. There is one text, however, that has implications for our understanding of the force of the Commandment in the political sphere. It is the account of the prophet's encounter with the chief priest Amaziah (7:10–15):

> ¹⁰Then Amaziah, the priest of Bethel, sent to King Jeroboam of Israel, saying, "Amos has conspired against you in the very center of the house of Israel; the land is not able to bear all his words. ¹¹For thus Amos has said,
>
>> 'Jeroboam shall die by the sword,
>>> and Israel must go into exile away from his land.'"
>
> ¹²And Amaziah said to Amos, "O seer, go, flee away to the land of Judah, earn your bread there, and prophesy there; ¹³but never again prophesy at Bethel, for it is the king's sanctuary, and it is a temple of the kingdom."

39

> [14]Then Amos answered Amaziah, "I am no prophet, nor a prophet's son; but I am a herdsman, and a dresser of sycamore trees, [15]and the LORD took me from following the flock, and the LORD said to me, 'Go, prophesy to my people Israel.'"

The crucial thing that happens here is not immediately noticeable. It is the disappearance of the Lord from the religious and political center of Israel's life. That happens in several ways. First, the divine judgment announced by the prophet in the preceding verse has been received and passed on to King Jeroboam by the priest Amaziah in a manner that removes the Lord's voice and agency completely. Instead of what the prophet declared in the name of the Lord—"I [the LORD] will rise against the house of Jeroboam with the sword" (7:9)—we have *"Amos has conspired* against you in the very center of the house of Israel" (v. 10; emphasis added). Further, where the Lord has spoken consistently of "my people Israel" (vv. 8, 15), the priest translates that simply as "Israel," so that the covenantal relationship that defines Israel's very being since the delivery from Egypt has also disappeared. And finally, Bethel has been turned from the Lord's sanctuary into "the king's sanctuary" and "a temple of the kingdom" (v. 13). It is not a matter of turning to other named gods. What has happened is that the Lord's claim over Israel, its politics, and its worship has been removed. The controlling power is not the Lord's. The political ruler and the religious leader are the center of all that happens. The sanctuary of the Lord has been taken over by the political leader. "The political lord is the center of meaning and value in this sanctuary, the one who gives it identity, not 'the Lord your God who brought you out of the land of Egypt, out of the house of slavery'" (Miller, *The God You Have*, 38). In subtle but definite ways, the political power and the religious establishment have taken away the Lord's place. And so the judgment will come (vv. 16–17).

Isaiah 40–66 has as one of its themes the claim that the Lord is God and there is no other. This is part of a theological apologetic to account for what happened to Israel in exile and in so doing to argue the case against the claims of Marduk or any other deity who might seem to be more powerful or merit Israel's allegiance, in light of what has happened. Along with the "good news" (52:7) that God will bring the people back from exile through "his anointed," Cyrus

(44:28–45:7), the prophet makes the case for the Lord against the apparent dominance—and thus attractiveness—of Babylon's gods. The issue is less the failure of the people to live by the First Commandment than it is the assertions of the Lord's claim to be God alone and thus the only one at work for weal and woe (45:7). The thematic sentence is "I am the LORD, and there is no other," repeated a number of times (44:8; 45:5–6, 14, 18, 21, 22; 46:9; cf. Deut. 4:35, 39). Its variation is "Besides me there is no god" (e.g., Isa. 44:6, 8; 45:5, 14, 21). Whether creation (e.g., 40:28; 45:6, 18) or the power behind the victory of Cyrus (44:28–45:7) or Israel's exile (e.g., 40:2), it is all the Lord's doing alone. In chapter 40, the prophet compares the Lord to the nations, the rulers of the earth, and the idols, the made gods of the nations. These are all nothing, a drop in the bucket, like dust on the scales (40:15) alongside the Lord. The idols and gods cannot deliver (57:13). As the Lord says through the prophet: "The wind will carry them off, a breath will take them away. But whoever takes refuge in me shall possess the land and inherit my holy mountain" (57:13b).

All of this is the reason for the people to trust in the Lord: "Then you shall call, and the LORD will answer; you shall cry for help, and he will say, Here I am" (58:9). The message of the prophet once more becomes the ground for the people's commitment to the Lord alone, trusting in this one alone and finding their hope for the future only there. The Lord used "the mighty hand," the "outstretched hand," and the "terrifying displays of power" for the people in Egypt so that they would acknowledge that the Lord is God and there is no other; so also now that power will be manifest in a new exodus, so that they may once again acknowledge that there is no other God than the Lord.

The Psalms as Meditation on the First Commandment

Martin Luther rightly said: "Moreover, what is the whole Psalter but meditation and exercises based on the First Commandment" (Kolb and Wengert, *Book of Concord*, 382). It is surely from the Psalms that Luther came to see how thoroughly the aim of the First Commandment is to bring about complete trust in the Lord and the Lord's care:

41

> ³Many will see and fear,
>   and put their trust in the LORD.
> ⁴Happy are those who make
>   the LORD their trust,
> who do not turn to the proud,
>   to those who go astray after false gods.
>   (Ps. 40:3–4)

The contrast between trust in the Lord, taking refuge in and cleaving to the Lord alone, and attaching oneself to other gods and other claims on one's allegiance and trust is a frequent theme in the Psalter. In Psalm 106 the sins of Israel are delineated on the one hand in terms of their turning to other gods and idols, and on the other hand in identifying all the ways the people did not respond to the Lord's wonderful works by trusting in the Lord. So also the psalmist mocks the idols of silver and gold that can do nothing, just like all those who trust in them, and then goes on to call on Israel—in contrast to the idol worshipers—to trust in the Lord, for "he is their help and their shield" (115:3–13; cf. 135:15–18). In similar fashion, the psalmist in Psalm 31 claims, "You are my refuge," and then sets his or her trust in the Lord over against those who pay regard to "worthless idols," on the way to declaring, in the face of the threats all around, "But I trust in you, O LORD; I say, 'You are my God.' My times are in your hand" (vv. 4, 6, 14–15a). Elsewhere the distinction between the righteous and the wicked is between the person who puts one's refuge in the Lord, who fears the Lord, and the one who "trusted in abundant riches, and sought refuge in wealth" (Ps. 52:6–9; cf. Job 31:24).

There is no place where the First Commandment is more directly and fully set forth than in Psalm 81:9–10:

> ⁹There shall be no strange god among you;
>   you shall not bow down to a foreign god.
> ¹⁰I am the LORD your God,
>   who brought you up out of the land of Egypt.
>   Open your mouth wide and I will fill it.

The psalm reinforces the strong connection between God's care of Israel and Israel's devotion to the Lord. The voice of the Lord sounds poignantly throughout the psalm, lamenting the failure of the people to "listen" (vv. 8, 11, 13; cf. Deut. 6:4) and continue to enjoy the Lord's blessing. In the background of the psalm is the

42

experience of the people in the wilderness and their testing the Lord at Meribah (see above and Pss. 95:8; 106:32).

One cannot leave the Psalter without calling attention to one of the more important but also more implicit expressions of the First Commandment within its pages. That is the way in which the psalms give voice to prayer and praise, to supplication and thanksgiving, all of which are manifestations of the fear of the Lord, of one's trust in God alone. Such acts declare that there is One to whom we turn whose power is beyond all human power and whose claim is such that the very being and purpose of human existence is to give praise and glory to this One, who is the Lord.

> Most of our other acts are quite ambiguous and capable of authentic duplication by others for whom the reality of God is a matter of indifference, irrelevance, or nonsense. But doxology and prayer make no sense in a world where God is not present or trusted. The act of doxology is a continuing testimony to another order than the one that assumes we have found all the answers in ourselves and have no other way to go than the path our human minds and wills can identify. One of the reasons we gather for worship on regular occasions is to remind ourselves in prayer and praise that the secular ability to live in a world without taking account of God is neither the last word nor the right one. (Miller, "In Praise and Thanksgiving," 123)

The Psalms anticipate the later Westminster Shorter Catechism with its first question: "What is the chief end of man?" To which, it properly answers, echoing the Psalter: "To glorify God, and to enjoy him forever." (For extended discussion of the First Commandment in the Psalter, see Miller, "Psalms as a Meditation.")

Listening to the New Testament

The temptation of Jesus. The account of Jesus' temptation in the wilderness (Matt. 4:1–11//Luke 4:1–13) is an echo of the earlier testing of Israel in the wilderness, to which we have referred above (Exod. 17:1–7). As that was a test of the people's complete trust in God to provide for every care and need, so also is this temptation a test of the Son's commitment to the Father. That the claim of the First Commandment is in view here as much as it was in Israel's testing is clear from the two quotations of Deuteronomy 6

43

that Jesus gives in answer to the devil's temptation. When the devil quotes Psalm 91 to urge Jesus to throw himself down from the pinnacle of the temple so that God will send angels to catch him, Jesus quotes Deuteronomy 6:16: "Do not put the LORD your God to the test" (Matt. 4:7//Luke 4:12). And when the devil offers him all the kingdoms of the world and their splendor and riches if he will simply bow down and worship him, Jesus then quotes Deuteronomy 6:13: "The LORD your God you shall fear/worship; him [alone] you shall serve" (Matt. 4:10//Luke 4:8). The First Commandment, in both its prohibitive and positive forms, is Jesus' guide.

All the devil does is in order to test Jesus as the Son of God: "If you are the Son of God . . ." (Matt. 4:3, 6). Jesus' response shows that his relation to God does not vitiate complete obedience and trust; nor does it provide special privilege, freeing him from absolute reliance on God and God alone. On the contrary, like any other creature, the Son of God gives ultimate allegiance to no other power but the Lord. The message becomes very clear as the incident serves to confirm the claim of the First Commandment. If the Son of God stands under complete obedience to the commandment, then he becomes a model for every human being and an example of Israel in obedience. Although most of the stories of the First Commandment to this point—but not all of them (cf. 2 Kgs. 18:5–6; 23:1–30)—seem to show the failure of human beings, of Israel, to live in such trust and obedience, this story now shows the way. Following Jesus is not to replace the object of our worship but is a commitment to follow no other gods, however tempting they may be, and to worship the Lord your God and the Lord alone. Whatever identity is made between Jesus and God, whether in the language of "Son of God" or of "Lord" (*kyrios*), the incarnate one embodies a faithfulness to the First Commandment that shows the way for all who follow him. This is the beginning of his ministry; it is the way he will go to the end.

God and mammon. For discussion of the force of Jesus' insistence that "You cannot serve God and mammon," see the end of the section above on "The Meaning of the Commandment."

The Great Commandment. All three of the Synoptic Gospels portray Jesus' citation or affirmation of the Shema as the "Great/First Commandment (Matt. 22:34–40; Mark 12:28–34; Luke 10:25–28). Several things are to be noted:

1. The first or great commandment for Jesus and his Jewish audience is the Shema, the normative positive form of the First

Commandment of the Decalogue. Its priority, evident in its place in the Decalogue, is reaffirmed by Jesus and those around him. What comes first, what matters most, is consistent in both Testaments.

2. In both Matthew and Luke, the interrogation that leads to Jesus' affirmation of the Shema is described as a test by persons in his audience. There is a link between the challenge here and the challenge of the devil in the temptation story. It is of a different sort and not as directly tied to the First Commandment, but it is a test to see if Jesus knows and affirms what is the most important word: Love the Lord your God with all you have and are.

3. While the debate remains open as to how best to translate *yhwh ʾeḥad* in Deuteronomy 6:4—"the Lord alone" or "the Lord is one"; in Mark 12:32 we are given both translations. Jesus responds to the question about the first of all the commandments with the Shema: "Hear, O Israel, the Lord our God is one . . ." (12:29–30). The scribe, however, in repeating and affirming Jesus' answer, says, "He is one, and besides him there is no other." To a large degree, this makes the debate about how to translate Deuteronomy 6:4 more philological than theological. That is, the Markan account legitimizes both translations and makes clear that both interpretations were a part of appropriating the Shema in that time. God is one and only.

4. Jesus' citation of the Shema sets it alongside his claim "You cannot serve God and mammon" to keep before the community both the need to *choose* and the need to give *total commitment*. There is no qualification in the call to love the Lord your God with all your heart, all your soul, all your mind, and all your strength. Both choice and commitment are aspects of one's obedience to the First Commandment.

5. Without being asked, Jesus adds to his quotation of the Shema the command "You shall love your neighbor as yourself" (Lev. 19:18), saying in the Matthean account that the second command is "like" the first (22:39). In joining this second command, which comes from the text in Leviticus most reflective of the Decalogue, with the first, Jesus affirms the wholeness of the Decalogue and gives to the community of faith a positive formulation of all the commandments about the neighbor alongside the positive expression of the First Commandment. Insofar as the second table of the Decalogue sets forth particular directives about treating the neighbor, one may not read them narrowly. They are central manifestations of the large command to love the neighbor, which includes all

45

sorts of positive ways to care for the well-being of one's neighbor, as the chapters on those commandments will show.

Jesus is Lord. The christological claim that serves to identify Jesus with the God of Israel is dealt with below in the treatment of the commandment protecting against misuse of the name of God (chap. 2). There is one text that merits attention in this context because of its clear focus on the worship of God alone and its appropriation of the Shema in order to claim an identity between the one God and Jesus:

> [4]Hence, as to the eating of food offered to idols, we know that "no idol in the world really exists," and that "there is no God but one." [5]Indeed, even though there may be so-called gods in heaven or on earth—as in fact there are many gods and many lords—[6]yet for us there is one God, the Father, from whom are all things and for whom we exist, and one Lord, Jesus Christ, through whom are all things and through whom we exist. (1 Cor. 8:4–6)

In the context of his attention to the church issue of whether or not Christians may eat food offered to idols, Paul makes the claim consistent with the Old Testament and Judaism of his time, to the effect that idols have no real existence. They are made images without power (see below). And with the Shema and the divine speeches of Isaiah 40–66 (see above), he can assert, "There is no God but one," something with which he knows his audience will agree. Then, however, he first acknowledges that there may be a lot of "so-called gods" around and goes on to the even stronger claim that yes, there actually are many gods and many lords. Here Paul recognizes what is at the heart of the First Commandment, awareness of the fact of many gods and lords who may make claims on the ultimate loyalty and obedience of human beings. We have already heard Jesus name one of them: Mammon.

> The pagan pantheon cannot simply be dismissed as metaphysically nonexistent and therefore morally irrelevant. It signals an actual phenomenon within the surrounding culture that must be faced and dealt with, not simply sidestepped. For this reason . . . the allegiance of local paganism to this or that "god" and "lord" must be met with nothing short of the Christian version of Jewish-style, *Shema*-style, monotheism. (Wright, *Climax of the Covenant*, 128)

46

In verse 6 Paul reaches the climax of his argument, first of all making clear that whatever may be the general cultural picture and the possibilities of other deities, "for us" that is irrelevant. Drawing on and expanding the Shema, he makes the double statement:

For us,

> there is one God, the Father,
>> from whom are all things and for whom we exist,
> and one Lord, Jesus Christ,
>> through whom are all things and through whom we exist.

N. T. Wright shows what is going on here:

> Paul . . . has glossed "God" with "the Father," and "Lord" with "Jesus Christ," adding in each case an explanatory phrase: "God" is the Father, "from whom are all things and we to him," and the "Lord" is Jesus the Messiah, "through whom are all things and we through him." There can be no mistake: just as in Philippians 2 and Colossians 1, Paul has placed Jesus *within* an explicit statement, drawn from the Old Testament's quarry of emphatically monotheistic texts, of the doctrine that Israel's God is the one and only God, the creator of the world. (*Climax of the Covenant*, 129)

As Wright notes, something similar happens in Philippians 2:5–11, which culminates in the confession "Jesus is Lord," as well as in Colossians 1:15–20, where "the Messiah himself is the dwelling place of the divine wisdom, the immanent presence of the transcendent God, the visible image of the invisible God" (Wright, *Climax*, 118). Through these and other texts, the church learns that when it obeys the First Commandment, worshiping the Lord alone, its Lord has not changed but is present now in the incarnate and resurrected Jesus of Nazareth.

Honoring the political rulers. The way in which the Ten Commandments speak about how persons are to respond to political powers is taken up below under the treatment of the Fifth Commandment, about honoring parents, and the reasons for doing so are given there (chap. 4). The subject, however, merits a brief mention in this context also because a couple of texts touch on the connection between response to God and response to political leaders. In all the cases, a clear distinction is made. Proper respect for the political authorities is to be expected, but this is not the

47

same thing as the service and worship of God. In Mark 12:13–17 (//Matt. 22:15–21//Luke 20:20–26), Jesus makes this distinction in response to a question about whether it is lawful to pay taxes to the emperor: "Give to the emperor the things that are the emperor's, and to God the things that are God's" (Mark 12:17). The two are not to be equated. The political leadership, so Paul argues in Romans 13:1–7, is "appointed" by God, and "the authorities are God's servants" (vv. 2, 6). The concrete implication of this is clear: "Pay to all what is due them—taxes to whom taxes are due, revenue to whom revenue is due, . . . honor to whom honor is due" (v. 7). Paul's point is affirmed and further clarified in the word in 1 Peter 2:17: "Honor everyone. Love the family of believers. Fear God. Honor the emperor." Lest there be any uncertainty, the text makes clear the difference between how we respond to the political ruler and how we respond to God. God is to be feared and worshiped. The emperor is to be treated like everyone else: with honor.

The Second Commandment: Make No Images

The Double Meaning of the Commandment

The succinct form of the Second Commandment is found in the sentence: "You shall not make for yourself an idol" (Exod. 20:4a// Deut. 5:8a). It is echoed with variations in other legal texts, specifically Exodus 20:23; 34:17; Leviticus 19:4; 26:1; and Deuteronomy 27:15. In all of these instances, the question inherent in the commandment is Images of what? The answer to that is twofold: images of the Lord, and images or representations of other gods. The latter is where the Second Commandment overlaps with the First, and the use of the plural "gods" in several of the texts just mentioned tends to confirm that interpretation, as in "gods of silver alongside me" (Exod. 20:23). The particularity of the Second Commandment, however, marking it off from the First Commandment, is probably to be seen in its prohibition of any representation of *the Lord*.

The clearest and most specific evidence for the commandment's inhibition of images of the Lord is found in the chapter in Deuteronomy immediately preceding the Commandments. Deuteronomy 4 is in effect a Mosaic sermon on the Second Commandment with resonances, inevitably and appropriately, to the First Command-

48

ment. Moses takes the people back to Sinai to remind them of what happened there, how the people stood before the Lord at the foot of the mountain while it "was blazing up to the very heavens, shrouded in dark clouds" (v. 11b). When the Lord charged the people to observe his covenant, the "Ten Words," the Lord spoke to them out of the fire. Moses makes the specific point: "You heard the sound of words but saw no form; there was only a voice" (v. 12). That fact then becomes the grounds for the warning:

> [15]Since you saw no form when the LORD spoke to you at Horeb out of the fire, take care and watch yourselves closely, [16]so that you do not act corruptly by making an idol for yourselves, in the form of any figure—the likeness of male or female, [17]the likeness of any animal that is on the earth, the likeness of any winged bird that flies in the air, [18]the likeness of anything that creeps on the ground, the likeness of any fish that is in the water under the earth. [19]And when you look up to the heavens and see the sun, the moon, and the stars, all the host of heaven, do not be led astray and bow down to them and serve them, things that the LORD your God has allotted to all the peoples everywhere under heaven. [20]But the LORD has taken you and brought you out of the iron-smelter, out of Egypt, to become a people of his very own possession, as you are now. (Deut. 4:15–20)

The people are warned not to make "an idol (*pesel*) in the form (*tĕmûnâ*) of any figure" (v. 16). The terms for "idol" and "form" are the same as occur in the Second Commandment: "You shall not make for yourselves an idol (*pesel*), whether in the form (*tĕmûnâ*) of anything . . ." (Deut. 5:8). The further elaboration prohibiting making the likeness of anything—human or animal—on earth or in the sky or on the ground or in the waters under the earth also echoes the Second Commandment, which forbids making an idol "in the form of anything that is in heaven above, or that is on the earth beneath, or that is in the water under the earth" (5:8). What is of particular importance in this context is the opening clause in 4:15, which gives the reason why no such idol or form is to be made. It is because the people saw no form (*tĕmûnâ*) when the Lord spoke to them out of the fire. They only heard a voice out of the fire. The prohibition of idol making, therefore, clearly rests on an understanding that the Lord does not appear in any concrete visible form. So no human being may seek to represent the Lord in such a way.

49

Human-made images of the Lord in any form imaginable are forever excluded. The Lord chooses the manner of divine revelation and appearance.

In this text it is also possible to see how the prohibition of images of the Lord is expanded to refer to idols and images of any sort that are worshiped, that is, images of other gods. That is implicit already in 4:1–18, but it becomes explicit in verse 19, which talks not about made images but about the elements of heaven and warns against bowing down to them and serving them, using language typical for speaking about the worship of other gods, not just idols. Whether natural or made, these other gods are outside the perimeters of Israel's worship. That we are talking here about other gods and not representations of the Lord is further underscored by a tantalizingly brief note: these are "things that the LORD your God has allotted to all the people everywhere under heaven" (v. 19b; cf. 29:26). Whatever the story is about these other gods in relation to "the LORD your God," it has nothing to do with Israel.

Finally, in verse 20 both dimensions are undergirded and given their grounding. The community belongs to the Lord because the Lord has brought them "out of the iron-smelter" of Egypt. So no other relation can be claimed or serve to interfere with this one. Israel's worship of the Lord precludes any other worship and is on the Lord's terms and in the manner consistent with the way God has spoken and acted. However impressive or appealing images and elements may be, either as objects of worship or representations of the Lord, they violate the relationship established in God's delivering grace.

Implications of the Absence of Divine Images

Insofar as divine images may either be associated in an explicit way with other deities than the Lord of Israel or become objects of worship in themselves, the prohibition of images of any sort is a strong barrier to the encroachment of other objects of worship on the exclusive worship of the Lord. As such, the Second Commandment is a strong *safeguard of the First Commandment*. Since nothing in the natural world may become an object of worship and our ultimate trust, so it is with any humanly created entity. Whether it is an intended representation of the Lord or an idol of some other deity, that which is made and "idolized" takes one away from the true worship of the one who is Israel's God, in exclusive and covenantal relationship with the "people of his very own possession" (Deut. 4:20).

The long sermon of Deuteronomy 4, however, shows that other things are at stake here. The *proper* worship as well as the exclusive worship of the Lord is violated when attempts are made to represent the Lord in some made "form of any figure" (Deut. 4:16). Both God's immanence and transcendence are breached or violated when human beings seek to make some representation of the Lord. Scripture more than once suggests that God has some form or image. It speaks, for example, of God's "face" and "hand" and "back." Such a way of speaking is important since it opens the theological possibility of thinking of God in personal language, a significant antecedent to the incarnation, which is itself confirmation of the persona of God. Yet that image is not available to us apart from its incarnate form. Deuteronomy 4 is a helpful guide to how we think about the divine appearance. There we encounter the paradox of the mountain "blazing up to the heavens" and at the same time "shrouded in dark clouds," literally, "darkness, cloud, and thick cloud" (v. 11). The paradox implicit in these expressions is crucial: utter darkness and the brightness of fire. The Lord speaks to the people out of the fire, a powerful image, something bright and visible, capable of being seen and illuminating; but it is also dangerous and untouchable, a reality that is not subject to being "made" or handled in any way. Nor is it in the form of any likeness. To make an image is indeed an effort to domesticate God, to tame the fire and control it. Making an image of God is like playing with fire. It is dangerous; one is sure to get burned.

As the most extended biblical interpretation of the Second Commandment, Deuteronomy 4 makes several other points. One is that *the Lord alone determines how God shall be seen, revealed, known, and accessible.* "Since you saw no form when the LORD spoke to you . . . out of the fire, take care and watch yourselves closely, so that you do not act corruptly by making an idol for yourselves . . ." (4:15). Human efforts to represent God in the form of anything are a corruption because God has determined how to be accessible. Thus Israel's modes of worship are given and not made. They arise out of the Lord's way with the community, not by its ideas and creations. As Brevard Childs has put it: "The prohibition of images is grounded in the self-introductory formula, 'I am Yahweh,' which

51

summarizes God's own testimony to himself. The contrast to this true witness, the substitution of an image—regardless of whether spiritual or crass—is judged to be a false witness, hence a delusion" (Childs, *Exodus*, 409). Or to put this divine self-determination in another way: "Graven images are not to be created, because the reality sought by such construction has already been created by the steadfastly-loving God" (Willis-Watkins, *The Second Commandment and Church Reform*, 37).

What is also explicit and formative in the Mosaic report of Deuteronomy 4 is the realization that the way in which God will be available and known to God's people is *through the word.* "You heard the sound of words but saw no form; there was only a voice" (4:12). "From heaven he made you hear his voice to discipline you. On earth he showed you his great fire, while you heard his words coming out of the fire" (4:36). It is in this speech of Moses that the revelation and accessibility of God only through the word becomes explicitly articulated in such a way that it shapes the rest of Scripture and the mode of encounter between the Lord and the Lord's people. These verses accent the voice in the fire. God is available to the community through the word spoken by God, not by any visible form. The focus of the church on the Bible and on preaching is rooted in this claim that the word of God is how the Lord is revealed and present. That point is given a symbolic and powerful confirmation in Deuteronomy 10, when "the ten words" (4:13, my trans.) are written on stone tablets by *the hand of the Lord* and put in the ark of the covenant (10:1–5). Rather than such an act being demythologization of the ark as the place of the invisible presence of God, it clarifies that invisible presence as through the word, starting with the "ten words" but certainly not ending there. The line between Deuteronomy 4 and John 1 is obvious. A theology of the Word is rooted in this biblical interpretation of the Second Commandment and becomes the obvious and necessary way of interpreting the revelation and presence of God in Jesus Christ.

Finally, Deuteronomy 4 opens up a critique of idolatry that becomes prominent in the prophets: *the utter powerlessness of idols.* In Moses' warning to the people about becoming complacent and falling into the corruption of idolatry and thus provoking the Lord to anger, he promises that such actions will lead to their perishing from the land and being scattered among the peoples. "There," Moses says, "you will serve other gods made by human hands, objects of wood and stone that neither see, nor hear, nor eat, nor smell" (4:28). A sharp contrast is implied between the Lord, who is not reduced to representation, and the gods, which are made by human hands. The point is not so much that the Lord does these things—seeing, hearing, and so forth—though there are many such indications, as it is that made objects are completely inanimate, lifeless, powerless, capable of doing nothing. Why would one worship such as that? is the implicit question. The point is reiterated in the prophets. In Second Isaiah, the Lord addresses the community in exile and asks, "To whom will you liken me?" (Isa. 46:5), and goes on to describe the idol makers, who take a lot of gold and silver and give it to a goldsmith, who then "makes it into a god," which they fall down and worship (v. 6). In the next verse we read:

> 7They lift it to their shoulders, they carry it,
>   they set it in its place, and it stands there;
>   it cannot move from its place.
> If one cries out to it, it does not answer
>   or save anyone from trouble.
> . . . .
>   9remember the former things of old;
> for I am God, and there is no other;
>   I am God, and there is no one like me.

The contrast between the powerless idols and the Lord is suggested in the inability of the idols to answer or to save from trouble when a worshiper cries out for help, one of the most characteristic features of Israel's God (e.g., Exod. 2:23; 3:7, 9; 22:23, 27; Pss. 3:4; 5:2–3; 9:12; 18:6; 34:4–6; etc.).

The difference is also implicit in the fact that the idols have to be carried, a point already noted in Isaiah 46:1: "Their idols are on beasts and cattle; these things you carry are loaded as burdens on weary animals." This is in sharp contrast to the Lord, who is not carried but *carries*:

> 3Listen to me, O house of Jacob,
>   all the remnant of the house of Israel,
> who have been borne by me from your birth,
>   carried from the womb;
> 4even to your old age I am he,
>   even when you turn gray I will carry you.

53

> I have made, and I will bear;
>> I will carry and will save.

(46:3–4)

The prophet builds a powerful metaphor of God's saving and caring activity in behalf of Israel as an act of carrying and bearing them from beginning to end. The Babylonian people make gods and carry them; the Lord makes a people and carries them.

Jeremiah makes the same point:

> ⁵They [i.e their idols] are like scarecrows in a cucumber field,
>> and they cannot speak;
> they have to be carried,
>> for they cannot walk.
> Do not be afraid of them,
>> for they cannot do evil,
>>> nor is it in them to do good.
> ⁶There is none like you, O LORD;
>> you are great, and your name is great in might.

(10:5–6)

The prophet then goes on to say that "the instruction given by idols is no better than wood" (Jer. 10:8; cf. Hab. 2:18–19). Here and elsewhere (Jer. 8:19; 14:22), Jeremiah uses the term *hăbālîm* for "idols" and in 10:15 calls them *hebel*, the Hebrew word most often associated with Ecclesiastes and meaning "vanity," "a breath," or "vapor." The idols are no more substantial than a whiff of wind or air, utterly worthless.

The Psalms do not often speak about idols, but in the one place where the matter is discussed at some length, the same point is made:

> ³Our God is in the heavens;
>> he does whatever he pleases.
> ⁴Their idols are silver and gold,
>> the work of human hands.
> ⁵They have mouths, but do not speak;
>> eyes, but do not see.
> ⁶They have ears, but do not hear;
>> noses, but do not smell.
> ⁷They have hands, but do not feel;
>> feet, but do not walk;
>>> they make no sound in their throats.

54

[8]Those who make them are like them;
   so are all who trust in them.
            (Ps. 115:3–8; cf. 135:15–18)

As in all of the texts mentioned, the contrast with the Lord is either the starting point or the ending. The idols are earthen, constructed, mute, inanimate objects. They can do nothing (cf. Rev. 9:20). The Lord, "our God," is in the heavens and "does whatever he pleases." What sense would it make to put one's trust in such useless, constructed objects (cf. Hab. 2:19)? In all of these texts, there is a kind of apologetic undergirding the First and Second Commandments. Obedience to these commandments is thus not only a proper response to what God has done and God's way of being accessible to the people; it also makes sense. Or to put it in reverse mode, as the Bible does, it makes *no sense* to give any homage to, put any trust in, or have any expectation of such objects as idols if one stops and thinks about it in a serious or rational way. How can they do anything?

The Trajectory of the Second Commandment

Stories of image making and image worship. The story of the Second Commandment has many episodes. The first is immediate and liturgical, the making of the golden calf by Aaron and the Israelite people and the consequent liturgical shout: "These are your gods, O Israel, who brought you up out of the land of Egypt!" (Exod. 32:4). There is an obvious incongruity between the plural expression of the people, "These are your gods," and both the fact that Aaron has cast an image of a single calf (v. 4) and then says after their exclamation, "Tomorrow shall be a festival to the LORD" (v. 5). The plural anticipates Jeroboam's similar shout after making the two bull images for Bethel and Dan (1 Kgs. 12:28). But whatever the history of the text, the present confusion attests once more to the interaction of the First and Second Commandments and the difficulty of separating the worship of other gods and the worship of images of God. Aaron the priest intends the calf to be an image to facilitate the worship of the Lord; the people interpret it as an image of other gods. Image making is the start of a slippery slope. The story of the golden calf tells us that the First with the Second Commandment, forming the principal commandment, was the first to go under, disobeyed in the impatience of the people, in their

55

search for a god who would get the show on the road, in their effort to set the agenda and arrange the schedule for the Lord, who moves in freedom and cannot be found in or on any image constructed by human beings.

Brief note should be taken of Gideon's making an ephod from the golden earrings that the people of Israel had taken as booty from the Ishmaelites and/or Midianites (Judg. 8:22–28). While the ephod was probably a divinatory device, the story seems to understand its reception in a larger way. As Carolyn Pressler notes: "Gideon's ephod becomes an idol, an object of worship rather than a tool of worship. The Israelites 'prostitute' themselves before it" (*Joshua, Judges, and Ruth*, 182). The text reports that the ephod became a "snare" to Gideon and his family, language used earlier in the book with reference to the gods of the nations (Judg. 2:3).

The danger of tools of worship becoming objects of worship, as Pressler puts it, is never more apparent than in the story of King Jeroboam's calves, which he had constructed out of gold and set up in Bethel and Dan (1 Kgs. 12:25–33). These may well have been pedestals for the divine invisible deity, but in the course of time, as the books of Kings and the Prophets attest, they became objects of worship and sacrifice and thus the primary cause for the fall of the northern kingdom (cf. 2 Kgs. 17:16, 21–22; Hos. 8:5; 10:5–6; 13:1–2).

An economic dimension: silver and gold. The stories above and other texts reveal an economic dimension to the Second Commandment. Idol making is closely associated with silver and gold, with wealth. The golden calf in the wilderness and Gideon's ephod are both made from gold and silver jewelry, plundered from the Egyptians (Exod. 3:21–22; 12:35–36) and the Midianites (Judg. 8:24–28). The prophets often inveigh against idols made from silver and gold (e.g., Isa. 2:20; 30:22; 31:7; 46:6; Jer. 10:4, 8–9; Ezek. 7:19–20; Hos. 2:8; Hab. 2:19). In the first statute after the giving of the Commandments in Exodus 20, the Lord tells Moses to instruct the people, "You shall not make gods of silver alongside me, nor shall you make gods of gold" (20:23). The idols or images are thus icons of excessive wealth. The simplicity of the worship of the Lord is revealed in the next sentence in Exodus 20: "You need make for me only an altar of earth" (v. 24). The temptation is to show off wealth by extravagant idols or to seek wealth by going after the valuable idols of others, as Moses shows when he says with regard to the images of the nations that Israel encounters: "The images of their gods you

56

shall burn with fire. Do not covet the silver or the gold that is on them and take it for yourself, because you could be ensnared by it; for it is abhorrent to the LORD your God" (Deut. 7:25). The idols are one of the first and primary objects of the avarice and greed against which the Tenth Commandment warns. Making idols, therefore, is seen to be tied to an economic situation of wealth and affluence, which gives a particular and quite concrete twist to Jesus' words about not being able to serve both God and mammon.

A *political dimension: kingship.* The Second Commandment also has a political twist in its trajectory through the story of Israel. Ronald Hendel has described the ancient context as follows:

> The close relationship between the image of the god and the image of the king is an important part of the ideology of kingship in the ancient Near East. The king was regarded as the earthly representative of the gods, and as such the image of the god was a symbol of the legitimacy of the earthly king. The divine image was pictured and was treated as a king, therefore serving as a reminder of the divine authority of the king. ("Social Origins of the Aniconic Tradition," 381)

On the one hand, Israel's nonimaged god resists the impulse to validation of the acquisitive and consumerist impulse by dedicating one's wealth to divine representation and thus reinforcing one's affluence by "the work of our hands" (Ps. 90:17) elevated to divine status. On the other hand, the prohibition of divine images undercuts the validation of political figures and political status by refusing to allow any identification between such figures and roles and the God who authorizes but also judges and destabilizes political authority.

A *theological dimension: theological images.* While in some sense everything about the First and Second Commandments is "theological," there is a particular way in which it has a theological impact on the life and faith of the community. While the visual and three-dimensional images are in view, it is possible to create divine images with words and thoughts as well. Thus theologians and clergy may be especially susceptible to idolatry by developing images, theological systems, and constructions of God that objectify the transcendent and make us deceive ourselves into thinking that we can see God *theologically,* with our concepts if not our eyes and hands. In the making of mental images, the Puritans saw a violation of this commandment, and while that may go too far, it is a proper

57

caution. The Second Commandment relativizes and criticizes every linguistic and theological system we can imagine. It is the main reason why the community of faith may not let any linguistic image of God—not even "Father"—be absolute and immune from the hammer of the Second Commandment. It is difficult to work without mental and verbal images. Scripture itself is full of them. Some are more fruitful than others. The danger is in thinking that somehow the image incorporates the reality, or that it is immune from critical scrutiny, or that the theological image is a means of getting one's way with the Deity so imagined. The chief divine imagery of Deuteronomy 4 is a warning that playing with divine images of any sort is playing with fire. Theology is a very dangerous game and always teeters on the brink of idolatry, with the tendency, intentional or not, of seeking to get at God for our own well-being and program.

In the prohibition against making images—theological or otherwise—we have the biblical form of what Paul Tillich called "the Protestant principle," the theological form of which is justification by faith. What Tillich meant by this was not some single principle within Protestantism. By "Protestant principle" he meant what Protestantism is and what it is all about, something that endures even if Protestantism disappears.

> The Protestant principle, in name derived from the protest of the "protestants" against decisions of the Catholic majority, contains the divine and human protest against any absolute claim made for a relative reality, even if this claim is made by the Protestant church. The Protestant principle is the judge of every religious and cultural reality, including the religion and culture which calls itself "Protestant." (*Protestant Era*, 162)

It is just such an "absolute claim made for a relative reality" against which the Second Commandment is set.

In the image of God. There is, of course, a creature made in the image of God. The intensity of the prohibition of images is finally matched only by the significance of God's creation of something "in our image" (Gen. 1:26–27). The language for "image" is not the same as occurs in the Second Commandment, but the substantive meaning is no different. There is a divine likeness, but it is not made by human hands. It is God's own doing, an image that is not to be worshiped but is both God's agent in the rule and care of all the rest of creation and God's loving and loved reflection. While centu-

58

ries of speculation show the multitude of possibilities for thinking about how the human creature images God, at least two things are clear: (1) The one in God's image is created and put in this world to represent God's rule over all that God has made; and (2) The male and female image of God is a creature made for relationship with God. While God's care of all creation is clear from Scripture, starting with Genesis 1, there is no other creature with whom God has such intimate and caring connection than the imaged one. Thus any human effort to make an image of God for worship or manipulation is a violation of both God's reality and the human purpose. And if we search for something that in some way images God in an accessible way, we will find that we have to deal with one another. To put it in reverse, all our encounters with other persons are an engagement with one who is made in God's own image.

The Rest of the Commandment: The Reason Why

The Second Commandment concludes with an extended motivational clause giving a powerful reason why persons should obey this commandment, a rationalizing of the divine command that occurs in the following three commandments as well. The heart of the matter is the jealousy of God, a divine attribute reiterated several times as the reason for not worshiping other gods or idols (Exod. 34:14; Deut. 4:23–24; 6:15). The jealousy of God, the demand for exclusive devotion, is the theological flip side of election. Those who are elected in love elect to love. Those who are chosen choose. Those to whom commitment has been made commit. There is a proper jealousy to the covenantal relation that is appropriately seen in marriage. It has two dimensions. One is seen in the positive side of the jealousy of the Lord in the prophets and elsewhere, that is, the "zeal" of the partner for the other member of the relationship, the zealous pursuit of the good and well-being of the one who is loved as well as the commitment to preserve and even restore the covenantal relationship (McBride, "Essence of Orthodoxy," 147). Isaiah speaks of "your zeal for your people" (Isa. 26:11; cf. 9:7; 37:31–32). That zeal, however, also involves a jealousy for the sole affection of the partner, an unwillingness to share a love that is meant to be a perfect trust. The covenantal understanding of marriage assumes an uncompromising commitment in love. It is that uncompromising commitment in love that is in view when the Lord is jealous for

Israel's complete trust. (For further discussion of the jealousy of God and idolatry as a form of adultery, see chap. 6, on the Seventh Commandment.)

The word about the Lord "punishing children for the iniquity of parents, to the third and the fourth generation of those who reject me" (Exod. 20:5//Deut. 5:9) is disturbing because of the moral conviction that only the guilty party in a sin or crime is to be punished, not the innocent, even if related. Several observations place this reference in the larger context.

1. There is often a *generational outworking* of the consequences of sin. In the context of the Commandments, that would always be understood as by the agency of God and not some neutral, inherent connection apart from divine activity. The principle of transgenerational punishment is present in Scripture in story (2 Sam. 12:10; 1 Kgs. 14:7–18; 2 Kgs. 9:7–9; cf. Lam. 5:7) and creedal-type formulations (e.g., Exod. 34:5–7; Num. 14:18) more than in legal settings (Lev. 26:39–40).

2. A *tension is built into the trajectory* of the Second Commandment on this issue. Concern about the justice of God at this point was there in Israel as much as it is present now. So in the Deuteronomic Code, for example, there is insistence on punishment not being transgenerational (Deut. 24:16). Children are not to be punished for the sins of their parents or vice versa (cf. Jer. 31:29–30; Ezek. 18:1–24).

3. Within the formulation itself *significant modification takes place* in the course of its repetition in Scripture. In Exodus 34:6–7 (cf. Num. 14:18) "visiting the iniquity of the parents upon the children and the children's children," which usually implies all future generations (e.g., Ezek. 37:25), is modified by the restriction "to the third and fourth generation": those still living during the lifetime of the parent committing the sin.

4. The Second Commandment provides *further modification* by the addition of the phrase "of those who reject me," suggesting that "cross-generational retribution applies only to descendants who act as their ancestors did" (Tigay, *Deuteronomy*, 437).

5. The *restriction of divine punishment* so that it no longer operates across generations is made specific and clear in a Mosaic homily on the matter that clearly alludes to the Decalogue. Deuteronomy 7:9–10 says:

> [9]Know therefore that the LORD your God is God, the faithful
> God who maintains covenant loyalty with those who love him
> and keep his commandments, to a thousand generations, [10]*and
> who repays in their own person those who reject him. He does
> not delay but repays in their own person those who reject him.*
> (emphasis added)

The restriction of punishment only to the individual offender—the
Hebrew text has the singular—is emphasized by its being repeated
("in their own person") and by the word, "he does not delay."

    6. In the formulation as a whole, both in the creedal expres-
sions and in the commandment, the point is made that *God is bent
toward mercy and grace* and the expectation of a covenantal partner in whom love will dominate rather than hate or rejection. That
commitment will be the larger picture, and infidelity will be the
lesser reality. The steadfast love of God, the covenant loyalty of the
Lord, extends to a *thousand generations* of those who return that
love and loyalty—in sharp contrast to the *one* who rejects.

Idolatry in the New Testament.

The Second Commandment per se does not come into view in the
New Testament, but idolatry clearly does. There are teachings that
continue the claims of the Old Testament that idols are mute and
powerless in contrast to "the living and true God" (1 Thess. 1:9;
cf. 1 Cor. 12:2; 2 Cor. 6:16; Rev. 9:20) and that they are made of
gold and silver and so are of economic value (Rev. 9:20; cf. Rom.
2:22). Several lists of vices to be avoided include idolatry along with
other sins that are violations of the Commandments (e.g., Gal. 5:20;
Col. 3:5; 1 Pet. 4:3). The closest thing to the commandment itself is
probably found in the final words of 1 John: "Little children, keep
yourselves from idols" (5:21; cf. 1 Cor. 10:14). This follows on the
assertion "He is the true God and eternal life" (1 John 5:20). It is
a matter of some debate as to whether the subject of this sentence
is the Father or the Son, but in the light of the whole of the letter,
there is no doubt that it means to claim, against the opponents of
this message, that in Jesus one encounters the true God and not an
idol. "Jesus is not an idol, because he is not a static, frozen image
of divinity, like the image worshiper's statue or even the iconoclast's

61

Torah scroll; rather, he is a living, incarnate, ever-changing reality" (Marcus, "Idolatry," 162). On the contrary, the dangerous idols to be avoided are found among those who do not see the true God in Jesus Christ.

For Paul, idolatry plays a key role in his account of the origin of "ungodliness and wickedness" in Romans 1:18–27. There he claims that exchanging "the glory of the immortal God for images" (v. 23) is not only foolish (v. 22) but also leads to lust, impurity, and degrading passions (vv. 24–27; cf. Wis. 14:12–31). When that happened, "they exchanged the truth about God for a lie and worshiped and served the creature rather than the Creator" (v. 25). "The key to the human malaise is idolatry, which is to be understood as having as lord someone or some thing other than the Father of our Lord Jesus Christ" (Achtemeier, *Romans*, 39).

"The notion that idolatry either leads to or includes all other sins aids in the process of generalizing and transforming it into a metaphor" (Marcus, "Idolatry," 155). That is most obvious in the places where greed is equated with idolatry (Eph. 5:5; Col. 3:5), an echo of the interest in and coveting of the silver and gold of idols in the Old Testament as well as Jesus' words about not being able to serve both God and mammon (see above). The ease with which idolatry is particularly associated with greed (Col. 3:5) is reflective of the close connection between avarice and the love of money and the assumption that one can place one's ultimate trust in wealth, seeking one's happiness and security in the acquisition of things (see chap. 9, on the Tenth Commandment). The equation of greed and idolatry is not a dismissal of economic needs and their proper manifestations in human life. Both the political realm (kingship/Caesar, as in Mark 12:13–14) and the economic realm (money/possessions) are necessary facets of human flourishing. They are also spheres of life in which it is all too easy to turn what one needs into gods in which one places ultimate trust, making unconditional what is contingent and relative (Reinhold Niebuhr, *Nature and Destiny*, 1:178).

CHAPTER 2

Hallowing the Name of God

You shall not make wrongful use of the name of the LORD your God, for the LORD your
God will not acquit anyone who misuses his name.

Exodus 20:7//Deuteronomy 5:11

No other commandment seems to have as much potential for being treated with both great seriousness and utter casualness as does the commandment having to do with the use and misuse of the name of God. The tradition of swearing an oath on a Bible—in court or elsewhere—or concluding an oath with the words "So help me God," a reflection of this commandment's impact, is at least part of the grounds for a charge of perjury, lying under oath in a court of law. And while perjury is not as serious a crime as murder, its implications and potential consequences, including unintended judicial murder (capital punishment), are such that it is treated as a serious crime meriting serious punishment. At the same time, one who would never intentionally lie under an oath involving God's name might easily and casually use that name in an expletive or curse and without further thought or any reaction from the community. Standing in an abrasive tension with this capacity for casual disregard for the name, however, is the fact that this is the only commandment that contains a very direct and particular sanction, assuring God's own judgment upon whoever breaks the commandment. From the start one assumes that the Third Commandment is of no less weight and significance than any other.

In taking up the Third Commandment for closer examination and understanding, one needs to pursue three lines of investigation and interpretation:

1. There is much debate about the *actual meaning* of the commandment, most immediately and obviously evident in some of the varying translations of Exodus 20:7

> You shall not make wrongful use of the name of the LORD your God, for the LORD will not acquit anyone who misuses his name. (NRSV)

> You shall not swear falsely by the name of the LORD your God; for the LORD will not clear one who swears falsely by His name. (NJPS)

> Thou shalt not take the name of the LORD thy God in vain; for the LORD will not hold him guiltless that taketh his name in vain. (KJV)

2. The fact that these constitutional directives for the community of faith, the Commandments, include a specific piece that focuses upon the name of God means that some inquiry into the *significance and place of the divine name* is appropriate.

3. Here, as elsewhere, the meaning and force of the commandment is not fully or adequately uncovered apart from an exploration of *the trajectory of meaning and effects that flow from it, the specifics and illustrations, and possible implications* that may be discerned in story and law, proverb, Psalm, and prophecy.

The Meaning of the Third Commandment

The Context of the Commandment

Like others, the commandment having to do with the use of God's name—the Third Commandment in the numeration used here—reaches or looks both backward and forward. The individuality and particular focus of each commandment should not obscure the many ways in which it shows itself to be part of a whole, reflecting an order, participating in various internal groupings, and revealing numerable associations and resonances to other commandments. In this case, the commandment about the use of the name flows in a rather direct way out of the Prologue or self-presentation formula at the beginning of the Decalogue and out of the prohibitions against having other gods and making and worshiping idols or images. The true worship of God is still at issue when one comes

64

to the Third Commandment. If the First Commandment has to do with having no other gods and the Second with not replacing the Lord your God with images—of the Lord or anything else—and worshiping what is made rather than the Maker of heaven and earth, the next commandment reinforces the first two while taking up another aspect of the reality of God with which the community has to do in approaching and responding to its Lord: the name of God.

The intimate connection of the Third Commandment to the preceding prohibitions and the degree to which this commandment may be seen as an aspect and reinforcement of all that has gone before is evident in one of the places where the Name Commandment is present along with and in relation to the preceding commandments. In the first reiteration or explication of the Commandments in Deuteronomy after the Lord has spoken them to the people, Moses says: "The LORD your God you shall fear, and him you shall serve; and by his name you shall swear" (Deut. 6:13, my trans.). The words "fear," "serve," and "his name" suggest that the first three commandments are being reiterated but now in positive form. The translation given above, however, attempts to reflect the force of the Hebrew syntax, which places emphasis on the objects of the verbs. The matter becomes even clearer with a translation like that of the NJPS version: "Revere only the LORD your God and worship Him alone, and swear only by His name." While the first three commandments are clearly indicated, the point that runs through all three sentences and holds them together is the emphasis: the Lord alone, the Lord only. In this mode, they are understood to say one and the same thing: the Lord alone is to be the focus of your worship. The Third Commandment is thus tightly bound to the first two, reinforcing them in a particular area but making the same point in the process. What it means to have no other gods but the Lord is now carried into a particular sphere: the place, function, and use of God's name.

The name of God is no small matter relative to how the covenantal community loves and fears, worships and serves the Lord. This commandment is given to that community to warn against endangerment of the relationship to God by a misuse of the name and to direct its proper use of the name in loving and worshiping God. Analogously, Jeremiah's call for Judah to return to the Lord and remove their abominations (Jer. 4:1)—both demands having

65

in mind the First and Second Commandments—is immediately followed by the call to "swear, 'As the LORD lives!' in truth, in justice, and in uprightness . . ." (4:2), again associating the Third Commandment with the preceding commandments.

The verse from Deuteronomy 6 cited above also contributes to the more specific understanding of the Third Commandment in two ways:

1. The command "and by his name you shall swear" indicates that one major sphere in which the name of God comes to play— and thus an important activity in which speaking God's name can be improper and wrong—is in speaking oaths in which the name of God is uttered to ground the oath. Other texts confirm this sphere of human activity as a context in which the name of God plays a prominent role (See below).

2. The particular form of the Third Commandment, with its positive mode and its emphasis on "by *his* name (alone)," suggests immediately that the negative counterpart of swearing "by his name" is swearing by the name of someone else, of some other god, some other power. So if this text points to swearing oaths as an activity being covered by the Third Commandment, it also indicates that it has to do with the exclusive worship of the Lord alone. That is confirmed by Joshua 23:7, where the Israelites are warned against making mention of the names of the gods of the people or swearing by them or serving them or bowing down to them. In this instance, swearing is specifically by the name of other gods.

The close ties between the Third Commandment and the ones preceding it do not mean that there are no ways in which it is connected to the commandments that follow. The Name Commandment also points forward and leads into another part of the Decalogue. There are formal and linguistic associations as well as content ones. A careful reader, for example, will observe a shift in person from the preceding verses when one comes to the Third Commandment. The Prologue and the commandments against having other gods and making and worshiping images are given in *first*-person speech: "*I* am the LORD . . . ," "before *me*," "*I*, the LORD your God," "those who reject *me*," "those who love *me*," "*my* commandments." Beginning with the commandment having to do with the name of God, the three commandments that follow all speak of the Lord in the *third* person. They continue to use the phrase "the LORD your God," only more extensively than in the Prologue

66

and the First and Second Commandments, where it occurs twice. In the next commandments having to do with the name of God, the Sabbath, and parents, "the LORD your God" occurs no less than seven times in the Deuteronomic version (three times in the Exodus version). These same commandments also all include motive clauses giving reasons for obedience, something that occurs elsewhere in the Decalogue only in the prohibition against making and worshiping idols.

These connections between the Third Commandment and the next two are more literary than substantive. They may reflect the composition and redaction of the Decalogue out of smaller groups of two and three commandments as well as the impact of Deuteronomic or Deuteronomistic editing (frequency of "the LORD your God"). There are, however, further associations between the Third Commandment and the Sabbath Commandment that are to be noted in seeing the complex wholeness of the Decalogue. Specifically, in terms of content, the Sabbath Commandment has also to do with the "use" of something in relation to the deity, in this case, the Sabbath and its proper preservation from misuse. An analogous connection to the Sabbath Commandment is the way in which the latter also is subject to casual inattention on the assumption that careful observance is not a matter of large consequence. Like the Lord's name, the Lord's Sabbath is subject to profanation. Hallowing the name of God is as crucial for the community's relation to God as is hallowing or sanctifying the Lord's Sabbath.

There is yet one more important connection of the Third Commandment with what follows, in this instance with the second table of the Decalogue and the Deuteronomic form of the Ninth Commandment, against bearing false witness. While the expression in the Exodus (20:16) version of the Ninth Commandment, *ʿēd šāqer*, clearly means "false witness [*ʿēd*]," in the Deuteronomic version (5:20) the term *šeqer/šāqer*, meaning "falsehood," "deception," does not appear. Instead the word *šāwʾ* is used, the same word that occurs in the Third Commandment (Exod. 20:7//Deut. 5:11), which says, in a fairly literal translation, "Do not lift up the name of the LORD your God *laššāwʾ*." What exactly *le/la* (= to) *šāwʾ* means is the central issue in translating, understanding, and interpreting the Third Commandment, the task to which we now must turn. Whatever it means, however, the repetition of this word invites an association of this commandment with the subject matter of the Ninth

67

Commandment and suggests that while the Third Commandment has to do with the proper reverence and worship of God, the activity involved may also have to do with the neighbor.

Translating and Understanding the Third Commandment

The issues raised in examining the immediate context of the Third Commandment lead directly into the question of its specific meaning. As the translations cited earlier suggest, that is not immediately clear. At least the prohibition is sufficiently ambiguous to have produced different readings of just what kind of activity or disposition is in view.

The expression "lift up the name" is not common, occurring in only two other places (Exod. 28:12, 29; Ps. 16:4b). The uses in Exodus 28 are not relevant, but the usage in Psalm 16:4b, "I will not lift up their names on my lips" (my trans.), provides a close parallel to the commandment and confirms that in this context the phrase means to name something, to pronounce or say the name. The critical issue, then, is what sort of speaking or saying the name is inappropriate and unacceptable. What does it mean to speak or say the name of God *laššāw*ʾ?

The use of the word *šāw*ʾ in the Deuteronomic form of the Ninth Commandment as a substitute for the word *šeqer*, which appears in the Exodus version and clearly has to do with deception and falsehood, already indicates that *šāw*ʾ can refer to something that is false, to lying and deception. That understanding of the word tends to be confirmed by the first occurrence of the word *šāw*ʾ after its use in the Decalogue:

> ¹You shall not spread [lit., "lift up"] a false [*šāw*ʾ] report. You shall not join hands with the wicked to act as a malicious witness. ²You shall not follow a majority in wrongdoing; when you bear witness in a lawsuit, you shall not side with the majority so as to pervert justice; ³nor shall you be partial to the poor in a lawsuit. (Exod. 23:1–3)

The juridical context in which the *šāw*ʾ report is mentioned here suggests that it refers to a false report, one that may be given as testimony in court. One must be careful not to restrict the initial sentence too much. A *šāw*ʾ report may be spread in other ways than in court. But the larger context suggests that such a report, wherever made known, is not true.

In a quite different context, Job lays out some of his case for having lived a righteous life as follows:

> If I have walked with falsehood [*šāwʾ*],
> and my foot has hurried to deceit [*mirmâ*]— . . .
>
> > (Job 31:5)

The word *mirmâ* clearly means "deceit," and the parallelism of the whole line suggests that is what is meant also by *šāwʾ* in the first colon. Closer to the spheres of meaning implicit or explicit in the Ninth Commandment are Deuteronomy 6:13 (cited above) and Leviticus 19:12. As we have already noted, swearing an oath by the Lord's name is what Deuteronomy 6:13 presents as a positive form of the Third Commandment. Since this is an injunction to swear by YHWH's name, the implicit prohibition cannot be not swearing oaths at all. It must be either swearing by some other name or swearing in a deceptive way, not living up to one's oath. While the former is clearly suggested by the emphasis in the syntax, the other meaning is also intimated by comparison with another text, Leviticus 19:12: "You shall not swear falsely by my name [*laššāqer*], profaning the name of your God: I am the LORD." Here clearly is the negative counterpart to Deuteronomy 6:13 and strong support for understanding *šāwʾ* not only as deception but also as deception in the process of using God's name in swearing oaths.

Swearing oaths by the Lord's name was a common phenomenon in Israel. There are some forty-plus occurrences of persons swearing by the name of the Lord, customarily saying *ḥay-yhwh*, usually translated "As the LORD lives." Examples from Jeremiah are indicative:

> Although they say, "As the LORD lives,"
> Yet they swear falsely.
>
> > (Jer. 5:2)

Then, if they will diligently learn the ways of my people, to swear by my name . . . (Jer. 12:16)

Lo, I swear by my great name, says the LORD, that my name shall no longer be pronounced [lit., "called"] on the lips of any of the people of Judah in all the land of Egypt, saying, "As the Lord GOD [= YHWH] lives." (Jer. 44:26)

In this last instance, we encounter not only the human oath by the name of God but a divine one as well. So also in Isaiah 48:1, there is a reference to those "who swear by the name of the LORD," though the actual oath is not included in this case. It can hardly be doubted, therefore, that the term *šāwᵓ* in the Third Commandment encompasses making false statements, more specifically swearing oaths in the name of God that in some way or ways are false.

At the same time, one notices that there are clear and well-known Hebrew formulations for "swearing by the name of the LORD" and for prohibiting swearing falsely by the name that are quite different from what is found in the Third Commandment. That commandment, for example, does not use either of the formulations one finds in Leviticus 19:12: "You shall not swear falsely by my name," or "You shall not profane the name of your God" (my trans.). Nor has it used other verbs occurring in other texts that speak in some fashion of wrongful use or appropriation of the name of God. Whatever reasons may be inferred about the nonuse of other viable expressions, it suggests that the formulation in the commandment may have a broader meaning and that the acts in view are not reducible to swearing oaths.

Confirmation of that is found in the fact that *šāwᵓ* has another range of meaning having to do with identifying something, someone, or some act as empty, useless, in vain, to no purpose. So the psalmist protests to God, "For what . . . [*šāwᵓ*] have you created human beings" (Ps. 89:48 [47 E]). The meaning of the preceding and parallel cola is uncertain, but the immediately following line says:

> Who can live and never see death?
> Who can escape the power [lit. "hand"] of Sheol?
>   (v. 49 [48 E])

The context thus suggests that *šāwᵓ* in this instance has to do with the ephemerality and transitoriness of human existence. It is empty, vanity, in the sense that Qoheleth views life in Ecclesiastes 1:2:

> Vanity of vanities, says the Teacher,
> Vanity of vanities! All is vanity.

Indeed the term for "vanity," *hebel*, in Ecclesiastes is joined with *šāwᵓ* in Jonah 2:9 and Psalm 31:7 [6 E]. The latter text reads:

70

> I hate those who have regard for [lit. "keep"] worthless idols,
>> but I trust in the LORD.
>>> (my trans.)

The expression "worthless idols" is *hablê šāwʾ*, literally, something like "breaths of emptiness/uselessness" or "empty vapors." *Šāwʾ* in this context points to the emptiness and ineffectiveness of the idols, as does the word *hebel*. The point is underscored by the joining of the two words, which have basically the same meaning in this context. Elsewhere the word *hebel* in the plural (*hăbālîm*) is used as a surrogate for "idols" (Deut. 32:21, with the parallel phrase "what is not god/God"; 1 Kgs. 16:13, 26; Jer. 8:19; 10:8; 14:22) or to describe the idols as useless and empty (Isa. 57:13; Jer. 10:15 = 51:18; 16:19). The instances in Jonah 2 and Psalm 31 are not the only cases where *šāwʾ* refers (or may refer) to idols. In Jeremiah 18:15, the Lord condemns Israel/Judah with the following words:

> But my people have forgotten me,
>> they burn offerings to a delusion/nothing [*šāwʾ*].

While not referring to idols, a number of occurrences of *šāwʾ* appear in a context that speaks of an activity that, like the idols, is useless or to no effect (Ps. 60:13 [11 E]//108:13 [12 E]; 127:1 [2x], 2; Job 35:13). Job speaks of his life as allotted "months of *šāwʾ*" (7:3), comparing the days of human existence to days of a slave or laborer who longs for some shade or hopes for wages, but to no effect.

Elsewhere, Job says:

> Let one not trust in *šāwʾ* [what is empty, vain], leading oneself astray,
>> For that one's reward will be *šāwʾ* [nothing, emptiness].
>>> (Job 15:31, my trans.)

Even more relevant for understanding the usage of *šāwʾ* in the Third Commandment are occurrences in Jeremiah where the particular idiom of the commandment—*šāwʾ* preceded by the preposition *lĕ/la*, that is, *laššāwʾ*—is used and clearly with reference to what is useless, in vain, and to no effect. So the Lord bemoans the fact that previous punishment of the people had no effect:

> In vain (*laššāwʾ*) I have struck down your children;
>> they accepted no correction.
>>> (Jer. 2:30)

71

And in Jeremiah 4:30–31, Judah/Jerusalem is mocked for adorning herself for her lovers, presumably foreign powers, for such dressing up is utterly in vain (*laššāwʾ*) because

> your lovers despise you;
> > they seek your life.
> > > (v. 30)

When Jeremiah's prophetic activity is compared to the work of a refiner, it is in order to show that all the refining is *laššāwʾ*, futile, because "the wicked are not removed" (6:29). Finally, in Jeremiah 46:11, Egypt is said to have used many medicines *laššāwʾ*, in vain, because "there is no healing for you."

The uses of the word *šāwʾ* thus show that the word has a range of meanings, but the various uses indicate a relatively narrow continuum rather than significantly different meanings. There are close connections between what is untrue and what is empty and without substance, between what is false and what is worthless. Both kinds of things are in some sense unreal. There is nothing there rather than something. One may say of a document, a contract, or the like that it is "not *worth* the paper it is written on," or of what someone has said that it is not "worth a plugged nickel." Does that mean it is a bunch of lies, or that it cannot be backed up, or that it is all words and no substance? It could be any one of the three or all three at the same time. They ultimately mean much the same thing.

What is clear from the many uses of *šāwʾ* and the nonuse of more specific and/or pejorative terms is that the expression "lift up the name *laššāwʾ*" involves a range of related actions, but it is intentionally and properly more vague and less concrete than, say, "swear by the name." The phrase is open to a variety of concretions or, as Thomas Elssner has put it, "a whole palette of possible speech acts" (Elssner, *Das Namensmissbrauch-Verbot*, 84). It remains now to explore in more detail what those possible concretions are—some of which have already been identified—what they involve, and their significance.

The Name of God

Before that is done, however, there is one element of the prohibition proper with which we have not yet dealt: the *name* of God, the central subject matter of the Third Commandment. While there are various names and epithets for the deity in the Old Testament, such as Elohim and El, both of which mean "god" or "God," the particular and specific name that is in view is the name indicated by the Tetragrammaton, *yhwh*, or, as it is more commonly transcribed, YHWH. This does not mean that other names are unimportant or not in some fashion also protected by the Third Commandment. The biblical story, however, makes clear that it is especially by the name YHWH that God is known and revealed, and the Third Commandment specifies that it is this name that is being protected.

Indeed much of the significance of the name lies in the degree to which the biblical story ties the revelation and knowledge of God to the name YHWH. Whether biblical criticism will continue to speak of three primary streams of tradition telling of the origins of creation and of Israel—the Yahwist, the Elohist, and the Priestly writer—is up for grabs, but it is worth noting that in the traditional form in which these documents/strata/sources have been laid out, all three of them give some accounting of the revelation of the name YHWH.

The simplest account is the one ascribed to the Yahwist. It is technically not a story of the revelation of the name YHWH in that the proper name of God is used from the very beginning of the Yahwistic story (Gen. 2:4b). The name is in that sense, a given, an a priori. So there is no moment when it is revealed. But there is a very brief note in Genesis 4:26, at the conclusion of the presumed Yahwistic creation story (Gen. 2:4b–4:26) to the effect that "at that time people began to invoke the name of the LORD" (*qārāʾ bĕšēm yhwh*). It is not clear what moment is meant by "at that time" (*ʾaz*). The sentence is placed after the report of the birth of Seth to Adam and his wife and then the birth of Seth's son, Enosh. Whether that specific moment is meant or not, the tradition here places the knowledge of the name YHWH and the worship of God by that name as something that was present from the beginning, from primeval times. Nothing more is said about the name, but several times the Yahwistic tradition reports about how the ancestors built altars and "called on the name of the LORD" (Gen. 12:8; 13:4; 21:33; 26:25). Abram's first act in Canaan is to build an altar, where he calls on or invokes the name YHWH. In the process, the narrative of J lifts up the name YHWH as the way by which God is known to the ancestors and the name by which the deity was worshiped wherever they built a shrine, altar, or sacred place of some sort.

73

The name of God comes to play an even greater role in the biblical story of the Exodus. There are two accounts of God's self-revelation through the name and of the name. The more extended account in Exodus 3 tells of God's revelation of the name YHWH in the context of an appearance to Moses at the burning bush, calling him to go to Pharaoh and lead "my people, the Israelites" out of Egypt and out of slavery (Exod. 3:10). It is in the process of Moses' questioning that God reveals the divine name:

> [13]But Moses said to God, "If I come to the Israelites and say to them, 'The God of your ancestors has sent me to you,' and they ask me, 'What is his name?' what shall I say to them?" [14]God said to Moses, "I AM WHO I AM." He said further, "Thus you shall say to the Israelites, 'I AM has sent me to you.'" [15]God also said to Moses, "Thus you shall say to the Israelites, 'The LORD, the God of your ancestors, the God of Abraham, the God of Isaac, and the God of Jacob, has sent me to you':
>
> > This is my name forever,
> > and this my title for all generations."
> > (Exod. 3:13–15)

The revelation of the name is sufficiently complex in the narrative and ambiguous in meaning that it has provoked much discussion. It is not necessary in this context to rehearse all those complexities and ambiguities, but two observations need to be made. First, the sequence of name identifications in verses 13–15—"the God of your ancestors," "I AM WHO I AM," "I AM," and "the LORD" or "YHWH"—represents a progression toward the concluding element. Whatever the possible linguistic relationships, the outcome is clearly the revelation of YHWH as the divine name. That is indicated by the sequence concluding with YHWH and is then confirmed by the note at the end of verse 15: "This is my name forever." Second, the name *ʾehyeh*, "I am," which is clearly understood here as related to *yhwh*, is given a significant contextual interpretation in verse 12. When Moses objects—rightly it should be observed—that he is certainly nobody to try to go before Pharaoh and take the people out, the Lord responds with the words *ʾehyeh ʿimmak*, "I AM/will be with you." The *ʾehyeh*, of course, is the same as the *ʾehyeh* = "I AM" that is used in verses 13 and 14 as an alternate form of the divine name. However enigmatic the name may be, it is given a very clear meaning in this context. YHWH/*ʾehyeh* is the one who is

74

"present with," specifically, in light of the context, present with the one whom God has called and in the most difficult, demanding, and dangerous situation. The name thus marks and denotes the companioning presence of God and points to the reality of God in the here and now of the human situation.

In Exodus 6, one more account of the divine self-revelation through the name YHWH is given, this time in the Priestly account:

> ²God also spoke to Moses and said to him: "I am the Lord. ³I appeared to Abraham, Isaac, and Jacob as God Almighty, but by my name 'The Lord' I did not make myself known to them. ⁴I also established my covenant with them, to give them the land of Canaan, the land in which they resided as aliens. ⁵I have also heard the groaning of the Israelites whom the Egyptians are holding as slaves, and I have remembered my covenant. ⁶Say therefore to the Israelites, 'I am the Lord, and I will free you from the burdens of the Egyptians and deliver you from slavery to them. I will redeem you with an outstretched arm and with mighty acts of judgment. ⁷I will take you as my people, and I will be your God. You shall know that I am the Lord your God, who has freed you from the burdens of the Egyptians. ⁸I will bring you into the land that I swore to give to Abraham, Isaac, and Jacob; I will give it to you for a possession. I am the Lord.'" (6:2–8)

Four times in these eight verses, one hears the claim "I am YHWH/ the Lord" (cf. v. 29). The name is the reality. The name tells who is God, who is at work, who will deliver the slaves. At first the people are not impressed by this revelation because they are too dispirited (see v. 9). Nor is Pharaoh (see 5:2). But the revelation of the name YHWH as the uncovering of the true reality of God is not over. There is a sense in which the whole book of Exodus is about this name and its significance for knowing and worshiping God and for the presence of God in the midst of the people.

When the Lord says in verse 7, "You shall know that I am the Lord/YHWH your God, who has freed you from the burdens of the Egyptians," the clear implication is that they will come to know who YHWH is and what this name really connotes only out of the story and events now unfolding. And the revelation of who God is in the name YHWH actually provides the thematic structure of Exodus 15. For as the story moves on, again and again one hears with regard to the ongoing events: "By this you shall know that I am the

LORD/YHWH" (7:17) or similar such words (7:5, 17; 8:6 [10 E], 18 [22 E]; 9:14, 16, 29; 10:2; 11:7; 14:4, 18). When at last the Israelites are free from slavery and the Egyptian army is destroyed in the sea, the Israelites sing a hymn of praise:

> ¹I will sing to the LORD, for he has triumphed gloriously;
>   horse and rider he has thrown into the sea.
> ²The LORD is my strength and my might,
>   and he has become my salvation;
> this is my God, and I will praise him,
>   my father's God, and I will exalt him.
> ³The LORD is a warrior;
>   The LORD is his name.
>
> (Exod. 15:1–3)

The story that began in the divine self-revelation through the name, the story whose sequence of events is borne by the words and deeds of the one who bears that name—all this now comes to its climactic conclusion in the people's shout: *yhwh šěmô*, "YHWH/the LORD is his name." The reality of God, of God's purpose and character, is uncovered by all that is said and done in and through the one named YHWH. The knowledge of God is in knowing and acknowledging the name YHWH.

The self-presentation formula at the giving of the Commandments then recapitulates this structure: "I am the LORD your God"—the revelation of the name now as the starting point for the teaching about how Israel shall live; and "who brought you out of the land of Egypt, out of the house of slavery"—the summary words that recount the deeds of the one who bears the name "the LORD your God." The Commandments thus begin with the revelation once more of the name of the power at work in the Exodus and now claiming Israel's covenant loyalty. The Decalogue itself establishes the meaning and significance of the name "the LORD your God."

Before the story concludes, however, there is one more episode that lifts up the name YHWH to show how it reveals who and what God is. When the people lose faith in YHWH and turn to other gods for help—in this instance the calf image made by Aaron and the people—resulting first in Moses' intercession to an angry YHWH and then his own angry destruction of the two stone tablets with the Commandments, the golden calf, and all the people who worshiped the calf, the final outcome of this terrible episode

76

is a new inscription of the Commandments and a new revelation of the name:

> ⁴So Moses cut two tablets of stone like the former ones; and he rose early in the morning and went up on Mount Sinai, as the LORD had commanded him, and took in his hand the two tablets of stone. ⁵The LORD descended in the cloud and stood with him there, and proclaimed the name, "The LORD." ⁶The LORD passed before him, and proclaimed,
>
> > "The LORD, the LORD,
> > a God merciful and gracious,
> > slow to anger,
> > and abounding in steadfast love and faithfulness,
> > ⁷keeping steadfast love for the thousandth generation,
> > forgiving iniquity and transgression and sin,
> > yet by no means clearing the guilty,
> > but visiting the iniquity of the parents
> > upon the children
> > and the children's children,
> > to the third and the fourth generation."
>
> ⁸And Moses quickly bowed his head toward the earth, and worshiped. (Exod. 34:4–8; cf. 33:19)

There is here a kind of starting over, the twofold revelation of God in the words (the Commandments) and the name. But the new is fully continuous with the past. While the Lord seems to set forth new commandments, they are fully consistent with and reflective of what has already been given in the Decalogue and the Book of the Covenant. Furthermore, in the redaction of these chapters, what the Lord tells Moses to write on the tablets is called "the ten words" an explicit move to identify what the Lord says in chapter 34 with what the Lord said in chapter 20.

So also the new proclamation of "the name" reveals it to be the same name, YHWH, the LORD. But in the proclamation, two things happen: (1) the name is given emphasis by its repetition in verse 6: "YHWH, YHWH," that is, "the LORD, the LORD"; and (2) the meaning of the name is explicated here in a quite different way than in chapter 3 but fully consistent with the way the story unfolds out of Exodus 3 and 6. That is, the revelation of the name is an opening of the character of God. The meaning of the name is in the reality

77

of the way this Deity is and acts. The proclamation of the name is the proclamation of the way God is in the world.

It is also directly tied to the presence or reality of God, as in Exodus 3:12, but here in a more theophanic way. Twice the text reports that the Lord proclaimed the name (34:5 and 6). Each time that proclamation of the name is preceded by reference to the Lord's actual presence: "The LORD descended in the cloud and stood with him there, and proclaimed the name, 'The LORD'" (v. 5); and then, "The LORD passed before him, and proclaimed, 'The LORD, the LORD'" (v. 6). The outcome of this appearance and the proclamation of the name is immediate and reported succinctly: "Moses quickly bowed his head toward the earth, and worshiped" (v. 8).

The foundational character of the Exodus story only serves to underscore the significance of the name of God. It is by this name that God is revealed. It is by all the words and deeds associated with this name YHWH that one shall know who and what God is, what God is like, and what God does. Through this name, human beings have access to the knowledge of God. By this name God is present, and through this name God is worshiped.

The Deuteronomistic voice, preserved in the book of Deuteronomy and the Deuteronomistic History that unfolds from it (Joshua, Judges, Samuel, and Kings) as well as in the book of Jeremiah, makes the name of God a kind of theologoumenon, a manifestation of the presence of God. So Deuteronomy speaks of Israel's place of worship as "the place where YHWH your God chooses to put his name there" (my trans.: Deut. 12:5, 21; 14:24) or "to cause his name to dwell there" (my trans.: Deut. 12:5, 11; 14:23; 16:2, 6, 11; 26:2), that is, "to place his name there." When Solomon begins his great prayer at the dedication of the newly built temple, six times he refers to building a house for the name of the Lord (1 Kgs. 8:16, 17, 18, 19, 20, 44). In the prayer itself, the king is explicit about God not dwelling on earth or being contained anywhere (v. 27). Several times he refers to heaven as the Lord's dwelling place (vv. 30, 32, 34, 36, 39, 43, 45, 49). Yet the king and the people pray in and toward the house = temple (vv. 28, 29, 33, 35, 38, 42, 44, 48), swear oaths in the temple (vv. 31–32), and confess and repent there (vv. 33, 35, 46–48). Twice the king includes "confess your name" as part of the process of turning, confessing sin, and repenting (vv. 33, 35). The reason for praying, swearing, and confessing in the temple or for turning and praying toward it is because it is the place of which the Lord said, "My name shall be there" (v. 29). There is a sense that the God who dwells in heaven but cannot be contained even there is present in the temple in and through the divine name. Because the name is there, access is granted to the God who bears the name and cannot be contained in any place. But because the name is God's and is in some sense God, it is holy (Lev. 22:2, 32; Pss. 33:21; 103:1; 105:3; 106:47; Ezek. 43:8; Amos 2:7), and so there is the danger of profaning it, a direct concern of the Third Commandment.

What is indicated above about the name and its intimate connection with the presence and reality of God and with divine access is attested in many different ways throughout the rest of the Old Testament. So Isaiah declares:

> See, the name of the LORD comes from far away,
>> burning with his anger, and in thick rising smoke.
>>> (Isa. 30:27a)

The name represents the powerful reality of God acting in judgment. Similarly, in the same book the prophet of the exile ties knowing God and who it is that speaks to knowing the name:

> Therefore my people shall know my name; therefore in that day they shall know that it is I who speak; here am I. (Isa. 52:6)

The name thus becomes a kind of surrogate, a representative of the deity and one that comes from God, a self-revelation and not a made representation. So the psalmists, who so often speak of trusting in the Lord, can just as easily say, "We trust in his holy name" (Ps. 33:21), and the prophets echo the same (Isa. 50:10). Praise and glory are given to the name of God throughout the Psalter (see below). The claim of the Exodus story that through the words and deeds "you shall know that I am YHWH," that is, that the reality of God is in this name and what that reality is and is all about—all this is manifest in the whole story of God's creative and redemptive work in the world. So one hears in the prophets how the Lord acts in many events so that Israel and the nations, indeed all flesh, "shall know that I am YHWH/the LORD" (1 Kgs. 20:13, 28; Isa. 49:23, 26; Ezek. 13:23; 14:8; 15:7; 16:62 [et passim]; Joel 2:27; 4:17 [3:17 E]; etc.).

If the story of Israel is a continuing revelation of who and what the name is and means, the teaching and instruction of God bears

79

the name as well. That is especially evident in the Holiness Code in Leviticus, where the legislation is underscored and grounded many times with the declaration "I am YHWH" (e.g., Lev. 18:2, 5, 30; 19:4, 10, 12, 14; 21:15, 23; 22:9). The name of God, therefore, is freighted with all the power and holiness that is God's. The community that cannot make anything to represent God and cannot put anything in God's place is freely given the name of God as representation and manifestation of the reality of God. This is how God is known, in and through the name YHWH. In some fashion, where the name of God is present, God is there, in complete freedom, but truly there.

When the name is spoken and drawn upon, one is claiming some knowledge of God or some claim on God. What is said with, by, and alongside the name of God implies some connection to the reality of God. When Moses hears the name proclaimed on the mountain, he quickly bows his head and worships (Exod. 34:8). That is not always the reaction to the name, but it is instructive and indicative of how the name makes God present or accompanies the presence of the name. If, therefore, the Commandments create a safeguard in the relationship with God against *using* things and images in place of the reality that can never be so represented and to whom such things can never provide access, it is just as important to protect against *misusing* what God has freely provided to represent, reveal, and provide access to the divine, the transcendent Holy One, whom earth and heaven cannot contain but who is known and present in the name YHWH, the LORD.

The weight of the name, the gravity of how the name of God is used by human beings, may have its clearest marker in the motivation clause that follows the prohibition of the Third Commandment: "for the LORD will not hold guiltless the one who lifts up his name *laššāwʾ*" (Exod. 20:7, my trans.). There are two things especially noticeable about this second part of the commandment. One is the way in which the close *repetition* of the substance of the prohibition—lifting up the name falsely/emptily—serves to underscore, emphasize, and so give weight to the command. Repeating the prohibition in the sanction makes sure that the prohibition is heard and underlines it several times. Such repetition does not happen with any of the other commandments. That does not mean they are to be taken less seriously, but it strongly emphasizes the seriousness, the gravitas, of one's taking up the name of God on the lips, for any purpose whatsoever.

Second, the Third Commandment is unique in being the only commandment with an explicit sanction clause. That uniqueness has no interpretive weight other than calling attention to a particularity that needs to be assessed. The presence of sanction in this commandment is one of the features that join it to the preceding commandment against making and worshiping images. These are the only two commandments in the Decalogue that indicate any kind of sanction at all. The sanction of the Second Commandment is of a general sort, promising punishment to those who hate or reject the Lord and steadfast love to those who love YHWH and "keep my commandments" (Exod. 20:5–6). Except for the jealous-God language, one would see no particular connection between the sanction and the prohibition of the Second Commandment.

That is not the case, however, for the Third Commandment. The sanction is related directly to the prohibition, as we have noted. Further, the punishment for disobedience is both *unstated* and *God's doing*. While the oath may often have to do with neighbor relations, obedience and disobedience are not always clearly discernible in the situation in which the oath is taken. There may be no clear way of determining whether the oath has been withheld (see below). So it is up to God to decide and to punish (cf. Deut. 1:17). The seriousness of human handling of the name of God is thus further underscored by the Commandment's unique sanction clause.

Using and Misusing the Name of God

Worship in the Name

The name of God comes quickly to the fore when one moves from the Decalogue to the Book of the Covenant (Exod. 20:22–23:33), immediately after the giving of the Commandments in the Exodus Sinai account.

> [22]The Lord said to Moses: Thus you shall say to the Israelites: "You have seen for yourselves that I spoke with you from heaven. [23]You shall not make gods of silver alongside me, nor shall you make for yourselves gods of gold. [24]You need make for me only an altar of earth and sacrifice on it your burnt offerings and your offerings of well-being, your sheep and your oxen; in every place where I cause my name to be remembered I will come to you and

81

bless you. [25]But if you make for me an altar of stone, do not build it of hewn stones; for if you use a chisel upon it you profane it. [26]You shall not go up by steps to my altar, so that your nakedness may not be exposed on it." (20:22–26)

When the name of God is first mentioned in the statutes and ordinances, several implications may be inferred from the reference and the context.

1. *The intimate connection between revering the name of God and the exclusive worship of the Lord is reiterated.* As in the case of Deuteronomy (see above under "The Context of the Commandment"), the point at which the First and Second Commandments begin to be explicated in the Mosaic instruction (Exod. 20:23), the name of God also comes into play (20:24). The name is thus not a separate matter from no other gods and no other images. In this association, one also hears, implicitly, no other *name*, an implication that becomes explicit later in the Book of the Covenant with a statute that is virtually the same as the First Commandment, only with specific reference to the divine name: "Do not invoke [or 'proclaim' (so Childs, *Exodus*, 47)] the *name* of other gods; do not let it be heard on your lips" (Exod. 23:13, my trans.; cf. Deut. 12:3).

At the same time, there is a positive, informing word about what "you have" when you may not "have" other gods and what you may and do worship when you may not and do not worship images. The name fills the space. The God with this identity is present in that place where the name is remembered (Exod. 20:24). It is not a numinous being. It is not some unknown mystery or other. The identity and reality, the character and way, of the God "you have" is uncovered in the name and all that name carries with it. The "me" and the "I" of the first two commandments are given content and meaning in the name "YHWH/the Lord your God."

2. *The primary place, the originating place, of the name of God is the sanctuary and worship.* We have already noted how the biblical story first begins to speak of persons calling on or invoking the name of God at the places where the ancestors built their altars (Gen. 12:8; 13:4; 21:33; 26:25). In other words, the Genesis stories of the worship of the ancestors are a narrative reflection of the meaning of Exodus 20:24, this statute in the Book of the Covenant. From the start the name of God is associated with the places and activities of worship. Although the community may call on the

name in other contexts, association with the concreteness and space of the sanctuary means that concreteness and that space can never be viewed simply in architectural or utilitarian terms. It is the place of the presence of God, a presence that is affirmed, recalled, and celebrated whenever the name is invoked, sung, praised, or pronounced in the reading of Scripture. Furthermore, it is precisely the regular frequent invocation and proclamation of the name in the place and activity of worship that reminds the community that the name of God has to do with the divine presence and the reality of God. Thus any uses of the name dissociated from that awareness become misuses and empty uses of the name. The holy name makes the place holy. Conversely, the place of worship is a regular reminder of the holiness, the weight, of the name. Encountering the presence of the Lord in the place where the name is remembered and proclaimed is a safeguard against devaluing the name in any other context.

3. *It is the name of God that specifically characterizes the true and proper worship of God.* The community of faith, church or synagogue, knows who it worships only through the words and deeds associated with the one whose name is proclaimed in worship. The faithful do not enter the sanctuary in worship of some numinous abstraction or some generalized notion of deity. There are such notions. There are concepts of God that come from various spheres—religion generally, philosophy and reason, the wider culture where religious and secular thinking overlap and interact. Central to Jewish and Christian faith is the conviction that the bearer of the name "the Lord" (YHWH) is God, is our God, and fills and exhausts the meaning of the term "God." The name is once again a continuing testimony and reminder of what it means to say "God." The philosopher Kwame Anthony Appiah begins his discussion of God with the significance of the term "God" as a proper name, on the assumption that we have to have some way of thinking of a person (or thing) "in order to be able to evaluate the arguments for his existence." The critical ways of "learning a name" are through knowledge by acquaintance and knowledge by description and, in the latter case, more specifically some individuating description that distinguishes the person from other persons who may have the same name. Appiah's philosophical approach has clear analogies to the experience of Israel and the later community of faith, who "learn the name" presumably by acquaintance (for example,

83

in worship and prayer) and clearly by description, that is, in Scripture (Appiah, *Thinking It Through,* 305–10). One may indeed find significant overlap between what has been revealed in the name, revealed of the one who bears the name "LORD," and culturally and rationally derived concepts of God. Scripture itself bears witness to the rootedness of the name, character, and work of "the LORD your God" in the more general religious world of which Israel was a part, a fact confirmed by historical investigation of the religion of ancient Israel (Miller, *Religion of Israel,* 23–29). The community's worship, however, is not of the one constructed derivatively but of the one self-revealed, made known—"that you may know that I am the LORD"—in the name and the story—past, present, and future—that tells of the word and work of the one bearing the name. The biblical tradition gives to the community of faith both the specific name, YHWH—the LORD, and the more generalized and shared term "God." The latter can and does function in Scripture and the church's worship as divine name, but there is always the danger that the community of faith may lose the particularity of the name or unwittingly substitute a generalized notion of deity for the one revealed in Scripture, the Lord, the God and Father of Jesus Christ.

4. *The proclamation of the name marks off the proper worship of God from practices that come from outside the story and apart from or over against God's self-revelation and instruction.* The purpose of this statute in Exodus 20 is to set out the proper mode of worship where the name "the LORD" is spoken, invoked, and revered. The verse in which reference is made to proclaiming the name—or causing it to be remembered—spells out succinctly and simply both the paraphernalia-architecture-instruments of worship, a simple altar, and the cultic practices appropriate to the place where the name is spoken and the God who bears the name is worshiped, sacrifices of a particular sort. By inference as well as out of the context, improper modes of worship where the Lord's name is proclaimed are ruled out. The context explicitly suggests this as it prohibits gods of silver and gods of gold, typical phenomena of other cults but having no place in the faithful and true worship of the Lord. The enigmatic verse 26, prohibiting going up by steps to the altar, may also refer to practices associated with non-Yahwistic cults, as may be the case also with the prohibition against using hewn stones (Childs, *Exodus,* 464–67).

84

The association of the name with the place and practice of worship as a way of delineating the proper worship of the Lord against improper practices is both evident and inferred from other parts of the Torah legislation. Giving one's child to Molech is forbidden because it would "profane the name of your God" (Lev. 18:21) or "my holy name" (20:3). There is much debate about what is meant by Molech and what practice is envisioned, but there is no doubt that the prohibition is against practices of other peoples that did not belong to the proper worship of YHWH. Leviticus 22 gives specific instructions about the handling of offerings by Aaron and his sons. These are prefaced and concluded by general words urging dealing carefully with the gifts and offerings so that they do "not profane my holy name" (22:1–2, 32–33). Further instructions are given to the priests in Leviticus 21, this time about abstaining from certain practices for the dead because the priests are holy and lacerating themselves or shaving their hair or beards would not only defile them but also "profane the name of their God" (21:6).

This prohibition in Leviticus 21:5–6 is important not so much for the particular practice involved but because it helps account for the way in which the Third Commandment is taken up in the Deuteronomic Code, Deuteronomy 12–26. These chapters, according to many scholars, seem to be structured in relation to the Commandments. The statutes are thus ordered by subject matter according to the topics and sequence of the Commandments. If that is the case, as it seems to be, the assignment of a particular chapter or sequence of verses as specifically explicating the Third Commandment has been problematic because of the absence of particular words and locutions that can be seen as referring back to the commandment about the use of the name. The common opinion, however, is that Deuteronomy 14, or some part of that chapter, probably represents whatever explication of the Third Commandment is to be found in the Deuteronomic Code (e.g., Olson, *Death of Moses*, 70–73; Braulik, "Sequence," 321).

While the connection is not direct or obvious, there are several reasons why Deuteronomy 14 may be seen as development and specification of the commandment about the use of the name.

a. *Better connection.* The simplest is that there is no place else that seems a better connection or fit. Deuteronomy 12 and 13 have to do with the requirement that Israel have no other gods than the Lord. Chapter 12 begins and ends with the divine insistence that all the cultic sites and paraphernalia of the nations being dispossessed by Israel be destroyed and never imitated by them. Chapter 13 reiterates the First Commandment in several explicit ways, warning the people against following the counsel of anyone in the community—prophet, kin, or anybody—who says, "Let us follow other gods and serve them." Chapter 15 clearly has to do with the Sabbath Commandment and the institution of a wider sabbatical practice. That leaves only chapter 14 as a candidate for the Deuteronomic explication of the Third Commandment.

b. *Development.* One should not be surprised if spelling out the commandment about use of the name tends to meld and fall together with the development of the commandments about having no other gods and not making and worshiping images. We have already seen a number of ways that these three commandments—two in some numerations—are held closely together, a cardinal example being the statute in Exodus 20:22–26, which is the starting point of this discussion. Furthermore, the explicit association of the name with proper places, structures, and practices of worship that we have noted in connection with Exodus 20:22–26 and sections of the Holiness Code in Leviticus is manifestly present in Deuteronomy 12–14.

c. *Holy to the Lord.* There is also a more explicit connection between Leviticus 21:1–6 (see above) and Deuteronomy 14. The Leviticus statute prohibits the priests from lacerating and shaving themselves as a ritual for the dead (see above) so as not to "profane the *name* of their God" (21:6). In that context, twice it is said, "They shall be holy (to their God)." The two following verses instruct about priestly marriage and make the point, *three* more times, that the priests are holy to their God and are to be treated as holy (vv. 7–8). The conclusion of both instructions is the declaration: "I who sanctify you, am holy" (v. 8).

Such emphasis on holiness is not surprising for instruction about priestly conduct within the Holiness Code. All of this resonates with Deuteronomy 14:1–2:

[1]You are children of the LORD your God. You must not lacerate yourselves or shave your forelocks for the dead. [2]For you are a people holy to the LORD your God; it is you the LORD has chosen out of all the peoples on earth to be his people, his treasured possession.

The specific statute has to do with exactly the same conduct that is regarded in Leviticus 21 as a profanation—and so misuse or wrongful use—of the name of the Lord: laceration and shaving for the dead. Furthermore, around that statute, which in the Deuteronomic Code applies to the whole community, not just the priests, are explicit words saying that such conduct is inappropriate "for you are a people holy to the LORD your God" and "you are children of the LORD your God." Those who are holy to the Lord may not profane the name of the Lord.

So the beginning of Deuteronomy 14 leads directly into statutes of various sorts that help to define and specify practices appropriate for the holy community and seek to sanctify rather than profane the name of the Lord. These are regulations having to do with what may or may not be eaten and are introduced (in v. 3) with the general injunction, "You shall not eat any abhorrent thing [or "abomination = *tôʿēbâ*]," indicating that the practices enjoined have to do with cultic purity, holiness, and cleanness. The whole collection of regulations then concludes with a return to the starting point, "For you are a people holy to the LORD your God" (v. 21), the inclusion thus serving to give the same emphasis to the holiness of the *people* effected by living this way as is given to the holiness of the *priests* in Leviticus 21.

The association of abominations or abhorrent practices with defiling or profaning the name of God is a concern of the prophets also. In Ezekiel's vision of the new temple, he is told that in this place the people and their kings will no more be "defiling my holy name by their abominations that they committed" (Ezek. 43:7–8).

Recounting the transgressions of Israel in an oracle to Amos, the Lord says:

> Father and son go in to the same girl,
> so that my holy name is profaned.
> (Amos 2:7)

The Torah concern for proper order in relationships is carried forward here in the family and sexual sphere. For the prophet Malachi, the indifference of the priests to the character or quality of offering they place on the altar is a profanation of the name of the Lord precisely because the offering is "offered to my name" (Mal. 1:11; cf. 1:2–14). But proper reverencing of the name is not confined to the matter of offerings. When the prophet's proclamation nears an end, it is in a vision of a book of remembrance of those who "revered the LORD and thought on his name" (Mal. 3:16; cf. 3:14; 1:14; 2:5). The conclusion makes it clear that *all* the acts condemned in the preceding chapter—adultery, swearing falsely, oppressing the poor, polluting the altar, robbing God of the tithe, and the like—are acts of those who do not fear the Lord or fear the name of the Lord.

Before leaving this point about the relationship between the proclamation of the name and practices of worship and piety, attention should be called to the latter part of the Book of the Covenant, where there is a further statute having to do with the name. What is particularly noticeable in this instance is that the statute begins a series of statutes defining proper worship practices of the community. In Exodus 23:1–13, a sequence of statutes having to do with issues of justice and compassion for the neighbor is followed by what seems to be a concluding general injunction: "Be attentive to all that I have said to you" (23:13a). The transition to the next section then follows in verse 13b and shifts the subject matter to the worship practices of Israel:

> Do not proclaim the name of other gods [or "cause the name to be remembered"]; do not let them be heard on your lips. (my trans.)

From that point onward, the statutes all have to do with festivals and offerings (23:14–19).

All of the texts under consideration in this section thus serve to create a strong connection between the name of God and the places and practices appropriate to reverencing and worship of the one whose name is the Lord. What marks the beginning of the Third Commandment's trajectory in the Torah's statutes and ordinances carries through the Book of the Covenant, the Holiness Code of Leviticus, and the Deuteronomic Code. Where the name of God is spoken and heard, proclaimed and present, attention is given to the modes and ways of being and worshiping. These are not fixed in a rigid sense, as some of the differences among the statutes make one aware. But the church listens to Israel's interpretation of the ways of using and misusing the name of God in these statutes to be reminded that its holy life has to do directly with the practices of piety and what, where, and how it carries out the formal worship of God. It becomes, for example, more alert to

- the question of simplicity, as in the earthen altar of Exodus 20:24;
- a sense of order and propriety in relationships and practices, as in the statutes about what its ministers or priests do in Leviticus 21 and the regulations about food categories in Deuteronomy 14; and
- avoiding the adoption and adaptation of practices that belong more to the culture, religious or secular, than to the biblical teachings about what is appropriate for reverencing the name of the Lord.

While there may not be specific direction for the church's life in these matters, it may and should attend to larger cautions and pointers that may be inferred from the Bible's teaching drawn out of the Third Commandment, instruction about what is fitting for the life and worship of those who reverence the name of the Lord, what holiness of practice reflects the holiness of the name.

5. *Speaking and proclaiming the name of God in worship is an avenue to God's presence and blessing.* The statute in Exodus 20:22–26 is quite explicit at this point: "In every place where I cause my name to be remembered I will come to you and bless you" (v. 24b). In such a straightforward manner, the community hears again of the promise it carries with it whenever it lifts up the name of the Lord in its worship. The prayer for God's blessing in and through the name is one of the central positive uses of the name. While blessing prayers may be offered without specific reference to the name (e.g., Ruth 4:11–12), such reference to the name or speaking the name in the blessing was the common practice, both in worship and in daily life. Such benedictions in the Lord's name are voiced in the Psalms. So at the end of Psalm 128, which is about the blessing that comes to those who fear the Lord, the psalmist says: "May the LORD bless you from Zion" (v. 5, my trans.; cf. Pss. 134:3; 115:14–15); and in the next psalm, the recital of the acts of the wicked and the "haters of Zion" concludes with identifying these folk in the following manner:

Those who pass by do not say,
"The blessing of the LORD be upon you!
We bless you in the name of the LORD!"
(129:8)

The practice referred to here as not occurring may be seen as a customary part of everyday life in the book of Ruth. When Boaz first appears in his grain fields, he says to the reapers, "The LORD be with you," to which they reply, "The LORD bless you" (2:4). Blessing in the name serves to *identify* the source of all good as well as to *pray for* continuing care by the one who is named in the prayer. It is the prayer of "those who pass by each other," with regular, continual invoking of the name in greeting and in farewell. In the prayer, "The LORD be with you," the one who so blesses invokes the name in its revealed meaning. The contextual explanation of the name of God in Exodus 3:12—*ʾehyeh ʿimmak*, "I will be with you"—becomes in the blessing a regular prayer for God to be what the name signifies: The Lord will be with you.

This use of the name to invoke God's blessing in daily life, the workplace, the act of meeting and leaving friends, and the like, has its important counterpart in the community's worship. When David takes the ark of the covenant into the city of David, he offers various kinds of sacrifices; when he has finished, he blesses the people "in the name of the LORD of hosts" (2 Sam. 6:18) and then goes home to bless his household (6:20). The community as it leaves its service of worship and the family in its life at home are both blessed in the Lord's name.

The significance and centrality of blessing in the Lord's name as an act of worship is indicated in two ways. One is in the Deuteronomic description of the responsibility of the priests. The priestly assignments are described in two places: Deuteronomy 10:8 and 21:5. While specific tasks are given in one or the other text—carrying the ark of the covenant in 10:8 and settling difficult judicial cases in 21:5—in *both* texts the priests are given two responsibilities: to stand before the Lord and "serve/minister to him" and "to bless in the name of the LORD" (my trans.). Along with the more general service of the Lord, the specific act of blessing, of invoking divine blessing through the name, is lifted up as one of the fundamental priestly acts (cf. Lev. 9:22–23).

Second, underscoring this responsibility and the place of the name in benediction, is the account in the book of Numbers of the institution of the Aaronic or priestly benediction (6:22–27). The centrality of the name is evident when the text is looked at as a whole:

²²The Lord spoke to Moses, saying: ²³Speak to Aaron and his sons, saying, Thus you shall bless the Israelites: You shall say to them,

> ²⁴The Lord bless you and keep you;
> ²⁵the Lord make his face to shine upon you,
>   and be gracious to you;
> ²⁶the Lord lift up his countenance upon you,
>   and give you peace.

²⁷So they shall put my name on the Israelites, and I will bless them.

Several things may be noted in this text:

a. *Assignment of blessing* the people as a specifically *priestly* or *ministerial* task in worship is here emphasized such that it becomes a kind of permanent ordinance.

b. *The focus on the name* of God is evident in three ways:

- YHWH, or "the Lord," is the explicit subject of each line of the blessing.
- The threefold repetition of the name is unusual and gives the name great weight.
- The act of blessing is characterized as "putting my name on the Israelites," clearly a reference to the threefold speaking of the name in the blessing.

c. *Effect.* When such a blessing in and through the name is uttered, it is effective. When God's blessing is invoked, "*I* will bless them" (Num. 6:27; cf. Exod. 20:24).

The prayer for divine blessing in and through the name is thus a ministerial responsibility of no small moment. Scripture signals this use of the name as a primary priestly act. So the use of the name is not a happenstance in ministerial activity; it is an expectation. More pointedly, it is one of the few responsibilities of ministry that comes as a divine assignment and not as a projected or rationalized job description. The weight of this priestly enterprise is underscored by the indication that such prayers are not perfunctory: they are effective. One prays the benediction in the name with the confidence that the bearer of the name will indeed bless. Conversely, the absence of such benediction in the name is an implicit wrongful use of the name and an explicit abandoning of a primary ministerial

91

responsibility. While one may not be able to say that blessing cannot occur apart from the prayer, the Scriptures tie the two together very directly. God's blessing is promised when it is invoked in the name of the Lord. In that act, the minister-priest prays for the Lord's providential care as the congregation moves from the sanctuary back into its ordinary life (Miller, *They Cried to the Lord*, 294–99).

6. *Blessing the name of God is an act of praise and thanksgiving to the one who has blessed us.* Especially in the Psalms one again and again hears individuals and the community, Israel and the nations, blessing the Lord or blessing "your name."

> Give thanks to him, bless his name.
> (Ps. 100:4)

> Bless the Lord, O my soul,
>   and all that is within me,
>   bless his holy name.
>   (Pss 103:1; cf. vv. 20–22;
>   104:1, 35)

> [1] I will extol you, my God and King,
>   and bless your name forever and ever.
> [2] Every day I will bless you,
>   and praise your name forever and ever.
> . . . .
> [10] All your works shall give thanks to you, O Lord,
>   and all your faithful shall bless you.
>   (145:1–2, 10)

> [1] Praise the Lord!
> Praise, O servants of the Lord;
>   praise the name of the Lord
> [2] Blessed be the name of the Lord
>   from this time on and forevermore.
>   (113:1–2)

Such expressions as the examples cited above are acts of thanksgiving to the one who bears this name. They are a form of continuing testimony to what God has done, and the frequent parallelism of "the Lord" and "his/your name" reinforces the centrality of the name of God and the identity and reality of God. To "bless the name of God" is to praise and honor the one who is so named. All the hallelujahs of Scripture and the church and synagogue are acts of praising the name of God. Having received God's blessing, the community now "blesses" God. This is not the same as our being blessed; it is not granting favor and goodness to God. The reciprocation implicit in the use of the same term for God blessing human beings and human beings blessing God is in our giving thanks to the one who has given blessings to us.

Oaths and Testimony

Use and misuse of the divine name occurs extensively in swearing oaths generally and more specifically in giving testimony under oath. The discussion above on the translation and meaning of the Third Commandment has already identified this as one of the earliest and very specific modes of using the divine name as well as one of the primary ways in which the Third Commandment is spelled out. Several of the references to swearing by the name or swearing falsely by the name occur in a Decalogue context (Lev. 19:12; Deut. 6:13; 10:20; cf. Jer. 7:9; Hos. 4:2). Leviticus 19:12 specifically prohibits a false oath because it profanes the name of God. The prophets also indicate the significance of swearing by the name as they indict the people for their false oaths in the name of the Lord (Jer. 4:2; 5:2; Zech. 5:3–4; cf. Jer. 7:9; Hos. 4:2; Mal. 3:5) or oaths in the name of other gods (Jer. 12:16; Amos 8:14; Zeph. 1:5; cf. Josh. 23:7; Hos. 2:19 [17 E]) and as they enjoin swearing truthfully (Zech. 8:17) and swearing only by the name of the Lord (Jer. 12:16).

Reverencing the name of God by swearing by the name and not swearing falsely is thus one of the important aspects of using (or misusing) the name of God. The biblical practice has continued in various spheres of the common life, the courtroom and marriage being among the most obvious. Oath taking is not confined to such formal contexts, however, for people often swear oaths in ordinary discourse, much as is the case for biblical oaths (e.g., Judg. 8:19; Ruth 3:13; 1 Sam. 14:45; 29:6; etc.). Our concern in this context is what it means to swear in the name of God and why that should be done rightly and not *laššāwʾ*, emptily or falsely. In biblical law, story, and prophecy, several aspects of the significance of oath taking in the name are evident.

1. *Oath taking in the name of God is a commitment to an action—short term or long term. As such it has to do with keeping promises.* Two stories provide rich examples of such commitment: one is a specific action of brief scope, the story of Rahab

93

and the spies at Jericho (Josh. 2); the other is a promise sworn and kept over many years, the covenant between Jonathan and David (1 Sam. 20).

a. *The whole story of Rahab and the spies* revolves around the oath and its reliability. Immediately noticeable is the way Rahab joins together the demands of the First and Third Commandments (Miller, "Story: Joshua"). Her "confession of faith" in YHWH (Josh. 2:8–11) concludes with the declaration: "The LORD your God is indeed God in heaven above and on earth below." The implication of that claim, which follows immediately, is to place the spies under oath in the name of the one who is God in heaven above and on earth below: Since I have dealt kindly with you, "swear to me by the LORD that you in turn will deal kindly with my family" (v. 12).

The rest of the episode then flows out of this request. The spies respond to her demand positively and with an oath. They do not name the Lord in the typical fashion of swearing oaths: "As the LORD lives." Rather they say, "Our life for yours to the death!" (v. 14, my trans.; cf. v. 13b), and promise to "deal kindly and faithfully" with Rahab if she does not give them away. The seriousness of the oath is evident in the way the spies stake their lives on the word of the oath. In their final words to Rahab, they couch everything in terms of the sworn oath (vv. 17–20). Because the oath is a mutual agreement, they spell out its implications: their release from the sworn oath if Rahab does not follow their instructions, their responsibility for the deaths of any of her family killed in the invasion if she does.

The oath sworn in the name of the Lord is a life-and-death matter in two ways: As in this story, it is often sworn in regard to an actual occasion in which the life of someone is at stake (Judg. 8:19; 1 Sam. 14:39, 45; 19:6; 20:3, 21; 24:21–22; 26:10, 16; 30:15; 2 Sam. 4:9; 12:5; 14:11; 15:21; 1 Kgs. 2:24). But the sworn oath may put the life of the oath taker at risk. That is spelled out in a particular way in this story and elsewhere (e.g., see below with regard to 1 Sam. 20:12–13), but the motivation clause of the Third Commandment—"for the LORD will not hold guiltless the one who lifts up his name falsely/emptily" (Exod. 20:7, my trans.)—makes the riskiness implicit in every oath taken in the Lord's name.

b. *The friendship of David and Jonathan* and their care for each other is thoroughly undergirded by swearing and oath taking. When David flees before a pursuing Saul, his fear is so great that he swears an oath that there is only "a step between me and death" (1 Sam.

94

20:3). In this instance his oath is not a commitment to action but an expression of his absolute conviction that he is about to be captured and killed. The oath is rhetorical, intended to persuade the listener that what is stated is reality, the true state of things. Such rhetorical force is at the heart of oath taking as it is designed to persuade and draw forth a commitment on the part of the one toward whom the oath is directed, in this case, Jonathan.

The rhetoric is successful, evoking an open and total commitment on Jonathan's part: "Whatever you say, I will do for you" (v. 4). David produces a plan, but it betrays a reticence about Jonathan's commitment to the covenant between them, a commitment to David's well-being. Whereupon Jonathan takes David into the field and swears an oath "by the LORD, the God of Israel!" (v. 12) to protect David, accepting the appropriate punishment of the Lord— "The LORD will not acquit anyone who misuses his name" (Exod. 20:7)—if he is faithless to his promise and betrays the commitment to David and to protecting his life. Their shared oaths create a covenant between them (1 Sam. 20:16), and the oaths are reiterated (vv. 17, 23). The episode concludes as Jonathan repeats the oath "both of us have sworn in the name of the LORD," that is, "The LORD shall be between me and you, and between my descendants and your descendants, forever" (v. 42). One of the submotifs of the whole David narrative then becomes this promise and David's commitment to it (2 Sam. 4:4; 9:1–13; 16:1–4; 21:7).

As these two stories presume and demonstrate, invocation of the Lord's name in the swearing of oaths is weighty, rhetorical, and consequential for those who make the oath and for those to whom it is made. Invoking the Lord's name in this manner moves what is said from statement, declaration, and intention to promise and commitment (cf. Num. 30:1–2 [2–3 Heb.]). Through the use of the Lord's name, the human act of speaking becomes a speech event in which, to use Lévinas's terminology, there is now a "third party," the Lord (Miller, "Good Neighborhood"). The word becomes act and an act with serious consequences—"the LORD will not hold guiltless"—beyond the seriousness of what is being promised in the specific oath. The human plane, the human relationship, becomes intentionally a matter before God. Because the oath often is set to evoke a countercommitment to action on the part of someone else, it also places the neighbor and the neighbor's well-being and faithfulness at stake.

95

2. *Oath taking in the name of God is an act of commitment to the truthfulness of what one says.* While this aspect of swearing and keeping oaths is closely related to promise keeping, the distinction between the two is immediately evident in the difference between the marriage oath or vow and the oath that is sworn by a witness in court. The former has to do with keeping promises, the latter with telling the truth.

This second aspect of oath taking receives prominent attention in the Prophets. Their indictment of the people often includes the swearing of false oaths. Sometimes specific reference is made to swearing falsely by the name of God (Zech. 5:4), but more often the sin is described simply as swearing (Zech. 5:3) or swearing falsely (Jer. 5:2; 7:9; Zech. 8:17; Mal. 3:5; cf. Ps. 24:4). Even when the name is not alluded to in the indictment, one may presume that the false oath is sworn in the Lord's name, as Jeremiah 4:2 and 5:2 make clear:

And if you swear, "As the LORD lives!"
   in truth, in justice, and in uprightness . . .
                   (Jer. 4:2; cf. Isa. 48:1)

Although they say, "As the LORD lives,"
   yet they swear falsely.
                   (Jer. 5:2)

The two tables of the Decalogue come together markedly in this context. For the false oath is most often associated with some sort of testimony or certification of the truth of something when it is actually a lie, leading to the endangerment of life, well-being, and property that comes with lies told against one's neighbor. As the following paragraphs show, the weight of this concern for truthfulness is evident in several ways.

Whatever intrinsic or consequentialist or utilitarian arguments might be put forth in behalf of truthfulness, in this context the central issue is *irreverence toward the Lord* and the Lord's name. Truthfulness and reliability are not simply matters in themselves. Invocation of the Lord's name makes a claim that there is a third party involved whose reliability is implicitly at stake in the oath. That the Lord's name is supposed to be invoked means that truth is not an issue separate from one's worship and reverence of the Lord your God. Justice and holiness, truth and reverence, are intimately associated in the invocation of the Lord's name in oath taking.

The false oath is often connected with *other acts against the neighbor*. This is especially the case with stealing from one's neighbor. In a number of contexts, swearing falsely is set alongside stealing or is seen as an aspect of various kinds of theft of the property of others (e.g., Hos. 7:1–2; Jer. 6:13//8:10; Zech. 5:3–4). The close connection between lying under oath, that is, perjury, and endangering the life and property of another is at the heart of the story of the mock trial of Naboth, whose life is taken and his property confiscated on the basis of two lying witnesses (1 Kings 21). The interconnection is explicit also in the statutes that flow out of the Third Commandment, for example, Lev. 6:2–5 [5:21–24 Heb.]:

> ²When any of you sin and commit a trespass against the LORD by deceiving a neighbor in a matter of a deposit or a pledge, or by robbery, or if you have defrauded a neighbor, ³or have found something lost and lied about it—if you swear falsely regarding any of the various things that one may do and sin thereby—⁴when you have sinned and realize your guilt, and would restore what you took by robbery or by fraud or the deposit that was committed to you, or the lost thing that you found, ⁵or anything else about which you have sworn falsely, you shall repay the principal amount and shall add one-fifth to it. You shall pay it to its owner when you realize your guilt.

The several examples lumped together all have to do with the way that lying, specifically swearing falsely, can be a means to steal, in a variety of ways, from one's neighbor. A similar statute appears in Leviticus 19:11–14 with an even more explicit reference to swearing by the Lord's name falsely. That, of course, is to be assumed for the statute in Leviticus 6 cited above. In all these instances, the sin or trespass against the Lord is precisely in the manipulation of the name of God for one's harmful acts against the neighbor. In the only prayer in the book of Proverbs (30:7–9), the sage specifically sees profanation—literally, "grasping"—of the name of the Lord as the outcome of stealing (v. 9b).

While the First Commandment is probably the commandment most prominent in the Psalter, a perusal of the Psalms reveals fairly quickly that lying is the most common complaint of those who cry out to the Lord about what is happening to them or speak of the ways of the wicked (e.g., Pss. 4:3 [2 E]; 12:3–5 [2–4]; 15:2–3; 27:12;

97

31:19 [18]; 32:2; 35:11, 19–20; 50:19–21; 52:5–6 [3–4]; 101:5, 7; 109:2; 144:8, 11; see chap. 8 on false witness).

There is another form of oath taking that is an act against the neighbor. It is the oath (ʾālâ) used as a curse to prove whether a person is guilty of something. The oath as curse becomes a form of ordeal, one that is most explicitly described in Numbers 5, which records a process for determining if a woman accused of unfaithfulness by her husband is guilty. She is made to take "the oath of the curse" (v. 21). The oath is actually cited, indicating that this is clearly a use, an invocation, of the divine name to bring about curse rather than blessing:

> The LORD make you an execration and an oath among your people, when the LORD makes your uterus drop, your womb discharge. (5:21)

The curse is to take effect if the woman is guilty.

The possibility of such a procedure being used as a weapon of harm against one's neighbor is suggested by a petition in Solomon's temple prayer:

> [31]If someone sins against a neighbor and is given an oath to swear [or "made to swear an oath"], and comes and swears before your altar in this house, [32]then hear in heaven, and act, and judge your servants, condemning the guilty by bringing their conduct on their own head, and vindicating the righteous by rewarding them according to their righteousness. (1 Kgs. 8:31–32)

As Josef Scharbert explains:

> Here ʾālâ is the curse which a plaintiff pronounces against his neighbor who is accused of wrong in order to force a divine judgment. . . . Job affirms that he has never asked for the death of an enemy by pronouncing this kind of curse (31:30). Ps. 10:7; 59:13 [Eng. v. 12) (both passages use the noun); and Hos. 4:2 (which uses the qal inf.) have to do with this kind of curse in unrighteous or unscrupulous accusations against another person. ("ʾālâ," 263)

Scharbert's summary formulation shows the large possibility for harm against the neighbor:

> One must ask God to put the curse into operation and to prove whether the person is guilty. It is obviously realized from the very first that a curse pronounced on an accused person may not be

satisfactorily proved. Therefore, such a curse could also be abused in making unjustified accusations. Once the accusation was made and the ordeal curse pronounced, the matter was put in suspense because the curse might begin to take effect on the accused only after a long time, in the form of illness or some other misfortune. In any case, the person accused carried a public blemish if his innocence was not evident. (266; cf. Brichto, *Problem*, 40–67)

3. *Taking and keeping oaths contributes to communal trust and the security of expectations within the community.* The significance of swearing truthfully in the Lord's name for creating a level of trust that enables the community to function for both the individual and the common good is already implicit in all that has been said to this point, but it needs to be underscored. In some instances, invoking the name of God in swearing an oath may be the only security the community has: there may be no other way to secure a matter except by the sworn oath and the confidence that the name of God provides a ground of security. In Exodus 22:7–13 (6–12 Heb.), provision is made for settling property issues when property has been in the hands of another for safekeeping or where there is a case of disputed ownership or a possible misappropriation. There is no clear evidence to determine who is in the right, whether the property kept for another was truly stolen by an outsider or stolen by the one to whom it was entrusted. The same is true for the issue of ownership and the claims made about that. Under those circumstances, the party or parties upon whom there may be some suspicion or who are possibly culpable are made to swear an oath "before the LORD" (v. 11 [10]). The name of the Lord thus becomes the guarantee of security, the basis for trust. The assumption is that one will tell the truth in the name of the Lord, and if not, then "the LORD will not acquit anyone who misuses his name." Even if falsely accused, the innocent party knows oneself to be standing before the Lord and the Lord's decision in the confidence of divine vindication.

There is no guarantee that such a system will work. Obviously, it did not always work, as the many references to swearing falsely demonstrate. But it is clear that when there are no witnesses and no evidence to determine a case, the community stands or falls on the security of expectations created by the invocation of the name of the Lord in an oath as a guarantor of reliability or the instrument of just judgment. Communal trust is grounded in the power and seriousness of the act of invoking the name to undergird one's claim for truthfulness (Welker, "Security of Expectations").

4. *Invoking the name of God in grounding human actions by oath can be a way of wielding political power for personal ends and goals by putting a divine imprimatur on the ruler's plans and decisions.* Communal trust and security of expectations are subject to violation at the political level as well as at the communal one. Once more, the story of Israel is illustrative of such misuse of the name of God. A perusal of 1 and 2 Samuel reveals how much oath taking in the name of the Lord takes place in the stories of Saul and David. There is probably more invocation of the name of the Lord in the form of oaths in those stories than in any other single context in the Old Testament. That reaches some climax in the account of the last days of David in 1 Kings 1–2. Seven references to oaths sworn in the name of the Lord appear in the report of the intrigue that goes on around the succession to the throne (1:13, 17, 29, 30; 2:8, 23, 42).

One set of references has to do with an oath of David's—or an oath Nathan and Bathsheba claim David swore—that Solomon should be king after him (1:13, 17). There is no previous record of such an oath, but David is persuaded to make the oath now (1:29–30). Another oath is taken by Solomon to ground his decision to execute his rival Adonijah to make sure he does not take the throne from him by the ruse of asking for David's concubine Abishag for his wife: "Then King Solomon swore by the LORD, '. . . Now therefore as the LORD lives, who has established me and placed me on the throne of my father David, and who has made me a house as he promised, today Adonijah shall be put to death'" (2:23–24). The claim to the throne is identified as a divine decision, based on the oath of David, which served to secure the throne for Solomon in the eyes of the people precisely by invoking the name of the Lord in the oath. So Solomon now invokes the name of God to help justify his decision to execute Adonijah and remove him as a possible threat to Solomon's reign.

The final set of oaths has to do with Shimei, who cursed David earlier (2 Sam. 16:5–13). On that earlier occasion, David swore not to kill Shimei (1 Kgs. 2:8). But on his deathbed, he indicates clearly to Solomon that he wants to be avenged against Shimei despite his oath. His words to Solomon are worth noting: "You are a wise man; you will know what you ought to do" (2:9). In the final part of this

100

succession narrative (2:36–46), it is clear that Solomon is indeed wise and clever in this regard and overcomes David's oath by using an oath-taking strategy of his own. He makes Shimei swear an oath "to the LORD" (*šĕbuʿat yhwh*, v. 43) never to go out of Jerusalem—a place where Solomon can keep close track of him—or he will die: "Your blood will be on your head" (2:36–38). Shimei stays there for three years but then at some point leaves the city to hunt for some slaves who have run away. This is reported to Solomon immediately, whereupon the king summons Shimei to the court, reminds him of his imposed oath, and has him executed. The act is explicitly tied to the establishment of David's throne forever through Solomon: "So the kingdom was established in the hand of Solomon" (2:46b).

The observations of Brevard Childs are an appropriate summary of the way in which the name of God has been used in this story of political power wielding:

> The theological issue arises because of the extreme ambiguity of each of the stories, and the basic incongruity of seeking God's confirmation of highly dubious human machinations. Thus David has sworn by Yahweh that he will not put his enemy, Shimei, to death by the sword. At his death he commands his son, Solomon, to carry out the deed. Although strictly speaking the oath is not broken, David resorts to a form of deception to execute his vengeance. The biblical narrative does not draw any moral implications, but the reader is left to ponder whether God's name has not, in fact, been dishonoured by such human casuistry. The tension arises from a practice which implies great deference towards God's name, but actually represents just the opposite. (Childs, *Old Testament Theology*, 69)

One may go even further to note the way in which the name of God is invoked, through the process of oath taking, as a way of giving a divine imprimatur to the acts of the ruler. No one can question what the ruler is doing because the name of God has been invoked, and that is serious business. But here the name is lifted up for political purposes, to secure the ruler's policies and plans, indeed in this case the perpetuation of the king's power and control of the empire. In the process the name is treated lightly and emptily as oaths by the name of the Lord are in effect broken and the process by which any party maneuvers around the oath in God's name involves itself a misuse of the Lord's name.

101

5. *Oath taking in the name of God is a pointer within the affairs of human life to the center of meaning and value, the object of one's devotion, trust, and obedience.* Here is the significance of the *injunction* to swear, of the positive command to swear and to do so by invoking the Lord's name. The act of swearing an oath in the Lord's name is not only a commitment to action, to keeping promises, and to truth. It is also a mark of identity and the development of a habit, the habit of commitment to the Lord in all one's doings. One must remember that the positive injunctions usually have as their point that one should swear by the name of the Lord and by no other. Such oaths mark one in a most fundamental manner. In all serious matters of life, one's identity in relation to "the LORD your God" is at stake and lifted up in swearing by the Lord's name. It is in that sense a *practice*, not just a moral obligation, a way of making sure that justice is done. One expects to take up the oath in the Lord's name because all the weighty matters that have to do with living in relation to others are matters of one's identity as a member of the people whose God is the Lord.

At this point particularly, one encounters a tension between what we have in the trajectory of the Third Commandment in the Old Testament and what we hear when Jesus teaches about this commandment and its practices in the Sermon on the Mount (Matt. 5:33–37; cf. Jas. 5:12). It is a mistake, however, to see Jesus as rejecting the claim of this commandment and the injunctions to swear by the name of the Lord. His insistence that one should not swear at all is a critique of the casual and all-too-common tendency to invoke something in an oath that is taken for all sorts of things (cf. Sir. 23:7–11) and even to discriminate as to whether an oath by one thing is more important and reliable than an oath by another (see Matt. 23:16–22). One notes that Jesus lists various things by which one swears—heaven, earth, Jerusalem, one's head, the sanctuary, and the gold of the sanctuary—none of which are the name of the Lord. Apparently oath taking had become a perfunctory matter, without the seriousness of the oath in the Lord's name. Thus Jesus carries forward the intention of the commandment in a radical but consistent fashion in behalf of both the carefulness of what one says—so also Sirach 23:9–11—and the truthfulness of whatever one says, a truthfulness not dependent upon invoking some ground of security.

Taking the Name Lightly

The openness of the term *laššāwᵓ* to wider meanings than simply falsehood, more specifically to meaningless and empty invocation of the Lord's name, means that one recognizes here also a warning against light, casual, nonserious uses of the divine name that do not take account of its weight, do not lift up the name in a way appropriate to its character as the name of the Lord.

In law and story, the text rejects the empty or casual use of the name of God, that is, any use of the name that belittles or treats lightly the name of "the LORD your God." The statute that is explicit about this is Exodus 22:28 (27 Heb.): "You shall not revile God." The verb of the statute is then central to the narrative in Leviticus 24:10–16 (see below). The two texts together indicate that what is in view is a spoken act in which the Lord, and specifically the name of the Lord, is used in a contemptible, belittling, and dismissive manner. The Hebrew verb of the statute is *qālal*, which in its various forms has to do with appearing light or trifling, and making and regarding someone or something as trifling, contemptible, to be scorned. While the particular form of the verb (*qillēl*) that occurs in these and related texts is often understood as cursing in a technical sense, the cursing here may be done in all sorts of ways and with all kinds of words, but it is always a way of treating lightly or with contempt, whatever the particular words used.

Some examples make this interpretation of the verb clear. When David first encounters Goliath, the Philistine scorns or disdains him when he sees that he is nothing but a boy (1 Sam. 17:42). He says to David: "Am I a dog, that you come to me with sticks?" Then the text says that the Philistine "cursed David by his gods" and said to him, "Come to me, and I will give your flesh to the birds of the air and to the wild animals of the field" (17:43–44). The context makes it clear that this cursing is an act of belittling, a disdaining of David, treating him with contempt. Likewise, in 2 Samuel 16, Shimei "curses" David. A form of *qillēl* occurs several times in this passage, translated by the NJPS sometimes as "insult" (vv. 5, 7, 13) and at other times as "abuse" (vv. 10, 11, 12). The story itself confirms that Shimei is hurling loud and contemptible insults at David. It is a form of verbal abuse. Finally, one may mention two other statutes, comparable to Exodus 22:28, that use this verb in the same way:

Exodus 21:17 reads, "Whoever *qillēls* his father or mother shall be put to death" (my trans.). Leviticus 19:14 commands, "You shall not *qillēl* the deaf." It is a matter of treating parents or the handicapped with contempt and in a trifling way.

While a number of other texts, such as Genesis 12:3; Judges 9:27; 2 Samuel 6:22; and Jeremiah 15:10, could be cited to confirm this understanding of the verb, it is the narrative in Leviticus 24 that brings this verb and its meaning into the use and misuse of the name of God. There one hears of an occasion when two persons got in a fight, one an Israelite and the other the son of an Israelite woman and an Egyptian man. In the course of the fight, "The Israelite woman's son blasphemed the Name in a curse" (Lev. 24:11). The blasphemer is taken into custody for what is obviously a crime/sin until it can be determined what the Lord's punishment will be. Through the divine word to Moses, it is learned that the man is to be stoned to death by the community, and in that context a longer discourse about the lex talionis and the equality of all before the law is given (vv. 14–22).

There are a number of things at issue in the text, including whether a non-Israelite is subject to the same requirements as an Israelite, but the pertinence to this discussion is the crime or sin that is committed. It is in effect a violation of the statute referred to above in Exodus 22:27 (28E). Only in Leviticus 24, the text is more specific in referring to the *name*. Two verbs are used, the second one being *qillēl* and the first one being a verb that "literally means 'to pierce,' and by extension, 'to specify, pronounce explicitly, identify'" (Halpern, *Leviticus*, 166). More literally, the text says that the man "pronounced the name and belittled [it]" (v. 11). Presumably, in the heat of the battle, the man let loose what is commonly understood as profanity, a nonserious use of the divine name, or a use of it in the context of fighting that can only be regarded as a trifling use of the name. It is as if someone in anger at a computer that is not performing correctly says in disgust "Jesus God!" a contemporary example actually heard by the author on the day of writing these words.

We can be no more confident of what exactly went on than some such supposition as proposed here. But there are three obvious and important aspects of the story: the name of God is the issue; it was treated in a light or trifling manner that did not take seriously that the name has to do with the very reality of God; and the seriousness of such action is measured by the penalty, in this instance a divine decision (see the motivation clause in the Third Commandment).

104

The story thus takes up a misuse of the name that is not confined to lying and oath taking, themselves seriously potential areas of misuse of the name. From this story, we learn that there are various ways in which the name of God may be misused so that God is treated lightly, in a trifling manner. The use of the name of God is not available for such purposes. It is a deadly serious matter when one lightly takes up the name of God on one's lips, in an unthinking manner, in anger, casually, as if the words do not mean anything. The tradition of interpretation of this commandment has always recognized that such empty and trifling uses of the name of God are sins against which the commandment guards the members of the community. In actual practice, the trifling use of the name is all too often regarded as a trifling violation of the Commandment. The fate of the violator of the commandment in Leviticus 24 is a warning against such a weak reading of the Third Commandment. The members of the community who live in obedience to the Lord your God, who are redeemed, blessed, judged, and saved by this God, are not to allow the name of this one to be a matter of casual, empty, belittling speech.

False Prophecy

Less commonly associated with the Third Commandment, false prophecy is, nevertheless, a serious instance of misuse of the name of God. That becomes evident in two ways. Not only does the prophetic word begin with the introductory messenger formula: "Thus says the LORD," but when prophecy is talked about, and especially when the issue of false prophecy arises, there also is explicit reference to and focus on prophesying "in the name of the LORD" or "in my name." The misuse of the name is clear in this instance for the texts regularly say that the prophets are prophesying in the name of the Lord though the Lord did not send them or speak to them (e.g., Jer. 14:13–16; 23:16; Ezek. 22:28), or the prophecy is explicitly called false and lying (e.g., Jer. 14:13–16; 27:15; 29:9; Zech. 13:3).

Moreover, the book of Ezekiel specifically identifies false prophecy as *šāwᵊ* and so provides a direct word association with the Third Commandment (12:24; 13:6, 7, 8, 9, 23; 21:28, 34; 22:28). Whether that word is understood more as lying or more as empty and vain or useless speech, it is the defining term for false prophecy in Ezekiel. Thus the prophet denounces those who prophesy without a vision, 105 that is, out of their own minds and imaginations (13:2; cf. Jer. 23:16). Then the prophet goes on to say of these prophetic projections: "They have envisioned [that is, "seen"] *šāwʾ* and lying divination" (Ezek 13:6). Further on, he says to the false prophets: "Because you have uttered *šāwʾ* and envisioned lies . . ." (v. 8). The interchange of the word *šāwʾ* with a word for "lies" indicates that the emphasis is on the prophecy as untrue; the reference to their prophesying out of their own hearts or imaginations points to the character of the prophecy as fanciful, made-up. Once again, the language conveys the overlap of speech that is false and speech that is made-up or not connected to anything real, speech without substance or grounding in reality.

The point is clear and crucial: Speaking the name, usually in the form "Thus says the LORD," once again grounds and secures what is said so that it is presumably trustworthy and reliable. The community can count on this word because, spoken in the name of the Lord, it is believed to be from the Lord and so a true word. When such words are either lies or made-up out of one's own imagination—and those are really the same thing—the community that follows the direction indicated by the words is in great danger. Once again the security of expectations and communal trust are deeply rooted in the way in which the name of the Lord is used or misused.

The commandment thus points to a critical danger for those who stand as spokespersons for the word of the Lord in the community of faith, those persons with a calling and office that places them in the position of declaring in some way the word of the Lord so that members of the community can learn from it what God is doing and what God expects. To the extent that the church understands its ministers to speak with a prophetic voice, the Third Commandment comes strongly into play. Where the false or empty words come from is not always clear, not even the degree to which such spokespersons perceive themselves as lying in behalf of God, but there is some clue in the two references to speaking from the mind or imagination (see above) rather than from a proper reception and perception of the divine word. Such words are simply made up out of whole cloth and are not a proper perception of God's word.

How is such imaginative and thus empty speaking of the word of God avoided? There may be some indication from the further references to false prophets and true prophets. In Deuteronomy 13 the community is warned about the prophet who produces good prophetic signs and omens and portents but says, "Let us go after other gods" (v. 2 KJV). Moses indicates that such an event is to be understood as a divine test to see "whether you indeed love the LORD your God with all your heart and with all your soul" (v. 3). Both the First Commandment and the Shema are here alluded to. Whatever is going on, the passage makes it clear that the issue is whether the prophetic voice is consistent with what has been revealed and given to the community to guide its life. Consistency with God's previous revelation is a fundamental test of the truthfulness and substance and reliability of what the community hears from its prophets. If there is no vision—and the church does not regularly expect formal visions of its ministers—there is still the issue of whether the words are simply made up in the imagination or whether they grow out of and are consistent with what God has said to the community in the Scriptures. To speak a word to the community that is simply the random, even interesting, thoughts of one's head rather than what is discerned from and consistent with God's revelation through Moses and the prophets of old is an empty/made-up, thus lying, act in God's name, a misuse of the name of God that can lead the church astray. That there may be disagreement about what that revelation says and means does not lessen the weight of the commandment here or the endangerment of the community's security before God.

There is possibly one other criterion to distinguish between the false and empty word of the divine spokesperson and the true and substantive and real word. It arises out of the fact that the community of faith has a history with prophecy and pays attention to how prophetic words have happened and been discerned and confirmed in the past. In Jeremiah 26 the priests and prophets want to put Jeremiah to death because he has prophesied against Jerusalem and the temple, saying it will be destroyed if, the Lord says, "you do not listen to me, to walk in my law that I have set before you" (v. 4). This is consistent with what has already been reported in Jeremiah 7, where Jeremiah's sermon about the temple is actually quoted. There he specifically calls upon the law about doing justly to sojourner, orphan, and widow and not going after other gods. So the word from Deuteronomy 13 about true prophecy being consistent with the previous revelation of God is attested here as well. But there is a further implicit pointer to the true prophetic word, one that is inferred from what happens then in Jeremiah 26, when the priests and prophets propose to kill Jeremiah (26:7–9). In response to that suggestion, some of the elders of the land refer back to the

107

word of doom about Jerusalem that came earlier from the prophet Micah in the eighth century (26:17–19). Though his prophecy was just as strong an announcement of doom for Jerusalem as Jeremiah's ("Jerusalem shall become a heap of ruins" [26:18; cf. Mic. 3:12]), Micah was not put to death. On the contrary, King Hezekiah feared the Lord and sought the Lord's mercy (Jer. 26:19). The elders see an important lesson in that story.

So there is a history of prophetic words that can help one judge the present proclamation of the word of the Lord. That history is clearly operative elsewhere, for example, when Jehoshaphat, the king of Judah, tells Ahab, the king of Israel, that even though four hundred prophets have given the two of them a positive word about going up against the Arameans, he wants to know if there is any other prophet of whom they may inquire for the word of the Lord (1 Kgs. 22:7). Ahab says there is indeed another one, Micaiah ben Imlah, "but I hate him, for he never prophesies anything favorable about me, but only disaster" (v. 8). In this conversation one sees an implicit criterion that is not fail-safe either but is obviously operative in this story as well as in Jeremiah's encounter with the religious and community leadership in Jeremiah 26. If prophets give the community/congregation what it likes to hear, especially in time of comfort and prosperity and especially when it is in conformity with the will of the political power, then one should check it out—very carefully. And those who so speak easy words in easy times to justify the desires of the political powers and claim to speak the word of the Lord may be in serious violation of the Third Commandment, lifting up the name of God emptily, when there is no substance to what is proclaimed as the word of the Lord.

Prayer and Praise

The name of God has important proper uses that are encouraged and protected by the Third Commandment understood in its positive meaning. The frequent idiom "to call on the name of the LORD," or "invoke the name of the LORD," often parallel to and the same as "to call on the LORD," or "cry to the LORD," is clearly invoking the Lord in prayer. Thus one of the primary "uses" of the name of the Lord, lifting up the name of God, is to invoke the name in a prayer for help. The significance of the name at that point is suggested particularly by the conflict between Elijah and the prophets of Baal

108

in 1 Kings 18, where Elijah makes the issue patently clear: "You will then invoke your god by name, and I will invoke the LORD by name; and let us agree: the god who responds with fire, that one is God" (v. 24 NJPS). The name is underscored because it identifies who it is that is God, who it is that is effective and powerful, able to respond when the name is called to. So in Psalm 99:6, the psalmist says:

> Moses and Aaron were among his priests,
> Samuel also was among those who called [*qārāʾ*] on his name.
> They cried [*qārāʾ*] to the LORD, and he answered them.

And in Psalm 116:4, the psalmist refers to his prayer in the situation of past distress:

> Then I called on the name of the LORD:
> "O LORD, I pray, save my life!"

In this instance, the content of the prayer is given. The reader is told what was done when the name of the Lord was invoked: an appeal in and to the name of the Lord for help. In similar fashion, the lamenter of Lamentations 3 recalls past prayers:

> ⁵⁵I called on your name, O LORD,
> from the depths of the pit;
> ⁵⁶you heard my plea, "Do not close your ear
> to my cry for help, but give me relief!"
> ⁵⁷You came near when I called on you;
> you said, "Do not fear!"

The name of the Lord is thus central to the prayer of the person in distress who cries out to the Lord by name, invoking the name of the one who can and does respond in help. That this is a self-conscious identification of the source of help over against other possibilities is indicated by the encounter between Elijah and the Baal prophets, but that is implicit in all such praying. The prayer does not go up to some numinous or mysterious other but to the one who is known in this story, who in the past has come to help and will do so in the future. There is a daring but necessary invocation of the name of God that serves to locate the source of help like no other. Calling on this name is thus an act of trust and confidence and assumes, with good reason, that such invocation of the name will elicit a response (e.g., Ps. 116 and Lam. 3:55–57). For it is in

109

God's delivering mercy that the name of the Lord is glorified. Thus the petition of Psalm 79:9:

> Help us, O God of our salvation,
>> for the glory of your name;
> deliver us, and forgive our sins,
>> for your name's sake.

When the psalmist prays "for your name's sake," it is a claim that the one who bears this name is this way—there to help and deliver. The character of the one who is "the Lord your God" is not determined by some definition of deity but by the words and deeds that come forth from the one who bears the name.

Proper "lifting up" or use of the name of God happens in *praise* as well as in supplication. The psalmist who at the beginning of Psalm 116 tells of invoking the name of the Lord in a situation of terrible distress then says at the end of the psalm:

> [12] What shall I return to the Lord
>> for all his bounty to me?
> [13] I will lift up the cup of salvation
>> and call on the name of the Lord.
>
> . . . .
>
> [17] I will offer to you a thanksgiving sacrifice
>> and call on the name of the Lord.

The name to which the psalmist cried out now becomes the name that is thanked and praised (cf. Ps. 54:1, 6). Such instances in which the name of the Lord is lifted up in praise and exaltation are too numerous to list (e.g., Pss. 7:17; 9:1–2; 18:49; etc.). To give thanks and praise to the Lord is to praise the name of the Lord. The beginning and end of Psalm 8 express such praise of the name of the Lord:

> O YHWH, our Lord,
>> how majestic is your name in all the earth! (my trans.)

It is such exaltation of the name of God that is in mind when the prophet says:

> Give thanks to the Lord,
>> call on his name;
> make known his deeds among the nations;
>> proclaim that his name is exalted.
>
> (Isa. 12:4)

110

Praise of the name of the Lord is so prominent both as an act and as an injunction—as a calling to others, a claim that is laid on the congregation and the nations—that it must be understood as a primary use of the name of the Lord. The community that avoids misuse of the name by empty and false uses does not avoid the use of the name of God. On the contrary, it cries out the name, and it sings out the name. For the name is the way by which the community knows its creator, its redeemer, and the one who receives all its worship. Praise of the Lord's name is one of the ways the community identifies both who commands its service and worship and who does not. There can be no substitution of some other name as the object of its praise and adulation. To speak the name and glorify the name is to ensure that it does not speak and glorify another name. Right use of the name is thus in a serious fashion a political act, but it is a political act that happens in praise and prayer, in terrible distress and in the gathering of the community in thanksgiving and prayer: "I will tell of your name to my brothers and sisters; in the midst of the congregation I will praise you" (Ps. 22:22). Exultation of the name in the congregation, in its worship life, prohibits the exultation of any other name as a claim on the congregation's obedience, service, and devotion.

Political use of the name of God is thus an important sphere of its use and misuse. The name of God marks off the one who claims the congregation's ultimate loyalty. It is not Caesar but the Lord whom this community serves. The one name relativizes all other names.

The Name of Jesus

Both the church's Trinitarian theology and the words of Scripture themselves bring the name of Jesus into the trajectory of meaning and action flowing out of the Third Commandment (Soulen, "Name"). The conviction that the God whose name is reverenced is known in three persons has at least two effects. One is to bring the name of Jesus into the same care and consideration that the name of God is given in the Commandments. The other is to provide the community with a name for God that it uses as much as it seeks to avoid misuse of the name. Focus on the name of Jesus belongs to the very beginning of the story and is there at the end. So the Gospel narratives not only give attention to the name of the child born to Mary; they also ascribe to him names that create an immediate

111

identification with the names of God in the Old Testament (see below), and at the end the name is the expression of divine sovereignty over all the world:

> [9] Therefore God also highly exalted him
>   and gave him the name
>   that is above every name,
> [10] so that at the name of Jesus
>   every knee should bend,
>   in heaven and on earth and under the earth,
> [11] and every tongue should confess
>   that Jesus Christ is Lord,
>   to the glory of God the Father.
>   (Phil. 2:9–11)

The name of Jesus, however, is not simply a fact reported biographically. It also comes to represent the reality of God as fully as does the name YHWH in the Old Testament.

A case can be made that the name of God and the name of Jesus are significant dimensions of the revelation of the tripersonal character of the Godhead. A significant and appropriate *tension* is brought about through the name. The name serves to effect both a *distinction* between and an *identification* of God and Jesus. The *distinction* is maintained as the name of God as revealed in the Old Testament, that is, the Tetragrammaton, YHWH, is not attributed to Jesus or appropriated by him in the New Testament though one may find implicit references to the Tetragrammaton in divine passive expressions (Soulen, "Name," 250–51) or in Jesus' "I am . . ." declarations in the Gospel of John (e.g., John 6:35, 48; 8:12; cf. Exod. 3:14–15). The term "God" is rarely applied to Jesus as name or title—but see Thomas's cry "My Lord and my God!" in John 20:28—although it functions as both name and title in the Old Testament. The distinction is further maintained in the names of the Trinity. The New Testament itself distinguishes between God and Jesus in its pre-Trinitarian formulations (2 Cor. 13:13) as well as in using titles—Father, Son, and Spirit—to describe a relational unity and distinction in ways that would be more difficult to do with actual names. Names would serve either to suggest a nondistinctional unity if, for example, "YHWH" were applied to Jesus, or a distinction without relationship if, for example, separate names were consistently used and nothing else.

At the same time, the name serves in several ways to effect a significant *identification* of Jesus with God:

1. *In the Gospel of John, Jesus' understanding of his identity and his mission is closely tied to the revelation of the name of God.* Twice in the final discourse Jesus says, "I have made your name known" (John 17:6, 26). The self-revelation of God in and through the divine name does not stop with the Old Testament. It is central to the presence and work of Christ, who says:

> Holy Father, protect them *in your name that you have given me*, so that they may be one, as we are one. While I was with them, I protected them *in your name that you have given me.* (17:11–12)

There is thus a marked continuity between the name of God and the name that Jesus bears. The Johannine discourse understands the divine name as in some way given to Jesus. It is not possible to tell exactly what is meant by the "name" in this context. Some have understood the name to be "Father," but that hardly fits the context and meaning of the verses above. The name remains the name it has always been, but now it is shared by Jesus. The significance of the name as identifying and characterizing the source and "object" of the community's worship is thus fully manifest in the New Testament.

2. *The names of Jesus are in strong continuity with the name of God in the Old Testament.* The name and the words and deeds of the one named YHWH are recapitulated in the names of the child of Bethlehem. The name of God as *>ehyeh <immak*, "I will be with you" (Exod. 3:12; see above), is also the name of God's messiah, "Emmanuel," "God is with us" (Matt. 1:23), And the name "Jesus" is the other chief clue—but only confirming what is already known in the story—to what the bearer of the name is about: "He will save his people" (Matt. 1:21; Luke 1:31), an identity that is fully consonant with the self-revelation of the name of God in the Exodus story.

3. *The term* kyrios *provides an explicit equation of the names of the Lord of Israel and the Lord of the church.* The use of the word *kyrios* for the Tetragrammaton in the Septuagint and its continued use in the New Testament both in reference to God—especially in Old Testament quotations but also in the infancy narratives and elsewhere—and even more heavily in reference to Jesus serves to create a linguistic identification of the name of God with Jesus. Because

kyrios is both an epithet and a substitute or surrogate for the divine name, as it is applied to Israel's God, it is the appropriate bearer of the continuity and identity between Jesus and God. This identification is a powerful theological reason why the church should be reluctant to let go of its use of the term "Lord" in reference to God, even with its problems. The theological loss would be large.

4. *The name of Jesus is used in ways comparable to the use of the name of God in the Old Testament.* Baptism is in the name of the Son as much as in the name of the Father (Matt. 28:19) and often is explicitly in the name of Jesus (Acts 2:38; 10:48; 19:5). Prophecy and mighty deeds are done in the name of Jesus (Matt. 7:22; Mark 9:38–39; Acts 16:18). Persons are healed in the name of Jesus (Acts 3:6). Jesus is present with those who are gathered in his name (Matt. 18:20). Belief is in the name of Jesus (John 1:12; 3:18; Acts 3:16; 1 John 3:23), and those who believe in him "call on his name" (Acts 22:16). Salvation is in and through the name of Jesus (Rom. 10:13; 1 Cor. 1:2). Proclamation is of the name of Jesus (Acts 8:12; 9:20) and in the name of Jesus (Luke 24:47), and prayer is specifically in the name of Jesus (John 14:13–14; 16:23–26). The prayer of Stephen as he is being stoned is instructive (Acts 7:59–60). His initial sentence is comparable to Jesus' prayer to God (Luke 23:46), citing Psalm 31:5, but it is addressed to Jesus: "Lord Jesus, receive my spirit." This is followed by a second prayer, "Lord, do not hold their sin against them," again comparable to some of Jesus' final prayers (Luke 23:34), but ambiguous relative to the one being addressed. Is his prayer to God or to Jesus? The Holy Spirit is sent by the Father in the name of Jesus the Son (John 14:26). The name of Jesus, like the name of God in the Old Testament, is to be proclaimed to the nations as well as to Israel (e.g., Ps. 105:1–3; Isa. 12:4; Acts 9:15) and to be praised (Acts 19:17) and glorified (2 Thess. 1:12). The consummation of the Lord's rule is envisioned when "at the name of Jesus every knee should bend" (Phil. 2:10).

The name of Jesus, therefore, is given to the community of faith in continuity with the name of God and so comes under the protection and instruction of the Third Commandment. All that belongs to the way that Christians use the name of God is proper for the name of Jesus. All vain, empty, and false use of the name of Jesus is prohibited. The community of faith lives by the Third Commandment whenever it prays and acts in accordance with the prayer it has been taught by its Lord: "Hallowed be your name" (Matt. 6:9).

Excursus: Pronouncing the Name of God

If the name of God is to be used in any fashion, that raises the question of whether and how the name of God is to be pronounced and whether one should substitute a title such as "Lord" for the name. That is a complicated issue, primarily because both the terms "God" and "Lord" have become names as well as nouns. So in this book, the custom of using the term "Lord" is adopted as a way of speaking the name of God. I would argue there is no inherent claim in Scripture that the name of God is not to be pronounced. But substitutions for the name, even as the Bible substitutes the term "God" for the name and uses it as a name, may properly represent the invocation and proclamation of the name of God. As for the actual vocalization and pronunciation of the Tetragrammaton (YHWH) by Christians, Robert Jenson's counsel in this regard is simple and wise: "Jewish feeling in this matter should be honored by Christians; the recent fashion of pronouncing the name in lectures and from the pulpit is deeply regrettable." It is important to observe that Jenson's comment in this regard is a matter of counsel and is not a theological argument (Jenson, *Systematic Theology* 1:44 n. 12).

CHAPTER 3

Keeping the Sabbath

8Remember the sabbath day, and keep it holy. 9Six days you shall labor and do all your work. 10But the seventh day is a sabbath to the LORD your God; you shall not do any work—you, your son or your daughter, your male or female slave, your livestock, or the alien resident in your towns. 11For in six days the LORD made heaven and earth, the sea, and all that is in them, but rested the seventh day; therefore the LORD blessed the sabbath day and consecrated it.

Exodus 20:8–11

12Observe the sabbath day and keep it holy, as the LORD your God commanded you. 13Six days you shall labor and do all your work. 14But the seventh day is a sabbath to the LORD your God; you shall not do any work—you, or your son or your daughter, or your male or female slave, or your ox or your donkey, or any of your livestock, or the resident alien in your towns, so that your male and female slave may rest as well as you. 15Remember that you were a slave in the land of Egypt, and the LORD your God brought you out from there with a mighty hand and an outstretched arm; therefore the LORD your God commanded you to keep the sabbath day.

Deuteronomy 5:12–15

With the Sabbath Commandment, we come to the end of the first table of the Decalogue, that is, those commandments that focus on the proper worship and love of God. At the same time, as shall be shown below, this commandment is a crucial bridge connecting to the commandments having to do with love of neighbor and the protection of our neighbor's well-being. In a variety of ways, the Sabbath Commandment is lifted up, and we are invited to think deeply about its meaning and implications. For example,

- Of all the commandments, the Sabbath requirement is the one with the most variation in the Exodus and Deuteronomy versions of the Decalogue. Rather than being a problem, however, the variations serve to create a rich theological and ethical directive for the community of faith.
- The Sabbath Commandment is the only one that explicitly includes both negative and positive aspects—prohibition and command—confirming that both dimensions belong to our understanding of God's requirements.
- The Sabbath Commandment, more than any other, draws together both the particularity and the universality of the commandments: that is, the Sabbath is a custom or practice belonging to a particular religious community, but it also provides for a fundamental human need: rest from our work.

117

- The Sabbath is the one commandment whose focus is on the good of the addressee rather than the worship of God or the good of the neighbor, though in fact all three dimensions are clearly present in the commandment.
- The Sabbath Commandment is the center of the Deuteronomic form of the Decalogue (see below) and influential in its teaching even though the Sabbath itself is never mentioned in the book of Deuteronomy outside the Decalogue.
- The Sabbath Commandment is the one commandment that is anticipated, actually given as a commandment and incumbent upon the people, before the Lord's address at Sinai (Exod. 16).
- The Sabbath is prominent and pervasive in the biblical text generally; it is more often referred to than any other commandment qua commandment except possibly the First and Second Commandments.

What Is Commanded

The Sabbath Commandment per se, apart from its motivation or rationale clause, is almost the same in the Exodus and Deuteronomic versions. There is not a conflict or difference in what is commanded, only in the grounding of that command, the motivation clauses that give reasons for obeying this commandment. Moreover, the differences in the motivation clauses serve to enrich the meaning of the commandment rather than causing problems in our understanding. In its two versions, the commandment part reads as follows:

> [8]Remember the sabbath day, and keep it holy. [9]Six days you shall labor and do all your work. [10]But the seventh day is a sabbath to the LORD your God; you shall not do any work—you, your son or your daughter, your male or female slave, your livestock, or the alien resident in your towns. (Exod. 20:8–10)

> [12]Observe the sabbath day and keep it holy, as the LORD your God commanded you. [13]Six days you shall labor and do all your work. [14]But the seventh day is a sabbath to the LORD your God; you shall not do any work—you, or your son or your daughter, or your male or female slave, or your ox or your donkey, or any of your livestock, or the resident alien in your towns. . . . (Deut. 5:12–14a)

There are two noticeable differences here. One is the presence in the Deuteronomic version of the clause "as the LORD your God has commanded you," on which see below on the Sabbath as center of the Decalogue. The other is the use of "remember" as the command verb in Exodus but "observe" or "keep" as the command verb in Deuteronomy. The two verbs really supplement each other and do not ask for different kinds of acts. They do serve, however, to make the hearer aware that there are two dimensions to the Sabbath: *memory* and *observance*. Not surprisingly, in both versions of the commandment there is a story feature in the motivation clauses that follow the command: in Exodus the story of God's creation of the world and in Deuteronomy the story of God's deliverance of Israel from slavery. The importance of remembering these stories and the practice arising from them is underscored in the rationale given in Deuteronomy, and the logic of the Deuteronomic version is evident. One "keeps" the Sabbath (v. 12) in order to "remember" the redemption (v. 15; see below).

A close look at the two versions reveals that there are in fact two commandments present, or two parts to the commandment now woven together: keeping the Sabbath and not working on the seventh day. These two elements reflect practices that may originally have been separate observances but are now merged in the Sabbath commandment. In the commandment, however, they are clearly and forcefully united into a single command, but with two emphases: setting a time apart for the Lord ("keep it holy . . . to the LORD your God") and resting on the seventh day of every week ("six days you shall labor and do all your work. . . . You shall not do any work"). What binds them together is the word and notion of "sabbath," a word that means to stop or cease but is also the name of a day. So "the seventh day is a sabbath to the LORD your God" means that day is a stop time but also the Lord's day. Whatever may be the history behind the commandment, the regular cessation of work in order to rest and the time set apart to the Lord are now fully identified and held together.

A Day to the Lord

Although the commandment is a unity, its two parts require attention and explication. One dimension of the commandment is the setting of a regular time that is dedicated to the Lord. This is conveyed both by the words "keep it holy" and "the seventh day is a sabbath to the LORD

119

your God." At this point the Fourth Commandment both has content and lacks content. The commandment is about what the community is to do with time, and one part of that is dedicating one day every week to the Lord. Keeping the seventh day holy means to set it apart from all the other days of the week by dedicating it to the Lord and the Lord's service. The Sabbath Day is like no other day. That the command is substantial and loaded is evident by even a casual observation of how persons take a day off and "stop" without doing anything that connects the day with the service of God. The first word about the Sabbath in both versions of the commandment is that it is to be sanctified, given over to the Lord. Because the Sabbath, or Sunday, is such a part of the human experience of time for many people, it is easy to ignore what a huge thing happens to time at this point. Whatever other cycles are present in the movement of time and whatever ongoing continuity is evident, it now has a regularity built into it, indeed a frequent regularity that is defined as God's time.

At the same time, one observes how little we are told in any detail about what this sanctification of time involves. What is one to do in setting aside every seventh day to the Lord? Clearly, as the rest of the commandment states, that means stopping all one's ordinary tasks and labors. That is the "not-doing" part of the commandment. What is involved in the "doing" part? How does one keep the Sabbath holy? As is true so regularly in the Commandments, the basic command gives a fundamental direction but leaves out many details about how it is one carries out the divine command. That has to be worked out in every time and place. The rest of Scripture helps to define and spell out for the community modes of sanctification, ways of dedicating a day "to the Lord." So it is necessary to keep reading to get some clues and ideas about what such dedication or sanctification involves. As we shall see, there are such clues in other parts of the Bible as the Sabbath is carried forward in Scripture and in the life of the community. Something very large is laid upon us, something that forever defines the time of our life, but we have to learn how to flesh out this time in a way that always sets it apart to the Lord.

Work and Rest

120   The second part of the commandment is the command to stop working on the seventh day of each week, which is the Sabbath. The commandment thus incorporates both the service of God and

human good in a single move. One cannot say that either takes precedence over the other. From the beginning, the point of the commandment is to make sure that time for the worship of God is provided in the midst of human activities. But the commandment is just as emphatic in its insistence on stopping work. Part of the sanctification of the day is the cessation of labor.

Despite some readings of the commandment, there is no reason to assume that it seeks to command work for six days and then stop for the seventh. "This must not be interpreted to mean that God commands us to work. Truly we are [already] born to that [end]" (Calvin, *Sermons on the Ten Commandments*, 116). Human toil is built into the system and the story of creation has made that clear (Gen. 2:15; 3:14–4:2). Work is required for human survival. The issue is not getting work done but making sure that it does not go on all the time and that one may let it go—and let it go regularly, "even in plowing time and in harvest time" (Exod. 34:21). The rhythm is unbreakable even when seasonal or other external circumstances would seem to preclude the rest. Work may have its rewards, but only if its limits, pressures, and demands are set under the safeguard of the Sabbath.

Compare Psalms 127 and 128, and one can see both senses about work. Labor is often burdensome or oppressive, and it can have its reward. "It is in vain that you rise up early and go late to rest, eating the bread of anxious toil" (Ps. 127:2). Such hard, driven, unrelenting labor has a kind of emptiness to it. This psalm, however, is set alongside Psalm 128, which exhibits many elements that lead one to associate it with Psalm 127 (Miller, *Interpreting the Psalms*, 136–37). There is recognition that under the providing, directing way of the Lord, "Happy is everyone who fears the LORD, who walks in his ways. You shall eat the fruit of the labor of your hands; you shall be happy, and it shall go well with you" (vv. 1–2). Work has its positive possibilities when understood in the wholeness of God's intention and under the sign of the Sabbath. If one approaches work in the context in which the Lord has ordered it, it has a different quality and a different character to it than the kind of drivenness that is described in Psalm 127. What protects that is the Sabbath.

The negative form of the Sabbath Commandment is the sentence "You shall not do any work." That prohibition is then *developed* and also given a *positive* dimension. The *development* serves to underscore the force of the prohibition by elaborating who is subject to the commandment: all the family members, all the servants, all the animals, and any immigrants in the community who might not be understood to be subject to the commandment. The point is clear: *everybody* stops work. Lest there be any assumption that the cessation is only here and there, applicable to the powers that be, the self-sufficient heads of families, and the like, both versions of the commandment itemize in a way that insists it is comprehensive, including even the animals! Whatever practices or customs divide the different strata of society in their daily life, they all disappear on the Sabbath. One practice is required of all.

That requirement, however, also provides an opportunity, a wonderful good: *rest*. Both the Exodus and Deuteronomy Sabbath Commandments make that clear in the rationales given for the Sabbath. In Deuteronomy the provision of the Sabbath is "so that your male and female slave may rest as well as you." And in Exodus the community is reminded that the seventh day of creation was when God rested (Exod. 20:11). Or as Genesis 2:3 puts it: "God rested from all the work that he had done in creation." The purpose of Sabbath to provide rest from work is reiterated in other Sabbath texts, for example, Exodus 23:12 and 34:21 both make the point that the seventh day is for rest. Exodus 23:12 underscores this restful purpose to the seventh day by reiterating it three different ways in a single verse: (1) "You shall rest [lit., 'stop,' [*šābat*]." (2) "Your ox and your donkey may rest" (my trans.). (3) "Your homeborn slave and the resident alien may be refreshed." The purpose of the Sabbath is rest for all. It is as much rest time as it is holy time.

And so the Sabbath is a *gift* of God as much as it is a *command*. In Deuteronomy the command is explicit: "Therefore the LORD your God commanded you to keep the sabbath day" (Deut. 5:15; cf. v. 12). The gift character of the Sabbath is implicit but clearly present in the notes of joy and blessing that run through those laws in Deuteronomy 15 and 16 that are an extension of the sabbatical principle (see below, "Holy Times"). In Exodus the character of the Sabbath as gift to the human community is explicit from the beginning. The first Sabbath reference in the whole of the Old Testament is in the story of the collection of manna in Exodus 16, where Moses says:

[25]Eat it today, for today is a sabbath to the LORD; today you will not find it in the field. [26]Six days you shall gather it; but on the seventh day, which is a sabbath, there will be none.

Some of the people did not trust the gift of the Sabbath and went out to gather the manna.

> [28]The LORD said to Moses, "How long will you refuse to keep my commandments and instructions? [29]See! The LORD has *given* you the sabbath, therefore on the sixth day he *gives* you food for two days." (emphasis added)

Here is an explicit statement, in a narrative, that the Sabbath is given by the Lord. In a larger way, that is clearly the point of the Exodus form of the commandment in reading the Sabbath in the light of God's creative work and identifying it as blessed by the Lord. The Lord's blessing of the Sabbath thus is the provision of the Sabbath as a gift for human existence. The Sabbath, at least in part, belongs to the providential work of God. It is a part of the continuities of life, given to bless human existence. Karl Barth has caught this very well in claiming that on this day we are to celebrate, rejoice, and be free to the glory of God (*Church Dogmatics*, III/4:50). While Sabbath is something to be done by us for our good and so comes to us as command (Exod. 20:8; Deut. 5:12, 15b), it is also something to be received for our enjoyment and benefit and so comes to us as blessing and gift (Exod. 20:11b). In fact the Sabbath comes to us *first* as gift, which is why Barth can say that human history under the command of God "really begins with the Gospel and not with the Law, with an accorded celebration and not a required task, with a prepared rejoicing and not with care and toil, with a freedom given . . . and not an imposed obligation, with a rest and not with an activity. . . . The aim of the Sabbath commandment is that man [*sic*] shall give and allow the omnipotent grace of God to have the first and the last word at every point" (III/4:52, 54). With such an understanding, the Sabbath Commandment lets us see how and why Paul Lehmann and others have observed that the Commandments are descriptive as much as they are prescriptive, describing what life is like under and in the grace of God as much as telling us what we have to do. It is not an exaggeration to say, "The Sabbath commandment explains all the other commandments" (Barth, *Church Dogmatics*, III/4:53). What is important to remember is that we need the prescriptive force of this commandment, the sense of duty and obligation, in order to be sure to receive the descriptive gift of the Sabbath rest.

123

Why Keep the Sabbath? The Exodus Rationale

Both versions of the Sabbath Commandment are noticeable for their extended motivation clauses. Such clauses occur in other commandments, specifically the prohibition of images, the protection of the name, and honoring parents. In each case the motivation works somewhat differently from the others. Two of the commandments, the prohibition of images and the commandment against misuse of the name of God, have motivation clauses indicating the dangers of not obeying the commandment. Conversely, the commandment calling for parents to be honored includes a clause pointing to the benefit of obedience. The motivation clauses of the Sabbath Commandment work differently from these others. They serve to give a reason for obedience, but it is less a matter of the consequences of disobedience or obedience and more an accounting for why the Lord has set this particular requirement upon the community. In both cases, the motivation clause is more of an explanation, a rationale, and one that roots the called-for practice in the story of God and humanity from the beginning, yet including the specific time the Lord acted to deliver Israel from bondage. Here is a positive requirement, a practice that is tied to the life and experience of a people and so merits some explanation in a way not necessarily required by the other commandments.

As already noted, the Exodus form of the Sabbath Commandment grounds it in God's work of creation, drawing on the conclusion of the first creation account in Genesis 1. If the Deuteronomic rationale (see below) connects the Sabbath to Israel's particular experience, the Exodus rationale connects it to the larger human experience. In other words, Sabbath is a custom to order the religious life of a particular people—"Remember the sabbath day, and keep it holy"—a point underscored as various cultic activities accrue to the Sabbath Day both in Scripture and in the experience of synagogue and church. But it also serves a basic human need, indeed a fundamental need extending beyond the human sphere and encompassing nature in various forms: time for rest.

The similarities and differences between the Exodus rationale and the Genesis account on which it appears to be based point to what is important in the commandment's rationale. While the verb most often associated with God's creative activity in Genesis is the verb *bārāʾ*, "create," both Genesis 2:2–3 and the Exodus Sabbath

124

rationale use the verb ʿāśâ, meaning "do" or "make." This is also the verb used in the commandment in the prohibition "You shall not *do* any work" (Exod. 20:10). There is no reference in the Exodus rationale to the Lord's "work" of creation, but the work of human beings mentioned in the commandment (*mĕlaʾktekâ*, Exod. 20:9–10) is clearly foreshadowed and anticipated in God's "work" of creation because *three times* in the Genesis 2 summary, reference is made to "his work" (*mĕlaʾktô*, vv. 2–3). The character of Sabbath as not only cessation of work in order to worship but also time for rest is underscored by the commandment's explicit reference to the Lord having "rested" (*nûaḥ*) on the seventh day. The Genesis account speaks only of God having "finished" and "ceased" (*šābat*, vv. 2–3; see NJPS). The two texts together equate stopping labor with resting. As both the commandment rationale and the Genesis creation conclusion make clear, it is only in the light of God's having stopped work and rested that the Sabbath Day is blessed and sanctified: "*Therefore* the LORD blessed the sabbath day and consecrated it" (Exod. 20:11; emphasis added).

In the Prologue to the Decalogue one can identify signs of an *ethic of response* alongside the obvious *ethic of command* operating in these guidelines for the life of the community (see discussion of the Prologue in chap. 1); with this creational rationale for the Sabbath Commandment, an implicit *ethic of correlation* or *correspondence* comes into play. The sabbatical practice of each family in the community, interrupting its work with a day of rest, is a self-conscious reflection and imitation of the work of God, who also interrupted—or better—finished the divine creative labor with a day of rest. The *imitatio Dei* of this commandment is indicated further in other texts. In Exodus 31:12–17, the Sabbath Commandment is repeated by the Lord, this time to Moses to pass on to the rest of the people. It is essentially what one finds in the Exodus Decalogue with three additional elements: (1) the penalty of capital punishment, which points to the absolute character of the commandments in distinction from other statutes (cf. Exod. 21:12, 15, 16); (2) the Sabbath as a perpetual sign to the people of God's creative work; and (3) the word that on the seventh day, the Lord not only ceased (*šābat*) from work but also "was refreshed" (*yinnāpaš*, 31:17). This expression occurs only two other times in Scripture. One of these is in the version of the Sabbath Commandment found in Exodus 23:12, where the Sabbath is in order to provide rest for

125

"your ox and your donkey" and also that "your homeborn slave and the resident alien may be *refreshed*" (*yinnāpaš*). As it was in the beginning, as it was the Lord's way, so now the community of faith is to take time to stop and be refreshed, rested, and renewed. God's creative work followed by time to rest and be refreshed becomes a model for the human way, with special emphasis that it serve for the weak and powerless ("homeborn slave and the resident alien"). If, as we shall see, the motivation of the Sabbath Commandment in Deuteronomy brings the neighbor into view as recipient of its benefits, this statute shows that the Exodus commandment does the same. The refreshment that comes from imitating God in the Sabbath rest is particularly for the slave and the alien or stranger. Furthermore, the imitation of God is also explicit in sanctifying the seventh day, for that is simply following God's lead, who "blessed the sabbath day and consecrated it" (20:11). In everything having to do with keeping the Sabbath, the community follows God's lead.

In this fashion, the imitation of God is set as an element of the ethical grounding of the commandments, though that is somewhat surprising insofar as it suggests that what human and beast require in order to make it and survive is also something that the God who made us also needs. It may not be possible to wrap our minds around that idea until we have come to terms with the realization that God also "works." We work and rest because God worked and rested.

Rooting the Sabbath practice in God's creative activity takes us in a somewhat different direction from what one usually finds in the motivation clauses seeking to persuade the community to keep the provision that has been given to them. Such clauses are most likely to be rooted in Israel's experience of salvation and deliverance, as is the case for the Deuteronomic Sabbath Commandment (see below). Here in Exodus, however, there is a different kind of theology of commandment, a cosmological one. Jon Levenson has suggested that here, as in other places, "biblical law . . . is of the same order as the laws of nature, the inner mechanism of creation. In this theology [of commandment], the commandments appear not as the yield of a historical event, or at least not exclusively so, but as the extension into human society of cosmic order, divinely ordained and sustained" ("Theologies of Commandment," 28). The keeper of the Sabbath thus brings one's life into "harmony with the intrinsic rhythm of the cosmos, instituted by divine fiat and observed [first] by God" (32). It is rather surprising that the Sabbath Command-

126

ment is where one may come closest to a kind of "natural law" operating in the Ten Commandments.

Why Keep the Sabbath?
The Deuteronomic Rationale

Formal Considerations

The particularity of the Deuteronomic Sabbath Commandment is not confined to its rationale. There are two important *formal* considerations that contribute to its significance and the role it plays in the whole.

1. One is that this commandment is a *bridge* between the first table of the law, which deals with the individual and the community's relation to God, and the second table, which has to do with the relation to the neighbor. That the Sabbath Commandment should follow upon the commandments guarding the exclusive worship of God and the use of the divine name is self-evident since it speaks about a day that is a Sabbath to the Lord your God, a day to be made and kept holy. But the purpose of the Deuteronomic form of the commandment as it grounds the Sabbath in the need to provide rest for your servants means that it also points *forward* and becomes a part of that group of commandments that have to do with the way one treats the *neighbor*, here embodied in "your servant/slave." So the Sabbath Commandment joins the service of God with relief from service for your neighbor/slave. Once again the preferential memory and attention of God is for the powerless. The only place the neighbor is ever defined in these commandments is in the Sabbath command, and there the neighbor whose good is being guarded is the slave in your midst, the servant who works for you and who elsewhere in Deuteronomy is identified as "your brother" (e.g., 15:12). In moving from the first table of the Commandments to the second, the Deuteronomic Decalogue effects an "illogical" move from God to neighbor, over against what one may rightly infer from the Exodus version. There the logic moves easily from the worship of God to honoring one's parents, the earliest and closest experience of the neighbor (see chap. 4). The Deuteronomic form of the Decalogue makes a kind of illogical move to the neighbor already in the Sabbath Commandment, which introduces the

127

neighbor first in the face of the slave. That rationally illogical move is surely rooted in the fundamental logic of the whole Decalogue: the starting point of the covenantal claims is found in Israel's status as freed slaves. The statute in Exodus 23:12 suggests that the neighbor who is slave is implicitly in view even in the Exodus version of the Sabbath Commandment (see above, "Work and Rest").

2. The second formal consideration vis-à-vis the Sabbath Commandment in Deuteronomy is that the Deuteronomic form of the Decalogue has been so constructed that the Sabbath Commandment is clearly the *center* of this body of instruction, formally and substantively. Norbert Lohfink has noted three ways in which the Sabbath is underscored and emphasized by being given a central position ("Decalogue").

a. The most obvious of these is the very extensive differences in the form and language of the commandment in distinction from the Exodus version. The reader/listener cannot help noting the significant changes in the Deuteronomic version, especially in the rationale.

b. The Fourth Commandment is given central place in the Deuteronomic version also by the way motifs from the beginning and the ending of the Decalogue are brought into the center of the Sabbath Commandment. The beginning of the Decalogue is echoed in the way the Fourth Commandment refers to the redemption from Egypt. The ending also, in a modest but clear way, is anticipated in the Sabbath Commandment by its reference to "ox" and "donkey," who are mentioned in the Deuteronomic version of the Tenth Commandment but not in the Exodus Decalogue. So by alluding to the beginning and to the ending in a way that the Exodus form of the Sabbath Commandment does not, the Sabbath is lifted up in the Deuteronomic Decalogue structure as the center that draws and holds things together.

c. The third way Deuteronomy makes the Sabbath Commandment the center of the Decalogue is structural: it creates five literary blocks or segments, of which the Fourth Commandment is the central block. In other words, the Decalogue in Deuteronomy divides into five parts: a long word, a short word, a long word, a short word, a long word. The first part—the Prologue, the First and Second Commandments—is a long block having to do with the proper worship of the Lord and where the first-person reference to the Deity is evident. The second part is the short Third Commandment. The third and central part is the long Sabbath Commandment. The fourth and short part is the commandment about the parents, and the fifth long part is the sequence of commandments about the neighbor. While these all seem very short, Deuteronomy has linked them into a single word or part by connecting them with conjunctions, reflected in the NRSV's repeated "neither," to say in effect that this is one long word with several components. So the Sabbath in this way is not simply one on the list but is the pivotal longer statement at the center, serving also as a bridge between the two tables of the Commandments.

What all this means is that the Sabbath is given preeminence in Deuteronomy. If the Prologue and the first two commandments form a kind of principal or great commandment, a second principal commandment is offered in the Sabbath Commandment. Or to put it another way, if the Prologue and the first two commandments, positively formulated in the Shema (Deut. 6:4–5), are the most important word of the Lord, the second most important word is the Sabbath command. The two principal commandments—sole worship of the Lord as God and sanctifying the seventh day—not surprisingly point us to the two chief features of the book of Deuteronomy: its radical claim for the exclusive worship of the Lord and its humanitarian sensibilities. The Shema and the many words of Deuteronomy about the sole worship of the Lord are rooted in the opening commandments: the humanitarian character so prominent in Deuteronomy is rooted in the Fourth Commandment. Along with the prophets, the command to keep the Sabbath is the primary biblical impetus for social justice in the human community. That will be increasingly evident as one explores the rationale for the Sabbath Commandment in Deuteronomy and its development in the statutes of the Deuteronomic Code (Deut. 19–26).

Substantive Reasons

The Deuteronomic rationale for keeping the Sabbath, for resting and setting that day apart to the Lord, is twofold, but the two reasons are intimately related. The first reason for taking the day off— the idiom is self-conscious—is "so that your male and female slave may rest as well as you" (Deut. 5:14b). Everyone needs rest, and the divine command seeks to provide that respite, so that each person may be refreshed, as the Lord was refreshed when resting after the creation (Exod. 31:17). In this motivation clause, however, the command recognizes that those who are free, householders, persons of substance and property, are capable of finding time off and getting their rest and refreshment. The reason for setting a regular day off from work and requiring it—at this point the focus is on not working—is to make sure that those who are not in that category, those who are indentured or in some sort of bondage and not free to provide their own time off, are given the same opportunity to relax and become refreshed as the free Israelite ("as well as you"). The point is clear in the Deuteronomic form of the Sabbath rationale, but it is also heard in the Sabbath statutes of the Book of the Covenant, and even more straightforwardly, as the whole purpose of the Sabbath rest:

> Six days you shall do your work, but on the seventh day you shall rest, so that your ox and your donkey may have relief, and your homeborn slave and the resident alien may be refreshed. (Exod. 23:12)

The second reason for keeping the Sabbath is closely related to the concern for providing rest for those unable to secure it for themselves and liable to excessive and oppressive labor. Keeping the Sabbath is a means of calling to mind the redemptive work of God in your behalf (Deut. 5:15a). The point of the Deuteronomic formulation is not that one should remember the deliverance from Egypt and so because of that keep the Sabbath. Rather, the Sabbath serves to recall the experience of slavery and deliverance. That is clear with the clause that follows: "Therefore the LORD your God commanded you to keep the sabbath day" (v. 15b).

The background of both rationales is Israel's own experience as recorded in Exodus 5. When Israelite slaves in Egypt sought time off to worship the Lord their God, when the people sought release from the service of the Pharaoh for the service of God, the forces of human tyranny and oppressive economic exploitation of slave labor were set against this request for time that is sacred and holy and restful, demanding for more work. Pharaoh said: "They cry, 'Let us go and offer sacrifice to our God.' Let heavier work be laid on them" (5:8–9). The service of God is rejected in behalf of a secular exploitation of human life and human work. That is what triggered the Lord's gift of the Sabbath. What is required is what is needed to make and to keep human life human—and not inhumane, as it was in Egypt.

130

The Moral Issues

The Sabbath and the Sabbath Commandment open up three related moral issues:

1. *The service of God is routinized in the common life.* The first thing that is said about the Sabbath in the Fourth Commandment is that it is sanctified; it is made holy, set apart. Or in the restatement of the command in the second sentence, it is "a sabbath to the LORD." The sabbath is given not only to provide a time for rest but to set in the patterns of daily life a time that is open to God. Here one must keep in mind again Exodus 5:1–9, the Lord's request that Moses and Aaron brought before Pharaoh and the response of the royal establishment as it placed harder labors upon Hebrews. In those verses we encounter precisely the opposite of what is intended in the Sabbath Commandment: the aberration of human existence, against which this commandment is set. Against the request for time that is sacred and holy (5:1), the forces of human tyranny set a demand for more work. The Sabbath is given and commanded not only to provide a time for rest but also time that is "for the LORD." There is a quality and sacredness to this time that moves it beyond simply the cessation of labor, which is its fundamental intent. That is why the Sabbath became one of the signs of the people of God.

Karl Barth shows why it is difficult for either Jewish or Christian existence to be experienced in a concrete and real way apart from this hallowing of the day:

> A day of rest based on merely humanitarian motives cannot as such be of real benefit or fulfill the need and right of resting from work. For what will such a day be used for except what it is actually used for?—various odd jobs and activities, all kinds of necessary and unnecessary meetings and assemblies, "sporting events" and rapt attendance at the same—enhanced by prospects of a lucky win on the tote—and finally and above all a motorized or unmotorized flight to distant scenes, ending up with an escape in alcohol and flirtation. How can it be otherwise? (*Church Dogmatics*, III/4:61–62)

Over against this, Barth goes on to say:

131

> The relationship of divine service to . . . (the) meaning of the commandment is also immediately apparent. It is participation

in the assembling of the congregation which gives this day's rest from work its positive meaning, and which openly distinguishes it from a mere inaction that can only be [hu]man's attempting whatever useless activities . . . [one] can. (III/4:62–63)

Sanctifying the Sabbath means setting aside on a regular basis some time that is consciously intended to celebrate the glory of God—what Abraham Heschel has called "a sanctuary in time" (*Sabbath*)—and to keep alive the memory of the created work (so the Exodus version) and the redemptive work (so the Deuteronomic version) of God. In this way the Sabbath was and is one of the marks of the people of God but one that is set in the ongoing and visible continuity of the common life. Like circumcision for the Jews, Sabbath was a visible sign of the covenant, of the relationship between the Lord and Israel. Notice how Ezra speaks in the long confessional prayer of Nehemiah 9:

[13]You came down also upon Mount Sinai, and spoke with them from heaven, and gave them right ordinances and true laws, good statutes and commandments, [14]and you made known your holy sabbath to them and gave them commandments and statutes and a law through your servant Moses.

Nehemiah thus affirms, in the midst of all the other commandments, both the centrality of the Sabbath, here as gift and command, as well as its distinctiveness, its separateness.

In Isaiah 56:1–8 the clear indication that the eunuch or the foreigner in the community is fully a part of the people and recipient of the full blessing of the Lord is if that person keeps the Sabbath. A regular time of rest is not in itself a sign of the people of God, a mark of the congregation. *Sabbath* is the sign, which includes the rest at its center. There really is a difference between taking a day off and taking a day off and *sanctifying it to the Lord*. Keeping the Sabbath joins with the blessing at each meal to be the most visible and regular means by which Jews and Christians acknowledge God in the midst of life. They are routines in the fullest sense of that word.

2. *All human work is relativized.* The people of ancient Israel were far more concerned about *release* from toilsome labor than about *ensuring* that the work got done. For those who think that divine judgments of Genesis 3 created a fixed order that cannot

132

be ameliorated, the Sabbath command is one of the things at work in God's way to offset their force. The power of work to control human life is forever relativized in the Sabbath. There is no eternal assembly line in the community that lives by these guidelines. The Sabbath helps to guard against one of the primary idolatries to which many, if not all, are prone: idolizing our work by making it the center of value and meaning for our lives. The Sabbath relativizes human work and makes it possible regularly to set aside our goals and plans, our ambitions and accomplishments, to think and care about the God who created us and God's work, about God's plan and our place in it. The Sabbath, therefore, is both a safeguard against one of the central ways in which we violate the First Commandment and also a barrier against the constant inclination to justify ourselves and to define ourselves by our work, what we do. The Sabbath cuts human beings loose from their work and calls them to do nothing but give praise to God. It is a constant reminder—and exemplar—of what the first question of the Westminster Shorter Catechism says is the goal of human existence: "to glorify God and to enjoy him forever."

So there is an *evangelical* meaning to the Sabbath Commandment. It sets us free from the slavery of work, and it reminds us regularly that God's redeeming grace saves us rather than any or all of our work. As the church celebrates the resurrection of Jesus Christ each Sunday, it carries forward the apperception of God's setting us free from sin and death and the praise of God as our reason for being.

3. *The sabbatical principle is God's provision of freedom and rest as a continuing possibility for human existence.* If Paul Lehmann's suggestion that what God is doing in the world is to make and to keep human life human (*Ethics*) is on the right track, then the Sabbath as command and gift is one of the most telling aspects of the divine activity. The primary trajectory set loose in and by the Sabbath Commandment is the principle of regular release from the things that enslave, oppress, and bind human life. It begins in the primary purpose of the Sabbath Commandment: You are not to do as was done to you in Egypt; you are to provide relief for those who do not have the power to secure their own relief. The Sabbath Commandment creates a principle of human existence, one that has two dimensions: (1) a regular release from work, a rest that can be counted upon always; and (2) inclusion of everyone in

133

that provision. The list of those who are released from work, and indeed forbidden to work, is long at every point—in the commandment itself and also in the statutes that reflect it, specifically Exodus 23:12 and Deuteronomy 15. All the members of the community, including the strangers from outside and even the animals come under the sabbatical principle of regular rest and refreshment from labors.

In its formulation in the Sabbath Commandment, the sabbatical principle becomes the specific Decalogue expression and starting point of the love of neighbor "as yourself": "so that your male and female slave may rest as well as you" (Deut. 5:14b). While the Great Commandment itself has in mind remembering that your neighbor is someone like yourself, here its specificity is in making sure that the neighbor who is not like yourself, one who is indentured to you, in servitude and not free to find his or her own refreshment, may rest just as you will do every seventh day. The embodiment of the second part of the Great Commandment in the Sabbath command is a further indicator of this commandment as a bridge to the second table and the beginning of those directives that have to do with how people treat one another.

Rooted in the Sabbath Commandment, the sabbatical principle becomes one of the primary manifestations of God's provision for justice and compassion in the human community. In its insistence on the provision of rest and release on a regular basis, in its special concern for slaves and servants and work animals, and in its openness to equality of treatment that includes the members of the community most open to oppressive treatment and least able to secure their own relief, the drive for justice and compassion is *built into the system* and *regularized*. It is not simply an ad hoc matter but something that is always being activated. As such, the commandment and the principle it evokes anticipate the possibilities of oppressive toil and economic bondage and cut them off at the pass, building into the "routines" of life just and neighborly treatment of those vulnerable to mistreatment, intended or otherwise.

What is initiated in the Sabbath Commandment, however, is not finally confined to a regular day of rest from work each week. Use of the term "sabbatical principle" is because the commandment opens up a large trajectory of social justice reflected in a number of statutes and oriented around rest and release. Several points on that trajectory show its significance.

134

The Book of the Covenant

The first place the sabbatical principle is encountered after its foundation in the Decalogue is in the Book of the Covenant (Exod. 20:22–23:33). The first of these ordinances, in *Exodus 21:2–11*, has to do with the release of indentured servants from their bonded-ness and their indebtedness: "When you buy a male Hebrew slave, he shall serve six years, but in the seventh he shall go out a free person, without debt" (21:2). The development of the second table of the Decalogue in the Book of the Covenant thus begins with the issue of slavery and how its perdurance is overcome by a systematic process of emancipation, one that is spelled out in detail to make sure the release is truly that and not a temporary or insubstantial act that does not truly provide release. The statute is not a perfect manifestation of release. The different treatment of women and wives in that patriarchal culture is clearly evident. At the same time, one observes that special and detailed regulations are put in place to make sure that the woman slave is not mistreated if she does not go free like other servants (21:7–11).

In *Exodus 23:10–11*, a statute directly tied to the Sabbath statute in verses 12–13 (see above), one finds the following:

> [10]For six years you shall sow your land and gather in its yield; [11]but the seventh year you shall let it rest and lie fallow, so that the poor of your people may eat; and what they leave the wild animals may eat. You shall do the same with your vineyard, and with your olive orchard.

Several things happen here:

1. The initial phrase "Six years you shall sow your land" echoes the form of the Sabbath Commandment in both versions of the Decalogue as well as in its expression elsewhere, including the immediately following verses (23:12; cf. 31:15; 34:21; 35:2; Lev. 23:3).

2. The Sabbath is extended from people and animals to the land, which is given a time of rest (cf. Neh. 10:31). The statute shows how fully the creation benefits from a regular time of rest. While the statute does not itself make the point, the land can be overworked and abused. Here, as in so many instances, the law is pragmatic in its effects. Human beings have learned that overworked land loses its productive capacity. Like its beneficiaries, the land needs a time of rest.

135

3. The "rest" is literally a "release" (*šĕmiṭṭâ*, Deut. 15:2), a term central to the application of the sabbatical principle in the Deuteronomic Code (see below).

4. Like the release of slaves in the earlier ordinance, the regular rest is here a release in the seventh *year*; so the sabbatical time is not confined to the weekly sabbath. It is operative in different ways and times, appropriate to the circumstances.

5. Release of the agricultural land serves a further purpose. It ensures that at some point *the poor* may have provisions. Whatever grows without planting during the fallow year may not be appropriated by the owner of the land. It is to be made available to those who do not have land. A practical need is met when the land has its rest. Furthermore, while domestic and work animals are already provided for in the Sabbath Commandment, now even the wild animals of the field are taken into account. In their case, it is like the poor, not so much time off as regular provision of food and sustenance, a dimension of the common good that is undergirded by other commandments and the statutes that grow out of them (cf. Lev. 19:9–10; Deut. 24:20–22; and chapters on stealing and false witness).

The Holiness Code

The rest of the land in the seventh year is regularized also in the Holiness Code in *Leviticus 25:1–7*.

> [2]Speak to the people of Israel and say to them: When you enter the land that I am giving you, the land shall observe a sabbath for the LORD. [3]Six years you shall sow your field, and six years you shall prune your vineyard, and gather in their yield; [4]but in the seventh year there shall be a sabbath of complete rest for the land, a sabbath for the LORD: you shall not sow your field or prune your vineyard. [5]You shall not reap the aftergrowth of your harvest or gather the grapes of your unpruned vine: it shall be a year of complete rest for the land. [6]You may eat what the land yields during its sabbath—you, your male and female slaves, your hired and your bound laborers who live with you; [7]for your livestock also, and for the wild animals in your land all its yield shall be for food.

136   The statute is similar to the one in the Book of the Covenant and probably dependent upon it as well as clarifying what is required: for example, not reaping the aftergrowth or gathering the grapes

of the unpruned vine. The complete rest is emphasized. Several other features are notable. First is that the Leviticus statute explicitly uses the term "sabbath" several times, thus making clear that the Sabbath Commandment is what is being spelled out in these laws about letting the land lie fallow in the seventh year. Further, whereas the Exodus statute focused on providing for the poor by the produce left on the fallow earth, here it is indicated that all persons are dependent upon what the Sabbath rest of the land yields. The Sabbath is for all, and all are dependent upon the uncultivated yield, rich and poor alike, slave and free, domestic animals and wild beasts. Finally, in this statute we have the same language as in the Sabbath Commandment of the Decalogue. The Sabbath year, like the Sabbath Day, is *layhwh*, "for the LORD." There is not some shift from social to religious concerns or vice versa. The sabbatical year is a cultic act also. It is a part of the devotion to the Lord and so holy. Nature, that is, the creation, participates in the Sabbath rest. While periodic fallowness is crucial for the fertility of the land, nothing is said about that here. "Its requirement is justified theologically, not economically—the sabbath" (Milgrom, *Leviticus 23–27*, 2153).

The Deuteronomic Code

Development of the sabbatical principle is especially evident in the Deuteronomic Code in *Deuteronomy 15*. Its opening sentence provides a crisp and succinct formulation: "Every seven years you shall grant a release" (RSV). The Sabbath Commandment is clearly the impetus for what follows in this chapter. As that commandment says, literally, "You shall *do* ["keep," NRSV] the sabbath" (Deut. 5:15), so here 15:1 says, "You shall *do* a release" ["grant a remission," NRSV]. As the Fourth Commandment calls for a "cessation/rest to the LORD" (*šabbat layhwh*), so now the statute in 15:1–11 calls for a "release to the LORD" (*šĕmiṭṭâ layhwh*, v. 2; cf. Exod. 23:11, above). Similarly, the provision for release of bonded servants from their servitude has the same motivation as the Sabbath release in the commandment: "Remember that you were a slave in the land of Egypt, and the LORD your God redeemed you" (15:15). This motivation actually appears three more times, always where the statutes explicitly call for justice and compassion toward the members of the community whose access and support is less certain: the widow, the stranger, and the orphan (Deut. 16:12; 24:18, 22).

137

In the statutes of Deuteronomy 15, the force of the sabbatical principle is carried forward so that it has implication for debts (15:1–11) and slavery (15:12–18). Limitations are placed on both in that the burden of debts, whether experienced in money owed or indentured service, may not be allowed to go on indefinitely. There is a regular time when the burden is removed and the debtor or worker is set free. So along with the release of all from labor on the Sabbath Day and the release of land in the sabbatical year, the Deuteronomic Code echoes the Book of the Covenant in providing release from two other burdens: indebtedness and slavery.

The release from indebtedness as spelled out in *Deuteronomy 15: 1–11* has several features to it:

1. Like the Sabbath the release from debt is a cultic or religious act, not simply a social one "for the remission proclaimed is of the LORD" (Deut. 15:2; NJPS).

2. The release is from the full debt, not simply the interest due.

3. At this stage the remission is only for the "neighbor" or "brother," that is, a compatriot, a "member of the community" (vv. 2, 3, 7, 9, 11), not for foreigners. The strong association of these statutes with relief and release for those who are so designated is why characterizing someone as "neighbor" and especially as "brother/sister" is such a crucial moral issue. Note how in verse 2 (RSV) "his brother" is added to "his neighbor," which is probably the earlier form of the statute. Deuteronomy wants to underscore the relationship because it is crucial to the rationality of the statute.

4. The statute assumes that such a way of acting really can overcome human need, if it is taken seriously (vv. 4–6). That is not undercut by verse 11, which has to do with persistent need "on the earth," not "in the land," suggesting that the way proposed in these statutes shows a way out of such unending need.

5. The realism of the statutes is found in the warning against the tendency not to offer a loan or provide for the need of one's compatriot when the sabbatical year is near and one will have to grant the remission of debts.

6. That realism is accentuated by the strong word urging a resistance to the inclination to be stingy with those in need. On the contrary, generous giving and loans are expected, underscored by the emphatic language of the original text, which speaks of giving liberally (v. 10) and opening wide one's hand to the poor (v. 11).

138

Deuteronomy 15:12–18 moves from the release of debts to the release of *slaves*. It is here and in the related texts that the institution of slavery begins to be subverted from within. Those in view in these verses are bond slaves, members of the community, someone who has bonded oneself to another because of economic debt; slavery is always an economic matter, however it is done. Several things happen here, however, that begin to undo the very possibility of slavery:

1. The "slave" or bond servant is, like the debtor, "your brother" and "your neighbor" (see above). Once again, it is clear how weighty that relationship is because, as with the remission of debts, the sabbatical practice does not seem to apply to foreign or conquered slaves (cf. Lev. 25:44–46; Deut. 21:10–14). Understanding someone as "brother/sister" or "neighbor" makes all the difference in the world.

2. Servitude cannot be unending: "If a member of your community, whether a Hebrew man or a Hebrew woman, is sold to you and works for you six years, in the seventh year you shall set that person free" (Deut. 15:12). Release comes around. Slavery, forced labor for someone else's economic benefit, cannot go on indefinitely. The system of economic bondage begins to come unglued once it requires the regular release of slaves.

3. The distinction between genders in the treatment of slaves breaks down: "If a member of your community, *whether a Hebrew man or a Hebrew woman . . .*" (15:12; emphasis added). The continuing trajectory of the commandment moves beyond the restrictions of the statute in the Book of the Covenant (Exod. 21:2–11; see above, "The Book of the Covenant"). The statute in Deuteronomy goes out of its way to make the treatment the same for the bonded woman as for the bonded man, repeating the point for emphasis and clarity at the end of the whole statute: "You shall do the same with regard to your female slave" (15:17). While the particularities of marriage and their implications are not brought into the statute as in the earlier one, the point is that women are to be treated the same as men in this situation.

4. The servant or slave is given choice: "But if he says to you, 'I will not go out from you,' because *he loves you* and your household, since *he is well off with you*, then you shall take an awl and thrust it through his earlobe into the door, and he shall be your slave forever" (vv. 16–17; emphasis added). The master does not decide the

139

fate of the slave. The choice to go free is made by that slave. Such a provision is in the statute in Exodus 21:5–6, but there such a decision is made because of love of wife and children, who belong to his master, and the bonded slave does not want to leave them behind. In Deuteronomy, a slave may remain with the master because of feeling at home in the household, being well treated—which is what the Sabbath Commandment in Deuteronomy is very much about—liking it there, and wishing to enjoy this good life in the future. In a symbolic act the slave is "nailed" to the house, belongs to it (15:17). The crucial thing is that the slave's right to well-being takes precedence over any prescribed or decreed freedom. Under some circumstances a release could lead to a socioeconomic decline for the slave if the one gaining freedom was not successful or had to eke out a living in great insecurity as a day laborer. It is the right of the *slave*, however, to make that judgment and that decision.

5. The slave whose sabbatical has come is not simply freed but is provided with a liberal economic base to begin life again, a provision that comes from the master of the slave: "And when you send a male slave out from you a free person, you shall not send him out empty-handed. Provide liberally out of your flock, your threshing floor, and your wine press, thus giving to him some of the bounty with which the LORD your God has blessed you" (vv. 13–14). The language "provide liberally" is an emphatic construction, underscoring lavish provision to be given the one who has served the master. It is presumed that the work of the bonded servant has been beneficial to the master, a presumption implicit in the words about "the bounty with which the LORD your God has blessed you." That bounty is to be shared in a large way. This is not a matter of having served one's time and being given a suit of clothes and ten dollars, as used to be done for released convicts. The release is God's decree, and the new life of the servant is to be genuinely new and rewarding, partaking of the bounty of the master whether by remaining in the household or going free on one's own.

Acting in this way to provide release for the economically bound is highly motivated in both recollection and anticipation of what God has done and will do. Such motivation is especially characteristic of the Deuteronomic Code (Deut. 12–26) and not confined to chapter 15. Obedience is not simply expected; it is also urged and encouraged by both positive and negative rationalization. This particular chapter offers a good example of how the motivation formu-

140

lations undergird the moral life described in the commandments and the statutes and stories that grow out of them. Three kinds of reasons are brought to bear to encourage following these statutes of remission and release in the seventh year:

1. If repetition is any clue, the primary reason for following these statutes is the assurance that living this way has brought and will bring God's rich blessing on one's life (vv. 4, 10, 14). One may presume that such blessing, expressed in bounty of flock, threshing floor, and winepress, is God's gift but also a working outcome of living according to these rules. Living and acting this way will bring into reality God's gift of blessing, which in the Old Testament has much to do with tangible benefits of the good life. Obedience brings about a positive good from the Lord your God.

2. The Sabbath Commandment is echoed here: one of the reasons for release of the bonded servant from unceasing labor is in the memory of the people's former life as a slave people in Egypt *and* that the Lord your God redeemed you, delivered you from the unceasing hard labor of life in Egypt. The power of memory here probably works both ways. In remembering the time of bondage and deliverance to freedom, those who are now masters will be moved to release their slaves or servants to a life of freedom from slavery. Impelled by memory, such action becomes also a kind of *imitatio Dei*, yet not in the fullest sense. The sabbatical release is not redemption, but it is an echo of the release from Egyptian bondage, an act that grounds the whole of the Decalogue but especially those commandments and statutes having to do with the experience of economic bondage. As in the Sabbath Commandment, however, this memory is probably also to be understood as an *outcome* of the sabbatical release. Acting in this way will call to mind the goodness of God not only in blessing the people with the good life but also in delivering them from their slavery. The regularity of the Sabbath evokes the memory as much as the memory evokes obedience.

3. A different but no less important kind of motivation is offered in Deuteronomy 15:9 to discourage being hostile and selfish toward the "needy neighbor." There we are told that if one gives nothing to the brother or sister in need, "your neighbor might cry (*qārāʾ*) to the LORD against you, and you would incur guilt." From other statutes we are told that such cries to God are indeed heard and attended (Exod. 22:21–27). This outcry to the Lord is not necessarily a cultic process by which the law is supported. It is likely

141

that such calling to the Lord is done in private, though this is a debated issue. The sanction is a reminder that the legal-juridical structure is undergirded by another structure, one that is present throughout the course of Scripture. When affliction and hurt occur, when the oppression of the poor is such that the cries of pain go up to God, the structure of human pain and divine compassion kicks in—a structured relationship most evident in the Psalms and other places where we encounter the prayers of those in trouble and here enfolded into the more formal structure of law and its obedience (Miller, "Prayer and Divine Action").

This same motivation occurs in Deuteronomy 24:15 as grounding for the requirement to pay the poor their wages properly and on time. In both cases the one who fails to do this will be in a state of guilt or sin. Over against the first category of motivation clauses discussed above, there is here a massive sanction of a negative sort. Like the positive ones, however, it is a feature of the relationship to God, though it may have an ultimate outcome within the formal procedures of the society for the punishment of the guilty.

Finally, this feature of these statutes having to do with bonded servants and the poor—the cry of such effecting divine assistance— is set as the feature of Israelite law that indicates the greater justice or righteousness of the ordinances and statutes of Israel. The only other time that there is any reference in Deuteronomy to "crying out" (*qārāʾ*) to the Lord is in Deuteronomy 4:5–8:

> [5]See, just as the LORD my God has charged me, I now teach you statutes and ordinances for you to observe in the land that you are about to enter and occupy. [6]You must observe them diligently, for this will show your wisdom and discernment to the peoples, who, when they hear all these statutes, will say, "Surely this great nation is a wise and discerning people!" [7]For what other great nation has a god so near to it as the LORD our God is whenever we call to him? [8]And what other great nation has statutes and ordinances as just as this entire law that I am setting before you today?

As Norbert Lohfink has observed, "calling out" or "crying out" in this text is to be understood, in light of the statutes, as the cry of the poor and the slave ("Poverty"). That cry, not unknown elsewhere in ancient Near Eastern law, is here regarded as the primary testimony to the righteousness of Israelite law. An extralegal protection against economic endangerment of the poor and the indentured is

142

the primary indicator of the righteousness of the system of justice set out in the statutes and ordinances. And, as elsewhere in Scripture, prayer is as much a moral matter as it is a spiritual one (Miller, "Property and Possession," 33–34).

The Jubilee Year

There is one more significant piece to the working out of the sabbatical principle. It is the enactment of the jubilee year, described in Leviticus 25 (cf. Lev. 27:16–25; Num. 36:4). The detailed elaboration of the jubilee year requirements follow immediately upon the statute providing for a sabbath for the land every seven years. The jubilee year occurred every fiftieth year, determined by counting seven weeks of years, literally, "seven sabbaths" of years (Lev. 25:8). The fiftieth year, like the Sabbath, was to be hallowed (Lev. 25:10). On the Day of Atonement in the fiftieth year, there was a proclamation of "release" (*děrôr*), or liberty, for all the inhabitants of the land (Lev. 25:9–10). While the sabbatical year and the year of jubilee may have had different origins and reflect different times and circumstances, they have been melded together in this context. As they are now brought together in Leviticus 25, the release of the jubilee has three facets:

1. *A Sabbath for the land (25:1–7; 18–22; cf. vv. 11–12).* We have already looked at verses 1–7 above. Here the primary interest is in seeing the land release in relation to the jubilee proclamation, as an outgrowth of the Sabbath (see above) but also as a part of a large, multifaceted program of release and restoration of land, property, and persons in order to bring things back to a kind of social and natural order that provides for all and does not keep any part in submission and servitude unendingly. As much as any manifestation of the sabbatical principle, the jubilee year allows for everyone and everything to start afresh and refreshed, to halt things as they are in order to find release from the burdens that otherwise might never be let go. That begins with the land, with the need of God's creation to have its rest, even as the Creator rested. The *imitatio Dei* is not confined to the human creature: it is a requirement of creation.

2. *Redemption of property (25:10b, 13–17, 23–34).* The heart of the matter is stated in the initial call for the jubilee year (v. 10b) and then repeated in verse 13: "In this year of jubilee you shall

143

return, every one of you, to your property." The jubilee proclamation ensures that no person or family loses their land forever. There comes a time when, whatever the circumstances by which the individual or family had to let go of the land—and the concern is clearly having to let go of the land to deal with economic problems and so becoming indebted—that person's land or that family's land is restored, and the owner can begin afresh with the land. It is not permanently lost because of economic pressures.

Now the basic principle of return of property is the critical matter, but dealing with the issues is more complicated, and so there are extended statutes spelling out various situations and ways of dealing with them. For example, since the jubilee comes only twice in a century, it is desirable to provide earlier release if possible, and so there are regulations allowing for families, next of kin, to help redeem the land and return it to the owner (vv. 25–27; cf. Jer. 32). If that does not work, the jubilee will eventually get the property released and returned (v. 28). In verses 14–17, there is further provision for how to handle debts and return property or possessions with proper compensation. Again, the jubilee year is determinative in figuring out what is an appropriate charge. All of these particular cases aim at relieving economic burdens and using the year of jubilee as a means of providing full "release" from them.

A distinction is then made in verses 29–34 between houses in walled cities and houses in villages. The former are not subject to the jubilee. They may be redeemed within the first year if the original owner wishes to do so and is able, but after that they may remain permanently as the property of the new owner. This exception seems to undercut the jubilee. What it indicates, however, is the focus of the jubilee on the *land*. In other words the jubilee has to do with access to the land God has given, which is what one finds in the open villages and farms, agricultural land that provides a living. It does not apply to urban conditions. Houses in the open villages may be redeemed and are released in the jubilee. Houses in the walled villages are not released in the jubilee. The distinction probably reflects the historical context where the city or urban experience belongs more to the Canaanite surroundings and less to the Israelite history, where land and its use were the primary concern. "Since the jubilee was intended to preserve the economic viability of the peasant farmer, there was no need to protect urban property from alienation" (Milgrom, *Leviticus 23–27*, 2198). One should note that

144

in virtually all of the various statutes of Leviticus 25, the starting point is a member of the community becoming impoverished or falling into difficulty (vv. 25, 35, 39, 47). That is not the case for the statute having to do with walled and unwalled houses. "In other words, destitution plays no role; the sale of a home is considered a business transaction" (Milgrom, *Leviticus 23–27*, 2198).

3. *Redemption of hired or bound laborers (25:10b, 35–55; cf. v. 6).* The third aspect of release has to do with situations of dependency and the possibility of extrication from that dependency in order to start afresh. The first instance in verses 35–39 calls for the family to help out when a near relative becomes dependent, providing support in the form of interest-free loans of money or food, also without seeking profit. It is likely that the loans would have been in order to buy seed to plant crops so as to sustain the family and livestock (Chirigno, *Debt Slavery*, 328). There is no reference to the jubilee release here because it is presumed that the impoverished citizen has not needed to let go of his land at this point.

If these measures did not work, however, then the poor farmer might have to sell his land and himself. That contingency is dealt with in verses 39–43 and 47–55. Two things are what matters in that situation. One is that those who have had to "sell themselves" are not to be regarded as slaves or even indentured servants but as hired help, employees. The point is underscored in two ways: (a) the emphatic construction "You shall not make them serve as slaves" (v. 39), or as NJPS translates, "Do not subject him to the treatment of a slave," is made up of four words, three of which have the root *ʿābad*, which is the word for "serve" or "slave"; and (b) the requirement here is grounded in the word of the Lord: "For they are my *servants*/slaves whom I brought out of the land of Egypt" (v. 42, cf. NRSV). This people as a people are servants of the Lord and cannot be slaves of any other. The second matter here is the declaration that whoever is in this situation does not stay that way forever. Like all the other situations described here, the jubilee sets the poor "hired laborer" free to return to his family and the property. The burden is removed on the one hand; on the other hand, access to the land and its life-sustaining capacities is restored. It is possible to say stop to the burden of debt and servitude and begin again with resources that had been lost. This is the sabbatical principle at work to place within the vicissitudes and vicious cycles of human life opportunity for release and renewal.

145

The statutory section in verses 47–55 follows this up, only dealing in this instance with the situation of an Israelite who has sold himself to a resident alien. The right of redemption is spelled out in a way reminiscent of what we find in verses 14–16 and 25–28. Once again, when all else fails to provide release, the jubilee takes effect:

> [54]And if they have not been redeemed in any of these ways, they and their children with them shall go free in the jubilee year. [55]For to me the people of Israel are servants; they are my servants whom I brought out from the land of Egypt: I am the LORD your God (Lev. 25:54–55).

Here also one sees how the claim that appears in the Prologue to the Commandments defines Israel's life, not only their relation to God but also their treatment of one another. From beginning to end and at all times the Commandments are God's instruction to freed slaves about how one lives as servant and free. Thus Jacob Milgrom has put it:

> The legal aspect of redemption operates in the Exodus: God owns Israel because he is their go'el [redeemer]. Freedom means solely a change of masters; henceforth the Israelites are slaves of God. . . . Implied is that Israel owes no obligations to any other power but God. . . . Israel serves its God by obeying his commandments. (*Leviticus 23–27*, 2226–27)

There is a qualification in the way these statutes provide release. In verses 44–46, a distinction is made between an Israelite citizen and a foreigner or a resident alien, that is, an immigrant who resides in the midst of Israel. In both cases it is possible for an Israelite to keep such a person as a perpetual slave and pass this slave on to one's children. Here we find, as in a few other places, references to captive or chattel slaves from outside the community of Israel. They stand outside the statutory guidelines for handling free Israelites who have been drawn into debt slavery. The distinction is evident in verse 46:

> You may keep them as a possession for your children after you, for them to inherit as property. These you may treat as slaves, but as for your fellow Israelites, no one shall rule over the other with harshness.

The laws of the year of release do not apply to the resident aliens or persons from other nations who have been bought as slaves.

Although the exceptions here do not vitiate the power of the jubilee to provide freedom for the bound, they stand in some clear tension with the general directions of the laws of manumission and release. Yet there are countervoices, at least with regard to the resident alien, the immigrant living in the midst of Israel. In Leviticus itself, specifically in chapter 19, highly influenced by the Decalogue, one reads:

> [33]When an alien resides with you in your land, you shall not oppress the alien. [34]The alien who resides with you shall be to you as the citizen among you; you shall love the alien as yourself, for you were aliens in the land of Egypt: I am the LORD your God.

Though Leviticus 25:46 seems to make a distinction between treatment of a fellow Israelite and of an alien, Leviticus 19 is emphatic in equating the resident alien with an Israelite, specifically forbidding oppressive treatment and calling for an attitude equal to the treatment of the neighbor: love. It is hardly an accident that the command to love the alien like yourself should occur in the same chapter a few verses after the command to love your neighbor like yourself (19:18). What is regarded as the embodiment of the commandments (e.g., Rom. 13:9), the great commandment, is specifically applied to the stranger in two of the three places where this commandment is given in the Old Testament (Lev. 19:34; Deut. 10:18; cf. Lev. 19:18). Similarly, Leviticus 24:22, again in the divine voice, declares the underlining conclusion: "You shall have one law for the alien and for the citizen: for I am the LORD your God" (cf. Exod. 12:49; Num. 15:16). Here is a classic case of texts coming into conflict with one another. While confronted with the tension and conflict, one cannot dismiss the contrary statute of Leviticus 25:44–46; yet one must also acknowledge that the controlling force is clearly the large command, whose application becomes the heart of the matter for the whole of the divine instruction of God's people: You shall love your neighbor/the alien as yourself.

Finally, one cannot ignore the large theological foundation on which all of the jubilee legislation rests. It is found in Leviticus 25:23: "The land shall not be sold in perpetuity, for the land is mine; with me you are but aliens and tenants." In the midst of perhaps the strongest chapter in the Bible asserting the right of Israelites to

147

have and to hold to land as their property, we hear a unique claim from Israel's Lord: The land is mine. Here is a tension that cannot be dissolved. The right of the human creature to the provision of life, represented here and throughout the Old Testament as land, is set over against the claim that no one owns the land except the Lord. To make the point stronger, the Israelites are relegated to the category of strangers or resident aliens on the land that belongs to the Lord. So the release that comes in the jubilee, overcoming the oppressive burden of debt and reclaiming one's land, is set in the context of a different understanding of ownership. Thus every treatment, every use of the land, is not finally determined by human ownership, even as that ownership is being protected. Beyond all human claims to the land, the land is God's, and human beings are but tenant residents. Israel's hold on the land is provisional and depends on their fulfillment of the covenant obligations (Milgrom, *Leviticus 23–27*, 2187).

Social Justice in the Ancient Near East

Before leaving the various ways the sabbatical principle worked to provide a systematic and regular release of economic burdens, we should note that providing some release from debts or from indentured service was not a peculiarity of Israelite culture. It is to be found in legal documents of various sorts in the ancient Near East. In the edicts of Mesopotamian kings to establish *mišarum* (justice) or *andurarum* (liberation), royal proclamations, provided for release of persons from debts or taxes, as well as forced labor and slavery and the release of land to its original owner (Hamilton, *Social Justice in Deuteronomy*, chap. 2; Weinfeld, *Social Justice*, chap. 4). There is even an Old Testament instance of such a royal proclamation of liberty or release for all those Hebrews who had been forced into debt slavery (Jer. 34).

Israel's manifestation of a principle of regular freedom from economic traps, therefore, finds its resonances with similar efforts among other communities and nations to provide release from economic bondage. At the same time, there is something operative in the development of the sabbatical principle in Israel that is a further step forward. The regularized seventh day of rest effects a widespread and many-formed principle of regular cessation of work and release of burdens together with recovery and refreshment

148

that outruns all other social milieus. It is in some sense God's own royal proclamation mandating constant enactment. The release of Hebrew slaves by royal proclamation in Jeremiah is seen as disobedience of the covenant requirements by the people in part because they immediately took the released slaves back into servitude but also because of the people's failure to provide the *regular* release set forth in the Deuteronomic statutes (Jer. 34:13–14; cf. Deut. 15:12). Provision of relief from economic oppression, or even its restricting burden when not genuinely oppressive, is set as a regularity in various ways and as a part of the worship of the God who rested on the seventh day of creation and set Israel free from slavery. The self-presentation formula at the beginning of the Decalogue—note its echo in Jeremiah 34:13—provides an identity for this God precisely in terms of the act of freeing from economic oppression so that there may be both rest and worship. Both the created order and the self-identification of the God of Israel ground and determine the extent and significance of the sabbatical principle as a regularized avenue for justice and freedom. Those who live by these commandments do so as a freed people, always being set free. The Sabbath is both a remembrance of that being freed and its constant enactment.

Holy Times

We have discerned at the heart of the Sabbath Commandment a double dimension: release from work and a day to the Lord, rest and refreshment and the worship of God. And as the sabbatical principle opens up further ways in which release and refreshment are brought about in the life of the community, so also the Sabbath Commandment leads to more occasions and opportunities for the community to set time apart for the Lord, for worship and remembrance, for quiet and celebration—aspects of the holy in the midst of the ordinary. As the books of Exodus, Leviticus, and Deuteronomy make clear, the Sabbath is the paradigm for various festivals and activities that belong to sanctifying a time for the Lord.

The most obvious way in which the legal codes identify the Sabbath as the ground for other festivals and rituals of sanctification is by their close association of the Sabbath requirements with statutes setting up the other festivals of the year. That is especially evident in the Holiness Code of Leviticus 17–26, where the primary formulation of

149

the Sabbath Commandment forms the introduction to the statutes providing for the major religious festivals of ancient Israel:

> [1]The LORD spoke to Moses, saying: [2]Speak to the people of Israel and say to them: These are the appointed festivals of the LORD that you shall proclaim as holy convocations, my appointed festivals. [3]Six days shall work be done; but the seventh day is a sabbath of complete rest, a holy convocation; you shall do no work: it is a sabbath to the LORD throughout your settlements. [4]These are the appointed festivals of the LORD, the holy convocations, which you shall celebrate at the time appointed for them. (Lev. 23:1–4)

What follows in the rest of Leviticus 23 spells out in some detail how the people are to celebrate various festivals or "holy convocations": Passover and Unleavened Bread, firstfruits, the first day of the seventh month, the Day of Atonement, and the Feast of Booths. The introductory verses may be a later addition to the text, but if so, that makes it all the more clear that Sabbath was to be seen as the foundation of all the holy convocations and celebrations of the Lord's goodness. The Sabbath reverberations are found in other ways in the chapter. One is the frequent characterization of the festival as "to the LORD," analogous to the "sabbath to the LORD" (Exod. 20:10; Deut. 5:14): for example, "a passover offering to the LORD" (Lev. 23:5)," "the festival of unleavened bread to the LORD" (v. 6), "an offering of new grain to the LORD" (v. 16), "the festival of booths to the LORD" (v. 34). Another reverberation of the Sabbath is the repeated instruction "You shall not work at your occupations" (vv. 7, 8, 21, 25, 35, 36). In addition, verses 26–32 speak of the Day of Atonement as a "sabbath of complete rest" (cf. v. 3), using the language of the Sabbath Commandment ("You shall do no work," v. 31; cf. Exod. 20:10; Deut. 5:14); and the provisions for the Feast of Booths call for a day of "complete rest" (*šabbātôn*) on the first day and the eighth day (Lev. 23:39).

Linking the sacredness of the "holy convocations" to the Sabbath is especially characteristic of the Holiness Code in Leviticus. This connection, however, is present elsewhere. In Exodus 23:12–17 and 34:21–23, the Sabbath statute is followed immediately by those setting up the three main festivals of the year. And in the Deuteronomic Code, the extended development of the sabbatical principle relative to remission of debts and release of bonded slaves

150

(Deut. 15:1–18) is then followed by an equally extended set of statutes for the three festivals in Deuteronomy 16:1–17. A transition between the two is made in Deuteronomy 15:19–22 with an ordinance setting up the consecration of the firstborn of the flocks and herds to the Lord. The connection to the Sabbath Commandment is evident in the consecration of these animals "to the LORD your God" and especially in the restriction "You shall not do work with your firstling ox" (v. 15:19).

Thus the various festivals and offerings are presented as growing out of the Sabbath requirement and, like the Sabbath, providing both times for rest and acts of worship and celebration. In this way they give us some idea of the kinds of acts that belong to a time set aside to the Lord, to the content and character of holy times. The focus of the Sabbath is on the rest and relief, but it is also a holy time belonging to the Lord. The festivals as "holy convocations" involve acts of worship and offering, but they are also times that provide release from labor and work. As time for rest and time for the Lord are conjoined, the Sabbath is actualized in the life of the community. Its character as both individual and communal is evident in the specification of those who rest, to make sure that no individual is forced to keep on working, and in the shared celebration in which all participate, rejoicing before the Lord and sharing in the Lord's blessing (Deut. 16:10–11, 14–15, 17). Not to be missed is the way the call to rejoice before the Lord at each of the festivals includes the kind of comprehensively inclusive list similar to what we encounter in the Sabbath Command of the Decalogue: sons and daughters, male and female slaves, Levites, strangers, orphans, and widows (Deut. 15:11, 14). And always in the background there is the communal memory of being slaves in Egypt and being freed by the Lord (Deut. 16:3, 6, 12). Each Sabbath we remember both our creation (Exod. 20:11) and our redemption (Deut. 5:15).

The Further Trajectory of the Commandment

1. *The seriousness of Sabbath observance is underscored* as several texts assign capital punishment as the fate of those who disobey the Sabbath Commandment. In two instances, the punishment is a part of the instruction of the Lord about the Sabbath.

151

[14]You shall keep the sabbath, because it is holy for you; everyone who profanes it shall be put to death; whoever does any work on it shall be cut off from among the people. [15]Six days shall work be done, but the seventh day is a sabbath of solemn rest, holy to the LORD; whoever does any work on the sabbath day shall be put to death. (Exod. 31:14–15)

[2]Six days shall work be done, but on the seventh day you shall have a holy sabbath of solemn rest to the LORD; whoever does any work on it shall be put to death. [3]You shall kindle no fire in all your dwellings on the sabbath day. (Exod. 35:2–3)

In the first of these texts, the penalty is ascribed to two activities—profanation of the Sabbath and work on the Sabbath—perfectly corresponding to the two emphases of the commandment: keeping the day holy, that is, not profaning it, and resting, that is, not working. The latter point is then reiterated in Exodus 35:2 with a further point added to underscore how complete the release from work is meant to be: You do not even build a fire. This latter point is elaborated in a brief narrative account of a man caught collecting wood on the Sabbath, presumably to build a fire, who is then stoned to death at the express command of the Lord (Num. 15:32–36). How serious and absolute Sabbath keeping is in the Lord's eyes is thus communicated in two ways: ultimate punishment for its breach and prohibition of even the smallest tasks one might take up.

You cannot do *anything* on the Sabbath or you will *die*. What does one make of these two extreme dimensions of the Sabbath command? A couple of things can be suggested in that regard. For one thing, capital punishment is, as far as one can tell, the expected punishment for disobedience of any of the commandments. That is made specific, for example, in Exodus 21:12–17, where violation of the commandments having to do with killing, respect for parents, and theft is in each instance to be punished by death. And in Leviticus 24:14–22 a narrative report of an instance of blaspheming recounts the execution—again at the Lord's command—of someone who violated the commandment protecting the name of God. Execution is one of the ways of pointing to the absolute and definitive character of the commandments and what they are after. It is crucial, however, that such punishment is not actually incorporated into the Commandments themselves. These fundamental guidelines or principles are simply set out as instruction, not case law,

152

which describes a crime and prescribes punishment. If the latter had been the mode of presentation of the Commandments from the start, they would probably have had much less impact on Israel and later communities. The Leviticus 24 text is especially relevant in this connection: like the Sabbath Commandment, handling the name of God does not seem to be something all that significant or wrong enough to evoke such terrible punishment.

That may be the point, however, of the texts that tell us about such extreme punishment for misusing the divine name and violating the Sabbath. They are the two commandments that seem to the modern world to be of fairly small moment. Killing, adultery, and theft are the kinds of acts that would seem to merit such punishment and often do so in different contemporary communities. Observing the Sabbath is a matter of small moment, one would think. Not according to Scripture, however. While violation of the Sabbath requirements does not always produce such an extreme outcome in the stories of the Bible, these three texts warn us against assuming that Sabbath observance is a matter of little consequence in the eyes of the Lord. Ask the wood gatherer of Numbers 15! What one hears today, therefore, is not a contemporary call for execution of persons who do not take the Sabbath seriously, but a call to those who live by these instructions to regard rest from all work and keeping the day wholly and holy to the Lord as crucial aspects of life in God's kingdom.

2. *The Sabbath is a sign and covenant* between the Lord and the community, marking its character as a holy people and signifying their binding relationship with the God who delivered them. The same text that underscores the death penalty for Sabbath violation—Exodus 31:13–17—speaks of the Sabbath as a sign and also as a covenant:

> [13]You shall keep my sabbaths, for this is a sign between me and you throughout your generations, given in order that you may know that I, the LORD, sanctify you. . . . [16]Therefore the Israelites shall keep the sabbath, observing the sabbath throughout their generations, as a perpetual covenant. [17]It is a sign forever between me and the people of Israel that in six days the LORD made heaven and earth, and on the seventh day he rested, and was refreshed.

The Sabbath as sign and the Sabbath as covenant are really two ways of saying essentially the same thing. It is "a sign between me and you" (vv. 13, 17), even as a covenant is the formalizing of a

153

relationship between two parties. Like the "perpetual covenant" (v. 16), the Sabbath is a sign forever (vv. 13, 17). And the text is explicit about what the Sabbath signifies and to what it testifies every time it is celebrated: "that I, the LORD, sanctify you" (v. 13). Every time the people rest, every time the people set the Sabbath Day apart and make it a day to the Lord, their identity as a holy people, a people to the Lord, is given public testimony. The prophet Ezekiel reaffirms this same claim (Ezek. 20:12) and adds a further formulation to make the point even clearer: "and hallow my sabbaths that they may be a sign between me and you, so that you may know that I the LORD am your God" (Ezek. 20:20). The Sabbath thus becomes one of the primary identifying marks of the people of God, a perpetual witness to the enduring relationship, a visible proclamation of their full devotion to the Lord. Sabbath keeping functions not only to rest and make holy a day but also to maintain and symbolize the devotion to the Lord that characterizes Israel and the church.

3. *The joy of Sabbath rest.* Keeping the Sabbath seems like an easy, even pleasurable thing to do, and there are countless witnesses to the joy of the Sabbath rest. Even so, other impulses work against acceptance of the gift of the Sabbath. These impulses are evident in the voices of the prophets (e.g., Jeremiah) and leaders (e.g., Nehemiah) and ring across the ages as evidence that the Sabbath Commandment is one of the most difficult to keep. Its promise, inherent and not explicit, is constantly undercut by the power of economic and personal desire.

In one of Amos's oracles, he indicts the rich for oppressing the poor, spelling out in detail the way of those "who trample on the needy and bring to ruin the poor of the land" (Amos 8:4). He does not accuse them of violating the Sabbath Commandment, but he does denounce their eagerness to get past the Sabbath so that they can go back to selling their many goods by devious and nefarious means (Amos 8:5). An aggressive, consumerist economy is not a discovery of the modern period, nor is the practice of deceiving the poor and taking advantage of them.

Sabbath observance is an issue in Jeremiah as well. The historical context of Jeremiah 17:19–27 is uncertain. It may belong to an exilic or postexilic context. Whatever its temporal setting, Jeremiah's proclamation of the divine word at the gates of Jerusalem, where kings and people go in and out of the city, is instructive about the Sabbath Commandment. The audience being addressed is compre-

154

hensive: kings of Judah, Judeans, and inhabitants of Jerusalem (v. 20). It is not altogether clear if the reference to the people not listening or heeding the word of the Lord refers to earlier generations or the prophet's own audience (v. 23), but the very preaching of this sermon is testimony to the ease with which the Sabbath could be ignored. So the Lord declares through Jeremiah that they must carry no burdens out of the house or do any work on that day (v. 22). The burdens probably refer to commercial products like grain and produce (see Neh. 13:15, 19). Further on in the text, this point is reiterated but this time with reference to bringing burdens in through the gates of the city, a further intimation of the commercial character of the burdens in mind (Jer. 17:24).

Once again Sabbath observance is a life-and-death matter, and the repeated reference to the gates of the city has large significance. "What the community does about the sabbath is made a criterion for its future existence. Careful observance of its sacred character opens up a restoration of the city and its rulers to an enduring existence as a community with city and temple as the cultic center of Israel" (Miller, "Jeremiah," 710). People will go in and out of the gates of the city in both prosperity and worship. If they do not keep the Sabbath holy, however, then "I will kindle a fire in its gates; it shall devour the palaces of Jerusalem and shall not be quenched" (Jer. 17:27).

Elsewhere in the prophets we hear words about the way in which keeping the Sabbath opens up the good for those who do so. "Happy" or "blessed" is the one who keeps the Sabbath, says the prophet in Isaiah 56:2. Further on, honoring the Sabbath and finding delight in it instead of pursuing one's own interests holds great promise for those who do so (58:13–14). So also keeping the Sabbaths is the way of access for both eunuch and foreigner into the community of those who serve the Lord (56:3–8). There, keeping the Sabbaths is paralleled by "holding fast my covenant," in this instance probably a reference to obeying all of the law or instruction the Lord has taught the people. The text seems to lift the Sabbath up as a piece unto itself, underscoring its place as indicator of the true worship of the Lord (cf. Neh. 9:14). In the trajectory of this commandment, once more we see how keeping the Sabbath becomes ever more firmly the identifying mark of the people of God.

Before turning to Nehemiah's engagement with Sabbath issues, we should note that Jeremiah's sermon in chapter 17 is a further

155

step on the trajectory of the Sabbath. The commandment is now expanded. That happens at the beginning of the divine speech:

> [21]Thus says the LORD: For the sake of your lives, take care that you do not bear a burden on the sabbath day or bring it in by the gates of Jerusalem. [22]And do not carry a burden out of your houses on the sabbath or do any work, but keep the sabbath day holy, as I commanded your ancestors.

The actual commandment as we know it from the Decalogue is found in the final clauses: Do not do any work but keep the Sabbath holy. Attached to the commandment now, however, is a more detailed and specific word forbidding commercial activity: labor, sales, or transporting goods in and out of one's home or the city. And that specification is conjoined with the basic commandment and characterized as what the Lord commanded the people at the beginning (v. 22b). In other words, "the general Pentateuchal prohibition of Sabbath work is expanded in new ways, and the entire result is presented as Sinaitic in origin!" (Fishbane, *Biblical Interpretation*, 132). What happens is that Sabbath observance is succumbing to economic and commercial pressures to the degree that the commandment needs to be reformulated so as to speak specifically about commercial activity as a violation of the Sabbath.

That is exactly what Nehemiah encountered after the exile, and indeed his denunciation of Sabbath desecration may well be dependent upon Jeremiah's speech (Fishbane, *Biblical Interpretation*, 131):

> [15]In those days I saw in Judah people treading wine presses on the sabbath, and bringing in heaps of grain and loading them on donkeys; and also wine, grapes, figs, and all kinds of burdens, which they brought into Jerusalem on the sabbath day; and I warned them at that time against selling food. [16]Tyrians also, who lived in the city, brought in fish and all kinds of merchandise and sold them on the sabbath to the people of Judah, and in Jerusalem. [17]Then I remonstrated with the nobles of Judah and said to them, "What is this evil thing that you are doing, profaning the sabbath day?" (Neh. 13:15–17)

156   What Nehemiah describes is, in effect, a Sabbath market, involving also Gentile traders' commercial transactions with the Jewish

inhabitants. The prohibition against selling goods on the Sabbath, already in place in Amos's time, as we have noted above, is now blatantly ignored, and Nehemiah remonstrates with the city leaders, not the priests, claiming that the disaster God brought upon them was directly due to this way of breaching the Sabbath. To change things he shuts the gates before the Sabbath and tells the merchants not to spend the night outside the gates, waiting for the Sabbath to be over.

In all of these texts, prophets and Nehemiah, we encounter already in biblical times the commercialization of the Sabbath. Indeed, the Sabbath seems almost to prompt people to buy and sell, shop and trade. The gift of the Sabbath is thereby turned into another form of unending activity focused on personal needs and not on the God who created the earth and rested on the seventh day, who delivered Israel from unending labor to set them free. Sabbath is a time of release from all work and all burdens. Israel found it difficult to accept the gift. So the prophetic voices reminded—and still remind—the community of faith that the Lord really does mean it: Let go of everything and sanctify this one day a week solely to the Lord. Part of what we see in the ongoing story of the Sabbath Commandment is that it is not as easy as it looks, but that was not and is not an excuse, if we listen to the prophets.

4. *The Sabbath of the land is actuated in the exile,* apparently out of the failure of the people to keep the Sabbath of the land. In both the epilogue to Leviticus in Leviticus 26:34–44 and 2 Chronicles 36:20–21, the exile is anticipated and seen as a punishment of the people, one in which the land, now devastated by the Babylonian forces, receives a seventy-year sabbatical to make up for all the years that the people disobeyed the commandment and did not let the land have its sabbatical. The judgment is a form of poetic justice, but that is not its primary force. The Lord punishes the people by removing them from the land—though scholars debate how extensive that removal really was—but that punishment has a positive feature. It allows the land to make up for the forgotten or ignored sabbatical years it was supposed to have had but missed because the people did not keep the Sabbath of the land. One may presume that once again commercial factors and economic possibilities trumped the Lord's "day" of rest for the land.

157

Jesus and the Sabbath

In the New Testament, Sabbath observance is presumed for the Jewish community, including Jesus and his disciples as well as Paul and his companions (Ringe, "Holy: Sabbath," 17–18). Not only are there several references to going to the synagogue on the Sabbath (e.g., Mark 1:21; 6:2; Luke 13:10; Acts 13:14), but in one of the more important of these, Luke 4:16–30, the text also speaks of Jesus going to the synagogue on the Sabbath Day "as was his custom" (v. 16; see below). There are also indications of care about what one does or does not do on the Sabbath, such as limitations on travel (Matt. 24:20; Acts 1:12), making sure that Jesus' body is in the tomb before the Sabbath (Mark 15:42; John 19:31), and the women going to the tomb to tend to the body only after the day of rest is over (Matt. 28:1//Mark 16:1–2; John 20:1). The Lukan account makes this point overtly:

> [54]It was the day of Preparation, and the sabbath was beginning. [55]The women who had come with him from Galilee followed, and they saw the tomb and how his body was laid. [56]Then they returned, and prepared spices and ointments. On the sabbath they rested according to the commandment. [1]But on the first day of the week, at early dawn, they came to the tomb, taking the spices that they had prepared. (Luke 23:54–24:1)

Various texts refer to teaching or praying on the Sabbath (e.g., Jesus in Mark 1:21//Luke 4:31; Mark 6:2; Luke 6:6; 13:10; and Paul in Acts 13:14–16; 16:13; 17:2; 18:4).

Sabbath keeping, therefore is a presumption of the Gospels. It is also a matter of controversy there, however. The issue is not whether one obeys the commandment or not. That is a given. The point of contention is *how* one obeys. What constitutes proper Sabbath keeping? That question becomes the center of some of the controversy stories in the Gospels. The arguments with the religious leaders are over (1) the appropriateness of Jesus' healing persons on the Sabbath; and (2) what kinds of actions might be engaged in without being understood as working on the Sabbath. The two are, of course, related. Before looking specifically at those controversies and what they tell us about Sabbath keeping, particularly in the Synoptic accounts, one should take special note of the way that, in the Gospels of Mark and Luke, Jesus' ministry of teaching and healing begins on the Sabbath (Mark 1:21–31//Luke 4:16–39).

The critical and defining text is Luke's account of Jesus' reading from the book of Isaiah in the synagogue at Nazareth. The text is explicit about this happening when "he went to the synagogue on the sabbath day, as was his custom" (Luke 4:16). The Sabbath setting is crucial for understanding what Jesus does on this occasion. The Isaiah reading is as follows (vv. 18–19):

> [18]The Spirit of the Lord is upon me, because he has anointed me to bring good news to the poor. He has sent me to proclaim release to the captives and recovery of sight to the blind, to let the oppressed go free, [19]to proclaim the year of the Lord's favor.

Two texts from Isaiah have been brought together in this reading: Isaiah 58:6 and 61:1–2, both in the Septuagint form. The clause "to let the oppressed go free" is from Isaiah 58:6, and the rest of the text is from Isaiah 61. The two texts are conjoined by a familiar principle for text association: catchword. In this case, the Greek word shared by the two texts is *aphesis*, translated as "release" and "go free." This is the Greek translation of the Hebrew word for the *release* of the sabbatical principle (e.g., *šĕmiṭṭâ* in Deut. 15:1). It is clearly the key word of the Scripture that Jesus reads. With Jesus' concluding words "Today this scripture has been fulfilled in your hearing" (Luke 4:21), the word "release" may be seen as the defining category for interpreting Jesus' work in Luke's Gospel. That release of which Isaiah speaks and which is embodied and enacted in the Lord's Sabbath is the intention and goal of Jesus' ministry. In the New Testament, however, the word *aphesis* (and its cognates) is also the common word for another kind of release, *forgiveness*, release from the oppressive bonds and chains of sin and guilt (Luke 7:48). Jesus' gospel is good news to the poor and to the poor in spirit. Whatever may be the origin of the differences between the beatitudes where we in one instance read "Blessed are the poor in spirit" (Matt. 5:3), and in the other, "Blessed are the poor" (Luke 6:20, my trans.), the two together are representative of the freeing ministry of Jesus, a ministry that assumes and carries forward the sabbatical principle of providing release from the bonds that hold and oppress human beings. What begins in the Sabbath Commandment is to be understood as at the heart of the ministry of Jesus and indeed his whole life, death, and resurrection. The release that Jews and Christians embody in keeping the Sabbath is consistent

159

with and reflective of the redemptive work of God that began in the exodus and continued in the life and work of Jesus Christ.

The account in Luke 4, paralleled in Mark 1:21–28, continues with the first of Jesus' acts of healing, also on the Sabbath (Mark 1:21//Luke 4:31) but in Capernaum. The release that God provides for human life is thus deeply tied to physical well-being. The various accounts of Jesus' arguments with the religious leaders when he heals on the Sabbath (e.g., Matt. 12:9–14; Luke 14:1–6; John 5:1–18) lift up and underscore his insistence that the Sabbath is the time for release and setting free.

The story that best conveys this point is probably the account of Jesus healing a woman who had been crippled for *eighteen years*. It is worth quoting in full:

> ¹⁰Now he was teaching in one of the synagogues on the sabbath. ¹¹And just then there appeared a woman with a spirit that had crippled her for eighteen years. She was bent over and was quite unable to stand up straight. ¹²When Jesus saw her, he called her over and said, "Woman, you are set free from your ailment." ¹³When he laid his hands on her, immediately she stood up straight and began praising God. ¹⁴But the leader of the synagogue, indignant because Jesus had cured on the sabbath, kept saying to the crowd, "There are six days on which work ought to be done; come on those days and be cured, and not on the sabbath day." ¹⁵But the Lord answered him and said, "You hypocrites! Does not each of you on the sabbath untie his ox or his donkey from the manger, and lead it away to give it water? ¹⁶And ought not this woman, a daughter of Abraham whom Satan bound for eighteen long years, be set free from this bondage on the sabbath day?" ¹⁷When he said this, all his opponents were put to shame; and the entire crowd was rejoicing at all the wonderful things that he was doing. (Luke 13:10–17)

The occasion is the Sabbath, the setting is the synagogue, the action is Jesus' teaching—all appropriate to what one would expect for Sabbath observance. But then there appears this obviously very crippled woman, whom Jesus sees and heals without her even asking. Not to be missed is the immediate outcome: "She stood up straight and began praising God," possibly in the words of or something like the songs of thanksgiving of the Psalter (e.g., Ps. 30), which were probably individual testimonies in the congregation by persons who had experienced God's healing or saving help.

160

That would seem to be sufficient to close the story—except that the leader of the synagogue indignantly challenges Jesus for healing on the Sabbath, saying such actions can be done on any of the other six days and should not be done on the Sabbath. Whereupon Jesus seeks to teach him, those listening at the time, and—through the Gospel narrative—the church in all times and places. He goes to the heart of the matter, interpreting his act and also the significance of the Sabbath. Interestingly, he does it by referring to the understanding of the Sabbath release that begins already in the Decalogue, which includes the work animals. His particular formulation, however, is an instance of common human decency to animals, letting them go to water when they are thirsty. Jesus makes an argument from the lesser to the greater: How much more should not this woman, who has been bound for eighteen years, now be cut loose and "set free from this bondage on the sabbath day"? That is what the Sabbath is all about. And as the story indicates, his words are immediately understood and accepted by all who hear.

In another instance, Jesus makes a similar argument, this time comparing his healing a man with a withered hand on the Sabbath to helping a sheep who falls into a pit on the Sabbath (Matt. 12:9–14; cf. Luke 14:5). His "how much more" claim is generalized this time: "How much more valuable is a human being than a sheep! So it is lawful to do good on the sabbath" (Matt. 12:12). In the Markan and Lukan accounts of this incident (Mark 3:1–6; Luke 6:6–11), the final statement is put in the form of a question: "I ask you, is it lawful to do good or to do harm on the sabbath, to save life or to destroy it?" (Luke 6:9; cf. 14:3; John 5:9–10). "The answer of the pericope is that one keeps the Sabbath by not failing to do good, an omission that is equated with doing evil, something clearly inappropriate on the Sabbath" (Ringe, "Holy: Sabbath," 19).

Just before the Gospel reports of Jesus healing the man with a withered hand, the question of what is lawful to do on the Sabbath is raised by the Pharisees when they see Jesus' disciples plucking grain and eating it on the Sabbath (Matt. 12:1–8; Mark 2:23–28; Luke 6:1–5). Several features of the story merit attention:

1. One is the mention of the *disciples being hungry* and needing food. The appropriate action on the Sabbath is not simply prescribed but especially has to do with the human situation. Sabbath rest was instituted to provide for human need. So also human need can lead to an action on the Sabbath that otherwise might not seem

161

appropriate. That is the point of Jesus' citation of David and his men eating the bread of the Presence in the house of God when normally that food would be only for the priests.

2. In the Matthean account, Jesus then offers further *illustration and support* by referring to the priests working in the temple on the Sabbath and yet being seen as guiltless of Sabbath violation. This leads him then to make the intriguing comment: "I tell you, something greater than the temple is here" (12:6). Robert Gundry suggests: "His purpose was to argue that though the disciples profaned the Sabbath, they—like the priests who worked in the Temple on Sabbath days—were guiltless because of a higher legal consideration: if the greatness of the Temple surpasses the sanctity of the Sabbath, the superior greatness of Jesus surpasses the sanctity of the Sabbath much more" (*Matthew*, 223–24). The point is reinforced by Jesus' citation of the Hosea (6:6) text: "I desire mercy and not sacrifice" (Matt. 12:7), an assertion from Scripture that mercy takes priority over ritualistic observance.

3. Both dimensions of Jesus' response are then given *concluding summary*. In each of the Gospels we hear him claim: "The Son of Man is lord of the Sabbath." This is a momentous assertion. By his actions—on the Sabbath and otherwise—and by his teaching, Jesus now is the one who directs our understanding of what the Sabbath is all about (cf. John 5:15–18). That direction, however, is not over against what the church and synagogue learn from the Old Testament. On the contrary, the Old Testament is all through this story, pointing the way to go. Its controlling force is underscored in the sentence that Mark adds to these concluding words: "The sabbath was made for humankind, and not humankind for the sabbath" (Mark 2:27). That has been the point all along. "To sanctify the Sabbath means to save life and do good, not just to rest but to *give* rest to others" (Bockmuehl, "Keeping It Holy," 116). Human need is not all the Sabbath is about, but it is at the heart of the matter. In Jesus' actions on the Sabbath Day, the commandment becomes an embodiment of the love of neighbor.

The Sabbath or Sunday?

162

Through the Commandments and Jesus' teaching and actions, the church has the Sabbath as God's gift of a time of rest and a holy day. Yet there is some tension between that reality and the church's observation of such a time and such a day not on the seventh day of the week, as is regularly the case in both the Old Testament and the New, but on the first day of the week. The move from seventh day to first day is deeply rooted in historical events and practices, which shall not be explored here, though we should recognize that the equation of Sabbath and Sunday was not always the case and that in the early life of the church, Christian worship on the first day of the week did not originally include rest, which came only later, from Constantine's time onward (see Rordorf, *Sunday*, 154–73). Our aim here is to comprehend theologically how the connections are made so that the church finds in its Sunday practices a fulfillment of the Sabbath Commandment.

We can begin by observing that the earliest name for the holy day of rest seems to have been "the Lord's Day" (Rev. 1:10), a designation that may have arisen out of celebration of the Lord's Supper on the holy day but is consistent with the force and character of the Sabbath, that is, a day holy to the Lord. The term "Sunday" has no particular theological force. While there is nothing wrong with referring to Sunday, for the church the terms "Sabbath" and "Lord's Day" are the appropriate ways of identifying this particular day of the week. They not only come from Scripture but also serve to bind our comprehension of the holy day and our appropriation of it to both the Old Testament and the New Testament.

In the New Testament, observance of the first day of the week as a holy day does not seem to represent annulment of the Sabbath, as Karl Barth has noted. In so doing, New Testament Christianity "was not rebelling against the order of creation, but was acting in profound agreement with what is said in Ex. 20^{8f} and Gen. 2^{1f} on the basis of the Sabbath commandment. . . . It saw and understood that in the resurrection of Jesus Christ it was concerned with the revelation of the truth and faithfulness of God in his blessing and hallowing of the seventh day" (Barth, *Church Dogmatics*, III/4:53). Celebration of the first day, the Lord's Day, as a holy time is, therefore, a natural move for those who have rejoiced in the redemptive work of God, begun in the deliverance from Egyptian slavery and continued in the resurrection of Jesus from the dead. Sunday carries forward Jesus' word that the Sabbath is a time for "good news" begun and fulfilled in his ministry. The confirmation of that good news is God's raising Jesus from the dead on the first day of the week.

163

As the New Testament portrays both Jesus' lordship of the Sabbath and his observance of it, one is not surprised to find the Reformers interpreting the commandment in a way that maintains both the freedom Jesus enacted and obedience to the aims intrinsic to the commandment. So Calvin asserted the following claim about the impact of the coming of Christ on our observation of the Sabbath:

> But there is no doubt that by the Lord Christ's coming the ceremonial part of this commandment was abolished. For he himself is the truth, with whose presence all figures vanish; he is the body, at whose appearance the shadows are left behind. He is, I say, the true fulfillment of the Sabbath. (*Institutes* 2.8.31)

At the same time and in the same context, Calvin maintained:

> Although the Sabbath has been abrogated, there is still occasion for us: (1) to assemble on stated days for the hearing of the Word, the breaking of the mystical bread, and for public prayers [cf. Acts 2:42]; (2) to give surcease from labor to servants and workmen. There is no doubt that in enjoining the Sabbath the Lord was concerned with both. . . . Who can deny that these two things apply as much to us as to the Jews? (*Institutes* 2.8.32)

Sunday continues to be the time of both rest and worship. The week is the time of God's creation. The day of rest still comes after six days of labor. In light of the Gospel, the "work" of God on the first day of the week becomes the norm for the time of sanctification and celebration while the "rest" of God on the seventh day of creation continues to be the model for our cessation from work. The holiness of the day is given a new substance but one consistent with its meaning from the beginning. It is the time in which the community gathers to remember the redemptive work of God, which is exactly how Deuteronomy understands the Sabbath Commandment. It is impossible for Christians to keep the Sabbath under the motivations provided by the Deuteronomic form of the commandment and not celebrate the first day of the week. That is the day of remembering what God has done for us, both when we were in slavery in Egypt and in our slavery to sin and guilt. Remembering is what the Sabbath-Sunday is all about. "Remember how the Lord your God brought you out with a mighty hand." "This do in remembrance of me." So the church's celebration of the first day of the week, the Lord's Day, is not a rejection of the Sabbath. It is a carryover of the Sabbath, precisely to ensure its observance.

"A Sabbath Rest Still Remains"

Celebration of the day of Jesus' resurrection as the Lord's Day inevitably and appropriately opened up an eschatological dimension to the Sabbath, something already present in the Old Testament. As Karl Barth has observed:

> When the first Christians called their holy day "the day of the Lord" they were certainly not unaware that in the Old Testament "the day of Yahweh" denoted the day of all days, on which there would be concluded in joy and calamity the history not only of Israel but also of the other nations, in a comprehensive and decisive act of God's judgment, but in righteousness, in the restoration of the order willed by Him, in the fulfillment of His promise, in the execution of His will which had this as its goal from the very first, and therefore to His glory and to the salvation of His people and all creation. (*Church Dogmatics*, III/4:56)

In texts such as Isaiah 58:13–14 and Jeremiah 17:24–26, careful observance of the Sabbath culminates in a grand vision of the people delighting in the Lord and dwelling in Jerusalem forever. Such depictions join with others, such as Isaiah 2:1–4//Micah 4:1–4, to point toward a time when all shall worship the Lord in joy and gladness, the Sabbath realized in its full intention and meaning. Some sense of this is present in the Jewish rabbinic legend recounted by Abraham Heschel:

> At the time when God was giving the Torah to Israel, He said to them: My children! If you accept the Torah and observe my mitzvoth [commandments], I will give you for all eternity a thing most precious that I have in my possession.
> —And what, asked Israel, is that precious thing which Thou wilt give us if we obey Thy Torah?
> —The world to come.
> —Show us in this world an example of the world to come.
> —The Sabbath is an example of the world to come. (*Sabbath*, 73)

So also the Old Testament in other ways sees the people's rest as the ultimate goal of God's deliverance. This is especially prominent in the Deuteronomic tradition, where the goal of Israel's entering the promised land is to find a rest at last (Deut. 3:20; 12:9–10; 25:19; Josh. 1:13, 15). Building upon the Old Testament texts, the Letter to the Hebrews takes up this vision of the Sabbath as a final rest for the people of God. In the story of Israel it sees some of the people's disobedience and thus resistance to entering into the rest that God has prepared (Heb. 3:11, 18; 4:2; cf. Ps. 95:11). The writer of the epistle understands the Sabbath rest as "good news" (Heb. 4:6) but good news resisted by acts of disobedience. Still, that promised rest is open and available:

> [9]So then, a sabbath rest still remains for the people of God; [10]for those who enter God's rest also cease from their labors as God did from his. (4:9–10)

The Scriptures thus understand the Sabbath rest as both present gift and also blessing yet to come. That Sabbath promise receives its seal and authentication in the church's celebration of the holy day of rest and worship on the first day of the week, thus forever identifying the Lord's Day with the climactic redemptive work of God in Jesus Christ, a work that is the ground of all hope. "The first day of the week should be a pointer to the last, final day for every person" (Wolff, "Day of Rest," 75). The rabbis were right. The Sabbath is indeed a glimpse of the world to come.

CHAPTER 4

Respect for Parents

Honor your father and your mother, so that your days may be long in the land that the LORD *your God is giving you.*

Exodus 20:12

Honor your father and your mother, as the LORD *your God commanded you, so that your days may be long and that it may go well with you in the land that the* LORD *your God is giving you.*

Deuteronomy 5:16

Honoring parents is the logical starting point for directing human life toward the other who is not God, the other who is most often described as neighbor, but may be brother or sister and, in the Commandments, is first of all mother and father. The commandment does not pose difficulties of translation and meaning, at least on the surface. But the effort to flesh out what is being expected in this second of two positive commandments in the Decalogue opens up a variety of issues. As with all the Commandments, the fundamental question is what is the *specific* focus of the commandment, if there is one; this question comes much to the fore with the *general* and *positive* command "Honor . . ." That issue, however, leads into other matters having to do with trying to comprehend and live by this divine command. One of them is the question of addressee. Who is being addressed in this commandment? While that question may be asked of all the Commandments, and one presumes a common audience for each of them, in the case of the Fifth Commandment, there is a particular twist. It is the question of the age of the child who is to honor the parent, because the honoring may involve different acts and modes of being at different ages. Is it comprehensive in that it is applicable to behavior of children toward their parents whatever the age of the child, five or fifty? A second question arising out of the effort to see what specifically is in mind is the openness of the Commandments. How does the language of the

167

commandment and the trajectory it opens up broaden the claim of the commandment beyond a single focus?

There is a further issue lurking in the background. A respected colleague wrote to me one time:

> From my own experience and observation, no text has done more damage to abused children than the words, "Honor your father and your mother." . . . I know that those words tormented me as a child, and I believe they have tormented others. . . . From my . . . work with the Hebrew of Exodus 20, two facts are clear to me: the first is that honor is not a synonym for obedience and the second is that the Decalogue is not addressed to children.

This poignant personal testimony raises a matter of large concern in the function of the Commandments in the Christian community and also reveals the potential connection between careful study of the commandment and dealing with its fundamental moral issues. Both the focus of the commandment and the question of its addressee are exegetical discernments that have become defensive weapons in the hands of this interpreter and make us aware of the relevance of one's interpretive decisions for right hearing and use of Scripture. In the background of any discussion of the Fifth Commandment is the question of the misuse of the commandment for the abuse of others. Interpretive discussion thus starts with a fundamental irony: The commandment whose purpose is centered on protection from abusive behavior is the one commandment most open to being a vehicle for promoting abusive behavior.

The Fifth Commandment as Bridge between the First and Second Tables

In the structure and movement of the Decalogue, the commandment to honor father and mother is, like the Sabbath Commandment, a bridge between those commandments that focus directly or primarily on our obedience and service to God and those that have to do with our relation to our neighbor. Many efforts are made to identify this commandment with either the first table of the Decalogue or with the second. Disagreements about where the commandment belongs in the structure of the Decalogue exist because a case can be made in either direction. The matter is further com-

168

plicated by the recognition that in some of the earliest interpretive history of the Fifth Commandment, in the references to it in the New Testament, one perceives a kind of looseness to its placement, suggesting it is not easily pinned down as either primarily theological in orientation and rising out of thinking about obedience to God, or primarily ethical and beginning the community's thinking about relations with the neighbor.

In Matthew 19:18–19 and parallels (Mark 10:19; Luke 18:20), the second table of the Decalogue, the so-called "ethical" table, is laid out by Jesus in response to the query of the rich young man about what commandments he is to keep. Jesus recites the second table from not killing through not bearing false witness. Then at that point he adds: "Honor your father and mother; also, You shall love your neighbor as yourself." In all three Gospels, the commandment to honor the parents comes at the end of the normal series. As such, it is somewhat loosened from its normal spot and, by its being set alongside the general commandment to love the neighbor, is given a somewhat broader or more overarching role. It is difficult to determine whether that means it is to be seen as synonymous with the love of neighbor, or as a representation of the first table of the Decalogue comparable to the love of neighbor as a summary of the second table. The ambiguity is perhaps a further indication of the way in which this commandment joins the first and second tables of the Decalogue, continuing our thinking about how we relate to God even as it opens up the relationship to the neighbor. Or it may be that the commandment genuinely stands on its own and is not to be slotted into one relationship rather than the other.

Indeed, the Fifth Commandment does clearly serve a *bridge* function. That is evident in several ways. Most obvious is the way it sets up the directives having to do with how one relates to and deals with other persons in the community. The commandment coming first after a series having to do with the service of God is one that concerns relationship to those with whom *all* persons are usually closest: one's parents. The starting point of life with the other is with those with whom one is already related and upon whom one has some dependence. One may have no other kinship relations, but one always has a mother and a father. The commandment presumes a functioning relationship between father and mother and child, and so it may have been applicable in one situation and not in another. Perhaps the father is gone; perhaps the mother has died.

169

The claim of the commandment is to be understood as taking such varied circumstances into account.

The question of the *addressee*, and especially the *age* of the addressee, means that closeness and dependence may vary in the relationship of parent and child. Indeed the starting point of the commandment, by general consensus and my agreement, focuses on the mature child's dealing with older and frailer parents; this means that presumptions about who is dependent upon whom will have to vary. Further, closeness of relationship may shift in the course of adult life. What is important at this point is that such shifting relationships and dependencies are to be governed by a fundamental responsibility incumbent upon each person in a given relationship that one did not create but cannot abandon. Being a "child" puts one in a relational category, not an age category. Love of neighbor does not begin outside the home but in the family circle. Its particularities and broader force remain to be examined in more detail.

The bridge character of the commandment, however, means that it is rooted in the series of prohibitions and commands that direct us about our life with God. The commandment not only takes its place as the starting point for life with the neighbor. One also moves from God to father and mother. That is both a natural sequence and highly loaded. One may feel the logic but worry about the implications. The image of bridge does not have its full force if the commandment is not as rooted in the first table and the relationship to God as it is in the second table and the relation to neighbor. The reasons for claiming the connection to the first table are several. These can be mentioned briefly to make the point, but some of them will need to be explored more fully in discussing the particular content and focus of the commandment:

1. *The ordering that places this commandment* in both the Exodus and Deuteronomic versions immediately following the sequence of commandments having to do with our relation to God at least raises the possibility that this commandment, like the others to this point, looks backward in some sense as well as forward, suggesting that one may still be talking about things related to the service of God. In this case, that connection turns out to be one of analogy, a connection that points to the difference as well as to the similarity, an important protection against misunderstanding and misuse of the commandment by equating parents with God. In the first century CE, Philo made an argument as follows:

170

After dealing with the seventh day, He gives the fifth commandment on the honour due to parents. This commandment He placed on the border-line between the two sets of five; it is the last of the first set in which the most sacred injunctions are given and it adjoins the second set which contains the duties of man to man. The reason I consider is this: we see that parents by their nature stand on the border-line between the mortal and the immortal side of existence, the mortal because of their kinship with men and other animals through the perishableness of the body; the immortal because the act of generation assimilates them to God, the generator of the All. (Philo, *On the Decalogue*, 22.106–107 [p. 61])

2. *There are close ties between the Sabbath Commandment and the commandment to honor parents,* some of which also reach back into the other commandments of the first table. Both commandments are positive in form, and they are the only commandments so formulated. Both commandments include motivation clauses to encourage obedience, a feature generally characteristic of the first table. Both commandments in their Deuteronomic form include the formula, "as the LORD your God commanded you," which does not occur in any other commandments. Martin Buber has seen in these two commandments a time structure within the Decalogue that is not present in the other commandments.

The two of them, and only these two among all of the Ten Commandments, deal with *time*, articulated *time*; the first with the closed succession of weeks in the year, the second with the open succession of generations in national durations. Time itself is introduced into the constitutional foundation of national life by being partly articulated in the lesser rhythm of the weeks, and partly realized in its given articulation through the greater rhythm of the generations. The former requirement is provided for through the repeated "remembering" of the Sabbath day as that which has been consecrated to YHVH; and the latter by the "honouring" of the parents. Both of them together ensure the continuity of national time; the never-to-be-interrupted consecution of consecration, the never-to-be-broken consecution of tradition. (Buber, *Moses*, 132)

Buber did regard these two commandments as together forming   171 a bridge between the "religious" commandments and the "ethical" commandments, the Sabbath Commandment referring "back to what went before" and the parents' commandment referring "ahead to those that follow." Close association with the Sabbath Commandment, therefore, does not preclude seeing the Fifth Commandment as pointing forward in the theological and ethical structure of the Commandments.

The commandment to honor parents also continues the use of the phrase "the LORD your God," which is characteristic of the first table of the Commandments from the Prologue through the Sabbath Commandment. After the Fifth Commandment, this phrase—and any reference to God at all—disappears. While that may well be expected for the short commandments dealing with the neighbor, it might also have been expected for the Fifth Commandment as well. While these connections to the first table and more specifically the Sabbath Commandment are more formal than material, such formal associations are part of the structuring, ordering, and interrelationship of the Commandments.

3. *Two texts merit a closer look.* The first one shows both the special place of the Fifth Commandment as well as its association with the Sabbath Commandment and the rest of the first table of the Decalogue. It is Leviticus 19, one of the most obviously Decalogue-related texts in the Old Testament. There the commandment to honor mother and father, using the language of "fear" or "revere," introduces a long series of statutes that reflect several of the commandments explicitly and represent specifications and developments of other commandments. Verses 2–8 show the connections clearly:

> [2]Speak to all the congregation of the people of Israel and say to them: You shall be holy, for I the LORD your God am holy. [3]You shall each revere your mother and father, and you shall keep my sabbaths: I am the LORD your God. [4]Do not turn to idols or make cast images for yourselves: I am the LORD your God. [5]When you offer a sacrifice of well-being to the LORD, offer it in such a way that it is acceptable on your behalf. [6]It shall be eaten on the same day you offer it, or on the next day; and anything left over until the third day shall be consumed in fire. [7]If it is eaten at all on the third day, it is an abomination; it will not be acceptable. [8]All who eat it shall be subject to punishment, because they have profaned what is holy to the LORD; and any such person shall be cut off from the people.

These verses deal entirely with matters belonging to the first table of the Decalogue, having to do with the proper worship of God. They begin with reverencing parents, pair it with the Sabbath Commandment, and then move back into the preceding commandments. Honoring parents is not connected to family statutes, though there are a number of these in the chapters immediately preceding and following this one.

A further structural aspect of Leviticus 19 reinforces the way that honoring parents is joined here with the first table. It is in verse 30, where there is a kind of reversal of the order found in verse 3: "You shall keep my sabbaths and reverence my sanctuary." Reverence of the sanctuary presumably has to do with it as the place where the Lord is worshiped and where the name of the Lord dwells. Through the use of the term "fear/revere" (*yārē'*), the order of Commandments Five and Four in verse 3 is reversed, and we now have Commandments Four and Three. The whole process serves to connect the Fifth Commandment very closely to the commandments directing the community's relation to God.

The way in which the commandment to honor parents draws together the proper service of God and care for the neighbor is intimated in another text as well:

> ⁶The princes of Israel in you, everyone according to his power, have been bent on shedding blood. ⁷Father and mother are treated with contempt in you; the alien residing within you suffers extortion; the orphan and the widow are wronged in you. ⁸You have despised my holy things, and profaned my sabbaths. (Ezek. 22:6–8)

These verses are followed immediately by other indictments that may be connected to the Commandments, but the NJPS rightly sets these verses in a separate paragraph. The bad treatment of mother and father leads into the bad treatment of other members of the community, particularly the weaker or more vulnerable persons. In that respect there is a clear move from the vulnerability of the aged parent (see below) to the vulnerability of other disadvantaged members of the community. Thus the commandment is an important bridge into the love of neighbor and in a particular way: vis-à-vis the vulnerable and powerless neighbor, the neighbor at risk of losing support and the means for life. At the same time, the

173

bridge out of the first table is identified as the paragraph concludes with the condemnation of Judah for despising "my holy things" and profaning "my sabbaths." The close connection of the Fifth Commandment to the Fourth is affirmed, and once again mistreatment of parents is brought into association with mishandling the things of God: "my holy things" and "my sabbaths."

One may add to these Old Testament texts evidence from the later Ben Sirach. A long section elaborating on the commandment to honor mother and father (3:1–16) is preceded in chapter 2 by a concluding section to the chapter that has to do with "those who fear the LORD" (3 times in 2:15–18), which probably has the First Commandment in mind. The connection to the first table is suggested again in 3:16: "Whoever forsakes a father is like a blasphemer, and whoever angers a mother is cursed by the LORD."

4. *A positive reinforcement of the associations* just described is found in the language used for the positive and negative forms of the commandment. "Honor" (*kabbēd,* Exod. 20:12//Deut. 5:16) and "fear/revere" (Lev. 19:3) on the positive side, and "curse" (Exod. 21:17; Deut. 27:16) on the negative side—these are basic terms to express positive (Lev. 19:30; Mal. 1:6; etc.) and negative (Exod. 22:28; Lev. 24:16) ways of relating to God.

The Addressee of the Commandment

The question of to whom a commandment is directed is not customarily an issue with regard to the Decalogue. Because it arises in this instance, we are led to think more broadly about the addressee(s) of the Commandments, individually and as a whole. It is widely recognized that the Commandments, however they originated, were in their origin directed toward mature adults, especially the male members of the community. The use of singular first-person masculine verbs and pronouns makes that evident in the Hebrew. The fact that the Tenth Commandment against coveting prohibits coveting someone else's wife but makes no reference to coveting someone's husband is further indication of the male addressee of the Commandments and, more specifically, the adult male, though one cannot presume that *only* males are meant to receive these divine words. The kinds of acts enjoined or prohibited generally have to do with activities—for example,

174

killing, theft, and adultery—that are usually carried out by adults. Reference to son and daughter and to male and female slaves or servants in the Sabbath Commandment and the coveting commandment assumes also that adults are the ones being instructed by these words.

So there are clues within the Commandments themselves that the recipients are adults and specifically the adult males. But that is not the whole story. The trajectory of the Commandments—as their transmission is reported and as their working out in story, law, and song, in specific statute, illustrative example, and proverbial wisdom is developed in the whole of Scripture—means that they are not finally locked into the adult male audience. Whatever was the original setting in life for these Commandments, their setting in the text now brings them forth as words addressed to the whole assembly of God's people. The elaboration of the Commandments in various places in the Scriptures makes it clear that they apply to everyone in the community, that not worshiping idols or other gods, keeping Sabbath, honoring father and mother, not committing adultery, not killing, and the like are matters applicable to the women as well as to the men (Miller, "Sufficiency," 34 n. 46). While the catechetical use of the Commandments tends to lead present audiences to see them as something to instruct the children, their cultural impact makes one sharply aware of how important they are perceived to be for the polity generally. The Commandments are not restricted by age or gender. They are taught to the young, who are part of the assembly of the people so that they have them in their heart whenever, whoever, and whatever age they may be when the issues with which they deal arise.

The starting point for the honor of father and mother, therefore, is the adult child and the particular responsibilities that accrue to that person relative to the care of parents. But the child grows into those responsibilities, and there is not some point at which the commandment is not applicable and some point where it suddenly takes effect. Part of tracing the trajectory of meaning and effects of this commandment is the exploration of how it opens up in terms of its addressee. That starts with the fact that its present formulation suggests it is not restricted to adult males but includes adult females. One of the primary stories of the Fifth Commandment, the book of Ruth, is a tale of a non-Israelite woman's care for her widowed mother-in-law (see below).

Honoring Parents: How Does It Happen?

Giving Great Weight

The Hebrew of the text is clear, and the translations agree on its meaning. In Hebrew, "honor" (*kabbēd*) seems to carry the freight it carries in English. So the task is to uncover what that content is and particularly in the relationship between child and parent. The starting point is recognizing the positive formulation of the commandment and thus the openness of the command. All sorts of things may be aspects of rendering honor to another. One may presume that the positive, with its more general openness, is intentional. At least it is what the present form of the text provides, thus presenting the hearer with a broad range of space in which to attend to the commandment. Whatever renders honor to a parent on the part of a child is implicitly commanded in the Fifth Commandment. Its aim, therefore, is broad rather than narrow. Other commandments may start out with an apparently narrow focus that then reveals itself to be broader as the commandments are elaborated; this commandment works in reverse. We are given a large command, to which we bring an existing and broad understanding of the meaning of honor and thereby learn how we live by the command.

At the same time, we are responsible for discerning from within Scripture itself some of the foci, some of the specifics, some of the primary concerns inherent in rendering honor. One can start with a particular nuance that is in the verb *kabbēd* that may not be obvious in Hebrew: Its literal meaning, "to make heavy," in the sense of regarding someone as weighty. We speak of something as a matter of great weight or even of a person as weighty. That does not refer to their body weight but to the importance of the issue, to the high regard or position of an individual. So to "honor" parents is to regard them as persons of great weight, to treat them with high regard.

We have noted above that the same term is used as a verb of action toward God (e.g., Mal. 1:6). Thus children, sons and daughters, are to treat their parents in a way that can be compared to their treatment of God. The specifics of such treatment are not given and may vary. But in both instances, they have to do with regarding God/parent very highly. The same broad giving of weight, honor, respect, and reverence to parents is indicated by the use of the verb "fear/revere" (*yārēʾ*) in Leviticus 19:3, a citation of the Fifth Command-

176

ment but with "revere" in the place of "honor" (see above), a verb that is fundamental for describing the proper attitude of human beings toward God. In 1 Samuel 2:30, the Lord says: "Those who honor me (*kabbēd*), I will honor (*kabbēd*), and those who despise me (*bāzâ*) shall be treated with contempt (*qillēl*)." This particular text catches our attention because of its general assumption that there are ways of responding to God—positive and negative—that are comparable to how God treats human beings. In this case, the particular concern is honoring parents, and it is worth noting that all the verbs in the quotation just given occur in texts that speak of how fathers and mothers should or should not be treated.

Dishonoring Mother and Father

Fleshing out the way in which honor is rendered, therefore, may be helped by a look at its opposite, at the negative formulations spelling out the meaning and force of the Fifth Commandment. There are several in the statutes of the Torah, but the Wisdom literature also speaks about how *not* to treat parents as a way of teaching honor indirectly and by its opposite.

In the Book of the Covenant—the statutes that immediately follow the Decalogue in their Exodus form and so begin elaborating the meaning of the Commandments—the two statutes, having to do with treatment of parents appear close together in Exodus 21:

> Whoever strikes (*makkēh*) father or mother shall be put to death. (v. 15)

> Whoever curses (*mĕqallēl*) father or mother shall be put to death. (v. 17)

The first of these statutes grows out of the largest theme of this section of the Book of the Covenant. Most of the statutes in Exodus 21:12–27 have to do with occasions when someone strikes or hits (*makkēh*) another person. They are safeguards against violence against the person of another and regulations for punishing such violence when it occurs, thus underscoring the significance of physical harm of other members of the community. The statutes deal with different cases and different levels of participation in the community. One of these cases is violence against one's father or mother. The verb for striking (*hikkâ*) does not automatically imply killing,

177

as other statutes make clear when they go on to prescribe punishment if death occurs. But most instances of the use of this verb have to do with serious harm, and even in the statutes of chapter 21 where death does not follow, the very reason for taking up that possibility is because it is likely to happen. In the case of striking a parent, there is no qualification about what happens depending upon whether the parent is seriously hurt or dies. The sanction of death indicates that this act, which is not a playful touch of a child but a serious blow inflicted to do harm, is terribly serious. There is no elaboration of that seriousness. One may suggest it is a reflection of disdain for authority, violation of the dependency, and the like. The rationale is not stated because it is presumed to be self-evident. In any event, such an action dishonors the parent in an extreme way and so represents a violation of the Fifth Commandment.

The second of these two statutes shows the connection to the Fifth Commandment even more obviously. The verb *měqallēl*, translated in the NRSV as "curse" but more accurately in the NJPS translation as "insult," is an action that is, in effect, the opposite of honoring. While it may involve formal cursing or malediction, especially in nominal derivative forms (e.g., Deut. 11:26, 28–29; 27:13; 28:15, 45; 30:1; etc.), the verb basically means "to be light, small, contemptible," and in its derived meanings, "to treat lightly, contemptibly." A more colloquial meaning would be "treat shabbily." Goliath does this to David, and in the context it is clear that he is scorning and ridiculing David, treating him very lightly and not taking him seriously as an opponent (1 Sam. 17:43). When the lords of Shechem *qillēl* Abimelech (Judg. 9:27), it is clear from the words they speak that they are not cursing him but belittling him and, as the NRSV properly translates, ridiculing him. So also when Leviticus 19:14 says, "You shall not revile [*qillēl*] the deaf," it has in mind dismissing or treating a deaf person shabbily.

The statute in Exodus 21:17 is thus precisely the negative counterpart to the positive form we encounter in the Commandments. That is confirmed by other texts using this same verb *qillēl*, and related forms, to describe behavior toward mother and father that is reprehensible and violates the Fifth Commandment (Lev. 20:9; Deut. 27:16, *qālâ*; Prov. 20:20; 30:11). Other verbs of similar meaning may be used to describe the wrong sort of behavior toward parents, for example, *bûz* ("despise/scorn," Prov. 23:22 and 30:17), *nābal* ("consider insignificant," "treat with contempt," Mic. 7:6). All these instances are the opposite of "honoring" parents and represent an open agenda of ways that children treat their father and/or mother shabbily and contemptibly, not respecting and dignifying them but denigrating them and regarding them very lightly rather than with great weight. Such behavior will usually be that of grown children who have the capacity to treat their parents in this way, though one needs to be careful about presuming a certain age when such accountability comes into play. The definition of "grown" and "mature" is slippery and refers to something that happens over time and differently with different individuals. There is not some fixed time in which childish behavior toward parents becomes adult contempt. One learns to honor early in order not to belittle later. In both its positive and negative forms, the Fifth Commandment teaches us about fundamental respect for father and mother, in full awareness that the implications of such respect or its opposite, contempt, vary and gain in significance as the children age.

Before going further in specifying how honoring father and mother may take place or, conversely, dishonoring and denigrating them, there are three important dimensions of this particular commandment that may be overlooked or lost in our understanding and appropriation of it. One is the danger of assuming that keeping this commandment is purely a matter of behavior and action without any emotional dimension. Yet one may assume that here as well as elsewhere there is a disposition involved in keeping the commandment that involves attitude and emotion as well as act. The former is confirmed and undergirded by the latter, but the feeling of honor and respect motivates the child to act in such a way that reverence and honor are demonstrated. The commandment teaches a way of responding to one's parent that joins feeling and act.

The second aspect of the commandment that may be missed or forgotten is a further facet of the function of this commandment in bridging between the relationship to God and responsibility to the neighbor. The connection to the *first table* and the similarity between what is expected with regard to the parent and what is expected with regard to God—honor and reverence—mean that the child's obedience to this commandment in part presumes or arises out of something about the position of the parent in the relationship, that is, *respect for the role and authority* of the father and mother as parent. The place of the commandment as opening up the *second table*, however, means that there is a significant tension at this point.

179

For, as is the case for all the commandments that follow, the one addressed, who is both child and neighbor to the parent, is being given direction relative to one's (or their) *responsibilities* to the other, in this case, the other being specifically mother and father rather than the neighbor generally. The right to honor may be implicit, as the right to life is an implicit corollary of the commandment against killing. But the formulation of the commandment means that here, as with all that follows, the good, the flourishing of the community that lives by these commandments, is worked out as the "you" being addressed is attentive to the good of the other, in this case the neighbor who is parent. As the one to whom the commandments are addressed, it is my responsibility to protect and enhance the well-being of the other in the community.

From this angle, obedience to the commandment is not because of inherent right or claim of the parent any more than that of the neighbor, but because of my responsibility for the safety and good of that parent/neighbor. Or to put it another way, the right of the parent may be presumed in the same way as the right of the neighbor, but the way into recognizing those rights is through the responsibility given to and taken up by each member of the community, not as parent with rights but as divine addressee with responsibility (Miller, "That It May Go Well," 103–24). "My" right as parent is protected, not as "I" claim it through the Commandments but as "I" am the beneficiary of the responsibility each member of the community assumes in response to the divine address, in this case, particularly "my" children. There is here, as in each commandment of the second table, a reciprocity to the responsibility, but it works in a particular way in this case. Reciprocal responsibility is carried forward through the generational structure of the family and is signaled in the motivation clauses of the commandment (see below, "The Commandment with a Promise").

Finally, one should not miss what is one of the most obvious aspects of the commandment: the inclusion of *both* parents as recipients of honor. All the forms of the commandment, negative as well as positive, include the mother with the father. The commandment, therefore, is not tied to any particular social structure but to the nature of the family. The mother as much as the father is due the honor and reverence of her children. There are points in the teaching about this commandment in the rest of Scripture where one parent, especially the father, is mentioned without the other.

Here the repeated reference to both father and mother joins them without reserve as the objects of the commandment.

Caring for Aged Parents

If the positive and negative formulations of the commandment leave it richly open as to the various kinds of acts that honor parents and, conversely, the different ways in which sons and daughters may treat their father and mother shabbily, what are some of the specifics that belong to such a mode of relationship between child and parent? Keeping in mind that the Fifth Commandment stirs us in a positive direction, how does one think out of Scripture about the ways in which reverence and honor of father and mother are actually expressed in human life?

We may begin with the behavior that seems to be much in mind when the larger picture is taken into account: the care and concern of adult children for their parents as they grow old. Not treating parents in a trifling manner does not mean simply general disposition or verbal modes. The feeling of respect and honor cultivated in the growth of the child continues on into maturity and is the impetus for the necessary protection and care of the now-aged and weaker parents. Honoring father and mother is expressed in concrete actions that enhance and thus give "weight" to the parents, in the most literal way possible: with respect to clothing, food, shelter, and maintenance of general welfare. While there has been a tendency among some to reduce the meaning of the commandment almost entirely to such care, at least in its original understanding, recognizing a broader and more open applicability to the commandment does not mean that one may ignore what is clearly both exemplary of and central to its meaning in any time and circumstance.

The responsibility for care of older parents as a basic intent of the commandment may be inferred from the implicit address of all the commandments first to adult members of the community and then, in the educational process, to the children as they grow up. That responsibility, however, is not laid out elsewhere in the legal statutes of the Torah or even in the Old Testament generally as the meaning or intent of the commandment, which is why one should resist seeing in this important responsibility the sole meaning of the commandment. There are places outside the Old Testament,

181

however, where the care of aged parents seems to be clearly indicated as a major responsibility of children and one of the primary manifestations of honor. In the legal material of the ancient Near East, a number of cases and documents set up arrangements having to do with parents and children. They seem heavily weighted toward responsibilities of the adult child to care for older parents and particularly for a widowed mother. That is especially so with cases and agreements where there is wording about "honoring" and "fearing." These terms often appear in documents having to do with inheritance arrangements. The child involved, often adopted but always mature, is to "revere" or "honor" the parent, sometimes a widowed mother, throughout her life in order to receive the inheritance. The details of what is meant by so honoring the parent(s) are not always spelled out. When they are, they tend to have to do with specific provisions of food and clothing to take care of the older parents as well as carrying out proper procedures for death and burial.

While we lack clear analogies in the legal material of the Old Testament, the parallel language of honoring and fearing clearly suggests the likelihood that when used in the Decalogue, those terms carry a similar concrete meaning: provision for the needs of older parents. When one goes to the *Wisdom literature*, there is further support for this meaning of the commandment. The only other occurrence in the Old Testament of the Fifth Commandment imperative "Honor . . ." is in Proverbs 3:9:

> Honor the Lord with your substance
> and with the first fruits of all your produce.

Association with the Fifth Commandment is twofold. One again hears an analogy between respect for parent and respect for God. In this case, however, one is told that honoring God happens in giving one's goods. That at least suggests that such honor, when extended to parents, involves giving one's substance as its concrete manifestation. There are further proverbs that point to the connection between honoring parents and providing for them but in a negative rather than positive form:

182

> A son who does violence to his father and sends away his mother
> causes shame and brings reproach.
>
> (Prov. 19:26, my trans.)

The shameful behavior of the child is in pushing his mother out in the cold, depriving her of his support, and leaving her on her own. The "violence" to the father is not specified and is a word that usually refers to general and terrible devastation. It can mean more specifically despoiling someone of their goods (Obad. 5), and that may be what is envisioned here also. Thus the violence to the father, which might be physical (cf. Exod. 21:15), could also be robbing him of the physical goods he needs for his sustenance in old age. Similarly Proverbs 28:24 teaches:

> Anyone who robs father or mother
> > and says, "That is no crime,"
> is partner to a thug.

This proverb, in the midst of others having to do with wealth and resources, presumably envisions taking family property and potential inheritance while the older parents are still alive. The claim not to have sinned or done any crime suggests that what is involved is an appropriation of the family resources when the grown son (or daughter) is old and strong enough to do it with impunity. This amounts to a kind of plunder of the family wealth. But the point of the proverb, as of the commandment, is not so much the family wealth or the entitlement of the son to take it over as he becomes adult as it is his responsibility to make sure that it is available for the welfare of the parents. These proverbs thus shed light on what may be involved in Proverbs 20:20:

> As for one who treats his father or mother contemptibly [*mĕqallēl*],
> > light will fail him when darkness comes.
>
> > > > > (my trans.)

The shabby treatment of the parents is just that dismissal and slighting of them in their time of greater need.

A *prophetic* voice undergirds this understanding of filial honor of father and mother. Failure to care for mother and father is one of Ezekiel's indictments against Jerusalem and its leaders (22:6–7):

> Father and mother are treated with contempt in you; the alien residing within you suffers extortion; the orphan and the widow are wronged in you. (v. 7)

183

Here treatment of parents is a societal issue. One presumes that none of the victims of wrong in this list is a single case. The indictment is against what has become common in Jerusalem. In all three cases—father and mother, resident alien, and orphan and widow—patterns of oppressive treatment have taken over. That certainly means mistreatment by ignoring these various members of society and their human needs, depriving them of support. The contemptuous or shabby treatment of parents referred to in verse 7 reflects the language of the Fifth Commandment in its negative forms (see above); the following descriptions of Jerusalem's treatment of resident alien, orphan, and widow confirm that what children are doing to their parents is a serious threat to their well-being, with dismissive and belittling attitudes reflected in abuse and lack of support for life.

Joining abusive treatment of parents with oppression of stranger, orphan, and widow in the same indictment suggests an important tension in the meaning of the Fifth Commandment. On the one hand, it may not be reduced to the issue of how widows are provided for; on the other hand, the grouping as a whole suggests that proper care of parents is largely a matter of the community's provision for its weaker and dependent members, those without adequate resources to sustain their lives without the help of their neighbors. In this case, the responsibility for that neighborly help rests first and foremost with the parents' children. From this angle one sees that even as the Sabbath Commandment—in its Deuteronomic form—sets in place family and communal provisions to ensure the well-being of those without the power or structural place to do that on their own—the slave or bonded servant—the injunction to honor father and mother continues that impetus to regularized support of the weak and the powerless, of those who by circumstances—in this case diminution of place and power through aging—may not be able to support themselves on their own.

The Fifth Commandment's protection of parents comes to life in the *biblical story*, in its more narrative texts, in various ways. When *Joseph* brings his whole family to Egypt so they will not suffer the ravages of the multiyear famine, his instruction to his brothers is as follows:

> [9]Hurry and go up to my father and say to him, "Thus says your son Joseph, God has made me lord of all Egypt; come down to me, do not delay. [10]You shall settle in the land of Goshen, and you shall be near me, you and your children and your children's children, as well as your flocks, your herds, and all that you have. [11]I will provide for you [sing.] there—since there are five more years

of famine to come—so that you and your household, and all that
you have, will not come to poverty." (Gen. 45:9–11)

Joseph's action provides for his brothers and their family as well as for
his father (47:12; 50:21). His address to his brothers, however, clearly
formulates his intent as a provision for the well-being of his father.
Thus he honors his father—Joseph's mother being long dead at this
point in the story (35:19)—with this concrete and necessary care. The
act is accompanied by deep emotional affection and respect for his
father (46:29; 50:1). Furthermore, the story tells, in great detail, how
Joseph carried out his father's wishes for a proper burial in his homeland (47:28–31; 50:1–14). Joseph's final act of filial responsibility gives
great "weight" to his father and honors him in death as in life.

A quite different story of parental care is at the heart of the
book of *Ruth*. There is no father or son—they are all dead (Ruth
1:3–5)—not even a mother and daughter, only a mother-in-law and
a daughter-in-law (1:15–18). That this feminine in-law relationship
is also presumed as part of the parent-child structure governed by
the Fifth Commandment is suggested by the prophetic indictment
in Micah 7:6. The story of Ruth suggests there is no automatic
responsibility in this relationship, for Orpah turns back on the journey and returns to her mother's house (1:4–5, 14–15). From beginning to end, however, the story is an account of the honor rendered
by a child (adult) to her (aged) parent. Naomi's release of Orpah
and Orpah's return home is less an indication of the inapplicability
of the Fifth Commandment than it is a reminder that child-parent
relationships are not all the same, and the circumstances in any situation may affect how the commandment comes into play. Naomi
releases her only remaining children, two daughters-in-law, from
any filial responsibility to her. This is because of her own decision
to return to her homeland, Judah, and her awareness that if her
daughters-in-law remain loyal to her and to their duty as daughters, it will probably wrench them out of their homeland forever
and without the support of husbands. Both her charity to Ruth and
Orpah and Orpah's rational decision are not morally questionable.

The situation thus calls attention to the act of caring for an
aged parent all the more. In this case, one does not have to guess
what honors the parent. Ruth's response to Naomi exemplifies such
honor and reverence, precisely because it happens in a situation
where failure to do so would not necessarily be an obvious act of

185

treating a parent shabbily. The circumstances give Orpah a way out. According to the story, she first is as insistent as Ruth in staying with Naomi. It is only after Naomi's second speech that Orpah decides to go back. Even then, she leaves her mother-in-law in tears and kisses, honoring her affectively to the moment of their departure. There is no indication of any breach in the relationship, and Naomi makes a good case for the wisdom of Orpah's decision. The story suggests that if Naomi had not made her speech calling attention to the exigencies of their particular situation and genuinely setting the daughters-in-law free from any obligation to her, Orpah might well have continued on. The legitimacy of Orpah's leaving her aged mother-in-law is all the more supported by the fact that neither she nor Ruth possesses resources to provide for their mother-in-law. Furthermore, their Moabite nationality puts them in an even more vulnerable position if they go back with Naomi to Judah.

The contrast with Orpah's sensible decision serves to highlight Ruth's honoring of her mother(-in-law). The weighty treatment of her mother(-in-law) is first expressed in her speech, stubbornly refusing to leave her mother-in-law, even when pressed to do so. The commitment is deep and total and permanent. If there is some legitimate analogy between the honor rendered to God and the honor shown to father and mother, Ruth may come as close as any figure in the Scriptures to manifesting such parental reverence. The appropriation of Ruth's speech in so many marriage occasions is a sign of its powerful articulation of commitment of one human being to another. But the use of Ruth's speech in the marriage context tends to blur the realization that, in its biblical setting, it is an expression of the child-parent relationship, not that of husband and wife.

The rest of the story has two primary themes. One of them is Boaz's rescue of the women, or to put it in the more biblical mode of speech, the "redemption" of Naomi and Ruth. On the way to that happy outcome, however, it is specifically Ruth's active, labored, and strategic efforts that bring this off. The whole intent of her actions is to provide for Naomi, her mother(-in-law), and for herself. That happens first by Ruth's going into the fields to glean behind the reapers, and second by Naomi's strategy for Ruth to steal up to the drunken and sleeping Boaz and invoke the next-of-kin relationship so that he would marry her and provide for them both.

186

Ruth's honoring her mother(-in-law) by providing for Naomi in her old age is then completed with the birth of her first child, a son.

Confirmation that the story of this biblical book is precisely about the care of the aged Naomi by her daughter happens at the end with the words of the women who extend blessings to Naomi when her grandson is born:

> [14]Blessed be the LORD, who has not left you this day without next-of-kin; and may his name be renowned in Israel! [15]He shall be to you a restorer of life and a nourisher of your old age. (Ruth 4:14–15a)

The significance of this child is twofold. In the larger story, the baby is identified as the future grandfather of David (4:17–22). So the narrative of Ruth and Naomi is given a significant place in the biblical drama. Indeed, it seems that the reader does not discover why this story is here until the final verses. Within the confines of the story itself, however, the child's arrival is greeted precisely because he will take over the filial responsibility of caring for his grandmother, Naomi, as she gets older. He has brought her "back to life" in the present, and he will provide for her in the future (4:15; Sakenfeld, *Ruth*, 81). The verb translated "nourisher" is the same verb that occurs several times in the Joseph story to speak of Joseph "providing" for his father and his family (Gen. 45:11; 47:12; 50:21; see above on Joseph). The recognition of Ruth's honoring her mother(-in-law) in both feeling and act reaches its climactic moment in the words of the women following the quote above: "For your daughter-in-law who loves you bore him, she who is better to you than seven sons" (Ruth 4:15b, my trans.).

Ruth's lifelong disposition is rooted in a devotion to and love for her mother-in-law. The final clause is a poetic way of pointing to the significance of Ruth's actions over this long period, from the departure from Moab to the birth of her son. It is to look after, sustain, and care for her mother(-in-law)—not leaving her alone, working to put food on the table, developing a strategy to secure a context for continuing provision for her and her mother(-in-law), providing a "grandson" to continue caring for her in the future. In this respect, Ruth fulfills the responsibility of a daughter to honor her mother and does so in many and various ways over an extended period of time, even up to her mother(-in-law)'s death. She has done this in a way that could not be matched if Naomi had had seven sons!

187

There is no explicit reference to the Fifth Commandment in the book of Ruth. The stories of the Ten Commandments often do not make reference to them. As the discussion above has indicated, however, Ruth's way is from beginning to end a window on what the Fifth Commandment is about. Katharine Sakenfeld has noted the limitations of the story as an exemplary moral tale but still regards it as a depiction of "the peaceable community" (*Ruth*, 9–11, 87–88). To the extent that is the case, it provides a model of the rich and happy outcomes that are possible when the honor and reverence of parents is taken seriously in a sustained way.

There are two features of the story that should be lifted up in conclusion. One is that parental honor is rendered in this instance by a *Moabite* woman. The nationality of Ruth is often observed for its significance in the Davidic (and later messianic) genealogy. It should also be noted in relation to the Commandments. No statement is made about the applicability of the Fifth Commandment, or the Commandments in general, beyond the confines of the Sinaitic community and their children. We are simply told a story that exemplifies as well as any text in Scripture what honoring parents means in very specific ways. In a rather by-the-way manner, we learn that such honor of parents may be found in the actions of others, of those outside the covenantal community. Indeed, much like the later story of a Samaritan neighbor (Luke 10:29–37), it is the outsider who seems to show best what is expected of those inside.

The other feature to be underscored is that this story of a child's honoring a parent involves *only women*. The commandment itself, of course, is explicit about the maternal parent as the object of honor as fully as the father. The story of Ruth lets us come to know, further, that this commandment is not addressed only to adult males. It is not applicable only to those who have the power structure and wealth in their control. Ruth and Naomi are rescued/redeemed by a male, of course. The patriarchal structure of family life is reflected there. But that rescue is accomplished solely by Naomi's planning and Ruth's actions. Lest one misunderstand the breadth of the circle of protection and responsibility envisioned in the Fifth Commandment, the story of Ruth and Naomi takes us outside the covenantal community, beyond the confines of male responsibility, and incorporates in-laws as well as the actual parents of the child to show us 188 what it is like to "honor your father and your mother."

There is one other brief narrative of a child's honoring his parents by making sure that they are physically cared for. In the account of David's conflict with Saul and his gradual rise to power, he flees from Gath to the cave of Adullam and finally to Moab. There he presents himself to the king with one request: "Please let my father and mother come to you, until I know what God will do for me" (1 Sam. 22:3). While his coterie is much larger than simply family at this point, he knows he has a particular responsibility to care for his parents and make sure they are safe and provided for. Securing their place in the court of the king of Moab ensures that they will be cared for. As in most of these episodes, there is little interpretive comment, only a report of an Israelite adult child doing what was expected of him in light of the covenantal stipulations of the Commandments. One does not need to presume any self-consciousness about obedience. Rather, David belongs to an ethos shaped by the Commandments and so reflexively acts in accordance with them.

We have already noted the explicit instruction about the Fifth Commandment in Sirach 3:1–16, but only to observe how it connects this commandment with the First Commandment. The text merits a closer look, however, because it represents one of the most developed pieces of instruction about the commandment. This long elaboration of what is involved in honoring parents has several features to which we will return, specifically its attention to the impact of the motivation clauses of the commandment on its meaning and promise. In this context, however, what stands out is the importance of adult children's attention to and care of older parents. That is central to verses 10–16:

> [10]Do not glorify yourself by dishonoring your father,
>   for your father's dishonor is no glory to you.
> [11]The glory of one's father is one's own glory,
>   and it is a disgrace for children not to respect their mother.
> [12]My child, help your father in his old age,
>   and do not grieve him as long as he lives;
> [13]even if his mind fails, be patient with him;
>   because you have all your faculties do not despise him.
> [14]For kindness to a father will not be forgotten,
>   and will be credited to you against your sins;
> [15]in the day of your distress it will be remembered in your favor;
>   like frost in fair weather, your sins will melt away.
> [16]Whoever forsakes a father is like a blasphemer,
>   and whoever angers a mother is cursed by the Lord.

189

Verse 12 speaks explicitly of the care of a father in his old age and for as long as he lives. That is then elaborated in the following verse, specifically with reference to the loss of faculties and the possibility that the mature child in full control of his or her powers may look down upon or belittle the senile parent, and thus the well-being of the father or mother is threatened by an attitude that will be reflected in dismissive treatment. In other contexts, the child is instructed not to "despise" father or mother (Prov. 15:20; 23:22; 30:17). Sirach now spells out what such despising may involve: a contempt for parents who are losing their senses and not able to function normally. In the Hebrew text, the word that occurs in Sirach 3:11b to describe disrespect of the mother is *měqallēl* (to treat lightly), the primary word used in the negative formulations of the Fifth Commandment in the Old Testament (Schechter, *Facsimiles*). The parental condition depicted in this instruction is a further reminder of the way the commandment to honor father and mother is pointed toward the protection of the weak, those without the capacity to manage and provide for themselves. Via the family, the Commandments create a safeguard aimed at the care and support specifically of the old and infirm, a protection properly wrought out in the context of the family but not limited to that nuclear relationship, as we shall see.

Here a further dimension is added to the teaching of the Fifth Commandment with the reminder that disgracing or treating parents badly, especially in old age, brings no honor to the child who does so. Quite the contrary, it will bring shame and disgrace. So there is an appeal to self-interest at this point. It makes sense to treat parents with honor and not demean them. Indeed, there are rich rewards for acting thus according to verses 14–15. The promise of good that is articulated in the Fifth Commandment's motivation clauses is taken seriously in this teaching of what it means for grown children. From beginning to end this explication of the commandment places a strong emphasis on the value, the good, and the honor that redounds to the children who treat their parents with gravity and honor and care for them, especially when they are not able to function and manage as they have in their prime.

Honoring parents by caring for them in old age is reiterated in Sirach 7:27–28:

190

27With all your heart honor your father,
    and do not forget the birth pangs of your mother.

²⁸Remember that it was of your parents you were born;
how can you repay what they have given to you?

The answer to the question in the last line is by caring for them in their old age. Here and in Tobit 4:3–4 the instruction to honor the parents is rooted in gratitude for all they have done for the son or daughter. This presumes the capacity of kindness and care to instill gratitude within the heart of those who receive such. The care of the parents is thus made explicitly reciprocal. Those who have received care, from the womb forward, are to reciprocate by providing for the adult parents. Tobit 4 is even more specific in expressly including burial as a part of that honor rendered to both mother and father.

The responsibility of children to care for their parents when for some reason they do not have their faculties is underscored in the account of Noah's drunkenness and the opposite responses of Shem and Japheth on the one hand and Ham on the other (Gen. 9:20–27). While the text is not very explicit about Ham's conduct, his "seeing" his father's nakedness and reporting it to his brothers is condemned with a curse by Noah, even as the careful effort of the other brothers to cover their father's nakedness without looking at him becomes the basis for paternal blessing. In this instance the blessing and the curse are to be compared with other examples of parental blessings of children, especially in Genesis (e.g., 27:27–40; 28:1, 6; 48:15–16; 49:1–28), as well as with the words of Sirach 3:8–9:

⁸Honor your father by word and deed,
that his blessing may come upon you.
⁹For a father's blessing strengthens the houses of the children,
but a mother's curse uproots their foundations.

The honoring of father comes into play in those situations where the father loses control of himself in a way that can bring shame upon him without the effort of the sons to tend to him in a respectful manner, as is demonstrated by Shem and Japheth. The story of Noah's sons, when heard alongside Sirach's instruction, accentuates both points made above: honoring the parent is a part of the community's protection of the vulnerable, and it may bring about rich blessing (or curse!).

Before leaving this aspect of the Fifth Commandment's directives, we should note that the support of older parents by their adult

191

children is a focus of attention in Jesus' argument about the law with the scribes and Pharisees in Mark 7:9–13. His concern is the larger matter of their setting a human tradition against the demand of God. His use of the commandment as illustration indicates an understanding of honoring as parental support. Jesus cites both positive and negative forms of the commandment (Mark 7:10). Then he accuses the leaders as follows:

> ¹¹But you say that if anyone tells father or mother, "Whatever support you might have had from me is Corban" (that is, an offering to God)– ¹²then you no longer permit doing anything for a father or mother, ¹³thus making void the word of God through your tradition that you have handed on.

His point is that the scribes and Pharisees are avoiding the support of parents by saying that it is all right to take money or goods that might have cared for parents and turn that into an offering for God. A human tradition is used as a way of nullifying the intent of one of the Commandments, that is, to lead children into continual support of their parents by whatever means is theirs. That responsibility is a divine command and may not be undermined by a human tradition, even one that is intended to render honor to God.

The argument between Jesus and the Pharisees is an indication of Judaism's continuing interpretation and discussion of what was involved in honoring mother and father. The key Talmudic comment defines honor specifically in terms of the care and support of parents: "Honor means that he must give him food and drink, clothe and cover him, and lead him in and out" (Blidstein, *Honor*, 38). As Gerald Blidstein puts it succinctly: "The fundamental motif of *kibbud* is personal service" (47). The focus is on the physical deed more than the financial expenditure, and the deed could include quite menial tasks like those of a servant to his master (cf. Mal. 1:6): washing and dressing or undressing, putting on the father's shoes. The question of how much the son was supposed to put out financially in behalf of the parents became an issue in the discussion, as is already signaled by the encounter between the scribes and Pharisees and Jesus. Daughters were also under obligation to honor and revere their parents, but Judaic tradition understood that marriage restricted or limited the ability of a daughter to care for her parents in a way that it did not

192

for the husband (Blidstein, *Honor*, 98). The rabbinic conversation about financial claims on the son is complex, but there seems to be a difference between the Palestinian Talmud (filial piety includes financial responsibility) and the Babylonian Talmud (it does not) on the matter (Blidstein, *Honor*, 64). The conflict at least suggests that the position of the scribes and Pharisees to which Jesus reacts critically was a serious one in Judaism but one that was contested and argued, often in very complex ways that tried to take account of the variations in circumstances, particularly whether or not the parents had resources and whether or not financial support on the part of the child would create severe financial difficulties for the child. These debates, which are not finally resolved, are important pointers to the complexity of the matter. Once again the commandment is seen to have a specificity to it but one that does not always say exactly how that particularity, in this case caring for parents, was to be worked out in every instance.

In sum, the commandments of the second table are aimed at protecting the well-being and good of other members of the community. The point where that is potentially at its shakiest in the family structure is as the father and mother age and move from independence and being in charge to dependence and the weakness of age. Different voices and texts lift up this responsibility, underscoring its importance and spelling out various ways in which honor to father and mother is evidenced in providing and sustaining them. Central to this obligation is the actual provision of the needs of life; failure to render honor is demonstrated in leaving the parents unclothed and unfed, treated shabbily, dismissed and sent away. Honor and contempt can be rendered to anyone, but the family relationship creates a setting where they are especially present or potential. Sons and daughters are given a basic direction. How they will follow it is open. The very general and broad directive of the commandment leaves it that way. That does not mean, however, that one is without concrete opportunity to show honor. The tension between the general instruction to honor and the specific responsibility to care for older parents leaves one where the moral space of the commandments always leaves us: in an identifiable space with room to work out the responsibility, to figure out what sort of care (the concrete and specific) truly renders honor (the general and shaping directive) to one's father and mother.

193

Listening To and Obeying Father and Mother

While there is little doubt that the responsibility of a daughter and son for the care of their parents as they grow older is at the heart of the act of honoring them, there are various indications that honoring one's parents cannot be reduced to that. As we have already noted, the general language of "honor," "revere," and "treat lightly" is sufficiently open to lead one into thinking about various ways in which such attitude-action is manifest, for good or ill. It is not surprising, therefore, that Scripture itself points toward other manifestations of honoring father and mother or, as is often the case, teaches about proper honor by pointing to its opposite.

A concrete example of the latter is offered by the only case in the Deuteronomic Code that deals directly with relation between a grown child and his mother and father.

> [18]If someone has a stubborn and rebellious son who will not obey his father and mother, who does not heed them when they discipline him, [19]then his father and his mother shall take hold of him and bring him out to the elders of his town at the gate of that place. [20]They shall say to the elders of his town, "This son of ours is stubborn and rebellious. He will not obey us. He is a glutton and a drunkard." [21]Then all the men of the town shall stone him to death. So you shall purge the evil from your midst; and all Israel will hear, and be afraid. (Deut. 21:18–21)

In this instance the son is of an uncertain age and clearly is in some way under the authority of the parents, which seems to be an implicit claim of this particular case. The conduct may reflect some immaturity, yet the drunkenness suggests that the child is old enough to engage in regular excessive drinking and gluttony. The modern era may have greatly reduced the age at which such things take place, but it is unlikely that these words in their original context would have to do with a child or even a young person. One may presume that the son is old enough to know what he is doing and the risks involved.

Here the issue is not really a matter of caring for parents. Apart from the drunken conduct, which is an implicit rejection of what the son's father and mother have taught him, three terms—stubborn, rebellious, and not listening/obeying—are used to describe his rejection of their authority. The text assumes that the parents— and as in the Fifth Commandment and in the Proverbs, that means

194

both father and mother—have some authority over the son and can expect him to listen to them and do what they say. We are not told the specific content of the rebellion. The drunkenness, however, is a chief clue. That is, there is a style of social conduct that presumably is contrary to what the son's father and mother have taught him. It is exemplified in but not confined to public drunkenness. The use of the words for "rebellious" and "stubborn" almost exclusively in reference to human acts and attitude toward God—only in this instance is the verb *mōreh* used without God as the object of rebellion—cannot help but suggest that there is some analogy between the authority and claim over the son and daughter on the part of mother and father and the authority and claim of "the LORD your God" over the people as a whole. As in the case of the son who is not a slave but whose proper care of his father is comparable to that of a slave for his master, so these parents are not "god." Their children, however, are to listen, respect, and obey their parents in a way that may indeed be compared to the way they obey and respect the Lord. The honor of parents is analogous to the honor of God because it is derivative of that honor and representative of it. Karl Barth has articulated this point as follows:

> The necessity and divine compulsion of this demand is rooted in the fact that from the standpoint of children parents have a Godward aspect, and are for them God's primary and natural representatives. The superiority which entitles them to this specific respect from their children really consists in their mission, not in any quality inherent in them, nor in their character as physical *parentes* (which, although it gives rise to vital emotional relationship to them on the part of the children, has nothing to do with this respect), nor in any particular moral quality possessed by them (which may again produce a special attachment on the part of the children but not necessarily the respect required by the command). The superiority which demands this respect consists rather in the correspondence of their parenthood to the being and action of God. (*Church Dogmatics*, III/4:245)

It has been suggested that this case is a reflection of wisdom teaching brought into a legal context (Jungbauer, *"Ehre Vater und Mutter,"* 56–47; Calloway, "Deut. 21:18–21"). Whether or not that is properly its origin, there are significant resonances between the way Proverbs instructs children about their father and mother and

195

aspects of this Deuteronomic statute. There are not many references to father and mother together in the Proverbs, but most of them continue the instruction of the Fifth Commandment. Several of them have to do with children caring for their parents, not belittling them or despising them, not sending them away or robbing them. They are negative reflexes of the general formulations of the commandment—not to treat father and mother contemptibly (Prov. 20:20; 30:11, 17)—or they are warnings against not caring and providing for one's father and mother (19:26; 28:24), which may, of course, be implied in any of the more general instructions, as we have noted above.

There is one piece of instruction where father and mother are both referred to *three times* (Prov. 23:22–25):

> [22]Listen to your father who begot you,
>   and do not despise your mother when she is old.
> [23]Buy truth, and do not sell it;
>   buy wisdom, instruction, and understanding.
> [24]The father of the righteous will greatly rejoice;
>   he who begets a wise son will be glad in him.
> [25]Let your father and mother be glad;
>   let her who bore you rejoice.

The text is significant for several reasons. It begins with the call to the son/child to "listen" or "obey" (*šāmaᶜ*) and so has in mind the responsibility of the child to respect the authority, counsel, and instruction that come from father and mother. In this respect, it echoes the Deuteronomic statute by identifying what the son has failed to do there. The varying translations of the Hebrew verb—in one instance, "obey," in another, "listen"—are important indicators of the proper vagueness of the term. Perhaps the term "heed" may best convey both dimensions: the need to pay attention to what the parents say and take it seriously, but also the responsibility for *doing* what they say, not simply hearing and going on one's way. The son and daughter listen to and learn from their father and mother. The instruction is very open as to what it is the children are to heed. At least, one may assume, they listen to the wise counsel of father and mother and to the story they have to tell about the family and the faith. They also pay attention to and follow the wisdom and guidance of their parents. What is not meant is either a disinterested listening to a lecture or a mindless obedience to whatever is said, as if the act of obedience is all that matters.

196

The instruction of the father and mother is wise, as the accent on wisdom and truth in the rest of the saying demonstrates. The importance of obedience is because the father and mother can teach the way to live. By virtue of their position and their experience, they have things to teach that will help the child live and prosper. Failure to listen and heed is a disregard for their authority as wise, experienced teachers and parents. While the "father who begot you" has a claim by virtue of that begetting, the instruction here does not focus so much on some inherent claim as it does on the good effects and outcomes of living by this structure of authority and respect. Whereas in Proverbs and elsewhere, especially in the Fifth Commandment itself, the focus is on the good consequences for the child who honors and heeds, in this text the proper respect and listening of the child will have positive outcomes for the parents, who will rejoice and be glad as they see the son act wisely.

Furthermore, the parallelism of the two parts of verse 22 neatly conjoins the responsibility to listen and heed—the father—with the responsibility to care for the aged parent—the mother. In this fashion, one sees the wholeness and coherence of filial responsibility to pay careful attention and follow the instruction of father and mother and the obligation to provide for them in their old age. The parallelism creates a kind of identity so that both things are part of honoring the father and mother. The attentive honoring and caring for aged parents will not happen for someone who has not listened and heeded the instruction of father and mother through the growing years and into adulthood. Conversely, the son or daughter who learns to pay attention to the wise counsel of father and mother will develop a pattern of respect and honor that will have its outcome in continuing care for the parents throughout their lifetime.

There is one other way in which this text joins hands with Deuteronomy 21:18–21. Before and after the verses under discussion, there is more specific instruction to the son. It is a strong warning against drunkenness and gluttony with some rather vivid description of the possible consequences: poverty and rags (Prov. 23:21) and terrible effects on mind and body and sight (vv. 29–35). The stubborn rebelliousness of the son in the Deuteronomic statute and the drunkenness are not two unrelated matters. Mother and father teach about the terrible effects of drunkenness—and its counterpart, gluttony—and the child who honors them and listens to them will avoid both. Is that because he is told to do so by his parents, or

197

because of the ill effects against which they warn? The choice is a false one. The parents have their place of authority because of the wisdom of their teaching, and their teaching is a function of their place as mother and father. The obedience of the son or daughter is because the parents have some very important things to teach.

Understanding the Fifth Commandment as a call to honor father and mother by heeding them in the manner described above is echoed in the New Testament without much elaboration. Twice we hear the injunction: "Children, obey your parents" (Eph. 6:1; Col. 3:20). In the case of Ephesians 6:1, the instruction is followed by a reiteration of the Fifth Commandment, so that the reader is clear what is the ground for the instruction, and the commandment is being interpreted directly in relation to honoring parents by listening to and obeying them. While the instruction may have younger children in mind, there is no reason to assume that it applies to one age over another. Younger and older children honor their parents by heeding their words. The call to obedience here is in direct continuity with what we learn from Deuteronomy and Proverbs about ways of honoring parents and not treating them lightly.

What about Disobeying Parents?

At this point an important question needs to be raised. Is obedience of parents *always* incumbent upon son and daughter? Are there not times when one should *not* listen and when obedience is not in behalf of the child's well-being? Should children ever resist parental authority?

There is no developed discussion of this issue, but there are some hints of how one might think about the question. The first and most obvious is that respect, honor, and reverence capable of being seen in analogy to God can only make sense when directed toward an object that expects and seeks the good. In other words, there is an assumption about the parents in the reference to their honor.

Second, honor and reverence, especially in the form of obedience, is incongruent with shameful counsel and behavior on the part of the parents. One may assume that obeying father and mother is a claim that rests upon the coherence of position and teaching.

198   Third, the frequent call of Proverbs to listen and heed father and mother is with reference to specific words, to instruction that is good and helpful, that brings joy and gladness. The commandment

itself promises a positive outcome for those who honor their father and mother. What is heard and obeyed brings long life and good for the one who obeys. Obedience has good results, so obeying makes sense.

All of these reasons, therefore, assume the appropriateness of obeying father and mother. That still leaves the question of an exception. That matter is taken up in the instance of teaching on the part of either father or mother that is inconsistent with the true and proper honoring of God. There are no explicit cases of this. In fact, the most overt reference to the possibility of a family member leading another member astray to the worship of other gods is notable for its lack of reference to the father and mother (Deut. 13:7–12 [6–11E]), suggesting, implicitly, that there is no expectation that father and mother would do such a thing. In a very different context, however, the blessing of Levi in Deuteronomy 33:8–11 speaks of the separation of the Levites as an act of renunciation of father and mother in order to be faithful in keeping the precepts and the covenant of the Lord.

> [8]And of Levi he said:
> Give to Levi your Thummim,
>   and your Urim to your loyal one,
> whom you tested at Massah,
>   with whom you contended at the waters of Meribah;
> [9]who said of his father and mother,
>   "I regard them not";
> he ignored his kin,
>   and did not acknowledge his children.
> For they observed your word,
>   and kept your covenant.
> [10]They teach Jacob your ordinances,
>   and Israel your law;
> they place incense before you,
>   and whole burnt offerings on your altar.
> [11]Bless, O Lord, his substance,
>   and accept the work of his hands;
> crush the loins of his adversaries,
>   of those that hate him, so that they do not rise again.

The reference is to events in the wilderness, and the text seems to combine different stories or traditions: the testing at Massah and Meribah (Exod. 17:1–7 and Num. 20:2–13), which does not mention the Levites, and the incident of the golden calf when the Levites

199

responded positively to Moses' call: "Who is on the LORD's side? Come to me!" (Exod. 32:25–29). As Moses commanded them, the Levites went through the camp to kill "your brother, your friend, and your neighbor." There is no reference here in Exodus to father or mother, but in that act the Levites were "ordained . . . for the service of the LORD, each one at the cost of a son or a brother." In the blessing of Levi in Deuteronomy 33:8–11, this rejection of kinship loyalties because the family has turned away from the Lord starts with the mother and father. The text is very concise. Nothing is said in the context about their teaching, but the story in the background makes it clear that parental authority does not hold sway when it turns against the Lord. Rejection of the authority of mother and father is very explicit in the text: "I do not see them" (v. 9, my trans.). For the Levites, honor and care of parents is now transferred to God, since the Levites have been set apart to the Lord's service (cf. Deut. 32:6, 18).

The parent-child relationship is used to make the same point in Ezekiel 20:18–21a:

> [18]I said to their children in the wilderness, Do not follow the statutes of your parents, nor observe their ordinances, nor defile yourselves with their idols. [19]I the LORD am your God; follow my statutes, and be careful to observe my ordinances, [20]and hallow my sabbaths that they may be a sign between me and you, so that you may know that I the LORD am your God. [21]But the children rebelled against me; they did not follow my statutes, and were not careful to observe my ordinances, by whose observance everyone shall live; they profaned my sabbaths.

The rebellion of the generation in the wilderness meant that their children were not to follow the statutes and ordinances, the teachings and precepts of their parents, for they were the way of idolatry. In that case, the son and daughter are not to listen to father and mother. Their authority is forfeited by their misguided teaching.

In a somewhat more indirect way, the story of the kings of Israel often measures the faithfulness of a king against the model of his father. While it is probably most often in order to identify the apostasy of the father being repeated by the son, there are instances where the son does not follow the model or exemplified teaching of his parents. So Asa removes his mother from being queen mother because of her idolatry, and this exemplifies the fact that he is true

200

to the Lord (1 Kgs. 15:13–14). King Jehoram gets a very mixed verdict, but the one positive thing that is said about him is that the wickedness he did was not like—in other words, not as bad as—that of his father and mother (Ahab and Jezebel). Each of these cases makes it clear that one does not automatically follow what parents say and do, or what they teach by their actions. When such counsel or example violates the proper worship and service of God, the reverence of the Lord, then one is not compelled to obey and may renounce the teaching and the authority of the parents.

The issue of obedience and disobedience of parents is at the heart of the account of the young Jesus in the temple (Luke 2:41–51). It is raised when his mother scolds him after they have finally found him. The incident is a typical family incident, the disappearance of a child when his parents—note how the story regularly speaks of Joseph and Mary as "parents," "mother," and "father," rather than by their names as usual—thought they knew where he was and that he was somewhere in their company. The response of his mother is to be expected. They had assumed he was with them and were undoubtedly distraught when he was nowhere around. There was nothing to do but go back to where they had seen him last, the temple. There they found him—after three days of wondering where their child was. Mary's anxiety and fear are visible in her scolding of Jesus when they finally locate him: "Child, why have you treated us like this? Look, your father and I have been searching for you in great anxiety" (v. 48). This apparent lack of respect for his parents, however, is in sharp contrast to what the Gospel says Jesus did when they found him: "Then he went down with them and came to Nazareth, and was obedient to them" (v. 51). Does this mean that Jesus changed from being a disrespectful and disobedient child to an obedient one? His response to his mother's scolding would not seem to suggest that: "Why were you searching for me? Did you not know that I must be in my Father's house?" (v. 49). Karl Barth is surely correct that "Jesus did not seek to evade the authority of his parents" (*Church Dogmatics*, III/4:250).

In a different sort of way than is suggested by the Old Testament stories, the First and Fifth Commandments come together. It is not finally a conflict but the fulfillment of the honoring of parents by honoring God. Obedience is not simply doing whatever is required; but it also is generally to be expected, as Jesus' immediate subjection in obedience to his parents' authority makes clear.

201

The disobedience in this case arises out of the direction of Jesus' parents, who have brought him to "my Father's house," and so he acts as appropriate in that context. His respect of them is qualified by the First Commandment, but in a positive way that ultimately grows out of his honoring his parents and does not set it aside. Barth summarizes the matter as follows:

> We have seen how this crisis arises in the story of the twelve-year-old Jesus with the emergence of tension and opposition between his obedience to God and obedience to His parents. But we have also seen in the same story the solution in virtue of which the child's obedience to his parents is transcended and qualified by its obedience to God, but at the same time included and grounded in it. (*Church Dogmatics,* III/4:259)

This story and its outcome are to be contrasted with Jesus' later conflict with the teachers when he criticizes them for allowing children to use money that could support parents for offerings (Mark 7:6–13). This is not a conflict between the First Commandment and the Fifth but a replacement of the divine word in the commandment with a human tradition that may seem to honor God but clearly dishonors parents (Barth, *Church Dogmatics,* III/4:250–51).

The Commandment with a Promise

When the writer of the letter to the Ephesians quotes the Fifth Commandment to underscore the instruction that children should obey their parents, he not only includes the motivation clause but also lifts it up and calls attention to it before quoting it: "This is the first commandment with a promise." There is no further comment at that point, but calling attention to the motivation clause(s) serves to suggest that this is an important part of the commandment and may indeed be drawn upon to instruct the children. The motivation clause is not to be regarded as excess baggage attached to this commandment but perfectly capable of being attached to any commandment. Such clauses do appear fairly frequently, especially in Deuteronomy, which in this instance expands the motivation from what is found in Exodus. That is not a reason, however, for ignoring the presence of such a stereotyped clause in this instance. As the Ephesians writer notes, such promise clauses are unusual in the Commandments.

202

Indeed, this is not just the "first" such clause, as Ephesians 6 claims; it is the *only* one (but see below), thus suggesting that the motivation or promise plays a real part in the commandment and is to be incorporated in the hearer's appropriation of it. In this regard, the motivation clause is like the ones connected to the previous commandments in that it grows quite specifically out of the content and aim of the particular commandment to which it is attached.

One may begin, in a sense, from outside the commandment proper by noting some similarities and differences between the motivation(s) of the Fifth Commandment and those in the preceding commandments having to do with images, the name, and the Sabbath. In all of these clauses, there is no explanatory intention, no spelling out or rationalizing the commandments themselves. Reasons for obedience are given; that is the point. But the sensibility identified is not aimed at spelling out what is meant by the particular commandment to which the motivation clause is attached. Rather, the rationality is more in terms of outcomes and consequences. The Sabbath Commandment is the most complex in this regard, having different motivations in Exodus and Deuteronomy. In the former, the encouragement to obedience is by offering the commandment as an imitation of God's own way, resting after a period of labor; in the latter, the primary motivation for rest is to ensure that the powerless, specifically the bonded servants, also have a chance to rest from their labors. For the commandments prohibiting the construction and worship of images and prohibiting misuse of the name, the motivation clauses introduce sanctions. They are largely negative, having to do with the Lord's judgment against those who do not keep these commandments. In the case of the Second Commandment, however, a positive outcome is also indicated for keeping the commandments. It is of a very general sort, though no less serious and important. It has to do with keeping the commandments generally—and that may have in mind much more than the Decalogue—and promises the Lord's continuing love and loyalty. In this sense, a positive promise for the future does not occur for the first time in the commandment to honor father and mother.

The Fifth Commandment, however, has a much more specific promise: life and good, or well-being. The context in which both things are possible and to be wrought out is the land. The presupposition of life and good is the space God gives where that can happen. The further presupposition is the generational responsibility, which,

203

precisely by its reciprocality, makes possible both a long life and a good life. The child's care of mother and father in their later years, providing physical needs, place to live, support for their well-being, and continuing respect—all this is the fulfillment of the promise. Without that care, mother and father have no chance for either long life or good life. With that care, provided in a way that treats the parents with great weight and does not belittle or denigrate them, length of days is genuinely possible, and enjoyment of that time from maturity through old age and to death is likely to happen.

But all that is about *parents* receiving the promise, whereas the commandment directs the promise to the son or daughter. The connection is obvious. For only as the sequence of generations lives by this commandment can each father and mother count on the promise. The son or daughter who honors becomes the father or mother who is honored. As they have nurtured respect and as they have provided for the good of their parents, they in turn will need the same and have the promise of the same. Their treatment of mother and father becomes a model by which their own children will learn to keep the commandment and what its keeping entails.

In her treatment of this commandment in her book *Smoke on the Mountain*, Joy Davidman begins with this fairy tale from the Brothers Grimm:

Once upon a time there was a little old man. His eyes blinked and his hands trembled; when he ate he clattered the silverware distressingly, missed his mouth with the spoon as often as not, and dribbled a bit of his food on the tablecloth. Now he lived with his married son, having nowhere else to live, and his son's wife was a modern young woman who knew that in-laws should not be tolerated in a woman's home.

"I can't have this," she said. "It interferes with a woman's right to happiness." So she and her husband took the little old man gently but firmly by the arm and led him to the corner of the kitchen. There they set him on a stool and gave him his food, what there was of it, in an earthenware bowl. From then on he always ate in the corner, blinking at the table with wistful eyes.

One day his hands trembled rather more than usual, and the earthenware bowl fell and broke.

"If you are a pig," said the daughter-in-law, "you must eat out of a trough." So they made him a little wooden trough, and he got his meals in that.

204

These people had a four-year-old son, of whom they were very fond. One suppertime the young man noticed his boy playing intently with some bits of wood and asked what he was doing.

"I'm making a trough," he said, smiling up for approval, "to feed you and Mamma out of when I get big."

The man and his wife looked at each other for a while and didn't say anything. Then they cried a little. Then they went to the corner and took the little old man by the arm and led him back to the table. They sat him in a comfortable chair and gave him his food on a plate, and from then on nobody ever scolded when he clattered or spilled or broke things. (*Smoke on the Mountain*, 60–61)

The rewards of honoring father and mother are the center of attention in the elaboration of this commandment in Sirach 3:

> [5]Those who honor their father will have joy in their own children,
>   and when they pray they will be heard.
> [6]Those who respect their father will have long life,
>   and those who honor their mother obey the Lord;
>   [7]they will serve their parents as their masters.
> [8]Honor your father by word and deed,
>   that his blessing may come upon you.

What the son and daughter do will redound through their own children. That may not be all that is involved in the joy, but that is a significant part of it. The reward or promise does not stop with that, however. Long life is reiterated as a promise generated out of respect for father and mother (v. 6). So also does the child receive blessing, explicitly from father and mother. In Sirach, this, like all the other rewards, is a result of honoring father in word and deed (v. 8). Such honoring of father and mother is understood to be an act of fearing and obeying God (vv. 6–7). Thus obedience to this divine command also carries with it the promise of atonement for sins (Sir. 3:3) and the hearing of one's prayers.

The clause of the Fifth Commandment itself sets the land as context for the two promises of good or well-being and long life. That is to be understood in the specific sense of the land given by God to the people of Israel but is not to be confined to that land. The promise continues in the life of the people in the Diaspora and beyond. Thus the community remembers the specific land as the reality of God's gift and a sign of God's gift. Away from the "land" of Israel, children still receive the promise of well-being and long life on the land that God provides as they honor their parents and so teach their own sons and daughters. The "land" points beyond any specific land to lift up the spatial context in which human existence is lived out. This becomes explicit in the citation of the promise of the Fifth Commandment in Ephesians 6:3, which gives the text of the Septuagint of Exodus 20:12, but stops with *epi tēs gēs*, omitting the adjective "good" (*agathēs*) and the following qualifying clause, "which the Lord your God is giving you." The phrase *epi tēs gēs*, therefore, is no longer to be translated as "on the [good] land" but "on the earth." Wherever and whatever the space and place of one's family life, God's promise of good things for those who honor father and mother is real. The community does not forget the particular land that was in the promise at Sinai, but it finds the promise of obedience in whatever land the Lord is granting for the life of one's family, for the continuation of the generations for length of days and for keeping life good and human to the end of those days.

One should not leave the matter of how the Fifth Commandment is encouraged and rationalized by its promise clause without recognizing that further motivation for its keeping is provided as the commandment is taken up as instruction in the New Testament. In the letter to the Ephesians, the promise of the commandment is itself lifted up to encourage the children to keep it. But there is an additional rationale as well as a qualifying clause. The rationale is "because it is right" (*dikaion*). In other words, along with the promise that undergirds keeping the Fifth Commandment, the children are told that this is appropriate to the relationship with God. It is the right or righteous thing to do. The grounding is not entirely consequential. One honors mother and father as an expression of the right relationship with God and in order to make sure that relationship happens. When Colossians 3:20 gives its motivation for children obeying their parents, it offers the same ground but in different language: "for this pleases the Lord" (RSV).

Both New Testament texts give a qualifying clause as well. In Colossians obedience is "in everything," and in Ephesians it is "in the Lord." Both qualifying clauses risk being misinterpreted, either too broadly or too narrowly. The "in everything" is a way of identifying obedience of mother and father as a general practice for children. It assumes the direction and instruction of Christian parents, whose counsel and direction will be itself "in the Lord." Both the direction and the obedience will thus be in the spirit of Christ, which is what it means to obey "in the Lord." The family's life is to

206

be Christlike. First of all, that happens in the way parents direct their children and then also in the response of the children.

Further Developments in the Story of the Fifth Commandment

The Commandment Becomes Explicitly Reciprocal

In the discussion above, the reciprocity of the Fifth Commandment has been underscored in the way that the parents' care of the children leads to the children's care of their parents. The argument has been made that parental care and right and good instruction are expected of the mother and father so that respect for their authority and listening to and obeying their counsel brings good rather than bad. The motivation clauses of the commandment underscore this expectation and presume that honoring mother and father has all sorts of good outcomes—in the relationship with God and in the future well-being of the child who keeps the commandment (Exod. 20:12b; Deut. 5:16b). The "good" is to be found in respect and honor and reverence of parents. That good is moral and experiential. From the commandment itself through the Proverbs and the stories, into the New Testament reiterations of the commandment, it is evident that listening to parents and obeying them is a good thing to do. Further, there is clear indication that poor parental direction is not to be followed or obeyed.

All of this is fundamental to understanding the Fifth Commandment as descriptive and good news and not as a demand with abusive potential. To further underscore that point, however, the appropriation of the Fifth Commandment in the Letters to the Ephesians and the Colossians makes the reciprocal character of the commandment explicit. It notes the possibility—and one may assume that possibility at times becomes actuality—of parents abusing their children and thus makes it clear that the responsibility commanded in this commandment is clearly a two-way street. Following the instruction, "Children, obey your parents," both letters set forth a parental injunction: "Fathers, do not provoke your children" (Eph. 6:4; Col. 3:21). The implication of mutuality is brought out lest there be any uncertainty about it.

Furthermore, motivation clauses follow this injunction in both instances. In Colossians, the reason for parents not provoking their

207

children, not abusing them, is "or they may lose heart." There is a pragmatic dimension here, an appeal to self-interest. Abusive parental behavior may lead to the children giving up on honoring their mother and father. The motivation as well as the instruction assumes the reciprocity and mutuality of the commandment. It will not work unless respect goes both ways, with parents not abusing their young, and grown-up children not treating their parents shabbily.

In the citation of the Fifth Commandment in Ephesians 6:1–4, the fathers are not so much given a reason for not provoking their children as given an alternative. The alternative is really an explanation of how one avoids provoking the children: "Bring them up in the discipline and instruction of the Lord." We are back in Proverbs, but with the further context that it is a Christlike way that is being taught. When that is what the fathers do with their children, they will not provoke them to anger but will evoke their respect and honor and loving treatment of their parents.

The Extension of the Commandment to Figures in Authority

One of the developments of the Fifth Commandment that has been much debated but cannot be ignored is the way in which it opens up the question of how human beings deal with and respond to figures in authority over them other than father and mother. For Luther, obedience to the civil authority was enjoined by this commandment because that authority "belongs in the category of 'fatherhood' as a walk of life, and is the most comprehensive of all" (Large Catechism, in Kolb and Wengert, *Book of Concord,* 407). He argues as follows:

> Furthermore, in connection with this commandment, we must mention the sort of obedience due to superiors, persons whose duty it is to command and to govern. For all other authority is derived and developed out of the authority of parents. Where a father is unable by himself to bring up his child, he calls upon a schoolmaster to teach him; if he is too weak, he seeks the help of his friends and neighbors; if he dies, he confers and delegates his responsibility and authority to others appointed for the purpose. In addition, he has to have servants—menservants and maidservants—under him in order to manage the household. Thus all who are called masters stand in the place of parents and must derive from them their power and authority to govern. They are all called

fathers in the Scriptures because in their sphere of authority they have been commissioned as fathers and ought to have fatherly hearts toward their people. (Large Catechism, 405–6).

Calvin also saw a further authority derivative from parental authority and to be honored by the command of God. In his case, this was, as in other instances, by way of applying the figure of synechdoche, the part as a reflection of and pointer to the whole (Miller, "Commandments in Reformed Perspective"). The authority of the father and mother is a pointer to the various authorities that govern our lives and are worthy of our respect and obedience. Such interpretation, therefore, has long been a part of teaching the commandment.

The primary exegetical grounds for connecting the respect for parents and respect for other authorities is in the Deuteronomic Code and the way in which it seems to lay out statutes and ordinances that develop and specify aspects of the Commandments and what they are about. As we have seen in regard to other commandments, Deuteronomy 12–26 appears to be structured according to the Commandments in their sequence. While the precise connections are more debated for the second table of the Decalogue and chapters 19–26 of Deuteronomy, those who have argued the case for connecting the Commandments and the Code agree almost unanimously that the elaboration of the commandment to honor father and mother is to be found especially in Deuteronomy 16:18–18:22. That does not mean there are no statutes in Deuteronomy outside this section that may be associated with the Fifth Commandment. As we have seen, there is a very specific statute in 21:18–21 that has to do with obeying and listening to mother and father. The main section, however, deals with honoring parents and seems to follow the treatment of the sabbatical principle (related to the Sabbath Commandment) in Deuteronomy 15 and the further rules about regular celebration of the cultic occasions in ancient Israel in 16:1–17.

The block of verses in 16:18–18:22 is almost entirely concerned with various offices in ancient Israel and their responsibilities: judges and the procedures for judicial process (16:18–17:13), the king (17:14–20), the (Levitical) priests (18:1–8), and the prophet (18:9–22). The treatment of these offices is less to assert their authority than it is to indicate how they are chosen and what belongs to the way they carry out their official duties. There is no discussion of parents in this block of material, so the connection is inferential in two ways: the presumed structure of Deuteronomy 12–26 according to the order of the Commandments, and the analogy from the authority of the parent to the authority of other representative ruling, guiding, and teaching figures in the community. Dennis Olson has stated the connection simply and well:

> The statutes and ordinances of 16:18–18:22 share with the commandment honoring parents a basic set of values concerning the role and purpose of authority, whether exercised in a smaller family context (5:16) or in a larger community or national context (16:18–18:22). (*Death of Moses*, 78)

There are various ways in which this part of the Deuteronomic Code resonates with the Fifth Commandment. Part of the motive clause of the Fifth Commandment—"in the land [or, 'in all your towns'; Deut. 16:18] that the Lord your God is giving you" (see Exod. 20:12; Deut. 5:16)—occurs several times in Deuteronomy 16:18–18:22. This expression is by no means confined to these chapters in Deuteronomy, but as Georg Braulik has pointed out, this particular section is structured around its use (*Die Gesetze*, 54). The sentences referring to the gift of the land introduce each of the offices: 16:18, judges and princes (16:18–17:13); 17:14, king (17:14–20); and 18:9, prophet (18:9–22). The reference to the land as the context for carrying out these offices is omitted only from the Levitical priest. That omission is probably because the Levitical priests were expressly prohibited from owning property and inheriting it (18:1–2; Braulik, *Die Gesetze*, 54). Ordering the discussion of the offices around the promise that is central to honoring parents recalls that promise and places the land of promise as the locus of leadership and authority for these various positions.

If the parental role has some analogy to God's place or is to be seen as reflecting the teaching and direction of the Lord, that is also a feature of the offices of the community. Their functions are strongly oriented toward God. That is indirectly suggested by the inclusion of the statutes having to do with cultic purity in 16:21–17:1 and the exemplary case for the judicial process in 17:2–7 having as its subject someone who goes after other gods. Furthermore, the difficult case goes to "the place that the LORD your God will choose" (17:8, 10), the sanctuary, and a warning is given against anyone "who

210

is presumptuous and does not obey the priest appointed to minister there to the LORD your God" (v. 12, my trans.). The offices and procedures have to do with maintaining the community's faithfulness to the Lord. Listening and obeying, therefore, is the appropriate response to and respect for the office of the priest and the decision he renders. The point is made again in the section dealing with the Levitical priest: his responsibility is twice described as "to stand and minister in the name of the LORD" (18:5, 7).

With even greater emphasis, the king's responsibility is also oriented *entirely* toward the service of God. Various matters are taken up as things the king is *not* to do. His single task is elaborated in a way that excludes any misunderstanding:

> [18]When he has taken the throne of his kingdom, he shall have a copy of this law written for him in the presence of the levitical priests. [19]It shall remain with him and he shall read in it all the days of his life, so that he may learn to fear the LORD his God, diligently observing all the words of this law and these statutes, [20]neither exalting himself above other members of the community nor turning aside from the commandment, either to the right or to the left, so that he and his descendants may reign long over his kingdom in Israel. (Deut. 17:18–20)

The king's only responsibility is wise rule according to the divine instruction. The same is true of the parent with the child. It is their wise instruction according to the torah of the Lord that gives them authority and merits their respect.

Finally, in the instruction about the prophet, we are told *three times* that he speaks in the name of the Lord. The Lord warns against "anyone who does not heed [or obey] the words that the prophet shall speak in my name" (18:19). At the same time, warning is also given against any prophet who does *not* speak in the Lord's name: no one is to attend to those words. The prophet's authority and right to expect obedience to what he says depends entirely upon the prophet's faithfulness to the Lord's way. Prophets who speak in the name of another god or tell the community something that has not come from the Lord (18:20) have no authority and are not to be honored or respected. They are not to be obeyed.

In sum, the position of authority is like that of the parents for their children. It is not because of something inherent in their positions but because they are part of God's rule of the community.

211

Learning honor of parents is an opening to learning how to respect authorities of other sorts. Furthermore, as one moves back and forth between the Fifth Commandment and this section on leaders, a very important reciprocity becomes evident. Olson has stated it accurately as follows:

> The primary thrust of the *commandment* concerning parents is that authorities are to be honored. The primary thrust of the *statutes and ordinances* that explicate the parents commandment is that authorities are to be worthy of the honor they receive. Leadership brings responsibilities. Deuteronomy thus moves beyond what ethicist Paul Lehmann describes as the false opposition between hierarchy and equality to a model of "reciprocal responsibility" involving both those who hold authority and those who are led. (*Death of Moses*, 78–79; cf. Lehmann, *The Decalogue*)

The analogy between father/mother and king thus raises the issue of parental responsibility to teach the way of the Lord. Seeing the Fifth Commandment from the perspective of the elaboration of the offices presses one toward a focus on the *grounds* for the respect owed to parents, on the reason that one should listen to and obey the parents. If one starts from the commandment itself, the weight of attention is on ways one can and should honor parents. If one starts from the offices that are analogous to the parents and the instruction that is given about them in the Deuteronomic Code, the weight of attention is on the role and responsibility of the father/mother or leader. One moves not only from the parent role to think about the role and authority and responsibility of the king but also in the other direction. The king's responsibility to keep God's instruction close at hand and learn it and live by it (Deut. 17:18–20) becomes a model for parents as much as respect for parents becomes a model for how subjects or citizens should respect the political ruler(s). By associating the family authority with the political authority, we are not only led to understand the authority of both as under God and derivative from God. We are also pushed to think about the nature and character of an authority that commands—and deserves—honor and respect as much as about the sort of honor and respect that is properly rendered to properly manifested authority.

212

The New Testament may provide some reflection of this connection between the respect due to parents and what is due to the authorities of the community, specifically in Romans 13, though it is implicit and not directly indicated in the text. For Romans 13 is Paul's most explicit reference to the Commandments. He cites the second table of the Decalogue, quoting four of the last five commandments as ways that love of one's neighbor is to be demonstrated and carried out. Although this section is not usually connected to the first part of Romans 13, it probably should be. There he gives his instruction about being subject to the authorities, Paul's version, in effect, of what Deuteronomy is about in Deuteronomy 16:18–18:22, though his focus is more on the responsibility of the subjects to respect the authorities than on the leaders to be faithful to their duties as God's representatives. The connection to the Fifth Commandment is not explicit, but placing this section immediately before the citation of the rest of the commandments is suggestive, especially when one notes that Paul concludes his instruction about rendering to the authorities what is due to them with language that is precisely what one finds in the Old Testament versions of the commandment: "respect [*phobon*] to whom respect is due," "honor [*timēn*] to whom honor is due" (Rom. 13:7).

The Human Family and the Family of God

It is especially in the New Testament that the question of how the natural family relates to the community of faith or to the "family of God" arises. Within the Old Testament, the latter is made up of the former, and the reverence of God is reflected in reverence and respect for parents. In the New Testament, the matter is more complicated, and from the beginning of the Gospel story, the call of Jesus creates a radical tension with the command to honor mother and father, especially when that presumes personal attention and caring for them as they grow older. Jesus' own life seems to create the tension—or reflect it—from the beginning. We have already noted that with regard to the account of Jesus remaining behind in the temple to talk with the teachers there. His action causes real anxiety and distress for his parents, while he understands what he is doing as proper attention to his "Father." At the same time, he does not see this as a breach of the Fifth Commandment, for he immediately goes home with his parents and is obedient to them.

213

The episode, however, foreshadows what is to come. Early in his career, tensions with the family are evident in the story of his ministry. Jesus' family is reported as responding to the huge crowds around him who were saying, "He is beside himself," by taking hold of him to get him under control (Mark 3:20–21 RSV). Jesus' relation to his family becomes the basis for an explicit teaching that distinguishes between his natural mother, brother, and sister and those who are his mother, brother, and sister by doing the will of God (3:31–35). At this point Jesus makes a clear distinction between the natural human family and the family of God. Priority is given to the latter. Jesus' teaching in this instance, however, is not a volunteered interpretation of the commandment or of family relations but because he has been pressed by his family through others. Jesus' words are not a rejection of the commandment so much as they are a clarification of relationships and priorities.

That clarification, however, is even sharper in a number of other texts where there seems to be a real tension if not conflict between honoring parents, with all that that involves, and discipleship to Jesus Christ. In the account of the calling of James and John, the narrative reports that "immediately . . . they left their father Zebedee in the boat with the hired men, and followed him" (Mark 1:19–20). The point is sharpened in Matthew's account by no mention of any hired men in the boat (Matt. 4:21–22). The sudden departure of James and John apparently leaves their father Zebedee by himself to do the fishing labors.

More explicitly in his teaching, Jesus identifies discipleship with separation from family and specifically from father and mother. This may be stated in radical and exclusive terms, as in Luke 14:26–27:

> [26]Whoever comes to me and does not hate father and mother, wife and children, brothers and sisters, yes, and even life itself, cannot be my disciple. [27]Whoever does not carry the cross and follow me cannot be my disciple.

The call to "hate father and mother" and other members of the family is a way of saying to turn these all aside and set them aside in order to follow Jesus. The same saying is put in a comparative rather than absolute way in Matthew 10:37–38:

> [37]Whoever loves father or mother more than me is not worthy of me; and whoever loves son or daughter more than me is not worthy of me; [38]and whoever does not take up the cross and follow me is not worthy of me.

The point is clear from both texts. Jesus' words are not an attack on the commandment to honor parents but an insistence that following him means letting go of all the things that matter, or in the somewhat-milder terms of Matthew, setting discipleship above other devotions, caring more about obedience to the Lord, or following after Jesus, than anything else. This is as much the point in the Lukan text, where it is not only family relationships but also life itself that is to be let go. The point is not about abandoning duties that God has commanded but about following God utterly as Jesus' disciple. It is a giving up like that of Abraham in Genesis 12:1: "Go from your country and your kindred and your father's house to the land that I will show you." Give up family relations, life (Luke 14:26), possessions (14:33), everything.

That such discipleship will mean abandoning family is clear from the texts cited. This is a letting go, a leaving behind, of things that hold one back in order to follow Jesus (Mark 10:29–31). It may mean letting go of responsibilities that customarily belong to honoring parents, like giving them a decent burial when they have died (Matt. 19:21–22//Luke 9:57–62). One does not hear so much a word against the commandment as a clarification of what the cost will be for the one who would follow. Jesus first says to the one who is eager to follow, "Foxes have holes, and birds of the air have nests; but the Son of Man has nowhere to lay his head." The follower, however, does not understand what is being demanded, that there is no home or place, only a following after, to the cross. He would qualify his following by tending to other matters, in this case, the burial of his parents. Jesus says there is something higher at stake here: the kingdom of God. The family to which all who follow Jesus belong is the family of those who seek first the kingdom of heaven (Matt. 6:33), who do the will of God (Mark 3:35).

All of these texts point us beyond the proper analogy between the reverence of God and the reverence of parents to the serious distinction between such objects of reverence. There really is a difference between the First Commandment and the Fifth Commandment. Radical love of God takes precedence over all human loyalties. In many ways Jesus' presentation of these hard sayings makes that point as vividly as any of the Old Testament stories. No trust or love or honoring of any human beings and what they represent can be more than the love of God, which is one of the primary Old Testament modes for speaking of discipleship. The specific language of

215

discipleship in both Testaments is the language of "following after." In the Old Testament that is always in reference to the First Commandment, to following after the Lord your God and the prohibition of following after other gods. In the New Testament that language now is directed toward Jesus. Its weight and force are most sharply evident in the sayings in which Jesus speaks of abandonment of all other things that hold us back, including family relations.

There is an obvious resonance and tension between the text in Matthew 8:19–22//Luke 9:57–62 discussed above and 1 Kings 19:19–21, a reflection of the tension that exists within the New Testament itself. After Elijah's flight from Ahab and Jezebel and his divine commissioning at Mount Horeb, he leaves the mountain and finds Elisha:

> [19]So he set out from there, and found Elisha son of Shaphat, who was plowing. There were twelve yoke of oxen ahead of him, and he was with the twelfth. Elijah passed by him and threw his mantle over him. [20]He left the oxen, ran after Elijah, and said, "Let me kiss my father and my mother, and then I will follow you." Then Elijah said to him, "Go back again; for what have I done to you?" [21]He returned from following him, took the yoke of oxen, and slaughtered them; using the equipment from the oxen, he boiled their flesh, and gave it to the people, and they ate. Then he set out and followed Elijah, and became his servant.

One cannot miss the comparison between what happens between Elijah and Elisha and what happens when the would-be follower of Jesus asks him to be allowed to go home and bury his parents. Jesus rejects this desire as a compromise on the cost of discipleship. Elijah accepts Elisha's request to say good-bye to his parents. Furthermore, the passage concludes with the word that when Elisha has finished his good-bye party, he "followed Elijah" and "served him" (19:21, my trans.). He in effect becomes his disciple, which means, as the story makes clear, that he moves into the full service of the Lord as the Lord's prophet.

What does this mean for our understanding of the Fifth Commandment? In one case, there is for the disciple no honoring of parents in the customary fashion; in the other case, there is honoring followed by true discipleship. Do the two texts force a choice upon the reader of Scripture, one who is both keeper of the Commandments and disciple of Jesus Christ? There is no easy answer to

216

that question. One must be careful about assuming that Jesus and the New Testament supersede and trump the Old Testament text. It is better to see in these similar but different texts a reminder of *two different* things about the human situation for those who live in the covenant and as a part of the kingdom. One is the reminder given in Elisha's actions, and Elijah's consent, when called by God to a dangerous discipleship, that we live in a complex network of relationships that shape our life, matter to us, and for which we are responsible. They begin with the first and closest of all human relationships, parent and child. The call of Christ does not mean a light and casual treatment of the human relationships that place claims upon us. In the service of Christ, a person does not forget that she is a child, a parent, a friend or give up such roles. The reminder of the New Testament text is that to live under God's rule and at the call of Christ is an *ultimate* claim, within which all truly good and necessary and penultimate claims are to be set. The relationships that cannot be set aside lightly also cannot stand as barriers of resistance to doing God's will in the world, to living as citizens of a kingdom that is not the same as the present political order, to being members of a household and family that incorporates those nearest and dearest to us but only begins there.

There is no certain way to work out the tension between the claim of the commandment and the claim of Christ. The two texts suggest it is both possible and impossible. What is clear, however, is that we have to live there, right amid the tension between honor of God and honor of parents, where God calls us to hold nothing so dear that it cannot be relinquished for the sake of the kingdom of peace and justice, where discipleship is not an abstract concept but a walk in the world along the dangerous track that Jesus carved out for us as the way of the kingdom—and also where father and mother, son and daughter, husband and wife really do matter in the dearest way, where those relationships are to be honored and nurtured, parents cared for, and children loved and instructed, all in accordance with the command of God, which is in no way superseded.

The final outcome, however, is not Jesus over against the commandment. There are ways in which Jesus' own life and teaching bring the commandment and discipleship together, ways in which he implicitly affirms the commandment and makes it his own. On two occasions, Jesus' act of healing restores a son to life and to the care of his parents. The first is the more obvious instance:

217

> ¹²As he approached the gate of the town, a man who had died was being carried out. He was his mother's only son, and she was a widow; and with her was a large crowd from the town. ¹³When the Lord saw her, he had compassion for her and said to her, "Do not weep." ¹⁴Then he came forward and touched the bier, and the bearers stood still. And he said, "Young man, I say to you, rise!" ¹⁵The dead man sat up and began to speak, and Jesus gave him to his mother. (Luke 7:12–15)

The text is explicit that the woman is a widow and that this is her only son. Jesus' final act is equally explicit: "Jesus gave him to his mother." Now the commandment takes over again. The care and honor due this mother will be hers through the son, whom Jesus has restored to life.

In a more abbreviated way, Luke also reports that when Jesus is confronted by a man whose child is possessed by a demon, he "rebuked the unclean spirit, healed the boy, and gave him back to his father" (Luke 9:42). This is an act of compassion, and like many of the healing acts of Jesus, it arouses astonishment on the part of the onlookers and is a pointer to "the greatness of God" (v. 43). While Jesus' healing may be no more than that, the word about "he gave him back to his father" may be more loaded than first appears, inasmuch as the father had pointedly told Jesus: "He is my only son." There is no reason to believe that healing would not have been offered if there were multiple children, but the incident is comparable to the widow's son in Luke 7, the restoration of an only child who now will be able to care for his parent.

Finally, in the Gospel of John, Jesus' last words before dying are an act of obedience to the commandment to honor father and mother:

> ²⁶When Jesus saw his mother and the disciple whom he loved standing beside her, he said to his mother, "Woman, here is your son." ²⁷Then he said to the disciple, "Here is your mother." And from that hour the disciple took her into his own home. (19:26–27)

The respectful son has now provided for the care of his mother. In the moment of utter self-giving in behalf of the world, the commandments are kept. The dangerous, costly way is not here in conflict with the commandments.

What happens in this incident, that is, what Jesus says and what his disciple does, is an important pointer to a further stage on the trajectory of the Fifth Commandment, the conjoining of the human family and the family of God. That is attested often in the stories of Acts, where again and again whole households are drawn into "the Way" and become disciples of Christ without losing their character as families and as parents and children. The family becomes a part of the family of God. That now can happen in ways other than through the natural family relationships. As natural families are extended in various ways, so the church becomes a kind of extended family. Jesus' care of his mother is carried out by a disciple who takes her into his home and gives her the honor and reverence that her child would give her. The beloved disciple acts in behalf of Jesus. The family of God incorporates human families, and it can act in place of natural families. Disciples of Christ may now render honor and reverence to fathers and mothers who are not their own but who need the care that the commandment expects from all children. They stand in behalf of others and keep the commandment in their behalf. In some instances the incorporation of the family into the family of God is such that the natural family in effect disappears as an important distinction within the family of God. So in 1 Peter, the natural family is taken over by the community, and instead of the command to honor parents, the community learns to honor all (1 Pet. 2:17; Jungbauer, *"Ehre Vater und Mutter,"* 324).

In a different but related way, the honor of parents by son and daughter becomes a wider responsibility for the Christian community as a whole in 1 Timothy 5:3–16, where particular attention is given to widows. The instruction is fairly detailed and has to do with the behavior of widows as well as with the way they are treated. The initial imperative "Honor" (*tima*) occurs elsewhere only in quotation of the commandment. So the Fifth Commandment is surely in view. The focus, however, is specifically on *widows*, that most vulnerable member of the parent genre. While there is much detail, in a nutshell the instruction calls families where the widow has children or grandchildren to carry out the honor, specifically in terms of support (v. 4). Not supporting members of the family is a denial of the faith (v. 8). In the final verse of the section, the point is made that any believer who has a widow as a relative should provide support so that the church should not be burdened with more caring.

At the same time, it is then assumed that if the widow is a "real widow," a widow in real need and at least sixty and without family, then it is the responsibility of the church to provide care and support (v. 16). Practicality, the Fifth Commandment, and the church's function as family come together in this instruction. The natural family and the family of God are blended into a whole without the believer losing a sense of belonging to both families.

Protecting Life

You shall not kill.—Exodus 20:13//Deuteronomy 5:17 RSV

In the common understanding of the Commandments, "killing" is at the top of the list. There is something so basic and elemental about taking a human life that one understands this commandment as fundamental, universal, obvious, given, without debate. That assumption is partly true and partly too simple. Interpreting the commandment is complicated because "killing" is complicated. All one has to do is think about the number of people who will invoke this commandment with vigor against abortion and worry little about capital punishment—or vice versa. The simplicity of the commandment fades quickly as soon as one tries to translate it. Matters become more complex when one tries to relate the prohibition to actual acts of taking life.

The Commandment in Its Context

At nearly each stage of moving through the Commandments, we have raised the question of sequence and order and how the commandments are to be related to each other. Before moving into the specifics of this commandment, which by any analysis has to do with the taking of life, one should ask about its placement. As soon as that question is raised, however, we encounter the instability of the tradition beginning at this point, with the prohibitions that follow upon the command to honor parents. In the two formal presentations of the Decalogue in Exodus 20 and Deuteronomy 5, there is no issue: both put the prohibition against taking life right after the commandment to honor parents. The fact that these accounts are the definitive and formal presentations of the Ten Commandments gives priority to this sequence. Its interpretive meaning is clear and obvious. As one moves out into the realm of life with the neighbor and into the basic guidelines for how one lives with others, the protection of human life is the starting point. Other important matters, such as protection of marriage and property or protection of the neighbor's freedom, logically follow upon the protection of life itself. They are penultimate matters, and the constitutional directives offered in these Commandments give a high value to human life and its preservation by opening up the relation with the neighbor at precisely that point. Therein one may well discern a reasonable and natural sequence. One may thus suggest that any analysis of moral responsibility and good behavior, or of its opposite, reprehensible behavior, "naturally" begins with taking and protecting human life. In nearly all societies the general taboo against taking human life seems to confirm such a law as being natural.

Whether or not that is the case, the point to be made here is that the way of the Lord as characterized definitively by the Ten Commandments gives high priority to the question of preserving or taking life by virtue of its location in the sequence. In a very basic sense the Commandments are all of the same weight. But the logic of how we receive them is also given in the sequence, as has been argued throughout this discussion. Whatever other reasons may suggest the importance and priority of protecting life, the Christian community learns that lesson when this commandment appears first in the list of things not to do to harm your neighbor.

Having made that clear, one must go on to recognize there are other presentations of the Commandments in the second table that reflect different sequences at precisely this point (see the discussion at the beginning of chap. 6 on "Marriage, Sex, and the Neighbor"). The existence of alternate sequences, including two variant orders in the Septuagint (Greek) translation of Exodus 20 and Deuteronomy 5, inhibits an overemphasis on the sequence of these three commandments in the primary texts, though it has been argued cogently that the sequence found in the Hebrew or Masoretic Text of Exodus 20 and Deuteronomy 5 is the most ancient order because it is reflected in the Deuteronomic Code (Kaufman, "Second Table," n. 31).

The Meaning of the Commandment

As indicated above, the most difficult matter in discerning the force and meaning of the Sixth Commandment is at the starting point, its translation. The commandment consists of a negative particle, "do not," and the second-person imperfect of the verb *rāṣaḥ*. The precise meaning of this verb, however, is where the complexities arise. The divided voice of the NRSV translation committee, which split down the middle on the matter, is indicative of the issue and its complexity. Usually the commandment is translated either "You shall not kill" (e.g., KJV, RSV, etc.) or "You shall not murder" (e.g., NRSV, NJPS). More recent translations have tended toward the latter interpretation, recognizing that the verb of the commandment is a more particular and specialized verb, a more technical term in a sense, than others commonly translated in English as "kill" (e.g., *hārag*, as in Exod. 22:23 [24E]) or "put to death" (e.g., *hēmît* from *mût*, as in Deut. 13:10 [Eng. 9]). (Analogously, there are a number of technical terms in English for different forms of killing: e.g., execution, abortion, euthanasia, put to sleep, and the like.) The problem, however, is that the verb does not have a single narrow meaning or usage "to murder." The matter is more complicated, and the force of the verb as it is examined on its trajectory of meaning and usage in the Scriptures broadens toward a wider understanding from the very beginning. Thus the tension between a narrower and a wider interpretation of the verb is an inevitable outcome and the locus of the community's effort to comprehend and obey the commandment. The meaning and force of the commandment, therefore, are discernible only as one looks carefully at its trajectory through Scripture. The commandment itself clearly prohibits some forms of taking life. What those are, how extensive they may be, and the broad function of the commandment to protect life requires an exploration of the movement of the commandment and its playing out in the statutes and stories as well as in the sayings of the prophets and the wise.

223

The Trajectory of the Commandment

Protecting Life in the Statutes and Ordinances of the Legal Codes

Numbers 35

Numbers 35 has to do with how the community should handle the killing of one of its members. It may well be one of the latest literary contexts in which the word *rāṣaḥ* appears; so one cannot argue a historical case from an "original" use to later meanings, at least not from this chapter. Such an argument, however, would be difficult to sustain whatever text one uses as a starting point. In terms of the movement of the Torah, however, Numbers 35 is where the verb *rāṣaḥ* is first encountered after its appearance in the Decalogue. Furthermore, the verb occurs in this chapter far more times than in any other context and with a significant variety of uses, two in particular but others as well. The use of the verb *rāṣaḥ* in this chapter also connects in significant ways with other cases of its use as well as with other language having to do with killing people. As such it leads both forward into Deuteronomy and back into the Book of the Covenant and the Holiness Code of Leviticus. It also demonstrates what the range of the verb becomes in the course of its use in Scripture as it takes up a matter that is central to the usage of the verb elsewhere as well: laws and practices of asylum.

The presentation arises out of setting the boundaries of the promised land and the allotment of that land to the different tribes (Num. 34). The Levites, who do not have a tribal allotment or inheritance because "the LORD is their inheritance" (Deut. 18:2), are to be assigned forty-eight towns, of which six are to be designated cities of refuge or asylum (Num. 35:6; Josh. 21:41). That provision then leads into an extended instruction from the Lord through Moses about how these cities are to function. In the course of that instruction, the central topic is the *rōṣēaḥ* (Num. 35:6), the participial form of the verb under discussion, literally, "the one who *rāṣaḥ*." The verb applies several times to two different figures and elaborates the distinction between them. They are both persons who have killed someone else, but only one of them, the "manslayer," may go to the city of refuge to save his life from the punishment of death. The other *rōṣēaḥ*, who is a murderer, is to be executed. In the course of making these distinctions and spelling

224

them out, one learns much about both the value of human life and what is at the heart of the commandment against killing.

The provision for cities of refuge, whose fundamental purpose was to protect someone who had killed another unintentionally, begins quite naturally—here as well as in other places—with the case of the *rōṣēaḥ* who has killed another person (lit., *makkēh-nepeš* = "one striking a person/life") inadvertently or by error, or as most translations properly say, "unintentionally" (35:11). The verb "to strike" (*nākâ*) and more specifically "to strike the life (*nepeš*)" is one of the most common modes of expression for taking a human life in contexts where the Sixth Commandment is in view either explicitly or implicitly. Here, for example, the term or phrase is used in verses 11, 15, 16, 17, 18, 21 (2x), 30.

In contemporary parlance, the technical term is "manslaughter." The text goes on to spell out what is involved in such prohibited killing, but it does so by contrasting manslaughter with murder, the other form of "striking a person" that is called *rāṣaḥ*. In the course of spelling out the differences between these two forms of action prohibited by the Sixth Commandment, the chapter is instructive about the context and dimensions of life-taking that belong to the continuing consideration of both individual and community as they seek to secure and protect human life from wrongful death.

The first category of *rōṣēaḥ* is described simply at the beginning as "a striker of a person in error (*bišgāgâ*)" (vv. 11, 15, lit.). Such a person is still a *rōṣēaḥ*, a killer, but because the striking and killing was "in error," inadvertent, protection from the serious consequences of killing another person is provided by the city of refuge, to which that *rōṣēaḥ* may flee. It is important, however, to distinguish between such unintentional killing and other forms of killing. The statute goes on to clarify and spell out the distinction. The initial clarification has to do with *procedure* and *means* (vv. 16–18; cf. v. 23). The text separates the inadvertent killer from the one who strikes another person with an "iron object" (v. 16), a "stone of the hand that could cause death" (v. 17, lit.), or a "wooden instrument of the hand that could cause death" (v. 18, lit.). Striking a person with an article such as one of these is to intend harm. These are dangerous weapons, and one may not go after another person with potentially fatal means such as stone, iron, or wooden implements. If death results, it is murder. And this is one of the acts prohibited by the commandment. The statute goes on to distinguish between such

225

actions and the *accidental* but *fatal* use of such an instrument (v. 23). The example mentioned is someone dropping a stone object (perhaps a stone tool), capable of causing death, on another person when they did not see that one and did not intend any harm. This slayer may seek asylum from the avenger of blood. Again, however, *both* situations describe actions for which the verb of the Sixth Commandment is used. There are important distinctions, and they affect outcomes, but *both* acts—intentional and unintentional killing—are prohibited by the commandment. The particular elaboration of the acts in this part of the extended statute calls attention to the issue of *how* the act is carried out and so brings the matter of *weapons*—actual, potential, and accidental weapons—into the frame of reference of the statute. The text repeatedly qualifies the instrument with the phrase "that could cause death" (vv. 17, 18, 23).

The first part of the text opens up the action prohibited by the commandment against killing to take account of the significance of weapons; the second part raises the matter of *motivation* and *intention* (vv. 20–23). The statute gives examples of actions such as pushing someone, throwing something at them, and striking with the hand. But in all these instances the distinction between the murderer and the manslayer is the intention or reason. Three times the issue is whether or not the action was done out of *hatred* (*bĕśînʾâ*, v. 20) or *enmity* (*bĕʾēbâ*, vv. 21, 22; cf. *lōʾ-ʾôyēb*, "not an enemy," v. 23). The elaboration of the commandment with regard to the way it takes effect in the life of the community gives significant attention to whether one has killed another out of hatred or because in some way that one was an enemy. Acting toward another in hostility—hatred or enmity—so that the other person ends up dead is a violation of the commandment. We have already noted that the absence of such a reason for killing does not mean that the act of killing is removed from the frame of reference of the commandment. On the contrary, whether the act was inadvertent, without harm being intended, or whether it was out of hatred and enmity, it describes one who is a *rōṣēaḥ*. In thinking about what is in view in the prohibition of the commandment, however, the motivation is lifted up as an indicator of the seriousness of the offense. The question of hatred of the neighbor as a precipitating factor in deadly violence against that person is underscored.

226   Alongside this, another factor is identified as distinguishing between the two kinds of *rāṣaḥ* or killing. It is the question of *premeditation* or, as is the case in the text before us, lying in wait (*biṣdiyyâ*

vv. 20, 22), or killing intentionally. Purposeful planning to kill another person heightens the act of killing and leads the community to take account of what precipitated this forbidden act of violence. Again, the matter of intentionality does not determine whether an act is "killing" (*rāṣaḥ*), but it significantly affects the outcome and once again introduces a factor into the community's thought and evaluation about how to deal with the fact of killing when it takes place in its midst. As such, it provides another aspect of the act of killing that belongs to understanding what is at stake in the commandment.

The fundamental purpose of Numbers 35 is to provide for places of asylum for those who have killed another person accidentally. Such provision, developed at length here but represented elsewhere several times, is by its very nature a testimony to the seriousness of taking a life, the presumption being that whoever does so will suffer the most severe punishment—blood revenge by a member of the slain person's family—even if the killing was not intentional, unless provision is made. The seriousness of taking life accidentally is further underscored in this text by the provision that the manslayer (*rōṣēaḥ*) cannot leave the city of refuge until the death of the high priest. Killing a person was an act of such extraordinary weight that it could not be reconciled through the sacrifice of an animal. In this instance the death of the high priest serves as a death for sins (Hossfeld, "*Du sollst nicht töten!*" 61).

Taking a human life is such a large matter that even the "legitimate" taking of life, the *legal execution* of either a manslayer who has left the city of refuge (v. 27) or a murderer (v. 30), is spoken of in this context with the verb *rāṣaḥ*. At this point, therefore, a serious tension is evident in the text, one that has implications for comprehending the trajectory of the commandment. Not only is the verb *rāṣaḥ* used in reference to unintentional or accidental killing of another as well as to murder; it is also used with reference to the act of execution. In its usage of the verb *rāṣaḥ*, therefore, the prohibition of the commandment brings into its range the killing of another person in various contexts and ways, not simply the act of murder. Both *accidental* and *legal* forms of killing can be and are described by *the same verb* the Decalogue uses to prohibit killing another person. The prohibition against killing thus stretches to incorporate both what would seem to be a killing that is impossible to prohibit—causing accidental death—as well as at least one form of killing that is permitted and legal—execution.

227

The Book of the Covenant: Exodus 20:22–23:19

As others have observed, the two large concerns of the statutes in the Book of the Covenant are life and property, the elaboration of the Sixth and Eighth Commandments (e.g. Crüsemann, *Torah*, 145–46). The most immediate contextual connection of the Sixth Commandment—and possibly the earliest form of the commandment—is found in the Book of the Covenant in Exodus 21:12–14: "Whoever strikes a person mortally shall be put to death" (v. 12). Connection to the Sixth Commandment is found not only in the topic, killing a person, but also in the use of terminology similar to what is found in Numbers 35, as well as a structure of thought and argument that is much briefer and simpler but analogous to the way in which the statute concerning the cities of refuge in Numbers 35 is developed.

The technical term of the commandment, *rāṣaḥ*, is not used in Exodus 21:12. Instead, one finds the language that occurs repeatedly in Numbers 35: "one striking a person" (*nākâ*; Num. 35:11, 15, 16, 17, 18, 21 [2x], 30). As also in Numbers 35, the phrase here indicates that death results from the striking. This is clearly an example of what the commandment prohibits and against which it seeks to guard. That such is the case is indicated further by the sentence of death upon one who so strikes another.

Then, in a manner similar to what one encounters in more detail in Numbers 35, a distinction is made between striking that was not intentional or premeditated (*ṣādâ*, cf. Num. 35:20, 22; 1 Sam. 24:11) but happened because God allowed or caused it to happen ("an act of God," Exod. 21:13), and the act of one who moves presumptuously or willfully against his neighbor in order to kill him and does so with deceit and treachery (Exod. 21:14). (The expression "act of God," which has carried over into contemporary use, should not be overinterpreted theologically and probably has to do with losing control, not knowing what one is doing and acting as driven by some outside force [Houtman, *Exodus*, 145–46].) The statute in Numbers 35 goes into more detail, but the law in Exodus 21:12–14 serves the same purpose. Like Numbers 35, it describes the kind of action that evokes the full punishment. Verse 14 heaps up language to indicate that harm, more specifically, death, was intended, that planning, deceit, and intentionality were clearly involved. And while there is no provision for setting up cities of

228

refuge, there is a presumption of the possibility of asylum for one who has struck and killed another, in this instance, fleeing to the altar of the Lord and remaining there (21:13). As in Numbers 35, the one who intended to kill is not allowed such safety but may be removed and executed.

Again, there is no language of the Sixth Commandment in this statute, but there is a concern for developing a way of protecting life and dealing with the situation when life is taken. The commandment seeks to ward off such revengeful killing. The statutes provide a way for dealing with the situation when the commandment has been violated. As such, they give us some indication of what it is the commandment seeks to keep from happening.

While the rest of the statutes in the Book of the Covenant do not deal directly with killing, there are places in these ordinances where the trajectory of the Sixth Commandment is in view. Some of them deal with cases where a person is physically harmed by another but death does not result. For example, one statute regulates compensation for a situation where two persons quarrel and one "strikes" the other with a stone or fist, but the person does not die (Exod. 21:18–19). This is clearly a further development of the statute in verses 12–14 having to do with killing. There is an outflow of the earlier statute as the legislation now regulates what happens when physical harm is done but without killing. Thus the trajectory of the commandment continues as the question of *harming one's neighbor in any way* comes into consideration. There is a difference, however, in the seriousness of taking human life as distinct from physical but not life-destroying assault. The latter does not evoke the death penalty. Rather, there is compensation to the injured party, in this case, covering the time off because of the injury (the victim's forced *šabbat*, v. 19) and covering costs of healing and recovery.

Other cases have to do with striking another or fighting with another and resultant injury (21:20–21, 22–25). They are handled in similar ways but with particular attention to the type of person involved, the first having to do with an owner harming his slave and the second with a conflict among males that results in harm to a pregnant woman so that she has a miscarriage. In both these cases, a lesser member of the community is protected, yet in the context of presuming that lesser status. In the case of the slave, if death does not result, nothing is done because the slave is the property (*kesep*, "money") of

229

the owner. If, however, death does result, there is a strong word about punishment. That word is that the slave "must surely be avenged" (v. 20, my trans.). What this actually means is a matter of debate. Brevard Childs has pointed out that the case is not simply a case of manslaughter, or it would come under the earlier statute having to do with that. He suggests that "the formula 'he will be punished' is strikingly vague and cannot be identified with the death penalty *per se*" (Childs, *Exodus*, 471). At the same time, one must note that the formula, while vague, is a very strong one. Thus the tradition at an early stage and frequently, particularly in the Jewish interpretation of this statute, has argued that the death penalty is in view. The Samaritan Pentateuch, for example, substitutes the expression "put to death" for the unusual formula of punishment that is in the text of verse 20, and many Jewish interpreters from the earliest stages till the present have tended to see here an indirect reference to the death penalty (Childs, *Exodus*, 471). While the difference from the customary formula for the death penalty—"He shall be put to death"—argues against interpreting this as indicating capital punishment, the significance of taking the life, even of a slave, is underscored with the emphatic formula of the text: "He shall surely be avenged." The slave who is property is also a human being. Thus the protection of life is given to the slave as well as to the free Israelite.

It is less clear what happens in the case of the miscarriage (vv. 22–25), but a fine is indicated if the injury is confined to the loss of the baby (v. 22). If there is further damage, however, and the further damage is not specified, then there is a larger penalty, indicated here by the talionic formula life for life, eye for eye, tooth for tooth, and so forth (vv. 23–25; see below, "Lex Talionis").

In what follows, there are other cases presented for handling death and bodily injury: loss of eye or tooth of a slave (and presumably other injuries, as in vv. 24–25), death of a person by being gored, and injury to one of the domestic work animals that results in the death of the animal. Presumably these are significant but also exemplary. Thus the Book of the Covenant is not a complete case book of Israelite law and so may be read as an indication of how one goes about different cases. At the same time, the particular instances that are taken up are crucial examples of physical injury and death that need to be specified even as they are indicative of how one might go about dealing with comparable but variant instances of injury and death.

230

A final concern for the protection of life is found at the beginning of the statutes having to do with protecting property in Exodus 22:1–2a. There it is indicated that if a thief is "struck down" (*hukkâ*) in the nighttime, the one who struck him down does not bring bloodguilt upon himself. If the sun had come up, however, then guilt would be upon the one who struck down the thief. As the following comment by Childs indicates, the lives of both owner and thief are being protected by this statute:

> The verses focus attention on the more important problem relating to theft, namely, the loss of life through a resultant act of violence. The law seeks to guard the lives of both parties involved. The householder is exonerated if he kills the intruder at night in the defense of his home. Conversely, the life of the thief is also protected by the law. If he is killed in plain daylight, then the slayer is held responsible for the homicide and is vulnerable to blood vengeance (Num. 35:27; Deut. 19:10). . . . To my knowledge no other law code seems to have a similar concern for the life of the thief! (*Exodus*, 474)

Deuteronomy 19:1–22:8

The section of the Deuteronomic Code that reflects aspects and situations arising out of the commandment protecting life is generally regarded as beginning at 19:1 and concluding at 22:8. All of the statutes in this part of the Deuteronomic Code, with the exception of Deuteronomy 22:8, have to do with matters of life and death or with the protection of life (so Olson, *Death of Moses*, 88–99; Kaufman, "Structure," 134–37; for detailed discussion, see Braulik, "Sequence," 328). This is the longest section of statutes in Deuteronomy 12–26 elaborating a particular commandment. With this material it is appropriate to include Deuteronomy 4:41–43 and Joshua 20:1–9, texts that, like Deuteronomy 19:1–13, deal with the cities of refuge and the provision for asylum.

The verb *rāṣaḥ* does occur outside this section of the Code, in Deuteronomy 22:26, but only by way of analogy between a man seizing an engaged girl and having sex with her and a man attacking and killing (*rāṣaḥ*) another person. It is not a further elaboration of the killing commandment. One notes, however, that the case to which the act of killing is analogous does involve an assault against a weaker member of the community, which seems to be a concern

231

identifiable on the trajectory of the Sixth Commandment, already uncovered in the statutes requiring strong punishment for someone who kills his slave.

Deuteronomy 19:1–21. The focus of these verses is on the protection of innocent life against various endangerments. They deal with cases that either lead to death (19:1–10, 14) or can be punished by death (19:11–13, 15, 16–21). So they move on a kind of continuum between the goal "that he may live (or remain alive)" (19:4, 5) and the requirement of "life for life" (19:21). The concern for protecting innocent life is immediately the focus of attention in the statutes having to do with providing cities of refuge for the one who has accidentally killed "his neighbor" without "hating" him (vv. 1–10 RSV). The word "neighbor" is regularly used for the one who is victim of the killing whether intentional or not (e.g., Deut. 19:4, 5 [2x], 11, 14 RSV) along with "brother" (vv. 18, 19 RSV) and "man/individual" (v. 15 RSV). The primary move of the statutes is to identify the victim as one who is in specific relationship with the one who has killed either as "neighbor" or "brother."

As in Numbers 35 and Exodus 21, there is further explicit instruction that refuge is not possible for one who has murdered, someone who has killed out of "hatred" (v. 11, *śōnēʾ*; cf. vv. 4, 6b; Deut. 4:42) or has lain in wait (v. 11). Four times in these statutes the question of whether or not the person "hated" or was at enmity with the one attacked is a crucial issue in the concern for protecting life and for dealing with those who take life. That is, attitude toward the neighbor/other is an important consideration in valuing and caring for human life.

In distinction from both the statute in Exodus 21:12–14 and Numbers 35, Deuteronomy 19:1–13 places the protection of the manslayer first (vv. 1–10). Only after extensively instructing about the cities to protect such a one does the chapter go on to refer to the murderer who is not to be protected. In this instance the primary concern is thus for the protection of life and secondarily for the punishment of the murderer. The execution of the murderer is pushed into the background. That, however, must be tended to in order to purge the community of the guilt of "innocent blood" having been shed.

Something of a surprise in the midst of these statutes clearly having to do with taking life is the presence in Deuteronomy 19:14 of the statute prohibiting moving a neighbor's landmark. The connection to the Sixth Commandment is indirect but quite real and important. There are at least two ways that the statute comes up in this context. The primary one is the degree to which boundary violation was (and is) a major cause of disputes between both individuals and communities and thus a provocation of both war and murder. Care in following this statute is an important form of preventing homicide (Kaufman, "Structure," 137). In addition to that, however, it is likely that inability to prevent such disputes or efforts to encroach on the allotted property of a neighbor will have special impact on the socially weaker members of the territory and thus endanger human life and the community's well-being (Braulik, *Die Gesetze*, 64). The crime being prohibited is clearly a form of theft, but it is one that undercuts human existence in the broadest sense because the allotted land is the primary provision for life. Thus a statute connected to another commandment, the prohibition of stealing, is brought into the frame of reference of the prohibition against killing, and the reader is led to reflect on the connection and the way in which once again the Commandments are not simply distinct rules but actually highly interconnected modes of living that interact constantly with one another, as the stories of Uriah (2 Sam. 11–12) and Naboth (1 Kgs. 21), among others, remind us.

There follows then a statute that seems—and is—a development of another commandment than the Sixth (19:15–20). It is a provision about bearing witness against a person in a trial. Once again, however, the issue is not confined to a single commandment. For the provision set forth here has as its major aim the prevention of *judicial murder* (see chap. 8, "Telling the Truth"). Several features of the statute are worth noting:

a. While false witness comes into the discussion, it begins with a provision that one may not be convicted of any crime on the basis of one witness alone. That is a clear recognition of the possibility of human error and the resultant death of an innocent person because of insufficient or erroneous testimony. The statute thus lifts up the significance of court testimony as a life-and-death matter. The history of legal activity confirms the fact that persons are harmed and often killed as a result of testimony by others. This early statute sets the matter at the heart of the life of the community of faith and shows that the commandment against killing is directly connected to what goes on in the courtroom.

b. The statute carries the matter further by recognizing the danger to human life that is possible when a malicious witness—literally,

233

"a witness of violence"—comes forward in a dispute. This is what the statutes we have considered earlier have in mind by intentional and premeditated harm. The witness wills to do violence to another and may cause the death of the one against whom the malicious testimony is brought. So the harm against another may be not only a *physical blow*; it may also be a *word* that does violence to a neighbor. Thus the statute provides for a careful judicial consideration. There are no guarantees, but the law recognizes the need for adjudication, for "thorough inquiry" into the matter (v. 18). Once again the significance of court testimony and procedure for the protection of life and the possibility of such procedures either doing harm or protecting from harm are lifted up.

c. One notes further that the legal protection in view is broadened from the earlier form of this statute in 17:6, where the provision of sufficient witnesses is only in an instance of capital crime and the possibility of the death penalty. The connection to that statute is important for it confirms that there is inherent in the concern for sufficient and truthful witnesses the endangerment of human life. Now, however, the statute has to do with *any offense*. The possibility of harm may happen at many levels, and the statute in 19:15–20 demonstrates once again that the trajectory of the Sixth Commandment does not work narrowly only with regard to the act of killing but has to do, as John Calvin and many others have observed, with many forms of bringing harm to the life of a neighbor (*Institutes* 2.8.9).

d. The connection of this concern for proper witness with the Sixth Commandment is further indicated by the fact that this is the last of the three occasions of the talionic formula "life for life," "eye for eye," and so on. In the other two instances—Exodus 21:23–25 and Leviticus 24:19–20—that formula is directly connected to statutes or narratives where the prohibition against killing is in view. So also here, the lex talionis comes to play when securing the neighbor's life from being endangered is the concern of the statute.

Deuteronomy 20:1–20. The statutes in this chapter join with the immediately preceding statute (19:15–20) in taking the Decalogue's concern for protection of life into the sphere of "those institutions—war and criminal justice—that constitute the only legitimate procedures for taking a human life" (Kaufman, "Structure," 135). It is too simple, as we have seen, to presume that the concern of the commandment is only for protection of life from high-handed, intentional, premeditated killing and that war is not in view as far as the commandment is concerned. The trajectory of the commandment does not lead immediately into a prohibition against war. On the contrary, it includes some explicit provisions for war in this chapter. The concern for endangerment of life and wrong killing in war, however, comes very much to the fore in these statutes. In verses 1–9 the statute focuses on exemption from military service. Somewhat surprisingly, there are several categories of exemption, all of which seek to prevent endangering the life of someone whose involvement in a venture having to do with human flourishing has not been fulfilled. The cases mentioned are building a new house but not having dedicated it, planting a crop but not having seen its produce, and paying a bride price or getting engaged but not yet having married. The rationale is set precisely around the endangerment of life. In all these cases, the soldier is to go home "or he might die in battle and another [enjoy the results]." The protection of life is brought specifically into the way in which a people engages in war, in this instance to guard against killing that cuts life short of its explicit promise. While that is true of any killing, there is an emphasis on this concern for fulfillment of life and its endangerment in war.

A further exemption is mentioned, but one of a different sort (v. 8). It involves sending home anyone who is afraid and disheartened. The rationale is once again explicit and has to do with protection of life. The fearful soldier may instill fear in his comrades, and then all will be in danger.

There follow, then, specific rules for the conduct of war centering on the effort to protect life if at all possible in the case of conflict among peoples. Attack and taking life cannot happen, even in the case of hostilities among nations, without first seeking peaceful settlement. Before one may besiege or attack another group, town, or city, one must thus offer terms of peace (vv. 10–11). War is a last resort, and if there is an acceptance of the terms for peace, then there must be no killing. Contemporary moral reflection properly will raise questions about any solution of war issues that leaves the victor able to turn captured peoples into slave labor (v. 11), but that should not diminish the way in which the trajectory of the commandment against killing comes directly to play in matters of war and, within the Jewish and Christian tradition, opens up the possibility of such things as just-war theory, the Geneva Conventions limiting the barbarity of war, and the like. The city that resists and

235

engages in battle will be subject to the common war rules, and there will be taking of life. Even there, however, concern for protection of life is central in that only those who themselves engage directly in war are vulnerable to loss of life, that is, the males. Women, children, and cattle are part of the booty of war, as in the case of those cities or towns that accept peace terms. They may not be killed.

The most difficult part of these war statutes to bring into the purview of the Sixth Commandment is the section in verses 15–18 prescribing the ḥērem, or ban, in the case of all the towns or cities of the peoples immediately around Israel. The text is explicit in calling for the annihilation or utter destruction of every living being (the ḥērem). The text is explicit also about both who is to be treated in this way—the Hittites, Amorites, Canaanites, Perizzites, Hivites, and Jebusites—and the reason: "that they may not teach you to do all the abhorrent things that they do for their gods, and you thus sin against the LORD your God" (v. 18). So while the result is the same, killing one's enemies/neighbors, something more is going on in this instance. The statute brings the first commandment into view by indicating that all of this mass killing has to do with complete obedience and loyalty to the Lord of Israel and the serious danger of eroding that allegiance by the encounter with the other nations (cf. Deut. 7:1–6).

One may not slide over this divine command to slaughter towns and cities and their inhabitants on the grounds of religious intolerance. There are few aspects of the Old Testament that are more troubling theologically and in terms of the claim and authority of the Old Testament than these verses and others like them. In this instance, we will not try to suggest a way of removing these trouble spots. It is not likely to be very successful, and others have addressed this issue from various angles (e.g., Olson, *Death of Moses*, 94–95; Miller, "God the Warrior"). Whatever critique is made will probably come from outside the text: attention to other texts that provide implicit critique, such as Jesus' words about loving your enemy; the impact of the Prologue to the Commandments, which serves to identify the Lord of Israel as the one who liberates from oppression, a critical profile that stands in some tension with the one who commands the destruction of whole peoples; continuing theological and biblical reflection on "Who is my neighbor?" leading to the opening of that question toward a more inclusive rather than exclusive definition; and so forth (for further discussion, see Miller, *The God You Have*, 16–18).

236

What is important in this instance, however, is to observe two aspects of these statutes that have been lifted up by Norbert Lohfink in his definitive study of the *ḥērem* (Lohfink, "*ḥāram*," 197). There he calls attention to the fact that in Deuteronomy and the Deuteronomistic History the destruction of the Canaanites by the Israelites in their occupation of the land happened only upon the refusal of the inhabitants to accept terms of peace. This is seen first in Deuteronomy 2:26–36, where Moses sends messengers to Sihon, king of the Amorites—one of the nearby peoples referred to in 20:17—to offer "terms of peace" (*dibrê šālôm*; cf. Num. 21:21–22). It is only after they have refused to accept those terms that the Israelites move against Sihon and the Amorites and "utterly destroy" (*ḥērem*) them. (One notes, of course, that the resistance on the part of Sihon is because the Lord has hardened his heart [Deut. 2:30], so a large theological issue still remains, one that is very much tied to Deuteronomic theology and perhaps to the circumstances in which the book came to life. One should also observe that in the Numbers account, there is no reference to the Lord hardening the heart of Sihon. Hardening the heart of the opposition is a particular Deuteronomic motif that resides in its firm claim that all that happens is by the divine command or will. [In this regard, see Miller, *Deuteronomy,* 36–42; and "Faith and Ideology."].) So also in the summary description of the entire occupation (Josh. 11:16–23), we hear, "There was not a town that made peace (*hišlîmâ*) with the Israelites, except the Hivites, the inhabitants of Gibeon . . ." (v. 19). Joshua 9 recounts the treaty of peace with the Gibeonites, one of the Hivite cities, which in turn was one of the nearby peoples who were subject to the ban as described in Deuteronomy 20:17.

The implication of all this is, as Lohfink has indicated, "Israel's obligation to offer peaceful terms of surrender to the enemy before a war (vv. 10f.) holds not only for the cities that are 'very far' (v. 15), but also for the cities that Yahweh has designated as Israel's inheritance (v. 16). The other form of war, namely *ḥrm* (v. 16f.), is to be practiced only upon rejection of terms" ("*ḥāram*," 197). The usual interpretation of this passage is that the cities near at hand are to be eliminated and everyone killed without regard to peaceful settlement. It is sometimes suggested that Joshua's treaty with the Gibeonites was a violation of the Deuteronomic law. In fact, the concern for peaceful settlement in war seems to have been comprehensive in the Deuteronomic statutes. The protection of life is not partial but comprehensive. It receives a particular underscoring as these statutes of war conclude with the word that the Israelites are not to cut down the trees in a cavalier way when they are engaged in military activities (vv. 19–20). The text provides its own emphasis on the point being made: "Are trees in the field human beings that they should come under siege from you?" (v. 19). Indiscriminate destruction even of nature is not to be allowed. The natural world is brought into the purview of the commandment against killing, and the limit on what might be acceptable destruction or the safeguarding of life of all sorts is at the heart of the Sixth Commandment in its trajectory through the Deuteronomic Code.

One should take note of Lohfink's further point with regard to the statute that permits the utter destruction of the cities and towns that are nearby:

> The war law Dt. 20:10–18 also limits the ḥērem strictly to the situation of the occupation and the inhabitants of the promised land. For later periods and other peoples, different rules apply. In principle, then, the very law that appears to demand the ḥērem in fact forbids it in the case of those to whom the law is actually addressed (Josiah and his contemporaries). ("ḥāram," 197)

The particularity and situational character of the statutes of the Torah is nowhere more apparent than in these statutes on war. They are informative and help us comprehend the things that come into play, the contexts and situations, the possibilities and issues that are involved in working out the Decalogue's command in all sorts of ways. They are instructional but not absolute. They belong to particular times and places. In later times and new contexts, the community takes up the commandment afresh, listening to what it has learned from its application along the trajectory and learning from that how to live by the commandment in a later time.

Deuteronomy 21:1–23. While it may not be apparent from a surface reading, the statutes of this chapter also serve to specify and illustrate the force of the prohibition against killing. As a whole they are also concerned with protecting life, though some particularities arise out of tangential but important issues evoked by the concern for protecting life. The initial statute, Deuteronomy 21:1–9, makes it clear that matters of life and death are still to the fore in the Deuteronomic Code at this point. The case has to do with when someone has been struck and death results (v. 1), the circumstance that is at hand in many of the particular statutes on the trajectory of the Sixth Commandment, as we have seen. In this instance, the concern is for how the community handles the discovery of a slain person when it does not know who is responsible. The statute is clearly a variation on the kinds of cases that are dealt with in the asylum statutes. The difference, and the problem, is the fact that one does not know who has killed the victim (whether intentionally or not). The concern of the statute remains the same. It is to deal with the danger of innocent blood having been shed (vv. 8–9) when somebody has been killed. The seriousness of such an act, as has already been indicated by the laws setting up the cities of refuge, is reflected in the fact that the whole community is in danger of being under bloodguilt, of being suspect in the unresolved case.

Killing a person thus has wide ramifications. Innocent blood that is shed and not dealt with justly, even if because of lack of knowledge or evidence, cannot be dismissed or treated lightly. It must be accounted for in some way. Thus a communal process is set up that is religious, judicial, and political in character. It involves elders and judges (v. 2), political leaders of the community, as well as the priests, who have a judicial function here and elsewhere in Deuteronomy (v. 5; cf. 17:8–13), all functioning to do "what is right in the eyes of the LORD" (21:9). The accounting has four elements: a rational process by the elders and judges to determine the closest town to the body and thus the most likely source of the crime; a complex ritual of atonement (vv. 3–6); a formal testimony by the community that it had nothing to do with this killing (v. 7); and a prayer for divine absolution rather than punishment because, in violation of the divine command that protects life, life has been wrongly taken (v. 8). While the locus of the complex process is the nearest town, the absolution is of the whole community, identified twice as "your people Israel" (v. 8). The unresolved killing is not a local matter. It is seen as a responsibility for the whole people, and absolution is a common responsibility and a common good.

Note that the testimony is before the only court that can operate in this instance, the divine court. When someone has been killed and the judicial system cannot account for or handle it, the matter cannot be dropped. The statute, therefore, reminds the reader and the community that obedience to the Lord's instruction about how one treats the neighbor is always a matter that in some fashion is before God and not simply a responsibility of the human

239

justice system. On the human plane the legal institutions serve to undergird the covenantal structure set by the Lord of Israel for its life.

Deuteronomy 21:10–21, while seeming to move into a realm other than the concern for life, is in fact an extension of the war laws, as is indicated immediately at the beginning of the statute: "When you go out to war against your enemies . . ." (on this group of laws, see Pressler, *View of Women*, 9–20). The first statute in this section (vv. 10–14) has to do with taking a woman from among the enemy captives as one's wife. From a contemporary perspective, the very subject matter is dubious. In its time and context, however, this particular development and specification of the Sixth Commandment is an important element in humanizing the "rules" of war. It also makes one aware of the range of concern that is in view when one is dealing with the practices of war. Here, there is an insistence on the worth of the human "booty." One may not treat a human life lightly, even when taken as a result of war. The captive woman is still valued and protected. She is not a sexual toy to be used in any way by the besieger of the city, though it is clear that she has been violated, coerced into sexual intercourse ("dishonored," v. 14 NRSV). The woman is to be cared for and brought into the family. If the capturer no longer desires (*ḥāpaṣ*, v. 14) the captured woman, he may not simply dismiss her or treat her cavalierly. Indeed, he *must* set her free and may not sell her as a slave.

The treatment of a captive wife, in all likelihood a second wife, opens up the question of how one handles the situation when there is more than one wife (vv. 15–17). Polygamy may produce a variety of issues, but there is a large and obvious one dealt with here. It is the matter of inheritance. Once again the statutes are aimed at making sure an injustice is not done with regard to provision for the next generation in the family when a husband cares more about one wife than about another. The inheritance right of the firstborn may not be overturned by favoritism. With this statute one is far from the question of killing but confronts one of the many ramifications that may flow out of the consequences of war. In taking up some of those ramifications, the Deuteronomic Code points in other directions as well, in this case marriage and family responsibilities. The context—the trajectory of the Sixth Commandment in the Deuteronomic Code—sees the issue arising out of the practices of war. It may surely come into communal life in other ways than as an

240

outcome of war. The elaboration and particularizing of the Sixth Commandment, therefore, continues to cast a wide net.

The previous statute has opened up the question of how parents handle their children. That is picked up in Deuteronomy 21:18–21, which treats the most anguished case possible: the continuously rebellious son. The statute has to do with parent-child relationships and so connects with the command to honor father and mother (see chap. 4). It also belongs, however, to the sphere of the Sixth Commandment and the protection of life. That is evident in several ways. The passage is followed by a statute that deals directly and entirely with capital punishment and its procedures. And it is connected to the preceding statutes by word and content associations around "woman/wife," "father/mother," and "son." Further in this statute is, however, a more direct connection to the concern for protecting. In distinction from the statute in the Book of the Covenant that calls for the execution of anyone who either strikes or curses one's mother or father (Exod. 21:15, 17), the Deuteronomic statute does not allow a onetime offense or act to be sufficient grounds for execution, legal killing. Only prolonged and total behavior of disobedience, rebellion, gluttony, and drunkenness—obviously a perverse and extensive rejection of parental guidance and with implicit wide-ranging effects—can be the grounds for execution. Once more, moral reaction to parents bringing about the execution of a son should not lead one to miss the point here. The statute is aimed as much at protecting life as punishing rebellious children. That is why it is in this section of the Deuteronomic Code rather than in Deuteronomy 16:18–18:22, which is where the trajectory of the commandment to honor parents is developed most (see the discussion of this statute in chap. 4, on the Fifth Commandment). A careful process in which both father and mother go before the elders of the community and together report on the extended and prolonged actions of their child is necessary before invoking capital punishment. The possibility of executing a son for misbehavior is thereby significantly limited and restricted. The statute thus sets a further guideline on the legal killing that takes place in capital punishment and thereby serves to protect human life from its easy destruction.

Finally, the large concern for killing and the immediate focus on capital punishment leads into the final statute in this chapter (21:22–23), which requires the community to make sure that the body of an executed criminal is not allowed to hang on the tree or

241

gallows over night. Once more the presence of a body, of someone who has been killed, even legally, is a potential danger to the land and the community.

Deuteronomy 22:1–8. This series of statutes begins a transition into the sections of the Deuteronomic Code that represent the elaboration and specification of the prohibitions against adultery (v. 5) and stealing (vv. 1–4). Verses 1–4 come into the trajectory of the prohibition against killing as an extension into the animal world of the concern for protecting life. As these verses relate to the prohibition against stealing, they reflect the positive side of the prohibition: protecting the property of the neighbor, not simply refraining from stealing it. In the context of the Sixth Commandment, however, the concern is for the endangered animal, which is either lost or fallen and so is to be helped. The statutes are emphatic in the repeated insistence: "You may not ignore/withhold your help" (vv. 1, 3b, 4). So also in the statute prohibiting taking the mother bird together with her young as food, both the animal and the community are in view. As its use in Genesis 32:12 (10E) and Hosea 10:14 makes clear, the expression "mother on the young" (v. 6) clearly means the mother together with the young and so the complete annihilation of the family. That is why the statute is in the trajectory of the Sixth Commandment and not the Fifth. It deals not with generational care but with inappropriate and unwarranted destruction of living things, even for the necessities of human life. While one may kill animals for food, the "large-scale killing of any species can lead to a serious diminution in its numbers and to eventual extinction" (Craigie, *Deuteronomy*, 289).

Finally, the statute requiring construction of a parapet for one's roof to avoid the danger of someone falling off and being killed is a clear example of a positive development of the prohibition against killing. The single purpose of the statute is the protection of human life, though that is expressed with the motive of the danger of bringing bloodguilt on one's household for having caused a death by negligence.

Leviticus 24:10–23

242　We have already brought this narrative-legal text into our discussion with regard to its relevance for thinking about the commandment forbidding the misuse of the name of God. In that context, it is the offense, belittling the name of God, that is the connection to the Commandments. The second part of this narrative, however, also takes us into the realm of the prohibition against killing and its corollary, protection against harm. The determination of punishment in this instance is provided by a declaration from the Lord (v. 12). When given, that declaration not only prescribes the death penalty for the blasphemer; it also goes on to a more generalized instruction about appropriate punishment, especially but not only for acts of killing. "The deed in and of itself—or the insulting of the deity—is not at all the center of attention now; rather it is the harm done to a person" (Gerstenberger, *Leviticus*, 366).

The text reads:

> [15]And speak to the people of Israel, saying: Anyone who curses God shall bear the sin. [16]One who blasphemes the name of the LORD shall be put to death; the whole congregation shall stone the blasphemer. Aliens as well as citizens, when they blaspheme the Name, shall be put to death. [17]Anyone who kills a human being shall be put to death. [18]Anyone who kills an animal shall make restitution for it, life for life. [19]Anyone who maims another shall suffer the same injury in return: [20]fracture for fracture, eye for eye, tooth for tooth; the injury inflicted is the injury to be suffered. [21]One who kills an animal shall make restitution for it; but one who kills a human being shall be put to death. [22]You shall have one law for the alien and for the citizen: for I am the LORD your God. (Lev. 24:15–22)

That the Sixth Commandment underlies this is surely clear. While the technical language *rāṣaḥ* does not occur, the frequently used substitute for that word, "one who strikes" (*makkēh*), regularly translated as "kills," is used in both verses 17 and 21. The concern of the statute here is about punishment, more specifically, punishment when a person or an animal has been killed, and beyond that, when a person has been physically harmed in some fashion, indicated here as often elsewhere by reference to eye, tooth, and so forth. Distinctions are made in that each case requires a different punishment.

The aim of the whole, however, is to recognize by judicial sentence the concern of the community for preserving life, or better, the value of life as indicated by what happens when it is taken. The starting point is the killing of a human being, the outcome of

243

which is *execution*. From that, the text goes on to speak about killing an animal, requiring "life for life" in this instance: restitution
by the "killer" providing a live animal in compensation for the one
he killed. Whether it is the expression "life for life" or the implicit
movement from killing a person to harming them physically, the
text goes on to deal with injury and, in accordance with what has
already been said, requires appropriate compensation, something
comparable to the injury done: "fracture for fracture, eye for eye,
tooth for tooth; the injury inflicted is the injury to be suffered" (v.
20). The statute concludes with an explicit insistence that it applies
equally to stranger/resident alien and to a permanent citizen, an
important underscoring of the extent of the implicit definition of
one's "neighbor." In matters of justice, lines of distinction are not
to be drawn.

Lex Talionis in the Legal Codes (Exod. 21:23–25; Lev. 24:17–21; Deut. 19:21)

Though the statute at the end of the narrative of the blasphemer in
Leviticus 24 essentially underscores what has already been demonstrated from other legal texts, it is the last text under consideration
here that specifically brings the lex talionis—"life for life," "eye for
eye," and so forth—into the picture. It is not without significance
that, while there are variations of the talionic formula elsewhere
(e.g., 1 Kgs. 20:39; 2 Kgs. 10:24; cf. Num. 35:33; Deut. 25:11–12),
the three primary talionic formulations as a principle of judicial punishment occur on the trajectory of the Sixth Commandment. The
provision for justice that is inherent in the talionic principle begins
with the valuing and protection of life and, as we have seen again
and again, moves out from there into concern for the neighbor's
physical well-being in all respects, the protection of one's neighbor
from harm of any sort. One cannot, therefore, leave the discussion
of the statutes having to do with protecting life without some specific look at this well-known and oft-discussed judicial principle.

It is customary for references to the lex talionis to identify it as
a primitive form of harsh punishment that needs to be eliminated
in favor of less retributive and less harmful punishments. Though
there are legitimate grounds for moving in that direction, the
assumption of primitiveness and harshness is dubious, particularly
if the principle is read as an early process out of which less primitive

and more humane procedures have evolved. It has long been recognized that the earliest law codes of the ancient Near East allowed
pecuniary compensation for homicide and other crimes against the
person and treated these as civil torts and not as criminal acts. The
Laws of Hammurabi represent a move in the other direction, prescribing the loss of eye or tooth if one has caused the loss of the eye
or tooth of another, presuming the other to be of the same class. If
the other person is of a lower class, then monetary compensation or
something else is possible. J. J. Finkelstein has proposed an understanding of the way in which the lex talionis functions in the biblical statutes in the light of the Near Eastern data, in this instance
specifically in reference to the section in the Book of the Covenant
where the lex talionis appears (Exod. 21:18–27):

> [T]he *aim* of the section in the Covenant Code is to mute the
> widely practiced custom of paying for injuries and wounds,
> whether they were inflicted deliberately or accidentally. These
> "laws" notwithstanding, that practice must—apart from some
> exceptional and isolated instances, which we may imagine
> occurred from time to time—surely have continued in Israelite
> society. The fact that the full formula, following that of "a life for
> a life," is commonly regarded as a late interpolation strengthens
> rather than weakens this view. It bespeaks the sense that however
> impractical and even inappropriate physical talionic punishments
> might be for the crimes of assault and injury, the principle never-
> theless deserves statement as a *moral* doctrine: if "a life for a life"
> is an eminently feasible method for "making the punishment fit
> the crime," *eo ipso* "an eye for an eye, a tooth for a tooth," and so
> on, despite the unfeasibility of the latter. A punishment is moral
> *only* if it fits the crime. The talionic formula is merely a dramatic
> and effective way of stating this principle, which is more explicitly
> formulated in Lev. 24:19–20: "When a man inflicts a permanent
> injury upon his neighbor the same shall be done to him." (Finkel-
> stein, *The Ox That Gored*, 25 n. 1)

The rabbis early on pointed to the difficulty of enacting talion in
any case except the life for a life (Milgrom, *Leviticus 23–27*, 2136–
40). They noted the problem of being able to carry out precise or
equivalent retribution when it is not life for life and argued the
case with examples to show that it was "impossible to execute talion
with absolute equality"(Milgrom, 2138). Portia's defense of Shylock
in Shakespeare's *The Merchant of Venice* is a famous example of

245

the problem: Take the pound of flesh but no more, not an ounce more and no blood. The unrealism of talion beyond the primary formulation "life for life" is obvious, as is also the importance of the principle as a theory of justice.

> It must have been the primary experience of jurists (not legists!) over the ages that talion in cases of personal injury was not only impracticable, but unjust. In other words, in such cases the very retributive equality that forms the basis of talion is totally vitiated. Indeed, since compensation was actually practiced in the ancient Near East from earliest times, it is likely that it was practiced in the courts of Israel also from earliest times. (Milgrom, "*Lex Talionis* and the Rabbis," 48)

In summary, then, one may suggest that two things are going on in the incorporation and expansion of the talionic formula. One is rooting the principle in the trajectory of the commandment against killing and protecting life. The formula "life for life" seems to be the governing notion. The other formulations that flow out from this, for example, "eye for eye," seem to be brought into or added to the primary formulation, which is "life for life." There is an appropriate inference from the protection of life toward the protection from harm and the effort to create a just penalty. That this is unrealistic does not mean that it is inherently harsh or primitive. One may acknowledge the moral principle involved while responding, as the tradition does, by developing other modes of just punishment, as seems to be the case in the Book of the Covenant (see above, "Book of the Covenant") and in 1 Kings 20:39, where the principle is stated: "Guard this man; if he is missing, your life shall be given for his life"—and then qualified by an alternative: "or else you shall pay a talent of silver." It is not surprising that there should be an alternative of pecuniary compensation in this instance because the missing prisoner is not a dead prisoner, and taking the guard's life or even enslaving the guard is not itself an equal-for-equal punishment. Within the many statutes and ordinances of the Old Testament, only one statute other than the lex talionis prescribes mutilation, and this is not strictly talion but a form of appropriate justice that is very similar to talionic mutilation (Deut. 25:11–12). So, and this is the second point, already within the biblical tradition—including within the very context in which the talionic formula is laid out in the Book of the Covenant—one

246

encounters modifications of the talionic principle according to circumstances but not in a direction that values life less or values one person's life less than another because of class, race, circumstance, and the like. There is no indication that this formula functioned as a general principle or practice in the Old Testament except as it suggested two things: (1) the appropriateness of punishment to the crime (ergo justice); and (2) the inhibition of wild justice and vengeance, punishment outrunning the crime (also justice). These principles, which are not stated explicitly in the lex talionis, may be inferred from it and leaned upon.

The principle that the punishment be appropriate to the crime is reflected in an explicit and particular fashion in Deuteronomy 25:1–3, where proportionality is required but also controlled from being excessive and humiliating:

> [1]Suppose two persons have a dispute and enter into litigation, and the judges decide between them, declaring one to be in the right and the other to be in the wrong. [2]If the one in the wrong deserves to be flogged, the judge shall make that person lie down and be beaten in his presence with the number of lashes proportionate to the offense. [3]Forty lashes shall be given but not more; if more lashes than these are given, your neighbor [lit., brother] will be degraded in your sight.

Ethical reflection upon or out of that piece of case law is contradictory but not useless. The statute speaks about the way in which human beings who bear the label "brother/sister" are to be treated, about the dehumanizing that comes with the infliction of physical pain, about the fact that physical punishment not only inflicts suffering but also has ramifications for one's standing before others and that the infliction of extreme pain is an expression of contempt for another human being. The contradiction is in the fact that the principles or directions thus inferred in turn question the secondary intent of the original case law. The primary intent of the law is to provide procedures for handling a dispute between persons, including the way to deal with the case and to provide punishment (vv. 1–2). The secondary intent is to spell out specifically what that punishment should be and why (v. 3). The directions inferred serve, however, to undercut the specifics of the punishment as they raise the implicit question why it is that forty-one lashes is degrading but not thirty-nine.

247

The Commandment in Israel's Story

The weight of this commandment for the life of the human community is evident in the degree to which the issue of protecting life against its endangerment is played out in the various stories and narratives of Israel's history. While there are all too many stories of murder and killing in the Old Testament, some seem particularly reflective of the concern or indicative of the range of applicability of the commandment protecting life.

Genesis 4:1–16

The story of Cain's murder of his brother sets the issue of life and its protection as an early item on the biblical agenda (Barmash, *Homicide in the Biblical World*, 12–19). In the Yahwist's account of the beginnings of creation and of humanity, the primal acts that identify the problematic of the human way before the Creator are the disobedience of the divine command by the first couple and their son's murder of his brother. There is little doubt that these stories are indicative of what went wrong and goes wrong. Genesis 4 sets the care of human life—and conversely its endangerment—as in some sense a first order of business on the human agenda and the fundamental concern of life with one's neighbor. A number of factors in the story undergird its claim that taking the life of another is both wrong and a terrible temptation in the interaction of human stories and experiences.

1. The temptation to kill another is placed in the context of the relationship with God as that temptation is itself identified by the Lord in the conversation with Cain, precisely to warn him about the danger before him. The Lord warns Cain and leaves him free while holding him responsible and instructing him about what is needful.

2. The enigmatic divine response to the two offerings of the brothers should not be allowed to divert attention from the clear issues of the story. Indeed, the inability to work out a neat reason for the Lord's preference of Abel's sacrifice is a narrative device that heightens the issue. It is in the face of this kind of conflict, one that is not rational and arises out of jealousy and human emotion and passion and especially anger, that murder happens. The issue is clear as God has defined it. Cain knows what is at stake and what

248

needs to be done. It is not the matter of the offering or of the Lord's reaction to it. It is the question of how the human creature will deal with the threatening situation. The Lord's words to Cain are a call for self-control, for dealing with rage and depression rather than letting go with it.

3. The story underscores murder as the primary concern of the negative formulation of the commandment. The story is a paradigmatic example of what the commandment is about as already uncovered in its various reflections in the statutes of the legal codes: it has to do with planned or premeditated action, plotting and lying in wait in order to do in another person with whom one is at enmity for one reason or another. Though the narrative does not actually tell how Cain plotted the murder of his brother, the history of the text preserves various proposals about an omission from the text at the beginning of verse 8 that would indicate what Cain said to Abel to lure him into the open field and away from protection. As for the act itself, the more technical language of the commandment (*rāṣaḥ*) does not occur. Rather, we have the common expression: "Cain rose up and killed him."

4. The story is not about *keeping* one's brother, as is generally and wrongly assumed (on this see Riemann, "Am I My Brother's Keeper?"). Human beings do not "keep" (*šāmar*) other persons unless they are concubines, prisoners, and the like. The story is about *not killing* one's brother. One misses the point if Cain's diverting question, clearly a ploy, is turned into a general moral lesson about keeping one's brother, a responsibility that belongs only to God (e.g., Ps. 121:5). At the same time, the specificity of the story's focus on not killing one's brother has as its corollary the responsibility for making sure that no harm is done.

5. Placing the Cain and Abel story at this point in the biblical narrative is intended to say something foundational about the human story and about human nature as much as is the case with the preceding chapters, a point well indicated by the frequent use of the "brother" language to refer to Abel and the fact that Cain is clearly the representative human being by his vocation as "tiller of the ground" (Gen. 2:5; 3:23; 4:2, 12; cf. 2:15; Miller, *Genesis 1–11*, 37–42). The story suggests that there is within the human psyche always the potential to do in the other/brother/neighbor, especially in anger. One may not assume that the commandment against killing is there for the few who actually commit murder. We are all

249

descendants of Cain. The trajectory of this commandment moves rather directly from this story to Jesus' instruction about killing and anger in the Sermon on the Mount (see below). Karl Barth has articulated this point when he observes

> on the basis of Mt. 5^{21-26}, that the so-called offender against the life of his fellows in the primitive sense is to be found in preliminary form in all men, even though it does not usually result in the crime itself. In most of us the murderer is suppressed and chained, possibly by the command of God, or possibly by no more than circumstances, convention, or the fear of punishment. Yet he is very much alive in his cage and ready to leap out at any time.
>
> This is revealed by the amazing ease with which, in spite of every deterrent, war has always been approved and even enthusiastically welcomed and vigorously prosecuted not merely by individuals but [also] by whole nations. (Barth, *Church Dogmatics*, III/4:413)

6. As the Commandments identify the kinds of ways one lives with the neighbor, so this story echoes them as it speaks of the way one lives with the "brother." That term is used *seven* times in the narrative. While the narrative background can speak simply about "Abel" in verses 1–7, the account of Cain's murder of Abel and God's response never speaks about Abel without identifying him as "his brother" or "your brother" and eventually drops the proper name altogether as the Lord identifies what Cain has done solely as a crime against "your brother" (vv. 10, 11). The biblical story thus sets the relationship with the brother/sister as a moral issue and a moral category and from the beginning defines that relationship as implying the requirement to do no harm to the one who is "brother/sister" or "neighbor." In some sense all the other responsibilities of human relationships flow out from this one, and the recognition of the other as brother or neighbor becomes definitive for how one lives in human community.

Genesis 9:1–7

The commandment protecting life is often seen as rooted in the sanctity of life as expressed first in Genesis 9:6, a sentence that needs to be seen and understood within its immediate context:

[3]Every moving thing that lives shall be food for you; and just as I gave you the green plants, I give you everything. [4]Only, you shall not eat flesh with its life, that is, its blood. [5]For your own lifeblood I will surely require a reckoning: from every animal I will require it and from human beings, each one for the blood of another [lit., "his brother"], I will require a reckoning for human life.

> [6]Whoever sheds the blood of a human,
>> by a human shall that person's blood be shed.
> for in his own image
>> God made humankind.

Whatever may be the case for the redactional and compositional history of the Pentateuch, in the movement of the biblical story and already in the Genesis account of the beginnings of the world and humanity, one hears something of a divine command comparable to what one encounters in the Decalogue.

The sentence occurs in the context of the divine blessing of fertility and growth in the human community, familiar from Genesis 1 and now reiterated and confirmed after the flood. This includes once more human rule of the animal world, though now the provision is in more negative terms—"The fear and dread of you shall rest on every animal of the earth"—and includes the right to eat animal flesh (vv. 2–3). What happens then is that this divine provision, the right of human beings to eat animal flesh, introduces into the human story a concession, the right to kill. That tension between divine gift and the concession to kill leads into what follows as a major caveat and a further divine instruction to make sure that the human community knows that the concession does not allow for the possibility of killing another human being (vv. 4–6). Several dimensions of the regard for human life and its protection may be found in this instruction:

1. As indicated by the introductory particle "only" or "but" (ʾak) at the beginning of both verse 4 and verse 5, this whole section is a restriction on the concession that human beings may now eat meat (Westermann, *Genesis 1–11*, 464). The point of verse 4 is, as the text states, you may not eat the flesh of an animal while its life is still in it, its life represented by flowing or pulsating blood. With verse 5 the divine instruction moves on to prohibit taking human life, indicating with high emphasis that the Lord will demand or require

a reckoning if the lifeblood of a human being is shed by either an animal or another human being.

2. With its threefold articulation of the verb *ʾedrōš*, "I will require" or "I will seek (a reckoning)" (v. 5), the Noah story in its conclusion unequivocally asserts *God's* rule over human life. The connection to the commandment against killing is formulated by Westermann as follows:

> The intention is clear: the command behind vv. 5–6, "Thou shalt not kill" is deliberately and emphatically reformulated so as to express God's unconditional lordship over the life of his people. In the context of the blessing bestowed on those saved from the flood, this can only mean that the command "Thou shalt not kill" holds for the whole of humanity unconditionally and without restriction. (466)

3. The instruction of God creates a large tension between the protection of life and the one possibility of taking life. The absolute restriction on taking human life is underscored by God's insistence that such an act can only be handled by taking the life of the one who has so acted. The formulation is in strict talionic form, as the translation of verse 6 indicates. The point, however, is not so much to give authorization to human beings to execute others as to assert God's valuation of human life and to recognize murder as a violation of God's claim over human life as well as of God's command. The tension between taking life and protecting life is in a sense unresolved in this talionic formulation.

This tension, set forth as divine command at the beginning, remains within the human community. The rule of God over human life is so clear and the value of life so high that nothing except human life can compensate. In such an act, however, the community, fallible in its procedures of justice, is always at risk of violating the first part of the tension. The text goes as far as one can go in Scripture in asserting the possibility of legitimate taking of life through judicial procedures. It does so, however, within the context of divine instruction that goes as far as it can go in protecting human life. Because the text gives no attention to the procedures and the problematic that is always present in the decision to take life even for a life taken, the community always faces the difficult and thorny problem of deciding on which side of the tension it will come down.

252

4. The reason why life is so valuable that taking it requires a life to be taken is because the human being, the bearer of life, is made in the image of God. The significance of this grounding may come from two directions. It may be seen as a valuing of human life because every human being is stamped in the image of God and so related to God in a quite specific way not only as the bearer of life but also as reflecting and mirroring the deity. Or one may understand the reason for this high view of human life as an endangering of the one who is given rule and dominion over God's creation, which seems to be the functional meaning of making humankind in the image of God (see Gen. 1:27–28). From either perspective, "the murderer by his action despoils God" (Westermann, *Genesis 1–11,* 468). The Sixth Commandment, therefore, is to be understood as having a theological rootage that is not simply tied to the general relation between the first and second tables of the Decalogue but also stands outside the Commandments themselves and is directly related to the theological anthropology of Scripture. The high anthropology of the Priestly stratum of the creation story in 1:26–28 has its corollary on the moral plane. The person who bears the divine image is thereby protected by the one whose image the person bears.

5. The other person whose life is not to be taken is identified in this story as "his brother" (v. 5). The instruction about valuing life is thereby a reflex of the earlier story about the murder of a brother in Genesis 4. While these two texts come from different strata of tradition, they now bounce off of and echo each other. What the Yahwist set forth in story form in Genesis 4 is offered in the Priestly part of the flood story as a piece of divine instruction. The categorization of "the other" as brother cannot be confined to family or clan relationships: it characterizes every human being. The one whose life is enduringly valued and protected is both made by God in God's own image and "your brother." On its story trajectory through Scripture, the commandment against killing is given a profound theological and moral framework.

Genesis 37

If the flood story has made it clear that the one whose life is to be protected from harm and endangerment is always one's brother, the Joseph story particularizes the threat to life safeguarded by the

253

commandment once more in relation to one who is brother in a familial sense. The narrative of Joseph and his brothers is long, but the piece of it that belongs on the trajectory of the Sixth Commandment is chapter 37. The relevant aspects of the story are obvious but important:

1. The threat to human life is once again an outcome of human passions and emotions. As in the story of Cain and Abel, jealousy is at the root of the decision to kill one's brother. Twice we are told that Joseph's brothers "hated him." They perceive their father's greater affection for Joseph (v. 4), and they hear him tell his dream, which suggests rather directly his eventual rule over them, thereby increasing their hatred of their brother (v. 8). In the statutes of Numbers 35:20–23 and Deuteronomy 19:1–21, especially verses 4, 6b, and 11 (cf. 4:42), the issue of *enmity* or *hatred* is a crucial factor both in initiating murder and in evaluating how to deal with it. The story of Joseph's brothers illustrates the kind of developing hatred that can lead to killing one's brother and thus to violation of the commandment.

2. The story is explicit that the hatred and jealousy leads to *planning and conspiracy* to murder Joseph (vv. 18–20), thereby illustrating further what the statutes of asylum lay out as the grounds for deciding about how to treat one who has killed another.

3. In resistance to this plan, Reuben uses the language familiar from both statute and narrative. He says, "Let us not smite (*nākâ*) his life" (v. 21, lit.; see comment on Num. 35) and "Do not shed blood" (v. 22, my trans.; cf. Gen. 9:5–6). The formulation makes Reuben's protection of Joseph's life an explicit reflection of the divine instruction about the value of human life in the flood story as well as an example of what the statutes growing out of the Sixth Commandment are talking about.

4. At the end of the story, with Joseph's interpretation of what has happened in terms of the mystery of divine providence (Gen. 50:20), one is led to wonder what might have happened if the brothers had not plotted against Joseph and sold him into slavery in Egypt, thus paving the way for his leadership in avoiding the famine. Such speculation could be endless. One *knows*, however, that God's intending and working good where the brothers intended and worked bad could never have happened in this way if his brothers had *killed* him out of their hatred. The story implicitly reminds us of the way in which killing another human being cuts off all possibilities for God's effective agency through that person.

5. The commandment against stealing lies in the background here as well as in the alternative that is both proposed and enacted.

> [26]Then Judah said to his brothers, "What profit is it if we kill our brother and conceal his blood? [27]Come, let us sell him to the Ishmaelites, and not lay our hands on him, for he is our brother, our own flesh." And his brothers agreed. (Gen. 37:26–27)

The worst crime against their brother would be to kill him. Second to that is what they in fact do, which is to "sell" him into slavery, thus violating the Eighth Commandment, whose original and still operative force is against stealing another person, especially if not always for economic gain, as in this instance (see chap. 7, on the Eighth Commandment). One observes further that the force of the "brother" relation as a guard against killing another human being is explicit in this story, though here it is specifically a flesh-and-blood or kinship relation. The family stories of Genesis deal with blood kinship. The instruction in Genesis 9:5 reminds us that the brother relationship does not stop at the family borders.

Judges 19–20

The first occurrence of the Sixth Commandment verb *rāṣaḥ* in a narrative context after the giving of the Commandments at Sinai is in the story of the rape and murder of the Levite's concubine at the hands of the men of the city of Gibeah (Judg. 19) and the tribal conflict that ensues from it (Judg. 20). As retribution for the violence done to the concubine, the Levite cuts her body into twelve pieces and sends it out to the tribes, calling for their help against the Benjamites. In the context of reporting on the Levite's speech to the assembled tribes, the narrator refers to him as the husband of "the murdered woman" (*hannirṣāḥâ*, 20:4). The reference may seem casual, but the "murder" is at the center of this story. It is a particularly violent act and triggers an equally violent response. The narrative around this murder becomes the primary indicator of the disorder in the tribal league that will lead to the beginning of kingship (21:25). In the story itself, the claim is made that nothing like this has happened in Israel since the exodus. Several dimensions of the story relative to the Sixth Commandment are significant for the explication of the commandment in the stories of Israel.

255

For one thing, this is clearly an instance of the vulnerability of the weak to the violence of the powerful, or more pointedly, of the weak woman to the strong man. The murder of the woman is the outcome of horrible gang rape, an act that is explicitly reported as something that went on all night long (20:5). Furthermore, it happens because of the Levite's willingness to give his concubine over to violent rape in order to save his own life. The story is hardly a casual instance of murder. It is indicative of the way in which the weak—whether weakened by gender, social status, property impoverishment, lack of family, or whatever—are the most likely victims of the breach of the commandment. That point is underscored in both the Psalms and Job, where we encounter specific reference to the violation of the Commandments. In Psalm 94, the judgment and vindication of God is called forth against the wicked. The specific crime or sin of which the wicked are accused is given as follows (v. 6):

> They kill the widow and the stranger,
> they murder (*rāṣaḥ*) the orphan.

When Job catalogs the sins of the wicked and the outcomes in chapter 24, his focus is almost entirely on the needy and the weak:

> The murderer (*rōṣēaḥ*) rises at dusk
> to kill the poor and needy. (v. 14)

While no one is invulnerable to attack and murder, the weak and socially marginal are especially open to the endangerment of their lives. The story of the Levite's concubine is a dramatic indication of how that is so. Protected by her master/husband, she is at risk by the same relationship.

This account of the rape-murder of a woman whose vulnerability is apparent not only by the gang rape but also by the Levite's power over her—whatever his actual relationship to the woman, he is clearly her male master—has connections to one of the statutes in the Deuteronomic Code (Hossfeld, "*Du sollst nicht töten!*" 30). In Deuteronomy 22:26 we encounter the only use of the verb *rāṣaḥ* in the Deuteronomic statutes outside the laws of asylum. The verse occurs in the context of an extended statute having to do with the treatment of the man and woman in cases where a man has intercourse with a young woman (*naʿărâ*) who is engaged (22:23–27), a section of the Code that has generally to do with the particularities

256

under the Seventh Commandment against adultery. The punishment varies, depending upon whether the woman was complicit or cried for help. The facet of the statute that connects with the story of the concubine's murder has to do with what is done when the deed happens in the field, in open country, and the man forces himself upon the woman. In that case, the man is executed, but nothing is done to the woman because she was out where no one could hear her cries for help. Presumably she was not complicit in the sexual activity and so was raped. The resonances with the story of the rape-murder of the Levite's concubine are found not only in the use of the verb *rāṣaḥ* but also in the characterization of the act in both the statute (Deut. 22:24) and the story (Judg. 20:5) as *ʿānâ*, as a "violation" or "oppression" of the woman involved. Further, in both instances the act is described with the expression *qûm ʿal*, "rising up against" (Deut. 22:26; Judg. 20:5).

The specific verse where the verb for "murder" occurs reads as follows (Deut. 22:26):

> You shall do nothing to the young woman; the young woman has not committed an offense punishable by death, because this case is like that of someone who attacks and murders a neighbor.

The act of raping the young woman is comparable to murder. In the Judges story it becomes murder. In both cases the victim is one of the vulnerable members of society, and the act is a violent attack against a person. Rape is in effect equated with murder. It is such an assault on a person, and it is clearly intentional assault. Hossfeld has suggested that one may indeed think of the act as killing the woman in some sense. It is not necessarily that the rapist has directly murdered the woman. Rather, he suggests, the raped young woman is like the poor, the widow, and the orphan, of whom Job and Psalm 94 speak. She is more likely "killed" through the social consequences of specific actions that robbed her of the possibilities of life (Hossfeld, 28–29).

The story of the Levite's concubine serves, therefore, to provide a sharp—not precise—illustration of the issues in the Deuteronomic statute. Both serve to do two things. They bring rape into the range of human destruction comparable to murder, and they add women to those categories of persons in society who are especially vulnerable to violent attack and murder. The commandment,

257

therefore, which is intended to protect every life, has an identifiable bent toward protection of just such persons in the community.

The focus of these texts against endangering the life of the weak and the vulnerable is reinforced by another dimension of the text. That is the cry of the woman who has been attacked (v. 27). This is the ṣĕʿāqâ, the cry of the victim or the oppressed, which is meant to evoke a response from either someone in the human community with the power to act, specifically the king but in this case anyone who can hear the cry, or from God. This context is the only occurrence of the word in Deuteronomy (also 22:24), but in 24:15, there is explicit reference to the crying out (qārāʾ) to God of the poor when their wages have been withheld. The young woman is one of those oppressed persons who cries out to some power to deliver her, but "there is no deliverer" (22:27b, my trans.).

First Kings 21

The language of the Sixth Commandment comes to play in a direct and significant way in the story of Naboth and the confiscation of his vineyard by King Ahab. Furthermore, the story is one of several showing the interaction of different commandment violations in a single plot whose outcome is the killing of another human being. In this instance the starting point is Ahab's coveting of Naboth's vineyard and his complicity in Jezebel's plot to kill Naboth in order to steal the vineyard from him when he refuses to give it up in a trade. The means by which the killing is accomplished is the courtroom and the false witness of two scoundrels who accuse Naboth of cursing God and the king. Thus the violation of several of the commandments by the king and his wife in the process of stealing Naboth's vineyard even incorporates an accusation against *him* of having violated one of the commandments. Naboth is sentenced to death for this crime or sin and then stoned. The whole matter is succinctly summarized when Elijah is sent by the Lord to confront Ahab in the coveted and now-possessed vineyard of the executed Naboth. The Lord sends Elijah to say to Ahab: "Have you killed (rāṣaḥ), and also taken possession?" (1 Kgs. 21:19a). Have you both murdered and stolen? In this instance the killing is a case of judicial murder. What was an execution by stoning is seen through the lens of prophetic justice as murder.

258

Although this story is not a matter explicitly of the vulnerability of the weak, it is clearly a narrative of power and the potential license to take life that such power may open up. It is also one more story that involves plotting, lying in wait, thus intentional and planned taking of life. The system of justice is taken over and becomes a vehicle for "legal" but wrong and immoral murder for the sake of theft. The ultimate aim of killing Naboth is important to keep in mind. Killing another may happen in anger and enmity, but it also is often a means of acquiring what one does not have and has to kill to get, whether perpetrated by the poor or the well-to-do. There is no asylum for such killing, and so the prophet moves immediately from the indicting question to the declaration of punishment of both Ahab and Jezebel, a sentence of death (1 Kgs. 21:19b–24).

Second Samuel 11–12

The story of David's adultery with Bathsheba and his subsequent plotting of her husband's death does not involve the use of the word *rāṣaḥ*, but what takes place in the story is comparable to the account of Ahab and Jezebel plotting to have Naboth killed in order to steal his vineyard. Once more the eventual killing arises out of a complex of commandment violations, specifically coveting another man's wife and adultery with her. Here it is an after-the-fact plot against Uriah to try to hide the pregnancy that results from David's adultery (or rape?) of Uriah's wife. When David's scheme to make it appear that Uriah is the father of the unborn child fails, he uses not the judicial system but the military system and his control over it to plot Uriah's death in battle. The specific language of the plot is that Uriah be struck down (*nākâ*) so that he dies (2 Sam. 11:15). This is the same language used in the statute having to do with the Sixth Commandment in the Book of the Covenant (Exod. 21:12) and often in the detailed statutes having to do with killing in Numbers 35 (see comments above). Royal power manipulates the machinery of politics and war in order to kill. The motivations are several; the outcome is once again the violation of the commandment to protect human life.

First Samuel 18–19

There are stories of killing or attempts at killing that reflect a specific dimension of the commandment elaborated in Numbers 35: the cities of asylum. The particularities of what is involved in killing someone are spelled out in more detail in the asylum laws precisely because they are designed to protect the killer against punishment in some cases but must be clear about when such protection is appropriate and when it is not. One of the criteria that identify a *rōṣēaḥ* whose act of killing is clearly murder is killing out of "hatred" (*bĕśîn'â*, Num. 35:20) or because someone is an "enemy" (*'ôyēb*, Num. 35:23; cf. vv. 21, 22, *bĕ'êbâ*, "in enmity"). The same point is made in the asylum statutes of Deuteronomy (4:42; 19:11; cf. 19:4, 6b). Another criterion determining when the act merits punishment as a crime and not an accident is when the killer lies in wait, a clear indication that the killing is intentional and with forethought.

The story of Saul's pursuit of David is reminiscent of other stories where the Sixth Commandment is violated. His jealousy of David resembles Joseph's brothers' jealousy of him (1 Sam. 18:6–9; cf. Gen. 37:4). Saul's ineffective effort to have David killed in battle is the plot that David uses successfully to have Uriah killed (1 Sam. 18:17–30; cf. 2 Sam. 11:14–17). When that plan fails, the text reports that "Saul was David's enemy (*'ôyēb*) from that time forward" (1 Sam. 18:29). Later in the story, David rejects the claim of some that "David seeks to do you harm" (24:10). "Seeking to do harm" is one of the explicit criteria in Numbers 35 for determining that a killing is murder (35:23). Over against David's innocence in the face of accusations that he wants to kill Saul, David complains that Saul is "lying in wait (*ṣōdeh*) to take my life" (1 Sam. 24:12 [11E], my trans.). The only other occurrences of this root are in the statutes having to do with the Sixth Commandment and specifying what acts are prohibited by it (Exod. 21:13; Num. 35:20, 22). The story of Saul's prolonged pursuit of David is thus an account of one person's extended effort to kill another whom he regards as enemy and with much plotting and lying in wait, yet also of the other person's vigorous efforts to avoid doing the same thing in retaliation. In the process, the story once more uncovers the effort of the powerful to kill the weaker party but also provides an account of a self-conscious effort on the part of the intended victim—who might be justified in killing in self-defense—to avoid strenuously any possibility of killing the one who seeks his harm. The story thus creates a highly ironic preparation for the later account of David's own—successful—effort to use his royal power to kill Uriah, a Hittite soldier in David's army who is totally unaware of the plot to kill him.

260

Second Samuel 13

The account of David's children Absalom, Tamar, and Amnon in 2 Samuel 13 is part of the outgrowth of David's sins against Uriah and Bathsheba. Amnon's rape of his beautiful sister Tamar and Absalom's subsequent murder of Amnon is a particularly sordid story, showing once more the violent outcome of rape, and in this case incestual rape. The only rationale for taking it up in this context is to notice how closely Absalom's killing of Amnon fits the criteria of murderous killing illustrated above. While one might make a case for Absalom's retaliation against Amnon as a kind of defense of his sister and retribution exacted for the crime against her, the story does not seek to justify Absalom's murder of his brother. Rather, it describes the killing as happening, as in other cases we have observed, because Absalom "hated" (śānēʾ, v. 22) Amnon and had him "struck down" and "killed" (v. 28), again using language that regularly refers to high-handed killing. Furthermore, the killing is carefully planned: luring Amnon to a feast and getting him drunk before killing him.

The story serves to underscore how the violence of killing arises so easily out of other kinds of acts: here as in Judges 19–20, the sexual oppression of woman as well as the urge for retaliation, likewise a large feature of the Judges narrative. Killing begets killing. Hatred erupts in violence. The commandment is set for the life of the community precisely to erect a barrier against such eruption. The life of the one who is "hated" or "an enemy" is potentially in danger, and the Sixth Commandment is the primary safeguard to restrain the eruption of that hatred and enmity into killing. Both the laws and the stories confirm the danger to the protection of life in such circumstances on the personal and individual level. One cannot avoid asking if the danger does not also arise at more corporate and communal levels. There is a fundamental tension that must not be overlooked between the clear condemnation of killing out of hatred and enmity and the engagement with others to kill them in battle precisely because they are the enemy. If many wonder whether the Sixth Commandment has anything to say about war, that is a very natural question. By definition, such killing is planned, intentional, an aspect of enmity, and involving all sorts of devices to plot and plan the death of the enemy. One may not easily rule the killing of war as outside the prohibition against killing in the Commandments.

261

The Commandment in the Prophets

Explicit reference to the Sixth Commandment is not extensive in the prophets. There are two occasions where it is part of what seems to be a partial summary of the Decalogue, though it is much debated as to whether these uses presume the prior existence of the Decalogue as a whole (Hos. 4:1–2; Jer. 7:8–9). In the case of Hosea, the prophetic speech is an indictment against the northern kingdom for the widespread breach of covenant, evidenced in various ways throughout the book of Hosea. In Hosea 4:1–2, that breach is identified with sins or crimes against the neighbor that are violations of the covenant stipulations reflected in the second table of the Commandments, including murder, a crime of which the priests are accused later in the book (6:9). The latter reference is rather enigmatic but depicts priests apparently lying in wait like robbers to murder persons on their way to Shechem. Whatever the circumstances, the context speaks of this as a transgression of the covenant (6:7).

Jeremiah's catalog of the people's violation of the Commandments (7:8–9) occurs in his famous Temple Sermon, where he speaks of the incongruity of such actions and the people's confidence that the temple, as the place of God's presence, ensures their freedom from retribution. Isaiah matches Jeremiah's later denunciation of the inhabitants of Jerusalem when he accuses the city of turning from a place of justice and righteousness to an abode of murderers, thieves, takers of bribes, and oppressors of the poor (Isa. 1:21–23). The Sixth Commandment is there in the prophets where one would expect it, as a part of the prophetic indictment of the sins of the people, more pointedly their violation of the covenantal requirements. The crime against the neighbor thus brings about the judgment of the covenant Lord.

Internalizing the Commandment

The prohibition against killing one's neighbor is not finally confined to acts. In texts already discussed, it is apparent that "hating" one's neighbor is integrally tied into the act of killing (see the discussion of Num. 35). The latter is an outgrowth of the former. In Leviticus 19, where the Commandments are most evident in the priestly traditions of the Pentateuch, more specifically the Holiness Code, the injunction is not against killing but against hating: "You shall not hate in your heart your brother/sister" (Lev. 19:17, my trans.). Here the trajectory of the commandment seeks to stop killing and protect life by internalizing and focusing on the prior interior mood that evokes the hostile act. The explicit internalization of caring for the neighbor that occurs in the commandment against coveting is thus present in the trajectory of other commandments as well. Attitude as well as act toward the brother or neighbor is placed under control. The connection between the attitude of enmity and the act of killing is clear and underscored in the various refractions of the Sixth Commandment. Here in Leviticus 19, the significance of attitude—"hate"—and internal feeling—"in your heart"—is such that it becomes the center of attention and the primary injunction, not the consequential act of killing. One may reprove one's neighbor or take the neighbor to court, but not take actions that incur guilt or exact vengeance (vv. 17b–18a). The interior emotion is further underscored with the warning against bearing a grudge (v. 18b) against someone.

Jesus' instruction about this commandment in the Sermon on the Mount follows along the same path. It is not just killing or murder that is ruled out but also anger and insult (Matt. 5:21–26). The internalization that Jesus underscores is already both implicit and explicit in the trajectory of the commandment but now lifted up as the particular focus and developed in terms of instruction about reconciliation to overcome the anger, hatred, and insult (see below, "A Look at the New Testament").

The commandment against killing, therefore, is seen to be wide-ranging, encompassing one's emotions and feelings quite directly. Restriction of the force of the commandment to acts of killing, intentional or unintentional, is too limiting. Protection of life involves the heart as well as the hand. Such protection begins before the hand is lifted as one learns control of one's attitudes and feelings and develops ways of dealing with them other than hostile acts against the person who may have inspired anger or hatred.

The Positive Force of the Commandment

263

It is not surprising that the Sixth Commandment became the cardinal example of John Calvin's claim that interpretation and application of the Commandments involves an argument from the commandment to its opposite (Miller, "Commandments in Reformed Perspective," 133–34). He puts it this way with specific reference to the commandment against killing:

> Therefore in this commandment, "You shall not kill," men's common sense will see only that we must abstain from wronging anyone or desiring to do so. Besides this, it contains, I say, the requirement that we give our neighbor's life all the help we can. To prove that I am not speaking unreasonably: God forbids us to hurt or harm a brother unjustly, because he wills that the brother's life be dear and precious to us. So at the same time he requires those duties of love which can apply to its preservation. And thus we can see how the purpose of the commandment always discloses to us whatever it there enjoins or forbids us to do. (*Institutes* 2.8.9)

Elaboration of the positive force of each commandment as well as its negative demand became a regular part of the teaching of the Commandments in the Reformed and Lutheran traditions. Luther's Small Catechism shows this succinctly with regard to the commandment against killing:

> You are not to kill.
> What is this? Answer:
> We are to fear and love God, so that we neither endanger nor
>   harm the lives of our neighbors, but instead help and support
>   them in all of life's needs.
>   (in Kolb and Wengert, *Book of Concord*, 352)

A number of the catechisms form their questions about the Commandments—like Luther's answer above—in terms of what the commandment requires as well as what it forbids.

"Those duties of love" to which Calvin refers in the quotation above are explicitly indicated in the way in which Leviticus 19:17–18 concludes. The statute that begins with the internalization of the commandment against killing by prohibiting hatred of one's brother or sister concludes with the second part of the Great Commandment: "You shall love your neighbor as yourself" (19:18b). The inference is direct and becomes the vehicle for the positive summary of the second table of the Decalogue. "Enmity is the motive force behind violent and murderous acts, and the best protection against this force is the cultivation of affection for those with whom one lives" (Patrick, *Old Testament Law*, 53).

The positive form of the protection of life is in fact already present in particular statutes discussed earlier (see comment on Deut. 22:1–8 above). Dennis Olson properly notes:

> The commandment "You shall not kill" entails by extension a positive commitment to enhance and protect life. Thus, Israelites are to care for and return a neighbor's stray or fallen animal ([Deut.] 22:1–4), protect mother birds so they can go on producing young (22:6–7), and build a parapet or guardrail on the roof of a house to prevent someone from falling off the edge and being killed (22:8). (*Death of Moses*, 98)

In the form of the statute to help the fallen animal of the neighbor that appears in Exodus 23:4–5, the "neighbor" is referred to as "your enemy." The love of neighbor becomes a specific act in behalf of the one who is at enmity with you.

The connection between the commandment against killing, with its positive force requiring protection of one's neighbor from all harm, and the general injunction to love the neighbor—this connection is carried forward quite explicitly in the catechetical tradition of the Reformed churches (e.g., the Geneva Catechism and the Westminster Shorter Catechism). They regularly follow Leviticus 19:17–18 in making a connection between not hating the neighbor and loving the neighbor. A good example is Question 107 of the Heidelberg Catechism:

> Q. 107. *Is it enough, then, if we do not kill our neighbor in any of these ways?*
> A. No; for when God condemns envy, hatred, and anger, he requires us to love our neighbor as ourselves, to show patience, peace, gentleness, mercy, and friendliness toward him, to prevent injury to him as much as we can, also to do good to our enemies (*Book of Confessions*, 4.107).

A Look at the New Testament

The commandment against killing is cited several times in the New Testament. Indeed, it is one of two commandments—the other being the prohibition of adultery—that are always cited in the partial lists of commandments found throughout the New Testament

(Matt. 5:21; 19:18//Mark 10:19//Luke 18:20; Rom. 13:9; Jas. 2:11; cf. *Didache* 2:2). In most of these instances, the commandment is simply quoted. It is especially in the Sermon on the Mount in Matthew 5 that the prohibition of killing becomes the focus of attention and interpretation. Jesus begins his teaching about the law with the commandment against murder or killing:

> [21]You have heard that it was said to those of ancient times, "You shall not murder"; and "whoever murders shall be liable to judgment." [22]But I say to you that if you are angry with a brother or sister, you will be liable to judgment; and if you insult a brother or sister, you will be liable to the council; and if you say, "You fool," you will be liable to the hell of fire. [23]So when you are offering your gift at the altar, if you remember that your brother or sister has something against you, [24]leave your gift there before the altar and go; first be reconciled to your brother or sister, and then come and offer your gift.

In this antithesis it is clear that Jesus in no sense sets the law aside or alters it. Rather, he continues the trajectory already developing in the Old Testament legal traditions. There one hears about not killing one's neighbor out of hatred or enmity (e.g., Num. 35). Now Jesus carries that further, teaching a way of not letting anger and hatred—which corresponds to anger or follows from it (Betz, *Sermon*, 219–20, 230)—take over and, implicitly, stopping the harmful actions that arise from those emotions. His teaching is not simply "Don't be angry at your neighbor." That is certainly there in his strong words about being angry or insulting one's brother/sister. Jesus goes further, however, in calling for acts of reconciliation with a brother/neighbor with whom one is at some enmity. The trajectory of this commandment in the New Testament thus takes us back to its first story:

> Simply stated, the source of murder is a broken relationship with the brother. The famous case of Cain's murder of his brother Abel (Gen 4:8–16) comes to everyone's mind, although it is not mentioned in the text. What then is the intent of the Torah commandment, "You shall not kill"? According to the SM [Sermon on the Mount], its intent—that is, God's will—is that one come to grips with the root cause of murder. It is this root cause that precipitated the prohibition. Once the root cause is identified as anger, the ethical demand follows: one must control anger. One

266

achieves this goal by avoiding situations that lead to anger, or, if the situations already exist, by defusing them through reconciliation and the restoration of the peaceful brotherly relationship. (Betz, *Sermon*, 230)

One notes further that in Jesus' teaching the move to effect reconciliation is not initiated by the one who is angry, as would seem to be the logic flowing from the earlier verses warning against being angry against the brother. On the contrary, it is the one who is the object of anger and enmity who makes the move toward reconciliation. The peacemaking initiative is by the one who is warred against. The reconciling initiative of the one who is threatened or in danger is another form of Jesus' teaching about turning the other cheek rather than retaliating. In this case, however, the protection of life involves anticipating the danger and making positive moves to erase the enmity and anger that can lead to harmful actions.

What Jesus initiates here continues in the New Testament and the Christian tradition generally as the community learns not to be angry or to deal with that anger in various ways so that it does not erupt in harmful activity. The instruction of Ephesians 4 is indicative of this with its words about not letting the sun go down on one's anger. Anger may happen, but it needs to be dealt with, as Jesus also indicates. Ephesians 4:26 gives the practical advice of not letting the day end with one's anger still seething. That is when it goes deeper. No word is said about acts of reconciliation, as in Jesus' teaching in the Sermon on the Mount, but further along in this very concrete instruction about the way of Christian living, a counter way is suggested, again following the implicit understanding of the Commandments as having a positive teaching along with the negative:

> [31]Put away from you all bitterness and wrath and anger and wrangling and slander, together with all malice, [32]and be kind to one another, tenderhearted, forgiving one another, as God in Christ has forgiven you. [1]Therefore be imitators of God, as beloved children, [2]and live in love, as Christ loved us and gave himself for us, a fragrant offering and sacrifice to God. (Eph. 4:31–5:2)

Jesus' teaching pointed toward specific acts of reconciliation; what we find here is a more general word that leads in the same direction: acts and dispositions of kindness, setting aside anger and

267

malice, and forgiving those whose words and acts may have aroused dangerous anger and bitterness, a way of living with one another that is directly reflected in Question 107 of the Heidelberg Catechism (cited above). Ultimately what is in view is the familiar word of loving the neighbor, here undergirded and underscored by the example of Christ, a love of neighbor that is self-giving rather than neighbor-harming.

> Christ's sacrifice for others is a model for our community love. . . .
> So in the light of the cross the bodily life of the neighbor, even
> of the enemy, is revealed as the prerequisite and the prototype
> of all the other values needing protection, even [to be] died for,
> in and for the neighbor, even the enemy. (Yoder, "Exodus 20:13,"
> 397–98)

Both Jesus' teaching in the Sermon on the Mount and the rules for life in community articulated in Ephesians 4 are echoed or recapitulated in 1 John 3:11–15, where hatred of one's brother is equated with murder and the counterway is a love that imitates Christ in the willingness to "lay down our lives for one another" (1 John 3:16). Love rather than hatred is what the Commandments are about, a fundamental principle articulated first in the Decalogue-like chapter 19 of Leviticus (vv. 17–18) and rearticulated by both Jesus (Matt. 5:43–48) and Paul (Rom. 13:8–10).

Finally, one notes that the lex talionis of the Old Testament is taken up by Jesus in the Sermon (Matt. 5:38–42). The guard against vengeance inherent in the talionic principle is assumed in his teaching (see above). The antithesis he puts forward, then, is in behalf of discerning what the love command presupposes and demands. Here nonretaliation is not simply a passive response to the act of the evildoer (Matt. 5:39). It is an aggressive move to overcome the evil with good (Rom. 12:20–21). The point is not so much nonviolence in general as it is desisting retaliation in specific instances. "The difference is that such desistance is in effect a positive method of fighting evil and helping justice prevail. This method corresponds to the 'intent' of the *ius talionis* and is thus an adequate way to fulfill the Torah prescription" (Betz, *Sermon*, 284).

An appropriate conclusion to thinking about the New Testament teaching may be found in Karl Barth's own concluding comment about the biblical instruction against killing:

In the final New Testament form in which we have to hear and understand it, the commandment: "Thou shalt not kill," reaches us in such a way that in all the detailed problems which may arise we cannot exclude the exceptional case and yet we cannot assert too sharply that it is genuinely exceptional. In other words, we cannot overemphasise the arguments against it, nor raise too strongly the question whether even what seems to be justifiable homicide might not really be murder. (*Church Dogmatics*, III/4:400)

CHAPTER 6

Marriage, Sex, and the Neighbor

You shall not commit adultery.—Exodus 20:14

Neither shall you commit adultery.—Deuteronomy 5:18

If one were to ask a stranger on the street to recite one of the Commandments, odds are she would come forth fairly quickly with either: "Thou shalt not kill" or "Thou shalt not commit adultery." Assuming that supposition is correct, one may go on to suggest some reasons for such a response. One would surely be the brevity of those two commandments. "Thou shalt not steal," therefore, is also a possibility. Other factors, however, lead one to think that commandment would not come as quickly on the lips of the stranger. Stealing is not perceived to be of the same significance or consequence as either killing or adultery. There is something so basic to both the acts of killing another person and having sexual relations outside the marriage that these two "rules" come readily to mind.

Not surprisingly, the possibility of seeing either adultery or murder as being basic violations of intersocial behavior is evident in the Bible as well, at least implicitly in the different orderings of the prohibitions following the command to honor father and mother. At least five different orders for the next three commandments have been identified within Scripture and the tradition flowing out of it. Four of the five have either adultery or murder as the first of the sequence, though some arrangements put theft as the second in the series. Various interpretations have been given for these variant orders, some of them compositional and others having to do with literary context or different ethical perspectives lying behind different times and circumstances out of which the various orders arose (Freund, "Murder, Adultery, and Theft"). All of them are interpretive, and none of them can be unquestionably justified. The order found in the two Decalogues of Exodus and Deuteronomy in the Hebrew or Masoretic Text suggests the priority of the neighbor's life followed by the priority of the neighbor's marriage. The fact that the legislation following the giving of the Commandments in both Exodus and Deuteronomy does not lift up theft as a capital crime tends to support an interpretation of the order found in the Decalogue as a reflection of priorities, but one cannot say that for a certainty. Any of the five orders can be justified by interpretation, including the order of Jeremiah 7:9, which places theft first, perhaps showing that the original meaning was theft of a life (see chap. 7, on the Eighth Commandment).

The sequence of protections of life, marriage, and freedom/property makes sense in terms of the seriousness of the offenses, even if other orders are possible. Because that is the order of the Decalogue in the Hebrew biblical text, we follow it. Both tradition and sensibility lead one in that direction. At the same time, the focus of the commandment on the protection of the family makes an attachment of this commandment to the honoring of parents quite plausible. Whatever the order, that familial context is shared by these two commandments. From the angle of the family, honoring mother and father and prohibiting adultery enhance its well-being and guard against its endangerment. From the perspective of the rights of the neighbor, protection of one's life is appropriately followed by protection of one's marriage.

The Addressee of the Commandment

As with other commandments, the commandment against adultery raises the question Who is being addressed? More specifically, as the commandment to honor father and mother raises the issue of whether small children as well as adult children are being instructed by the commandment, so this commandment leads one from the start to ask whether it includes women as well as men. It is often read as addressed only to males, whether married or not. Certainly the grammatical form of the verb is second-person masculine, as is the case with other verbal forms in the Decalogue. That the free male citizen of Israel was to the fore as the recipient of the Com-

272

mandments is clear. That is confirmed by the formulation of the commandment against coveting where specific reference is made to not coveting "your neighbor's wife."

Less obvious, perhaps, are the indications from the text, greatly reinforced by the tradition, that the prohibition addresses women members of the community as well. The most immediately evident indication of that has already been identified in earlier discussion. The Commandments are spoken to the whole community of Israel. There are times when the Old Testament is explicit about only male members being present before the Lord (e.g., Deut. 16:16–17). But that is not the case in either the Exodus or Deuteronomic presentations of the Commandments. In Exodus we are told that "all the people witnessed the thunder and lightning," and the conversation that follows God's speaking the Commandments refers only to "the people" (20:18–20). In Deuteronomy the text says that Moses summoned "all Israel" (Deut. 5:1) for the giving of the Commandments, and when the Lord finishes proclaiming them, Moses says, "These words the LORD spoke with a loud voice to *your whole assembly* at the mountain" (5:22). While it is possible to read "the people" in the Exodus presentation as having to do only with adult males (see 19:15), Deuteronomy is explicit on more than one occasion about the inclusion of women and children and strangers in the hearing and learning and doing of the law (29:10–13; 31:12–13; Josh. 8:34–35). Elsewhere are signs of women's involvement in the assembly of Israel and in its practices (e.g., Jer. 44:15, 20; Ezra 10:1; Neh. 8:2).

Although the primary or starting point of reference seems to be the activity of a man in violating the marriage of another man by having intercourse with his wife, in the trajectory of the commandment through the law and elsewhere, it does not stay so strictly confined. As with the commandments having to do with killing and stealing, one can identify a specific and confined focus that opens up rather quickly to a wider frame of reference. In this instance, there are two indicators of the wider applicability of the commandment. One is the formulation of the commandment itself. As others have noted, the common expression for sexual intercourse is "lie with" (*šākab*) + preposition + object ("her," "a woman," and the like; e.g., Gen. 19:32–34; 39:7–14; Exod. 22:15). There are other expressions as well, such as "take" (her; e.g., Gen. 34:2; 38:2), and "come to/ cohabit with" (her; e.g., Gen. 38:2, 15–16). All of these, however, regularly take an object, and it is female. The commandment itself

273

uses a verb that is less common in these situations, *nāʾap*, "commit adultery." It is a more general term and can stand without an object, thus leaving the possible object of the act of adultery open, relative to whether it is with a wife or a husband. Even when the verb *nāʾap* is used in an explicit drawing upon Decalogue language and reference, as in Leviticus 20:10, the subject is a man (*ʾîš*), and the object is "the wife of his neighbor." Here the specifying is a narrowing, but that is not the form of the commandment itself. One may well expect that a formulation on the order of Leviticus 20:10 was what was meant, but that is not what appears, and the difference is very noticeable. The formulation of the commandment is more general and more open.

This same verse in Leviticus 20, in a counterword to what has just been noted, happens to provide the other primary indicator that the commandment can and should be seen as addressing women as well as men. That is in the fact that the statute in Leviticus 20:10 prohibiting adultery says that the woman as well as the man shall be put to death. Both persons are seen as having violated the commandment/statute and are subject to its sanctions. Furthermore, both the man and the woman are called "adulterers" (the man, *nōʾēp*; the woman, *nōʾāpet*). Both persons have clearly violated the commandment. Inclusion of the adulteress in the punishment may be a later development in light of the use of a singular verb (so, e.g., Milgrom, *Leviticus 17–22*, 1747). In its history therefore, the text may show the dynamic of the trajectory of the commandment against adultery.

It is not possible, however, to make a historical argument as to "when" the commandment was understood to address the women members of the community as well as the men. Even if it were, the point would be of historical interest only and not of moral significance. The canonical form of the commandment in its context and these other clues within Scripture clearly set the commandment as a word to any member of the community.

The Basic Claim of the Commandment

274   The prohibition against adultery offers several important protections within the covenant community. The first of these is the protection of the marriage of one's neighbor. As the Sixth Commandment guards

the life of "your neighbor," so the Seventh Commandment guards the neighbor's marriage. The presence of a prohibition against adultery, which from all the instances in Scripture seems to mean sexual intercourse with someone who is married, is in immediate sequence after the prohibition against killing one's neighbor and serves to undergird and establish the importance and sanctity of the marriage relationship. This is not a protection of property. That is tended to in the next commandment. It is an explicit claim that the sexual activity between a man and woman who are married is central to the relationship and may not be disregarded. In the range of texts that speak about marital relationships in the Bible, one discerns a distinction between men and women: sexual activity outside of marriage is allowed for men as long as it is not with another married woman. This laxity, however, is tied to social structures where polygamy is a marriage pattern more than it is reflective of a permissive sexual culture. At some points, in some of the stories, men are given more leeway for sexual activity with women, but that is within a structure where multiple wives and concubines are permitted.

The seriousness of the intimacy of a marriage, specifically in the sexual sphere, is confirmed by the general condemnation of prostitution, which is casual sex with a woman with whom the male has no relationship. In prostitution, the family and the question of posterity are not seriously at stake (see below). And while there are occasions of men having sex with prostitutes without condemnation (e.g., Gen. 38), there are many instances in the laws, the prophets, and the wisdom writings where prostitution is condemned and men are warned against consorting with prostitutes (e.g., Lev. 19:29; Prov. 7:10; 23:27). Prostitution as well as adultery may serve as a metaphor for violating the relationship between God and the people (Exod. 34:15–16; Deut. 31:16; Jer. 13:27; Nah. 3:4).

The sacredness of marriage and the centrality of sexual relationships within the marriage is thus to the fore and lifted up in this commandment. While the commandment does not explicitly address fornication, an implicit word is sounded about where the sexual relationship belongs, in the marriage of a man and a woman. The commandment thus provides the starting point of a sexual ethic even as it emphasizes the importance of a person's marriage. Your neighbor's marriage has as much weight and protection as does his life.

At this point it is crucial to the understanding of the commandment that one incorporate what is omitted from the commandment

275

per se but very present in the statutes elaborating it as well as in the Tenth Commandment: "your neighbor." The sin of adultery—and elsewhere the Scriptures are clear about this being a sin (Gen. 20:9; 39:9; 2 Sam. 12:13; cf. Ps. 51:4 [and superscription])—is to be understood first of all from the perspective of responsibility for the well-being of the neighbor. The point of the commandment in its context and its history thus is first of all to protect one's neighbor's marriage from encroachment and endangerment by someone outside the marriage. Or to view the commandment from the perspective of the one addressed by the commandment, to teach a way of living that works to support and keep safe the marriage of others, that is, of one's neighbor. Appropriation of the commandment may very easily—and often does—start with interpreting it as a protection of *one's own* marriage, but that is not its primary frame of reference. All of the commandments in the second table are aimed at protecting the well-being of members of the community by placing upon each one a responsibility for the other/neighbor. Safeguarding marriage begins with and is centered in the care with which each person who receives the commandment is careful not to violate the marriage of any other person by having sexual relations with the wife—or husband—of a neighbor.

It is easy to forget the neighbor in this commandment, as it is in some of the others, and thus hear it as primarily a word about the protection of "my" marriage by "my" being careful not to stray and destroy "my" marriage by having relations with someone else, married or not. That is an obvious inference of the commandment and is reinforced by the absence of explicit reference to one's neighbor in the commandment itself. In the context of the Decalogue, however, "my" marriage is safeguarded by the reciprocity of the commandments, by "my" neighbor's being careful not to commit adultery with "my" wife/husband. Here, as elsewhere, the Commandments are given for the creation and preservation of community, for producing a good neighborhood in which one may live and dwell without endangerment, and especially without endangering one's marriage and family (see below on Deuteronomy). So their focus is upon how we covenant together to support and protect one another. The character of the Commandments as setting up responsibilities toward the other/neighbor is never more apparent than in this instance. As these obligations are taken up mutually, then the marriage and family of all members of the community are protected from harm.

The weight upon responsibility not to violate the marriage of another has, then, an implicit repercussion for one's own marriage. If engaging in intimacy with the wife/husband of another has effects upon that other person and the other's marriage, one may conclude that the act has also endangered the marriage of the one who committed adultery with the spouse of another. "My" breach of the commandment not only damages the relationship of my neighbor; it also bounces back to damage my own marriage and family relationship. Each marriage, therefore, is safeguarded both by avoiding adultery with the spouse of another and also by the reciprocity inherent in the Commandments. "My" neighbor is under command also not to commit adultery with "my" wife.

The Rationale for the Commandment

Any discussion of the rationale for avoiding adultery can only argue on implicit grounds. Like the commandments that surround it, the prohibition against adultery does not include a motivation clause. One may assume, however, that several matters are at stake in preserving the integrity of the marriage relationship by not committing adultery:

1. From the beginning of Scripture, the marriage of a man and a woman involves a *commitment to a relationship* that is not like any other—except our relationship to God (see below)—and involves an intimacy, signaled first in the sexual sphere but not necessarily restricted to that. The story of creation makes that point with its simple words about a man leaving father and mother and clinging to his woman/wife so that they become one flesh (Gen. 2:24). Elsewhere procreation is brought into the picture (e.g., Gen. 1:28; 3:16; 4:1), but the Yahwistic story of man and woman as husband and wife in Genesis 2–3 gets to the procreation of children rather late. It is first of all about a physical union and a helping relationship, "a helper as his partner" (2:18), that in some basic ways serves to define what it means to be human. Human being is as man or as woman, whether there is marriage or not. The intimate, caring, loving relationship in a marriage, however, is given by God in the

277

creation of man and woman and so is to be safeguarded in the daily life of the community. The language in which ʾādām responds to the creation of woman—"bone of my bones and flesh of my flesh" (2:23)—is specifically covenantal and thus identifies not only the physical union and the shared humanity but also the loyalty of the relationship and the exclusiveness of the union of the helping partners in marriage (Brueggemann, "Of the Same Flesh and Bone").

In its full sense, sexual intercourse is not simply an activity. It is a reflection of intimate and loyal relationship between two persons who share their life together as partners in an enduring relationship. Even where divorce may be an outcome of a relationship, it is not presumed in its initiative. Faithfulness to one another starts in the sexual relationship, but that is only the beginning of it. Much is often made of the fact that, in the Old Testament, sexual union is described as "knowing." One needs to be careful about carrying that particular use of the verb over into all forms of knowing, but it is no small matter that in the relationship of a wife and husband, their most intimate acts together are characterized as "knowing," for in that act whereby the two become one, there is a coming to know that blossoms in countless other ways. Adultery is a breach of that intimate knowing relationship. In this understanding of marriage, one can already see how adultery can become a prime figure of thought for speaking of the violation of the relationship between God and people. Indeed, the use of that image not only speaks about what is at stake in the First Commandment, but the image of adultery as a metaphor for disobedience and distrust of the Lord also is a way of learning about what is meant to be the character of the husband-and-wife relationship. It is an absolute devotion at the core of one's being, a trust in and loyalty to one another in all matters that cannot be manifest in any other relationship.

The commandment against adultery is a clear example of the way in which the Commandments often serve to delimit within a large moral space, to set bounds in a realm of much freedom. For the marriage of a man and a woman is a partnership in freedom, where the love for the other serves always and continually to set free. It is not bondage; it is a bond in freedom, a tie that releases (Barth, *Church Dogmatics*, III/4:190). Marriage is a specific act of creating moral space, of bringing about a realm in which life is lived in its fullest and most complex way around the deepest of relationships, which itself opens up into other relationships, whether in the

278

creation of a family or the participation with others in the good neighborhood. The only limit on this freedom, the only demarcation of the moral space, is in terms of preservation of the covenant commitment, in not violating the marriage of another in the neighborhood or one's own marriage in the process. Obedience to the commandment serves to preserve the freedom of the neighbor's marriage and "my" marriage. The prohibition against adultery thus leaves a large area for living in covenant and in freedom.

The significance of the marriage relationship and of its violation is evident in the Genesis stories of Abraham and Isaac's efforts to pass their wives off as sisters in order to avoid possible endangerment of the life of the husbands. Practical necessity does not preclude the unwitting taking of Sarah/Rebekah by Pharaoh/Abimelech from being a great sin. It has violated the marriage relationship (Gen. 12:10–20; 20:1–18; 26:1–11). Even in a story in which the focus is heavily upon the barrenness of a woman and the importance of children—the story of Elkanah, Hannah, and Penninah—the husband, Elkanah, seeks to comfort his barren and depressed wife with the words "Am I not more to you than ten sons?" (1 Sam. 1:8). One may dismiss this as husbandly insensitivity, easily said because Elkanah has sons through his other wife, Penninah. But if it is meant seriously, it is a claim on the part of one member of the marriage that the love between the two of them is deeper and much more important than having children.

2. As the story of Hannah makes clear, however, the *procreative aim of marriage* is evident early on. If the Yahwistic account of the creation of man and woman does not put weight on procreation, the Priestly report in Genesis 1 does. While no story of man and woman together as husband and wife is told in that chapter, the initial word to this being who is created as man and woman is, "Be fruitful and multiply and fill the earth" (1:28). So bearing children and the development of the family as well as the continuity of the human line in its family particularity is a significant dimension of the husband-wife relationship. The many accounts of barrenness and the sadness that goes with it (e.g., Gen. 30:1; 1 Sam. 1:6–7) are a testimony to the significance of bringing forth children in the marriage relationship. Indeed, this procreative aim of the man-and-woman relationship can become so dominant that it breaks out of the marriage bounds, as in the case of Sarah giving her handmaid, Hagar, to Abraham so that they may have a child through his sexual relationship with the

279

slave girl instead of with his wife. Even in this instance, however, the story, which does not seem to frown upon such activity in general, makes it clear that the human effort to create a child outside of the marriage relationship, as an apparent necessity in order to accomplish the divine promise of posterity, is not God's intention. The child who carries on the promise is the child of Abraham and Sarah, of the marriage of this man and this woman.

The procreative function of marriage is an important rationale for the prohibition against adultery. For the continuity of the family line is only clear and preserved when the marriage, specifically in its sexual dimension, is kept whole. There can be no certainty about whose child a newborn is if there has not been constancy in the marriage. Some of the laws having to do with marriage and adultery seem to point in this direction particularly. Thus the laws of Deuteronomy 22:13–29, having to do with forms of adultery, focus on the married or betrothed woman and not generally on the husband's sexual infidelity. The instance of an unbetrothed woman having intercourse with a man, whether or not consensually, is handled by the woman becoming the man's wife. Should there be a child out of the intercourse, the paternity is clear. Numbers 5:11–31 is a legal provision for handling a case when a husband suspects that his wife may have had intercourse with another man but cannot prove it. Again the underlying issue is that the wife may bear him a child that is not his own.

3. So avoiding adultery is also a way in which *the family is supported and enhanced*. Preservation of the marriage of one's neighbor serves to keep the other's family stable and whole. The breach of intimacy of husband and wife and their covenantal relationship and the risk of progeny who are not part of the marriage relationship both serve to undercut the health and happiness of the family. Nurturing the family as part of God's blessing on human existence—and everyone belongs to a family—is not handled simply by *preserving* the marriage covenant without blemish, but that is its starting point. The place of the family as the context for life in the world of Israel underscores the significance of this prohibition. It was in the family that economic security and safety of individuals was preserved. Securing the inheritance, caring for older persons, and the general support of one another by food, shelter, clothing, and the means of life took place in the family. They still do. Marriage is the beginning of the family as the nucleus of life and values and culture. Adultery

280

undercuts that nucleus, breaking the family bonds at their foundation. What was true in ancient Israel is true generally even when societal and cultural profiles have greatly changed. Thus pairing of the command to honor parents with the prohibition against adultery found in some arrangements of the Decalogue has a powerful rationale and may not be simply a traditio-compositional matter (cf. Lev. 20:9–10). At least the alternative tradition has a significant rationale in the way in which both commandments focus upon protection of the family, its members, and its continuity.

The Trajectory of the Commandment through Scripture

Breaking the First Commandment as the Sin of Adultery

Adultery, that is, sexual relationship that betrays the deepest covenantal relationship between two persons, is in both the background and the foreground of the Old Testament's many manifestations of the First Commandment and what it involves. The marital metaphor is the closest relational metaphor in the human realm, and the sexual urge is so strong within human experience that it is not surprising that sexual language and marital images should come to the fore as a way of speaking about the relationship between God and human beings or, more specifically, Israel. While the image of adultery and marital betrayal is most prominent within the prophets, there are clear indications of its presence from the beginning of the story of the Lord and Israel.

The Sinai Story

Divine jealousy. Even within the wider sphere of the First Commandment itself, including its extension back to the Prologue and forward into the command against making and worshiping images of anything, the marital metaphor and the concern for faithfulness that is equivalent to the faithfulness of marriage is present, specifically in the claim made in the Prologue, "I am the Lord *your God* . . ." The self-presentation thus is an identity in terms of relationship and one that can make claims in the way that a marriage is

281

relational and obligating, arising out of love that has been manifest and claiming response of love. The "your God" does not have to be seen simply in terms of the marital metaphor. It can also be viewed appropriately in terms of the imagery of a king or suzerain. The further unfolding of the Commandments, however, serves to bring the marital relationship further to the fore, specifically in the second divine claim of the Commandments. "I am the LORD your God . . ." is followed by "I am a jealous God . . ." The latter self-identification is to be seen in close relationship to the former one. As "your God," the Lord is appropriately jealous for "your" full affection, loyalty, and love. The positive form of this claim is in the language of the Shema, where the sum total of Israel's responsibility is encapsulated in the term "love." In the Commandments, the logic is "I am the LORD your God, . . . [so] I am a jealous God" (Exod. 20:2, 5). In the positive form of the First Commandment, in the Shema, the logic is from the other end: "The LORD is our God, the LORD alone, . . . [so] love the LORD your God with all your heart and with all your soul and with all your might" (Deut. 6:4–5). Both the formulation in the Commandments and the formulation in the Shema can only find their proper human analogy in the faithfulness of the marital relationship and the proper jealousy that belongs to any such relationship.

In the Song of Songs, when the poet seeks to express the depth of passion that belongs to love and equals love, it is with the language of jealousy:

> For love is strong as death,
>> passion [jealousy] fierce as the grave.
>> (8:6)

The term for "jealous" or "jealousy" (*qānāʾ*) can be used to express various kinds of zeal or ardor, but in several places it specifically refers to the jealousy of a spouse over the affection of a wife or husband when adultery has taken place or is suspected (Num. 5:14, 29–30; Prov. 6:32–35; Ezek. 16:38). The jealousy of a marriage has its positive and negative dimensions: positive in its zeal and passion for the partner; negative in its anger when the covenant is broken and the zeal and passion are not reciprocated. It is not surprising, therefore, that the name of God is "Jealous" (Exod. 34:14) and that attribute is so often taken up by the Lord, usually in first-person

282

speech (e.g., Num. 25:11; Deut. 4:24; 6:15; 32:16, 21; 1 Kgs. 14:22). It thus is a self-identification more than it is an ascription on the part of others. It is a part of the claim of God on the loyalty and obedience and affection of the people.

Lusting after other gods. On an occasion when Moses speaks of the Lord as jealous, he goes on to describe the people's covenant with other gods as an act of prostitution, lusting or whoring (*zānâ*) after other gods (Exod. 34:15–16; cf. Judg. 2:17). The reference to the jealous God is matched by the imagery of sexual lust or harlotry as a way of speaking of the abandonment of the covenant relationship with the Lord.

The great sin. The identification of adultery as a "great sin," not only in Hebrew but also in Egyptian and Akkadian texts, has already been noted. In Genesis 20:9, Abimelech, upon hearing that Sarah is Abraham's wife and he has come close to sinning, nearly to committing adultery against his neighbor, calls in Abraham and says to him:

> What have you done to us? How have I sinned against you, that
> you have brought such great guilt [sin] on me and my kingdom?
> You have done things to me that ought not to be done. (20:9)

When the Israelites break the First and Second Commandments by making and worshiping the golden calf, Moses tells them—twice—that they have "sinned a great sin": "You have sinned a great sin. But now I will go up to the LORD; perhaps I can make atonement for your sin." (Exod. 32:30). Later the same language will be used to refer to the "great sin" that Jeroboam made the people commit (2 Kgs. 17:21). This again is the worship of the calves that Jeroboam had set up, a violation of the First and Second Commandments, described indirectly but clearly as an act of adultery.

Prophetic Indictment

The metaphor of adultery provides one of the strongest vehicles for prophetic indictment, carrying with it all the anger and jealousy that arise when a marriage is broken by acts of adultery. The metaphor is most extensive in Hosea 1–3 and in Ezekiel 16 and 23, where the story of Israel's faithfulness is spelled out in detail as a story of broken marriage, punishment, and restoration. The image

283

occurs elsewhere as well, in briefer but no less explicit form, for example, in Jeremiah 3 and 13. In these instances, certain features stand out:

Breach of covenant. From the beginning, the commitment intended in the First Commandment was understood as covenantal. That is articulated late in the story in the indictment of Israel for its sins in 2 Kings 17:37–39:

> ³⁷The statutes and the ordinances and the law and the commandment that he wrote for you, you shall always be careful to observe. You shall not worship other gods; ³⁸you shall not forget the covenant that I have made with you. You shall not worship other gods, ³⁹but you shall worship the LORD your God; he will deliver you out of the hand of all your enemies.

Here the worship of the Lord alone is equated with the covenant, and its clearest implication is the rejection of the worship of other gods. In Ezekiel's extended development of the marriage-adultery metaphor in Ezekiel 16, the marriage is described at the beginning as a covenant: "I pledged myself to you and entered into a covenant with you, says the Lord GOD, and you became mine" (Ezek 16:8b). The language is precisely that of the marriage covenant. What then follows is a long and harsh indictment of Israel/Judah for its adultery, its violation of the forming relationship, the commitment to each other that began when the Lord first saw his bride, when "no eye pitied you, . . . but you were thrown out in the open field" (16:5). The commitment is couched as the Lord's initiative, but the covenant is a shared commitment, whose only limit is the bounds of the covenant. When Judah pursues other partners, making shrines and images and dressing them up, presenting their children as offerings to these images—and the chapter lays all this out in extravagant detail—the covenant is broken.

If today's culture knows covenantal relationship primarily through the covenant of marriage, it is not that far from what one finds in Scripture. Although there were then, as in more recent history, political forms of covenant, the appropriation of the marriage and adultery metaphor for speaking about faithful and faithless conduct on the part of Israel seems to rest very much on the understanding of marriage as a covenant that joins the two parties together in a binding relationship and in a commitment that does not allow either one to commit to any other in the same way. In the marriage of husband and wife, that commitment is represented especially in the sexual relationship but not only there. In the relationship between God and people, that commitment is represented especially in acts of worship but not only there. Both kinds of commitment are covenantal. That is, they are enduring, unique, and exhaustive. Thus their breach is a terrible betrayal of trust and devotion and commitment.

Adultery language. There is no mistaking the depiction of Israel's betrayal of its God in pursuit of other gods as an act of adultery, betraying the covenant relationship to "love" others. When the Lord indicts Judah for their whorings, the announcement of judgment is explicit: "I will judge you as women who commit adultery" (Ezek. 16:38). In the second extended use of the metaphor of the Lord as husband and Judah as wife, the Lord says, "With their idols they have committed adultery" (23:37), and "She is worn out with her adulteries" (23:43). Through the prophet Jeremiah, the Lord says:

> I have seen your abominations,
> > your adulteries and neighings, your shameless prostitutions.
> > > > (13:27)

Jeremiah offers even more explicit identification of Judah's idolatries, comparable to those of the northern kingdom earlier, as acts of adultery in 3:8–9:

> [8]She [or "I"] saw that for all the adulteries of that faithless one, Israel, I had sent her away with a decree of divorce; yet her false sister Judah did not fear, but she too went and played the whore. [9]Because she took her whoredom so lightly, she polluted the land, committing adultery with stone and tree.

While Hosea uses primarily the language of harlotry and whoring (*zānâ*) in referring to the unfaithfulness of Israel, when the Lord instructs Hosea to enact in his own life the way God will take with the people, the instruction is couched in the language of adultery:

> Go, love a woman who has a lover and is an adulteress, just as the LORD loves the people of Israel, though they turn to other gods and love raisin cakes. (Hos. 3:1; cf. Jer. 7:18; 44:19)

285

The rage of jealousy. The reaction of the one betrayed is the passion of jealousy. It is the negative side of the zeal for the relationship that is positively expressed in the loving commitment (see the reference to Song 8:6 above). The vehement and indeed violent response of the Lord to these adulterous betrayals, as they are depicted especially in Ezekiel 16 and 23 but not only there, is often noted. The critique of the male or patriarchal orientation of the mode of expression is justified. The point, however, should not be lost, for the passion of jealousy is on both sides in the marriage relationship. In the covenant commitment it is not possible to treat its betrayal lightly. Thus most of the jealousy language in relation to God is to be found in relation to the violation of the First Commandment. The one whose name is Jealous (Exod. 34:14) unleashes that jealous passion, whose depth is only otherwise comprehended by the character of true covenantal love. The meaning of the jealousy is only understood in relation to the depth of the love that has been betrayed. Not to see that in critique of the violence of the Lord's reaction is to risk a kind of superficial view of the covenant between the Lord and the covenantal partner.

The possibility of renewal. A critical feature of the marriage-adultery figure as a way of speaking about the relationship between the Lord and Israel is the fact that while the outcome of Israel's "adultery" in going after other gods is punishment, that is not the end of the story. Adultery as the great sin may be the best human analogy for trying to depict and comprehend the faithlessness of God's people, but if so, there is a reverse instruction as well. In several contexts where the people's betrayal is couched in the imagery of adultery, there is an eventual renewal of the marriage relationship on the part of the Lord. Divine forgiveness does not let the marriage relationship go forever even in the face of massive adultery. So in Jeremiah 3:12b–13, the Lord calls "faithless Israel" to "return":

> [12b]Return, faithless Israel,
>> says the LORD.
> I will not look on you in anger,
>> for I am merciful,
>>> says the LORD;
> I will not be angry forever.

¹³Only acknowledge your guilt,
>   that you have rebelled against the Lord your God,
> and scattered your favors among strangers under every green tree,
>   and have not obeyed my voice,
>   says the Lord.

The renewal of the relationship expects repentance, but it depends upon divine mercy and compassion. Elsewhere, this renewal is spoken of specifically in terms of renewal of the covenant relationship and not necessarily prior to the realization and repentance of the adulterous people. So the Lord says to "adulterous" Judah:

> ⁵⁹Yes, thus says the Lord God: I will deal with you as you have done, you who have despised the oath, breaking the covenant; ⁶⁰yet I will remember my covenant with you in the days of your youth, and I will establish with you an everlasting covenant. . . . ⁶²I will establish my covenant with you, and you shall know that I am the Lord, ⁶³in order that you may remember and be confounded, and never open your mouth again because of your shame, when I forgive you all that you have done, says the Lord God. (Ezek. 16:59–60, 62–63)

In similar fashion, the prophet Hosea speaks of the Lord's punishment (2:13) but then goes on to tell of God's compassionate drawing of the faithless wife Israel back into the relationship: "Therefore, I will now allure her, and bring her into the wilderness, and speak tenderly to her" (2:14). The renewed relationship, at God's initiative, is once more a return to the marriage covenant:

> ¹⁶On that day, says the Lord, you will call me, "My husband," and no longer will you call me, "My Baal." ¹⁷For I will remove the names of the Baals from her mouth, and they shall be mentioned by name no more. ¹⁸I will make for you a covenant on that day with the wild animals. . . . ¹⁹And I will take you for my wife forever; I will take you for my wife in righteousness and in justice, in steadfast love, and in mercy. ²⁰I will take you for my wife in faithfulness; and you shall know the Lord. (2:16–20)

The marriage metaphor for Israel's relationship to God returns in the postexilic prophecy of Third Isaiah but without the presumption of adultery. There the Lord speaks of the return of Israel to its land as a marriage:

> [4]You shall no more be termed Forsaken,
>   and your land shall no more be termed Desolate;
> but you shall be called My Delight Is in Her,
>   and your land Married;
> for the LORD delights in you,
>   and your land shall be married.
> [5]For as a young man marries a young woman,
>   so shall your builder marry you,
> and as the bridegroom rejoices over the bride,
>   so shall your God rejoice over you.
>
> (Isa. 62:4–5)

The Reciprocity of the Image of Adultery

The significance of the use of the adultery image as a fundamental means of communicating what was involved in the violation of the covenant must not be underplayed. The analogy is indicative of what is at stake in human adultery as much as it is an appropriate metaphor for the divine-human covenantal relationship. One gains some sense of what happens in the violation of the marriage relationship by adultery as one reads the frequency and passion of the Lord's denunciation of the community for its waywardness. At the most fundamental level, betrayal has happened. Breach of the marriage covenant between a man and a woman is like the betrayal of the community that was freed and loved and made into a people by the Lord's loving acts. To have a relationship with someone else's spouse is only finally comparable to giving oneself over to some other god, some other claim on one's life and commitment. One may gain some sense of the depth of sin in adultery by realizing that it is the primary image for speaking about the breach of the relationship that is most central for human existence, the love of God.

Equally, there is something about the reality of adultery that is large enough to portray what happens in violating the service of God. One may comprehend the jealousy and passion on God's part, the terrible sense of betrayal and anguish that God feels when the people betray the Lord by giving themselves over to other objects of devotion only by comparing that anguish to the human experience of discovering that one's spouse has taken up with another lover, has entered into the most intimate relationship with someone other than that one with whom a deep and constant commitment has been made. The notion and language of faithfulness has its pri-

288

mary locale in the love of God and the love of one's spouse. From each relationship, something is learned about the other. Faithfulness in other relationships is important as well and to be pursued. As in learning respect for persons in authority by the way in which we respect and honor our parents, so also faithfulness in all relationships is learned as it is practiced in the two relationships that are the deepest of our lives.

The reciprocity of the image and the reality is crucial also precisely at the point where the image seems to outrun the reality, in what happens after adultery has taken place. The assumption that punishment and dissolution of the marriage relationship are the only options is undercut in the way in which the mercy of God leads to renewal of the covenant, a return to the marriage relationship even in the face of great acts of adultery. Divine forgiveness for adulterous breach of covenant can mirror human forgiveness for similar acts.

Opening the Moral Space of the Commandment in the Statutes and Ordinances

The subject of adultery is prominent in the statutes and ordinances, especially of Leviticus and Deuteronomy. The Book of the Covenant includes a statute having to do with the consequences of a man seducing a virgin for whom a bride price has not been paid. Inasmuch as this is a case of a woman who is not betrothed or married to someone else, the matter is handled by way of having the man marry the woman. The case is clearly a guide for dealing with sexual and marital relationships before they get to marriage and ensuring that once a virgin has been seduced, she must be taken in marriage. The statute does not open up the space of the commandment about adultery in any significant way. The legislation in Leviticus and Deuteronomy, however, does serve to specify and develop the trajectory of the commandment in some particular ways.

The Holiness Code (Lev. 17–26)

In the statutes of Leviticus 18 and 20, the prohibition against adultery in the Commandments opens up specific and further directives that have to do with sexual and family relationships and their interaction. The Decalogue character of Leviticus 19 is often noted, but

289

the statutes in the chapters immediately before and after are also to be seen in relation to the basic directives of the Commandments. The protection of marriage and the sexual relationship between husband and wife leads into various kinds of related concerns that seem to grow out of this. Both Leviticus 18:6–23 and 20:10–21 cover much the same territory and have to do primarily with forbidding sexual relations with various members of the family, or as the introductory statute of Leviticus 18:6 puts it, one's own flesh. These include parents, children, grandchildren, aunts, sisters-in-law, and so forth. The fundamental point of all of these is to confine sexual activity within the family to the husband and wife. There are also prohibitions against sexual intercourse between man and man (no reference to woman and woman), man or woman and animal, or during a woman's menstruation. In Leviticus 20, these are incorporated into the prohibitions against family sex, but they are separated and put at the end of the family sex prohibitions in Leviticus 18. Several features of these statutes can be lifted up.

The family as context. The family is clearly to the fore in chapters 18 and 20 and the statutes that deal with sexual relationships. This is evident in several ways. The most programmatic indication of the family context is the way in which the sequence of laws having to do with sexual relations in Leviticus 20 begins not only with a fairly explicit formulation of the commandment against adultery but also precedes that with one of the negative formulations of the commandment to honor parents:

> [9]Anyone who curses father or mother shall be put to death; that one has cursed father and mother, so his bloodguilt is upon him. [10]If a man commits adultery with the wife of his neighbor, both the adulterer and the adulteress shall be put to death. (my trans.)

Jacob Milgrom understands the sexual prohibitions that follow verse 9, in verses 10–21, as coming under the dishonoring of parents as the "fundamental cause":

> The fact that a law regarding dishonoring parents heads a list of prohibited sexual unions is hardly an accident, but, on the contrary, is crucial in understanding the provenance of the entire list. It reflects a patriarchal society that relates all familial relationships, by the twin principles of consanguinity and affinity, back to one's father and mother. It adverts to the unstated premise that

290

> dishonoring parents—that is, the breakdown of obligations to one's father or mother—is able to lead to the breakdown of relationships with the other members of the familial chain, including the sexual taboos. (Milgrom, *Leviticus 17–22*, 1744)

Leviticus 18:6–18 does not include a form of the commandment to honor mother and father, but the different prohibitions of family relational sex begin with a general injunction against sex with someone who is "of one's own flesh" and then move directly to incest with a parent (mother). Prohibition of sex with one's mother is the longest of these statutes and incorporates six references to either father or mother.

The protection of the family that begins in honoring mother and father carries forward in the care with which one avoids engaging in sexual intimacy with other members of the family. Family relationships are not the entire concern of the sexual statutes of Leviticus 18 and 20—there are also prohibitions of male-male intercourse, sexual relations with animals, and sex with a menstruating woman—but they dominate and are clearly the focus of attention. The specifics of the text indicate this, as Samuel Balentine has noted:

> It is apparent that prohibitions of certain sexual practices promote healthy family units, which are essential for the covenant community that bears witness to God's presence in the world. . . . One clue concerning the threat of sexual misconduct to the stability of the family occurs in 18:18. In the context of the injunction against marrying two sisters, the text warns against relationships that produce "rivalry." The Hebrew root, which means "show hostility toward, vex," may be paradigmatic for the dissension in the family that is implicit in all these prohibitions: Whenever the bonds of love are conflicted by illicit sexual practices, the family is threatened by strife and hostility. (*Leviticus*, 158)

The very fact that sexual intimacy is the center of marriage and the starting point of the family means that the community needs to be careful not to let that intimacy spill over into other family relationships and so endanger the well-being and harmony of the family, as well as the proper paternity and maternity of children who keep the family going.

Protection of the neighbor's marriage. The concern of the commandment against adultery to provide protection for one's neighbor in the sphere of marriage and family is specified precisely in

291

the adultery statutes of the Holiness Code. In Leviticus 18:20 and 20:10, one finds the most explicit forms of the prohibition of adultery outside the Decalogue itself. In both cases, the statute refers to adultery with one's neighbor's wife. Although the focus is on sexual relations within the family, a concern that grows out of keeping sex in the family but in its proper place, between husband and wife only, the starting point in Leviticus 20:10, as reinforced by Leviticus 18:20 at the end of its family sex prohibitions, is concern for the well-being of the neighbor and the neighbor's family and marriage. That is implicit in the commandment and now is brought to the fore in the formulations in the Holiness Code.

The sexual temptation. More implicit in these statutes is the sense of the power and allure of sex. While the form of the law focuses on the sexual initiative of males, the passion of sex is not to be presumed as confined to the male. Nor may one assume that all the cases referred to in these two chapters involve involuntary sex on the part of the various women members of the family. The combination of the erotic force in the human body and the proximity and intimacy of the family relationships makes the family a seedbed for the release of sexual forces and thus extremely vulnerable to its disintegration and destruction. These statutes point to the power of sex, the proper place of sex, and the immediate danger of misdirecting one's sexual attraction and desire. The connection to the Tenth Commandment against coveting would be obvious even if there were no reference to "coveting your neighbor's wife" in that commandment. The problem of desire, which endangers the proper obedience of nearly all the commandments but especially the prohibitions against adultery and stealing, is large and is underlined by these numerous statutes prohibiting the expression of sexual desire in ways other than in the marriage of husband and wife.

Same sex relationships. Though in this context it is not necessary to go into every type of forbidden sexual relationship described in Leviticus 18 and 20, the only two places in the legal material Old Testament where there is any reference to homosexual or same-sex relationships are here, in Leviticus 18:22 and 20:13. In both verses there is condemnation of a man lying with another man as one lies with a woman. The presence of this injunction in both chapters and the confinement of the issue to these chapters suggest that one needs to look at this issue in this context. If the adultery commandment—as spelled out in a variety of ways around sexual rela-

292

tionships that do not fit the order of creation, serve procreation, or protect the family and marriage—includes some reference to same-sex engagement, one needs to ask what we learn and can carry from these texts on that important and controversial matter. At the same time, on this issue as on most significant moral questions, one cannot work out a full picture of the moral issues simply on the basis of a brief statute. So one must look at them in the context of the larger whole of Scripture. Several observations are appropriate:

- What is at stake or the ground of the prohibition of male-male relationships is a debated matter, but it may have to do with one or more of the following:

  a. The wasting of male seed and so the loss of the opportunity for procreation that normally would be assumed with intercourse (Seow, "Heterotextual Perspective," 25–26 n.1).

  b. The effect of shame that would come with a male assuming the position of a woman (Walsh, "Leviticus 18:22 and 20:13," 208).

  c. The violation of the orders and boundaries of creation that may be inferred from the creation of man and woman and the creation of sexual organs that belong to man-woman sexual intercourse (as suggested also by the prohibition of either man or woman having sex with an animal and as well as by the clear connection to various prohibitions against mixing things that occur in relation to the adultery commandment in Deuteronomy; see below, "The Deuteronomic Code").

- The statutes say nothing whatsoever about female same-sex relations, probably because they did not involve the spilling of seed. It may be, therefore, that this was not really a concern of the community in its protection of sex in marriage.
- The statutes have to do with sexual relations kept within the sphere of marriage and do not presume that male-male sexual activity could take place within such a context.
- Thus, there is within these statutes no reference to or thought of same-sex relations occurring within a continuing relation of affection and commitment and responsibility for each other. Like the provisions against intercourse with animals, they assume the male-male sexual activity as a specific, momentary act and not a part of a continuing relationship, though one cannot assume

293

that such a statute would not have been written if there was such presumption.

The particularity of these statutes, therefore—which, like the others in Leviticus 18 and 20, are instructive about the protection of sexuality within the intimate covenantal relation of marriage—needs to be viewed in a larger context that recognizes several things:

1. The statutes that spell out the implications of the Commandments illustrate implications of the Commandments in different times and contexts. They are instructive but do not have the same binding force that the Commandments themselves do. Or better, they both give some direction and lead us to thinking in our own time about the force of the Commandments, about how they are to be held and worked out in our own situation.

2. As many have noted, there are various points at which the specifics of these statutes are no longer held to be operative in the life of the Christian community. Thus the mixing of different kinds of seeds and cloth and animals (e.g., Deut. 22:9–11), which is prohibited as part of the Israelite and biblical distinctions, orders and boundaries, goes on routinely in our culture. We have not found many of these statutes to be binding or destructive of human relationships, or even violating a creational order. So there is no restriction on sexual activity when a woman is menstruating or when procreation is not possible. There is no restriction on a woman remarrying her former husband after a divorce (Deut. 24:1–4).

3. We have already noted that the creation story, relative to the creation of man and woman, is told in different ways. One focuses, at least implicitly, on the role of man and woman as procreators and rulers of the creation (Gen. 1). The other, however, does not lift procreation to the center but focuses more on the continuing relationship of intimacy, companionship, support, and shared life and responsibility, including complicity in disobeying God (Gen. 2–3). The way in which the Old Testament takes up the matter of adultery and sees it as an image and parable for the faithful relationship with God is consistent with Paul Lehmann's suggestion that the man-woman relationship as described and laid out in the creation stories can be understood as *foundational* rather than *limiting* or *restrictive*. It is paradigmatic for human relations rather than restricting them. In various ways employment of the adultery image

indicates that we have in the marriage relationship and its protection something that points us to various relationships and identifies the critical thing as keeping covenant and not harming the neighbor's relationship. This has much significance for understanding what matters with regard to same-sex relationships. To use Lehmann's terms again, it is a matter of the significant in the factual, in this case the character of the relationship more than the fact of it. The Levitical laws have to do with a particular kind of sexual act, not with the gamut of affections, feelings, acts, and commitments that belong to a relationship of two persons that is intimate and permanent, characterized by love and faithfulness (Miller, "What the Scriptures Principally Teach").

The Deuteronomic Code (Deut. 12–26)

To the extent that one can see in the Deuteronomic Code an arrangement of statutes along the lines of the order of the Decalogue, the commandment against adultery would find its development and specification in chapter 22 along with much of chapter 23, at least through verse 14 [15 Heb.]. Deuteronomy 22 contains several statutes having to do with marital relations. While the word "adultery" does not occur, the statutes of Deuteronomy 22:13–30 [22:13–23:1 Heb.] are clearly concerned with sexual activity outside of or related to marriage. Deuteronomy 23:1–15 does not seem to be obviously connected to the prohibition of adultery in the Commandments. The statutes there, however, represent an important carry through of the sexual aspect of marriage into matters having to do with purity and with proper boundaries in the cultic life of the people. The proper definition of marriage and the sanctity of the sexual relationship within it now lead into statutory instruction about further matters of proper definition, limits, and purity.

Adultery cases. The statutes in Deuteronomy 22:13–30 consist of the following:

> Six cases of illicit sexual relations between a man and a woman: (1) a husband's false accusation of his wife's lack of virginity at marriage, (2) a husband's true accusation of his wife's lack of virginity at marriage, (3) a man's adultery with a woman married to another man, (4) a man's illicit sexual encounter, in a city, with a virgin engaged to marry another man, (5) a man's illicit sexual encounter, in the open country, with a virgin engaged to marry another man,

295

(6) a man's illicit sexual encounter with a virgin not yet engaged to marry another man. (Olson, *Death of Moses,* 102)

As illustrations of ways of specifying the prohibition against adultery, they reveal several things:

1. They reflect a patriarchal and male-dominated cultural ethos, with men as the primary actors and controlling figures and the question of women's virginity (vv. 13–21) a prominent issue but not that of men. Not only is male virginity not an issue, but also a woman who has had sexual relations with a man before her marriage is vulnerable while the man is ignored, and she is stoned by the men of her town. As always, the specification of a commandment in the statutes is relative to its time and cultural ethos and is illustrative for the community in its further life, but not restrictive. The trajectory of the commandment goes through these statutes and learns from them, but it does not stop there or fix certain elements of the social structure as permanently determinative of the way this commandment "works."

2. As in Leviticus 20:10, the seriousness of adultery is reinforced with the death penalty for both participants in an act of adultery (Deut. 22:22).

3. The seriousness of sexual relations outside of marriage is indicated by the focus on sexual purity—that of the woman!—in a way not simply tied to reproduction. Hence sexual activity is supposed to be withheld until marriage is presumed. Even if there is no procreation, sexual intercourse is prohibited. In these statutes, it is only the woman for whom this requirement is set, but the focus on the woman's confining her sexual activity to marriage opens up the question of a reciprocal delimiting of sexual activity on the part of the husband. In other words, the seriousness and intimacy of the sexual life, which is here focused on the woman, is lifted up. It is further undergirded by the requirement of the male to marry the woman with whom he has had intercourse—and without the possibility of later divorce—if she was not already married or betrothed (22:29).

4. Adultery and proper sexual relationships are community concerns and have to do with the righteousness and holiness of the community as a whole. This is indicated in several ways in the text. The husband who makes a false accusation has slandered "a virgin in Israel" (22:19 NJPS). The woman who has had sexual relations

before marriage and is so discovered is executed because "she committed a shameful thing in Israel" (v. 21, my trans.). The purpose of execution, in all the instances where it is to be carried out, is "so you shall purge the evil from your midst/Israel" (vv. 21, 22, 24). The statutes clearly assume the husband or father's rights over the wife/betrothed and daughter. The matter, however, is not only a marital or family concern. Adultery is an offense against the community and brings shame upon the community as a whole, affecting its holiness and purity. That also seems to be what is at stake in the related statutes that follow in Deuteronomy 23.

Purity and order. The statutes before and after those having to do with adultery do not in fact address that topic. So their direct pertinence to the interpretation of the prohibition of adultery is slight. There seems, however, to be some sense in which the concern for proper relationships that centers so much in marriage and its protection carries over into a sense of order and proper relationship in other areas, many of which may seem to the contemporary reader to be of little significance. There is one that deals with the gender distinction being preserved against transvestism (22:5), thus calling for men and women to function within their gender roles, however that may be defined at a particular moment, and not to pretend to be of the other sex. The creational distinction so central to the function of nature and human life is not to be fuzzed over. God's order in creation matters, especially in regard to the creation of man and woman and their relationship to one another.

That concern is then seen to flow into other areas where there is a desire to keep things in their natural order (22:9–11) and to keep the place of the divine presence and meeting pure and holy (23:1–14). Such concern for the proper order of things stands in a legitimate tension with the experience of bringing different things together, so that relationships, usefulness, beauty, and other features of God's creation are accomplished not only in separation but also in new orderings. Here is where the contextual character of the statutes limits their usefulness. Those kinds of boundaries that do not interfere with the purpose, beauty, and usefulness of the creation may often be crossed. The statutes derive a concern for proper boundaries and relationships from the sexuality and covenantal intimacy of marriage. Covenantal marriage is foundational; the specific statutes are illustrative and not necessarily perduring and binding.

297

The Seventh Commandment in the Stories of Scripture

The Fathers and Mothers of Israel

The sin of adultery is a prominent feature of the stories of Abraham, Isaac, and Joseph. In the case of Abraham and Isaac, it is the issue at the heart of the accounts of a patriarch's passing off his wife as his sister in a foreign land for fear that he will be killed so that the ruler or someone in power can take his wife (Gen. 12:10–20; 20:1–18; 26:1–11). The origin and redactional history of these stories is a much-debated matter. The similarities in the stories, however, are sufficient for giving attention to them together in this instance without the need to uncover their complicated compositional history. In each instance, however, the particular thematic point of the story is handled differently. They are consistent at the point of the patriarch being afraid that persons will be attracted to his beautiful wife (so 12:11, 14; 26:7) and thus kill him. In the progress of the stories, however, what happens is different in each case. In the first instance, the king of Egypt actually takes Sarah, Abraham's wife, and makes her his wife (12:19), though nothing explicit is said about Pharoah's lying with her or going in to her. Abimelech, king of Gerar, has Sarah brought to him, but before he can have sexual relations with her (20:4), God appears to him in a dream to let him know what he is about to do and that he will die if he does so. In the third account, Isaac passes his wife off as his sister. The deceit is uncovered, however, not because Abimelech takes Rebekah for a wife but because Isaac is seen fondling "his sister" (26:8). In the first two accounts, the ruler acts unwittingly; in the final account, it never reaches the stage of adultery, but the possibility of that is explicitly stated at the end of the story (Gen. 26:10).

Several features stand out in the three narratives:

1. Taking another man's wife, whether or not knowledgeably, and having sexual relations with her is a sin. In one instance, it is called "a great sin" (20:9 RSV); in another, adultery is a potential source of "guilt" (26:10).

2. Adultery is adultery even when the spouse, in this instance, clearly the husband and possibly also the wife (see 20:5), consents to the arrangement. At least in these stories, the husband is not the possessor of his wife's sexuality with the freedom to do as he pleases. In these narratives the implicit restriction on such liberty is surely tied to the promise of posterity for Abraham and Isaac.

3. The patriarch does not regard his wife having relations with another man as so great a sin or crime as to avoid it at any cost. Fear for his life overrules inhibitions against letting his wife have relations with another man. At every point the story assumes the patriarchal social system and gives no indication at any point what the wife's reaction is to this sharp violation of her marital relationship. In each instance the story presumes her acquiescence but tells us nothing of her internal or external reactions to the plan.

4. Interpretation of the act of adultery or potential adultery as sinful is implicit (12:17) or explicit (20:3, 6) on the part of God. In each of these instances, some affliction comes upon the ruler who has taken Sarah into his household, even if he has not committed adultery (so Abimelech, who is threatened with death if he does approach Sarah).

5. Each of the rulers of a foreign land, Pharaoh in Egypt and Abimelech in Gerar, recognizes that taking another man's wife, having sexual relations with the wife of another man, is a crime or a sin. With regard to this act, the three stories assume a common ethos. That ethos is consistent with what is known of ancient Near Eastern society in general, where adultery was consistently regarded as a crime or sin.

These stories do not tell us something different or in more detail about adultery and the importance of protecting the marriage relationship. In this series of related stories, however, one may recognize that, according to the biblical narrative, the sin of adultery was generally acknowledged as something of great and dramatic consequence not only within Israel but also among its neighbors. Even when adultery does not take place and there is no divine threat, Abimelech rebukes Isaac for placing his people in danger of having committed adultery. In these stories it is the outsiders who lift up the sin and guilt of adultery. According to the tradition of Scripture, therefore, the protection of the marriage relationship was not peculiar to the Israelite ethos. The absence of any condemnation of Abraham or Isaac in the stories is surprising. The response of the rulers and Philistines to what Abraham and Isaac do, however, carries a strong implicit criticism of the action of the patriarchs as they describe the actions as bringing guilt and ask in each case, "What have you done to us/me?" (12:18; 20:9; 26:10). And in Abraham's case, the sister-wife episodes may have something to do with why God tests Abraham in Genesis 22.

Although there is only a brief reference to it, the report that Reuben slept with his father's concubine or secondary wife, Bilhah, is another instance of a breach of the marriage relationship, in this case as incest (see Lev. 18:8; 20:11; Deut. 22:30 [23:1 Heb.]). That such an act had communal implications and was destructive of the social fabric may be inferred from the word that is added to the simple statement of what Reuben did: "and Israel heard of it" (Gen. 35:22). The disruption such hearing would produce may be inferred from the preceding story of Shechem's rape of Dinah, which reports on what happens when Jacob "hears" and then when his sons "hear" of what has happened (Gen. 34). The outcome is violent conflict between the sons of Jacob and Hamor's household and then also Jacob's rebuke of his sons for bringing trouble upon their family among the inhabitants of the land. In like manner, the violation of the relationship of Jacob and Bilhah becomes a communal shame that is remembered in the blessing of Reuben in 49:4:

> Unstable as water, you shall no longer excell
>> because you went up onto your father's bed;
>> then you defiled it—you went up onto my couch!

The sin of adultery is the cause of Joseph's being thrown into prison, not because he commits adultery but because he resists the seductive efforts of Potiphar's wife to get him to do so. While he responds by pointing to all that his master Potiphar has done for him and entrusted to him, Joseph's rebuke of Potiphar's wife is not primarily because having sex with her would be unfair and a breach of trust. There are three facets to his refusal to lie with his master's wife (39:9): (1) "You are his wife"; (2) to have sex with her would be a "great wickedness"; and (3) it would be a sin against God. The story of Joseph and Potiphar's wife is thus consistent with the other stories except in the role reversal. The patriarch resists committing adultery while the foreign woman presses him to do so. The marriage of the neighbor, in this case, the Egyptian master Potiphar, is inviolable and not to be broken by Joseph's having sexual relations with his neighbor's wife.

Joseph's story is consistent with the others in recognizing that having sexual relations with another's spouse is both a crime or sin against the neighbor and a sin against God. It is not a matter of concern only within the family or clan relationship. With whomever it happens, the family is disrupted and the marriage broken. There are not, at least as far as one can infer from these stories, some circumstances in which such activity may be allowed, for example, with an unmarried slave (Joseph) or with agreement on the part of the parties involved (Abraham and Isaac), without consequences, either the pragmatic ones of shame, disruption, and even violence, or the judgmental ones of divine punishment.

The House of David

There are two powerful stories of adultery and sexual misbehavior in the long account of David's reign. They belong on the trajectory of the Seventh Commandment as dramatic instances of the effects of disobeying the divine instruction about how and where sexual relations among men and women are to happen.

David and Bathsheba. The most famous of these accounts is the report of David's taking Bathsheba (2 Sam. 11–12). It is an example of both the power of sex and the use of power for sex. David's lying with his neighbor's wife is a result of his being aroused by seeing Bathsheba bathing. She is obviously naked and, according to the text, very beautiful. David's desire for sex with this beautiful woman causes him to have her brought to him, and they have intercourse. The king's intention is simply to have sex with this gorgeous woman. The outcome of the act, however, carries it further. She reports that she is pregnant. The rest of the story recounts David's machinations to hide the fact that the child is his. Unfortunately, that is difficult to do because her husband, Uriah, is in the battlefield and refuses to enjoy the customary pleasures of life—food, drink, and sex—as long as the ark of the covenant and the armies of Israel and Judah are in the field. Failing to lure Uriah into sex with his wife, which would disguise the paternity of her child, he has Uriah killed, by deception, in the battle and then makes Bathsheba his wife. In the following chapter, David receives a visit from Nathan the prophet, in the course of which his sin is disclosed and a double punishment is announced. The punishment corresponds to the sin in that the king who took and slept with another man's wife will have his own wives taken and lain with by another man; and the child born of the adulterous act will die.

Several features of the account merit closer attention in this context:

301

1. David's act as a sin against his neighbor is lifted up in the story in three ways: (a) the identification of Bathsheba from the

start as the "wife of Uriah" (11:3, 26); (b) Nathan's emphasis on this point with the parable of the poor man's "lamb" and his identification of the woman involved only as "the wife of Uriah" (12:10, 15) or "his wife" (12:9); and (c) Nathan's announcement that David's punishment will be the Lord's taking of his wives and giving them to "your neighbor" (12:11), the only occurrence of *rēa*ᶜ in this sense in 2 Samuel.

2. The parable of the rich man taking the poor man's lamb is a pointer to the adulterous act as an abuse of power and wealth. The act would be no less adulterous under other circumstances, but in this instance David has used his power as king to take the wife of another man, even if he tried to conceal the fact. The story tells nothing of Bathsheba's reaction, but one must assume that she is forced into this act of adultery against her husband because of the power of the king.

3. The Tenth Commandment is fully in view and violated as much as the commandment against adultery. It is David's inordinate desire for this beautiful woman that leads him to take her and sin against his neighbor.

4. The outcome of David's adultery is the further violation of the commandment against killing or murder. In this as in other stories, one sees how the commandments form a protective fence around the neighbor; their breach by any act may involve other violations of the neighbor's right and good.

5. Whether Bathsheba perceives herself as a victim is not known, but David's adultery leads to tragic consequences for the woman whom he has taken for sexual pleasure as she finds herself pregnant with a child that is not her husband's and then, because of that, loses her husband—and her child.

6. Nathan's judgment speech is explicit about the way in which David's acts of adultery and murder are sins against God. In this case there is no reference to "the great sin," but both David and Nathan refer to David's actions as "sin" against the Lord (12:13). Further, the prophet speaks of David's "despising the word of the LORD" (12:9, 10) and "scorning" the Lord (12:14). One may presume that the "word" of the Lord in this instance refers to the "words" from Sinai commanding the people not to commit adultery and not to kill.

302

7. The downward movement of David's reign is the direct consequence of his acts of adultery and murder (12:11–12).

The account of David's adultery becomes a communal memory (cf. Ps. 51). It serves to interpret the commandment by telling and preserving the story of the great ruler's sin, thus reminding the community of the destructive power of sexual relations not guided by the Commandments and what they teach about the appropriate place of sexual intimacy. The tragic consequences underscore the instruction about adultery and are a pointed way of warning those who continue to read this story of the possibilities unleashed when the Commandments are not kept.

Amnon and Tamar. Immediately following the story of David and Bathsheba, the narrative account of David's reign tells the story of his son's excessive love for his half sister Tamar (2 Sam. 13). Amnon plots a way to try to seduce Tamar, but it does not work. She rejects his advances and forthrightly labels what he is doing a sacrilege (my trans. of *nĕbēlâ*), something that "is not done in Israel" and will bring her shame (13:12–13). His action is a "violation of the sacred taboos that define, hedge, and protect the structure of society" (McCarter, *II Samuel*, 323). Unable to obtain Tamar's acquiescence because of her awareness of the communal rejection of incest, Amnon rapes Tamar and then casts her out, loathing her after the act as much as he desired her before it. In great distress and shame, she goes to her brother Absalom and tells him what has happened. Hating Amnon because of what he has done to Tamar, Absalom quietly plots a way of revenge and has him killed.

The incident is not a matter of adultery. We have already seen, however, how the statutes of the Holiness Code open up the matter of carefulness in sexual matters to the avoidance of sexual relations with members of the family. The plain statutes of the Code are here enlivened by dramatic and terrifying story. The incest is not a theoretical, contextless moral misstep to be avoided. It is an act of a brother's violent rape of his half sister that leads to her shame and distress. It is a communal sin as well, an act against the norms of community life. There is no reference to divine reaction or judgment, but the reference to the potential act as a *nĕbēlâ*, something not done in Israel (13:12), lets us know that this is a sacrilege, outside the definition of what is proper for God's people. The devastation that flows out from the incest is immediate and extensive: Amnon's loathing of his violated sister, Tamar's shame and distress, Absalom's resultant hatred of his brother, his eventual murder of Amnon in revenge, and David's sorrow over the loss of one son and

303

the disappearance of another. Before this whole story is over, David loses another son, Absalom, after his effort to take over the throne of his father (2 Sam. 15–18). The sequence of incest and murder—violence leading to violence—is reminiscent of the preceding chapters. The consequences altogether are terrible and drawn out. The summary statement of Kyle McCarter is to the point:

> The initial sacrilege, therefore, will precipitate the destruction of the entire social unit, the family. And because this particular family is the royal family, the social fabric of all Israel will finally be threatened (chap. 20). (*II Samuel*, 328)

The story of David reaches its climax in the chapters immediately before 2 Samuel 11–13, with David's appointment as king (chap. 5), the taking of the ark into the sanctuary (chap. 6), the divine promise of an eternal Davidic house (chap. 7), and then the military victories recounted in 8:1–11:1. Then David sees Bathsheba. The two stories of adultery and incest and their complicated and unhappy outcomes provide a tragic turning point in the David story. It is all downhill from there. Furthermore, that decline is only partly described as divine judgment. What happens is the human *consequence* of adulterous activity as much as it is divine *punishment*. The lesson of the Commandments is played out in a large way in the house of David.

The Prophets Cry Out

The prophets' references to adultery are not confined to its metaphorical use in relation to the violation of the First Commandment. They also decry the acts of adultery that seem to have been all too common among the community. Their denunciations do not carry any special character to them. What is most noticeable is how regularly—and this is true to some degree of other commandments—committing adultery is joined with the disobedience of other commandments. Adultery thus is symptomatic of a wider covenantal unfaithfulness and societal disintegration. This is particularly obvious in such places as Jeremiah 7:9 and Hosea 4:2, which are classic prophetic references to the second table of the Decalogue, referring to murder, stealing, adultery, and swearing falsely. In Jeremiah 5 the prophet lifts up the adultery and prostitution practices of the people and sees them as an outflow of the disobedience of the First

Commandment. In that same chapter is a further particular association of adultery with lying or swearing falsely (5:2–3) that we see elsewhere in the prophets, specifically in Jeremiah 23:14 and 29:23, as well as Malachi 3:5. Hosea 7:4 lists the adultery of the people along with dealing falsely and stealing, though the adultery here may refer to the betrayal of the Lord (Mays, *Hosea*, 105).

In Ezekiel 18 and 22 one finds several instances where adultery is listed in the indictments along with other sins (18:6, 11, 15; 22:11). In these cases what is to be especially noted is that while other commandments are explicitly in view, such as honoring father and mother and not profaning the Sabbath (22:7–8), the catalog of the people's sins refers more to matters that are identified in the statutes and ordinances (18:9, 17). Yet these references to oppressing the poor, not restoring pledges, extorting from the stranger, wronging the widow and orphan, taking interest and bribes, and the like take up matters that belong on the trajectory of the Commandments, especially the commandment against stealing. Further, 18:6 and 22:10–11 cite prohibitions against incest as well as other prohibitions associated in the Holiness Code with the commandment against adultery.

At least two implications may be drawn from the prophets' references to adultery. One is the way in which adultery seems to be part of a larger disintegration of the social fabric, part of a culture in which the neighbor is unprotected in various ways. Especially obvious is the degree to which adultery goes along with deceit. That is so universally the case that one is not surprised to see it uncovered by the prophets, but their testimony is a reminder of the interaction of deceit and unfaithfulness (cf. Ps. 50:18–20). The community of trust is broken in several ways when the marriage relationship is broken. The second implication is a point that is fundamental to the whole discussion of the Commandments in these pages. It is the prophetic identification of the way in which the Commandments are referenced not only by their explicit citation but also by the statutes and ordinances that flow out from them. Ezekiel lists commandments, but alongside them he places statutes and ordinances that spell out the force and particularity of the commandments, thus calling attention to the strong connection between the commandments and the statutes and ordinances, a connection signaled from the start of the story when both types of instruction are set forth in the Torah.

Wisdom's Handbook for Faithfulness in Marriage

Proverbs 5–7 offers a manual of instruction for the young about matters sexual and marital. The two belong together, and that is what the instruction seeks to make clear. It is aimed at the young man, so its pertinence for the woman is inferential, suggesting that the issue of proper sexual relationship and faithfulness in marriage was in the context of Proverbs more a male issue than a female one. That was probably the case generally, but both story and law have shown us that the woman could also violate her marriage, and the instigator of improper sexual activity in these verses is a woman who entices young men when her husband is away (7:10–23). So the explicit instruction for the young man has something to say as well, if primarily by implication, also for the young woman.

The handbook begins with a warning against being lured into sexual relationships with the "strange" or loose woman (5:1–14), a danger signaled early in the teaching of Proverbs (2:16). This is followed in turn with a directive about turning one's full attention and desire to one's spouse (5:15–23). The chapter is thus a version of the negative and positive forms of the commandment against adultery, beginning with the dangers of forsaking one's marriage and being lured—and that is indeed the way that Proverbs sees falling into adultery—into sexual activity with a "strange" or "foreign" woman, with someone "outside" the marriage and family relationship.

The degree to which Proverbs here and elsewhere describes the lure and seductiveness of the "outside" woman suggests what more contemporary analyses of sexual mores and practices have indicated: sexual activity often seems more desirable with someone outside the established sexual relationship. Sex with the stranger or sex with the other who is not the normal sexual partner is very tempting and so a danger to which each person is vulnerable. This has much to do with the instruction of Proverbs putting so much weight on the ways and wiles of the other woman as well as on the dangers, the consequences that flow from wandering away from the proper sexual relationship (6:29), with the one to whom one is pledged and committed, with whom one's sexual enjoyment and procreation is appropriate: the husband or wife. The marriage relation is one of the places where attention toward the "other" or "stranger" is a wrong rather than a good. When the "other" draws one away from one's proper commitments and destroys the faith-

306

fulness of the covenanted relationships, the other is a category of unrighteousness.

The weight of temptation in the sexual sphere is so large and basic that instruction in this area puts some weight on resisting that outside lure. It does so in two ways. One is by recounting the bad outcomes that proceed from being drawn into sexual relations with the "strange woman." These are laid out at some length: the way to death, the loss of wealth to strangers, self-contempt, and disgrace before others (5:1–14). Motivation for proper sexual activity only within the marriage includes attending to the possible consequences of going outside. One cannot always move from the way the consequences are set forth poetically in Proverbs to the specific outcomes, but they are sufficiently suggestive, as when the teaching says, in effect, that you cannot play with fire without getting burned (6:27–28). In this opening section of chapter 5 as elsewhere, the social consequences of adultery are identified:

> Now I am at the point of utter ruin
> > in the midst of the public assembly.
> > > (v. 14)

The specific reference is vague, and some have seen an allusion to judicial proceedings. It is more likely that the one who looks back on the effects of his adulterous acts finds himself publicly shamed, losing his place in the community, his reputation to start with, and probably other forms of honorable standing as well.

The other way this instruction fights the lure of sex with the outside person is to remind the hearer of the joys of sex with the one inside, with one's own partner (5:15–23). There may be some dimension of concern for proper or legitimate offspring (vv. 13–14), but the weight of the argument for sex at home is because of the erotic pleasure it brings. There is enough sexual fun and pleasure with the one you love that it is not necessary to go outside the marriage. Sex is just as good with the wife or husband. Here the text is fairly explicit in its erotic tone. It speaks first in poetic manner:

> Drink water from your own cistern,
> > flowing water from your own well.
> > > (v. 15)

307

Water and good cisterns and healthy wells were crucial for Israel's well-being. The cistern/well here is one's own spouse, poetically figured as a source of fresh and flowing water, quenching whatever sexual thirst one may have. The well is deep; the water abundant; there is no need to search elsewhere. In similar fashion, the Song of Songs speaks of the woman as "a garden fountain, a well of living water, and flowing streams from Lebanon" (4:15). This being the case, there is no need for the man to let his seed flow in any other stream (Prov. 5:15).

The poetic instruction then moves to more explicit and erotically inviting language:

> [18]Let your fountain be blessed,
>   and rejoice in the wife of your youth,
>   [19]a lovely deer, a graceful doe.
> May her breasts satisfy you at all times;
>   may you be intoxicated always by her love.

The reference to the wife's breasts is stronger than the customary translation, and the image of flowing liquids continues, this time from the woman's breasts. The term for "satisfy" is another word for intoxicate or even saturate. The image would be clearer with something like "May her breasts drench you at all times." The teacher then asks "Why should you be intoxicated, my son, by another woman" (5:20) and at the end of this instruction points to the outcome of such a move as death because being so intoxicated has led to the loss of the necessary discipline to make life work. In other words, there is plenty of erotic, intoxicating sex flowing from the well of one's own marriage, exemplified here in one of the more erotic aspects of sexual activity, caressing and enjoying a woman's breasts. So why turn elsewhere when there is a full well at home? The adverbial expressions "at all times" and "always" (v. 19) serve to underscore the point that is being made.

Though the instruction of chapter 5 shows the dangers to one's own life and marriage when one engages in sex with someone other than one's spouse, whoever that may be, while underscoring the enjoyment of sex with one's spouse, chapter 6 moves to the specific act of adultery with the wife of a neighbor (vv. 20–35). The previous more general instruction about keeping and enjoying sex within the marital relationship now moves more pointedly to a strong warning against violating the marriage of another by having sex with the spouse of a neighbor. Four times there is explicit adultery language (6:24 Greek, 26, 29, 32). Here the argument is more severe than in chapter 5. It is not a matter of proclaiming the enjoyment of married sex but a clear warning against losing control in the face of an attractive married woman. This is playing with fire, and you cannot do that without getting burned. When the sexual breach is with the wife of another, then one risks the anger and destruction of the neighbor whose marriage has been violated (6:34–35) as well as disgrace and contempt before others. The social significance and consequences of breach of the marriage relationship are underscored. Furthermore, committing adultery is stupid. Wisdom's perspective comes into play with the words that whoever does this "lacks sense [lit., mind]" (6:32a). It is a form of suicide (6:32b), and the final verses of the chapter play that out in terms of disease, disgrace, and the revenge of the neighbor whose marriage has been violated (6:33–35).

A piece of the teaching here can be missed if the focus is simply on the words about adultery per se. That is the fact that the passage provides a way to avoid falling into this terrible disaster. That way is through the protection of the commandment and teaching of mother and father. What is certainly in mind is holding all this teaching forever in one's mind and heart. The imagery, which draws on the way in which the Shema is meant to function in the life of the community, has another dimension to it. The parental teaching is really a kind of apotropaic symbol, which one always wears so that it guides and watches over and keeps one from harm, in this case, the harm of being tempted by the sexual attractiveness of a woman who is not one's wife (and, mutatis mutandis, a man who is not one's husband). Thus the Commandments, carried forward and enfolded into the more extended teaching of mother and father, provide an armor against the dangers of seduction and temptation. That such armor may have been manifest in a visible form of the teaching is certainly a possibility. The visibility and rereading of the Commandments and the Shema were a tradition that is now extended into the parental teaching, which itself was instruction about the ancient and continuing direction of the Commandments.

In this section of Proverbs, the teaching of the mother and father comes to a conclusion in the long poem of chapter 7. It is vivid and particular, building on the previous two chapters but in a more dramatic way describing the various enticements that may lead a man into the arms of someone other than his wife. The outcome, however, is no different. It is death in some form or another. So the teaching is reiterated but in a more extended and lively way.

309

The Song of Songs: A Lesson in True Love

What the book of Proverbs opens up by way of its encouragement of a good and enjoyable sexual relationship with one's spouse is celebrated in beautiful poetic form in the Song of Songs. One need not go into great detail in this context. The important thing is to recognize that wisdom's lesson about the joy of sexual intimacy with one's spouse is spelled out now in rich language. It exalts the delight that lovers have in each other and especially in their bodies and the physical intimacy of their relationship. There is no dwelling on the marital state of the two lovers, but their contentment with one another and their commitment to one another is presumed and intimated in such expressions as "I am my beloved's and my beloved is mine" (Song 6:3) and the declaration "My dove, my perfect one, is the only one" (6:9). Most of the Song is a dialogue in which each exults in the physical beauty and desirability of the other, each longing for and finding the highest joy in seeing and touching the other and sharing a physical relationship. The picture of such physical and sexual enjoyment is given to the community that reads the Song as an intimation of what true physical love is all about. The sexual relationship may or may not result in procreation. That is, however, not even on the agenda here. Rather, the sheer joy of physical love is lifted up and made desirable and good, inviting and alluring. Such enjoyment of the other in these sensual and physical ways is at the heart of the binding of lovers in marriage. What lures them together remains at the heart of their relationship and is to be enjoyed to the fullest. Ellen Davis has put the matter this way:

> The thing that intrigues and embarrasses us about the Song—precisely the fact that its language is so private—is surely also the key to its unique value. The Song is the strongest possible affirmation of the desire for intimate, harmonious, enduring relationship with the other. The fact that it is found within the canon of scripture suggests that genuine intimacy brings us into contact with the sacred; it is the means through which human life in this world is sanctified. (*Proverbs*, 235)

Her last point is not to be overlooked. Through the centuries the interpretation of the Song has seen here rightly a metaphor for the relation between the soul and God or the community and God. That being the case, one hears its words about the joy and beauty

310

of the physical and sexual between lovers underscored in a rather astonishing way as something that is appropriate for speaking about the relationship with God. The intimacy of the sexual is a pointer to the intimacy of the sacred. The sacred seen at its best as something expressed in the erotic joy and pleasure of sexual intimacy says something about the value and place of true sexual pleasure between lovers. What the mother and father in Proverbs extol by way of drinking from one's own cistern and being intoxicated by the physical pleasure of one's spouse is developed in the Song in such a way that one cannot be deceived about Scripture's real affirmation of the enjoyment of such sexual and sensual pleasure.

Into the New Testament by Way of the Tenth Commandment

The Danger of Desire

The subject of adultery is not confined to a single commandment in the Decalogue. It comes to the fore again at the end, when the Commandments turn to the matter of desire and its possibilities for effecting harm against the neighbor. That is all the more the case when one moves from the Exodus version to the Deuteronomic one. In the former, desire for the wife of the neighbor and other things belonging to the neighbor is prohibited after the prohibition against desire for the neighbor's house (Exod. 20:17). In Deuteronomy 5, the prohibition against coveting the neighbor's wife occurs first and is separated from the rest of the coveting prohibitions (v. 21). It has often been argued that this move reflects Deuteronomy's higher view of women. Whether or not a case can be made for such an interpretation of the book as a whole, the Deuteronomic shift in the Decalogue serves to highlight and underscore the prohibition against coveting the wife of the neighbor. It lifts up the danger of sexual desire for another person's spouse. Too often such desire is so strong that the one who covets will move to take the neighbor's wife, as in the case of David and Uriah. The Deuteronomic Decalogue thus begins the problematic of desire in general with what may be the most intense desire of all: sexual desire. What is good and appropriate and one of the greatest pleasures of human existence is capable of being turned into a destructive act. It is not

311

enough simply to avoid adultery. One must also place human desire under control because desire provokes the act.

What happens in the heart and mind, which often leads to wrong actions, becomes the focus of attention when Jesus takes up the matter of adultery in the Sermon on the Mount (Matt. 5:27–30). The word about desire is underscored as Jesus calls the lustful look an act of adultery. This is not a break with the Commandments; it is a reinforcement of the direction opened up by the Tenth Command-ment: lustful desire for another's spouse already begins to undercut both the marriage of the one who so desires and that of the one who is desired. The distinction between the desire and the act is clear, but the assumption that desire is acceptable is not. There are two reasons for that. One is already implicit in the coveting command-ment, and that is the ease with which inordinate desire, lust, opens up into acting (cf. Prov. 6:27–28). The other is the close connec-tion between mind and heart and one's intimate relationship with another in marriage. The relationship with one's spouse is already compromised if there is a lustful desire for someone else.

The radical control of desire that is sought in both the Com-mandments and Jesus' interpretation of them should not be compromised as one deals realistically with sexual desire. Sexual attraction is so much a part of being human and always at work in the human psyche and body that one may want to dismiss the force of the teaching here in the face of a more realistic psychology, a clearer awareness of the way the brain and body work. Thomas Long provides a helpful way of hearing the force of Jesus' words in full without ignoring what we know of sexual desire:

> Jesus speaks . . . not of psychological introspection, but of people's basic attitudes, the choices that we make about what we allow to take root in our imaginations, to shape our thoughts, to govern our actions, and to mold our relationships. For Jesus, lust is a cov-etousness at the heart of a person, a distortion of the human will, in other words, an intention to break a sacred covenant poised just this side of action. The notion of sexual feeling constantly bubbling up from a spring in the unconscious mind is a modern idea, unknown to people in Matthew's day. The notion of posses-sive sexual desire being fed, petted, nurtured, and trained until it is straining at the leash ready to spring into destructive action is as old as humanity itself—and obsolete, claims Jesus, in the kingdom of heaven. (*Matthew*, 58)

The Question of Divorce

Divorce is not a practice that receives much attention in the Old Testament. It is presumed as a possibility in the legal statutes of the Pentateuch, at least for the husband to be able to divorce his wife (Deut. 22:19, 29; 24:1–4; cf. Jer. 3:1). The question of divorce comes into the discussion of adultery because in both the Old Testament and the New an equation is made between the two. Malachi 2:10–16 makes no explicit reference to adultery. But there is a strong statement about preserving the covenantal relationship between husband and wife because it is a reflection of the covenantal relationship with the Lord.

> [11]Judah has been faithless, and abomination has been committed in Israel and in Jerusalem; for Judah has profaned the sanctuary of the LORD, which he loves, and has married the daughter of a foreign god. . . . [13]And this you do as well: You cover the LORD's altar with tears, with weeping and groaning because he no longer regards the offering or accepts it with favor at your hand. [14]You ask, "Why does he not?" Because the LORD was a witness between you and the wife of your youth, to whom you have been faithless, though she is your companion and your wife by covenant. [15]Did not one God make her? Both flesh and spirit are his. And what does the one God desire? Godly offspring. So look to yourselves, and do not let anyone be faithless to the wife of his youth. [16]For I hate divorce, says the LORD, the God of Israel, and covering one's garment with violence, says the LORD of hosts. So take heed to yourselves and do not be faithless. (2:11, 13–16)

Here again, marriage is a metaphor, or in this instance, a reflection of the binding relationship that the community has with its God. Rather than marriage faithfulness being a way into thinking about faithfulness to God, however, the concern of the prophet is for faithfulness in the marriage relationship.

The particular issue that prompts these strong words, including the Lord's statement "I hate divorce," is the action of some of the men in the postexilic community to divorce their wives in order to marry women from outside Israel. Lying behind the concern of these verses is the deep issue of preserving the distinctiveness of Israel. In this case, however, there is a more immediate problem. It is what the text several times calls "treachery" (*bāgad*; 2:10, 11, 14, 15, 16), translated appropriately as "faithlessness" in the NRSV. So while there is

313

no explicit reference to adultery per se, divorcing a wife in order to marry another woman is an act of treachery to "your companion and your wife by covenant" (2:14), and further characterized as an act of "violence" (2:16). The husband has violated the marriage relationship by setting his spouse aside in favor of another woman. It may be done publicly and according to law, but it is an act of treachery and condemned by the Lord of Israel. The divine resistance to divorce is to be recognized; the particularity of that resistance is also to be underscored. It is resistance to divorce as an overt act of treachery toward one's spouse by turning to another woman.

The connection of divorce and adultery is more explicit in the New Testament, specifically in some of Jesus' teachings. There the argument is not far different from what we find in Malachi, at least in Jesus' debate with the Pharisees in Mark 10:2–12 and its parallels in Matthew 19:3–12 and Luke 16:18. The context is the effort on the part of the religious leaders to test Jesus on how to interpret the Mosaic law. In this context it is not necessary to go into all the interpretive issues around these texts. One may assume from these texts, as well as Matthew 5:31–32, that Jesus did not see divorce as the way of the kingdom and thus challenges the easy abandonment of a wife by her husband (Long, *Matthew*, 58–60; Hays, *Moral Vision*, 347–78). The main point to note in this context, however, is that, as in Deuteronomy 24:1–4, divorce is dealt with precisely in relation to remarriage. In all three texts the pronouncement by Jesus that adultery has been committed is when someone "divorces his wife and marries another" (Matt. 19:9; Mark 10:11; Luke 16:18) or "divorces her husband and marries another" (Mark 10:12). The text does not say that the divorce in mind is in order to marry someone else, but the Malachi text suggests that this is at the root of the matter: the easy dismissal of a spouse in order to marry someone else. The Markan text lets us know that divorce as a form of faithlessness is not finally confined to the acts of husbands but also includes the way in which the wife deals with the covenant of her marriage. The complex issues of divorce are not fully uncovered or dealt with in these teachings, but the danger of making divorce a legal way of faithlessness and treachery to one's spouse is opened up before the community and rejected as a way of acting in the kingdom of God.

314   Divorce comes up also in Paul's teaching to the Corinthian Christians (1 Cor. 7:10–16). It is not couched in terms of adultery, however, so it is less pertinent to our thinking about the trajectory

of the prohibition against adultery. Paul's instruction at this point does, however, represent an instance of the early church's dealing with moral complexity and trying to work out a stance of discipleship that does not flinch from following the way of the Lord but seeks to deal with the realities of life as it is encountered. It also begins to open up the possibility that remarriage may not be always an act of faithlessness to one's former spouse. Richard Hays's summary comment on the passage uncovers its significance for our thinking about moral issues:

> Paul's judgment in the case of the believer married to an unbeliever shows that the church may need to exercise flexible moral discernment in particular cases not sufficiently dealt with by the command of the Lord. This has significant implications for our thinking about the problem of remarriage after divorce. Paul does not tell us, for example, whether the believer whose unbelieving spouse chooses to separate is then free to remarry. . . . That question remained on the agenda for the Corinthians' own discernment. If remarriage is allowable in that case, might there be others as well, such as in cases of abuse or abandonment of one spouse by the other? The teaching of Paul and the gospels clearly excludes divorce and remarriage as a legal strategy for serial polygamy. But this still leaves many questions unresolved, and Paul's careful reflection about the issues addressed in verses 10–16 offers a model of how our thinking about such matters might proceed. (Hays, *First Corinthians*, 132)

An Evangelical Word

The story of the Seventh Commandment has its primary New Testament episode in the account of Jesus' controversy with the scribes and the Pharisees over the woman caught in adultery (John 8:1–11). The incident is, like so many others, a conflict story in which the religious leadership again seeks to trap Jesus in a violation of the law. He avoids the trap, and that is the chief point of the story. The story ends, however, not with a debate or with Jesus getting the last word with the scribes and Pharisees. It ends rather with Jesus' unexpected words to both the religious leaders and the adulterous woman. In both cases, the words send the others away. In one case, however, the leaders leave convicted of sin; in the other, the woman leaves freed from the burden of her sin and guilt.

315

These are not, however, Jesus' last words on this occasion. The episode concludes with his words to a person who has explicitly violated this commandment against adultery. His words to her— "Neither do I condemn you. Go your way, and from now on do not sin again"—together with those to the leaders are typical of the way in which the law maintains its fundamental claim but always within the context of the gospel. Jesus explicitly does not condemn her. What Jesus does is release the woman who has sinned. Today, he has come to preach good news to this adulterous woman, to proclaim release to the one who is bound by sin and guilt (Luke 4:18). Here, therefore, is the evangelical word that is sounded in the story of the Seventh Commandment. The woman is now free to go and does not stand under human or divine condemnation. The great sin is overcome by divine grace here imparted in the words of Jesus, who also calls the adulterous woman to a new life. She has sinned. The law makes that clear. Now, however, she is released from the burden and the punishment of that sin by the gracious words of Jesus.

In this episode we have Jesus before a violator of the Seventh Commandment. Under condemnation and threat of death, she is set free in every way, free from the sin that has undone her, released from the threat and condemnation. Here, therefore, is the story in the New Testament that does not vitiate the law that guided Israel's life; indeed, it is a story about the one who intensified the demands of the law in the Sermon on the Mount. His encounter with the adulterous woman, however, lets us know that even those most important rules for human life whose requirement is unambiguous and whose violation is clear still stand under the grace of God. No ethic of the law can afford to leave this story out, for it is the one place in the whole tradition where we become absolutely clear that under this Lord our disobedience is capable of being overcome and overwhelmed by the freeing grace of God.

CHAPTER 7

Property and Possessions

You shall not steal.—Exodus 20:15

Neither shall you steal.—Deuteronomy 5:19

There are many rich and necessary interconnections between or among the Ten Commandments. Inasmuch as human conduct and the moral life are not a complex of unrelated thoughts and actions, such interaction and overlap of concern and subject matter is inevitable. While instances of this are already evident in the discussion of other commandments, that interaction becomes increasingly clear as one moves to the final three commandments. Any extensive investigation of the commandment against stealing leads one directly into matters having to do with false witness and its trajectory, and vice versa. The commandment against coveting, of course, is directly related to greed and actions in which one engages out of avarice and cupidity. So the last commandment looks back on many of the Commandments and carries them to a different level. In many respects, it would be appropriate to deal with all three of these commandments together in a single chapter. That, however, would involve skimming over particular features belonging to the individual commandments. So each commandment is taken up separately here. In the process, however, I will identify and discuss interaction with other commandments—including commandments that come before—and ways their overlap is reflected in the Scriptures. Because it is not necessary to deal with the interaction of these three commandments in each chapter, the extensive connections between stealing and false witness are treated primarily in the

317

next chapter. The reader is referred to the section on "Lying and Stealing—Honor and Property" in that chapter for further exploration of the trajectory of the Eighth Commandment.

The Meaning of the Commandment

The commandment "You shall not steal" is one whose force seems clear and whose moral pertinence is universally accepted. For example, one standard work says: "The ethical consciousness of all men concurs that stealing is wrong" (Hamp, "gānabh," 45). And in one of the more helpful books on the Commandments where a hundred pages are devoted to discussion of the individual commandments, there are never less than five pages for any particular commandment except the one against stealing, which takes up only two and a half pages (Schmidt, *Die zehn Gebote*). The matter is a little more complicated than that, however, for this commandment has a specificity that opens up into a broader horizon of application from the beginning, and its trajectory of meaning and effect is already underway when we encounter it in the Decalogue. The substantive word of the commandment, "steal," (Heb.: *gānab*) means exactly what it suggests: to take from another and to do so by stealth, that is, under cover. There is an immediate problem, however, having to do with the implicit sanction or punishment for disobedience of this command. The other commandments are clearly identified as a kind of absolute law, for when we find forms of them in the Book of the Covenant or the Deuteronomic Code, they regularly are crimes for which the penalty is death. For example, Exodus 21:12 and 15:

> Whoever strikes a person mortally shall be put to death. (Sixth Commandment)
>
> Whoever strikes father or mother shall be put to death. (Fifth Commandment; cf. Deut. 21:18–21)

Or with regard to the Sabbath Commandment, the one who profanes the Sabbath is to be put to death (Exod. 31:14; cf. Num. 15:32–36). The matter seems to be handled differently with regard to theft, however.

318

In the statutes of the Book of the Covenant, there are several cases in Exodus 22 that deal with theft of property—for example,

theft of a work animal or a food animal. In each case, there is economic restitution by the thief, not capital punishment. The one
other case where an act of stealing is involved—and the word for
stealing is clearly used—follows the two cases cited above about
striking a person or striking father or mother and, like them, prescribes the death penalty: "Whoever steals a person, whether that
person has been sold or is still in possession, shall be put to death"
(Exod. 21:16, my trans.). Deuteronomy reiterates this point in the
only statute in the Deuteronomic Code that specifically refers to
stealing: "If someone is caught stealing another Israelite, enslaving or selling the Israelite, then that thief shall die" (24:7, my
trans.). The original force of the commandment, therefore, and still
operative by its specification in the two related codes of law, is the
freedom or protection of the individual, the theft of a *person* and
the conversion of the "personal" good into property for economic
exploitation. No member of the community shall appropriate any
other member of the community illegally or against their will for
economic gain or advantage.

The *story* of this commandment begins early in the Old Testament, when Joseph says from prison in Egypt: "I was stolen out of
the land of the Hebrews" (Gen. 40:15). That story is revealing for
the way in which it depicts the effects of stealing a person, what we
commonly call kidnapping: the loss of home and family, enslavement
in Egypt, subjection to imprisonment through the false accusations
of his master's wife. What is particularly noticeable in this story and
in the laws that have to do with stealing persons is that stealing
a person's freedom is virtually always a matter of economics, the
theft of a person for economic gain, turning the stolen object into
a human machine of productivity. Judah's comment to his brothers
is, "What *profit* (*beṣaᶜ*) is there if we kill . . . [him]? Come, let us
sell him" (Gen. 37:26). The statutes prohibiting stealing a person
in each instance assume that the purpose is to sell or ransom the
individual. Thus every attempt to enslave, to restrict the freedom,
and to coerce and force economic production from one's brother or
neighbor—such is a violation of the Eighth Commandment. The
slave trade thus gets its first blow under the hammer of freedom
and economic protection that is the Eighth Commandment, and
the Commandments are seen to uncover a complex of legal and
justice-shaped specifics about slavery that begin with the free Israelite but move out into other relationships that involve both the

319

nonfree and thus nonequal Israelite and the outsider or foreigner. For the question of persons as property is also taken up, as we have seen, in the Sabbath Commandment and the complex of statutes that unfold its moral ethos.

The trajectory of meaning and action that is unfolded out of the Eighth Commandment, to which the Sabbath Commandment attaches itself, thus begins in a specific and critical safeguard of human freedom that is hidden but real. It is real, as the other laws indicate. It is hidden because we only discern it from the other statutes. For there is, obviously, no object to the word "steal" in the commandment itself. That absence of a restricting object opens up the trajectory to include the prohibition against the covert act to rob a person of that one's *property* as well as of his or her *life*. So the law develops a body of casuistic law that identifies all sorts of ways in which one might steal from another and prohibits them or requires restitution when the theft happens and the thief is caught. Two illustrative examples, one complex of laws from the Book of the Covenant (Exodus 21–23) and one from the Deuteronomic Code (Deuteronomy 12–26), will help to make this point.

The Legal Trajectory of the Commandment

The Book of the Covenant (Exod. 20:22–23:33)

In Exodus 22:1 and the verses that follow, the Book of the Covenant begins a set of laws or statutes, running through verse 15, that have to do with theft and restitution. This is where the word for "steal" (*gānab*) in the Eighth Commandment comes into play most often in the Book of the Covenant. Several things may be observed:

1. In one instance the object of theft is "money or goods" (v. 7). In most cases the object is an ox, a donkey, a sheep (vv. 1, 9, 10), or a coat (once: v. 9, "clothing"). The reason for that repeated reference to animals is fairly obvious. These animals are the work and food and clothing animals, the means of economic support. Specifying of the commandment against stealing is thus seen to focus particularly upon its way of protection, not of property generally, though that is indicated in verse 9 with reference to "any other loss," but specifically of *the means of livelihood and production* for each member of the community. At least at this point on the trajectory and within

the moral space created by the commandment, it is not a matter of general property rights but of what human beings, a family, needs for support, to provide food and clothing.

2. The concern for theft opens up more generally the matter of *loss of property*—loss again of the means of subsistence such as work and food and clothing animals but also grain in the field—whether by intention, as by theft, or by accident, such as livestock grazing or fire (vv. 5–6). The Eighth Commandment thus leads into the large area of *restitution and restoration* as well as the *maintenance of justice* and *fair dealing*.

3. A series of these statutes has to do with *safekeeping and borrowing* the goods of another (vv. 7–13). In other words, relation to a neighbor's property and possession is not just a matter of possible theft or accidental damage, but also the relationship of trust and what Michael Welker calls the "social virtue" of readiness to help and to assist a neighbor, for example, by loaning an animal to help in cultivation or by keeping something for someone who is away on a trip. The endangerment of this social virtue is addressed in these statutes as cases are dealt with where one cannot easily determine what has happened. If goods kept for someone are stolen, how does the owner know this was not simply a theft by the neighbor who was keeping them? Statutes might have been set up saying the safekeeper was required to make full restitution. Then who would ever agree to help out this way and risk loss? Or the practice might have been the other way: The person who asked for help put oneself at risk. Too bad. Bad luck. Either alternative, however, would create a communal climate of mistrust and reticence to help or seek help, breaking down the fabric of social trust on which a moral ethos depends. The difficult issue is given cultic and public mode of resolution, the persons being brought before God for a decision. In one statute (22:10–13), provision is made for "an oath before the LORD"; so the *Third* Commandment, against misusing the divine name, comes into play to undergird the protection of property further. Perjury can and did happen, but the danger of mistrust is addressed since the community now knows that the matter is also under divine sanction and the community can remember the divine decision. Further, should mistrust be directed toward one who was truly innocent, that member of the community can live strengthened in the knowledge of one's own righteousness before God (Welker, "Recht," 398–401).

321

4. The references to ox and donkey and sheep, which are central to the theft and property laws, carry forward to the other references to these animals in statutes that follow. One provides for giving the firstborn of sheep and oxen to the Lord, thus relativizing the possibility of setting an absolute worth on even those things that sustain and provide for life (Exod. 22:30). In this act the members of the community are reminded that their access to the land is through God's allotment, that the first word about property is that it belongs to the Lord and only to the Lord—but importantly, secondarily to the family and the community. This is symbolized precisely in the *relinquishment* of the property that the statutes work so carefully to *safeguard*. Thus the Eighth Commandment is seen to lead not only to *ad hoc protection* of property but also to *regular relinquishment* of it. In these statutes, inalienable right to property is given up while its protection is ensured in a pragmatic and coherent complex of individual, communal, and divine interaction. And the community is reminded that its access to property is not by any *right* at all but by God's gift and in God's providence.

5. The *ox* and *donkey*, who are the primary focus of the theft cases, appear again in Exodus 23:4–5, verses occurring in the midst of a set of instructions that clearly have to do with the Ninth Commandment, against false witness, one of the many places where the concerns of the Eighth and Ninth Commandments overlap. These are two brief case laws having to do with the way in which one responds to the property, not just of a neighbor but also of one who is identified as an "enemy" (v. 4), who might be a person in the community with whom one is at enmity. The second one has to do with finding an animal of "one who hates you" resting while carrying a load (v. 5). This is a notoriously difficult verse, and the interpretations are varied. It appears as if the statute is meant to instruct the person in such a situation to provide some kind of help or release, but it may mean to leave the animal alone and not to interfere with the property of someone with whom you have a hostile relationship. With the first of these statutes, however, directing that one should return the straying ox or ass of an enemy to its owner (23:4), the trajectory of the commandment against stealing moves now into matters that not only have to do with protection, restitution, and relinquishment of property, but also set forth a more positive need to *take responsibility* for tending to that property, even if it is the property of one with whom one is at enmity. The divine instruction about loving one's enemy begins not

322

in the New Testament but in the moral dynamic opened up by the Eighth Commandment. Here, in effect, is a precursor to contemporary "Good Samaritan" laws, the legal accountability for attending to and not ignoring the need of one's neighbor.

This statute in the Book of the Covenant has its parallel in the Deuteronomic Code in a section that has to do largely with the Sixth Commandment against killing (22:1–4). Protecting life overlaps with protecting property. Because it is so closely connected to Exodus 23:4–5, it is appropriate to take it up in this context.

> ¹You shall not watch your neighbor's ox or sheep straying away and ignore them; you shall take them back to their owner. ²If the owner does not reside near you or you do not know who the owner is, you shall bring it to your own house, and it shall remain with you until the owner claims it; then you shall return it. ³You shall do the same with a neighbor's donkey; you shall do the same with a neighbor's garment; and you shall do the same with anything else that your neighbor loses and you find. You may not withhold your help.
> ⁴You shall not see your neighbor's donkey or ox fallen on the road and ignore it; you shall help to lift it up. (Deut. 22:1–4)

The Deuteronomic statute makes taking responsibility for property applicable explicitly to the brother or sister in the community, to one's compatriot now as well as to one's enemy. The Deuteronomic version expands the statutes in two ways: (1) to include the coat or garment of one's neighbor or anything that is the neighbor's; and (2) to require that one take the straying animal into one's own safekeeping until it is possible to get it back to the neighbor. It also clearly reads the second of the Exodus statutes as having to do with an animal that is not just resting under its burden but has fallen because of the load and so needs help. The Deuteronomic language is striking at one particular point. The term translated twice as "ignore" and once as "withhold your help" is, literally, "hide oneself." The threefold repetition underscores the responsibility of the neighbor to move in positively and take actions to help secure the neighbor's property and keep it safe from harm, a facet of the trajectory that is developed in the Reformed tradition and elsewhere. *Passivity and inaction* are prohibited, which means that positive action for the good is expected. Nor is this simply responding to the neighbor's request for safekeeping of property.

323

The Eighth Commandment thus does not simply inhibit one from mugging a person on the street or robbing a bank—exceedingly important inhibitions but responses to the commandment that work in a more passive way. It also serves to effect a more systemic activity to ensure the economic sufficiency of one's neighbor, a systemic activity that is not even vulnerable to likes and dislikes, to favoritisms and antipathies, to hostilities and enmity between members of the community. One might call this *the economics of the straying ox*. The force of the commandment is not simply that if I, that is, the one addressed by the statute, steal the property of my neighbor, I have to make restitution. It is also that if I find my neighbor's ox straying, *I cannot hide myself from the reality of my neighbor's economic endangerment.* I have to take the ox in, watch over it, and protect it, making sure that the property is returned so that my compatriot is able to use this ox to provide for the needs of life. The same is the case with my brother or sister's donkey or a coat or any kind of property that belongs to the neighbor. I am drawn into active responsibility for securing his or her economic well-being by securing and protecting the property of my neighbor, what Deirdre McCloskey calls "imaginative entry into the interests of others" ("Avarice," 316). The Eighth Commandment here carries forward into the creation of a communal disposition to watch for the economic endangerment of other members of the community and not to hide from it behind gated communities and the walling-off, literally or figuratively, of the ghettos of the economically endangered. Luther put it succinctly and well in his comment on this commandment:

> We are commanded to promote and further our neighbor's interests, and when they suffer any want, we are to help, share, and lend to both friends and foes. (Luther, "Large Catechism," in Kolb and Wengert, *Book of Concord*, 419–20)

The Deuteronomic Code (Deut. 12–26)

As the preceding discussion has intimated already, there is significant overlap between the commandment against stealing, with its frame of reference, and other commandments. For that reason it is necessary to look at several parts of the Deuteronomic Code to uncover its various ways of developing in specifics and practice how

324

one protects the property of one's neighbor. The exemplary and interpretive statutes of the Code that explicate the commandment against stealing lead into and overlap especially with those that grow out of the commandment against false witness. That is both because they follow each other in the sequence and because there is often a correlation between stealing and lying.

Deuteronomy 23:19–24:7 [23:20–24:7 Heb.]

The part of Deuteronomy regarded by most interpreters as developing the commandment against stealing is 23:19–24:7, though not all the statutes in these verses seem to deal directly with its concerns. For example, the last statutes in the Deuteronomic Code dealing with marriage matters and growing out of the preceding commandment against adultery make their appearance in 24:1–5, thus providing a kind of transition from thinking about matters of sexuality and marriage to property concerns (Braulik, "Sequence," 322). That transition is further accentuated by the real possibility that the husband who seeks to remarry his divorced wife after her second marriage ends, à la 24:1–4, might thereby profit from this relationship a second time, gaining access to any property acquired by his former wife in her second marriage (Westbrook, "Prohibition"). Marital relations are at the center, but property and possessions are in view as well, as they usually are in marital issues. The proper treatment of property as a focus of the statutes is anticipated a few verses earlier, in 23:15–16, providing sanctuary for an escaped slave. Counter to the general pattern of ancient Near Eastern law, slaves were not permanent property to be reclaimed if they had broken loose from their slavery.

The property concerns of this section are evident especially in 23:19–25 and 24:6–7. In the first of these blocks (23:19–20), the matter of *loans* is taken up, and the community is instructed not to profit off the situation of one's neighbor, one's brother or sister. Once again it is clear why the designation "brother" (or "sister") is a moral category and involves special responsibilities. While one might engage in commercial enterprises involving profit-making loans with someone outside the community (v. 19; cf. 15:6; 28:12), several texts make it clear that within the community, loans were made only to the poor, those in need of financial or economic support, and were for the benefit of the recipient, not the one who gave

325

the loan (Deut. 24:10–13; Exod. 22:25). Such support of the needy by loans was expected but could not be taken advantage of. This form of economic support of the needy without economic gain for the creditor is most clearly articulated in Leviticus 25:35–38:

> [35]If any of your kin fall into difficulty and become dependent on you, you shall support them; they shall live with you as though resident aliens. [36]Do not take interest in advance or otherwise make a profit from them, but fear your God; let them live with you. [37]You shall not lend them your money at interest taken in advance, or provide them food at a profit. [38]I am the LORD your God, who brought you out of the land of Egypt, to give you the land of Canaan, to be your God.

Here the statute makes it clear that loans within the community are incumbent upon its members as a way of providing for those in economic distress and so are to be granted where needed but not at a profit. That would be a form of theft, as is indicated by the attention given to matters of loans, pledges, and interest in these statutes dealing with the Eighth Commandment.

The statutes in Deuteronomy 23:21–23 and 24–25 [22–24 and 25–26 Heb.] parallel the one just dealt with having to do with loans without interest in that they "all deal with the unlawful taking or withholding of property rightfully belonging to another, that is, 'theft'" (Kaufman, "Structure," 140). The first of these might seem initially to deal with other matters than property and theft. In fact, however, it has to do with prompt fulfilling of a vow, "usually a sacrifice or equivalent monetary payment" (McBride, "Annotations," 291). In this instance it is "property" that now belongs to God and may not be kept as one's own (cf. Num. 30). The contemporary equivalent is the church pledge, which is a dedication of one's property to God so that it now is no longer one's own, and the pledge or vow, freely made, is to be kept. Not stealing means not keeping for oneself what one has committed to the Lord.

The instruction in Deuteronomy 23:24–25 [24–25 Heb.] continues the concern for proper attention to the property of others, allowing someone passing through a field or a vineyard to take some of what is there, presumably to assuage hunger. Here one may presume, as in cases above, that there is some need, some hunger that may be eased but only that. Access to the neighbor's property is only to fulfill a basic need, and one may not enhance one's own wealth

326

or goods by taking excessively from the vineyard or grain field. To make clear what is meant, the statute gives practical direction: No one may fill a container of grapes or use a sickle to cut down the neighbor's grain. That would move the situation from the availability of the neighbor's property for basic needs to a profit-making use of someone else's economic goods, in effect, theft. The statute is a beautiful balance between making one's goods available to those in need and protecting one's goods from wrongful appropriation. The Eighth Commandment points in both directions.

Transition Verses: Deuteronomy 24:6–7

The closest statute to the actual commandment against stealing—24:7, referring to stealing or kidnapping and selling a person (discussed above)—comes at the end of this section and provides a transition into the following block of statutes, those generally associated with the Ninth Commandment. While this section is discussed in detail in the next chapter, its relation to the matter of property needs to be lifted up in this context as well. Overlap with the Ninth Commandment is evident in the subject matter of both sections—23:19–24:7 (stealing) and 24:8–25:4 (false witness)—as they each deal with property and pledges, grain and vineyards, ways of taking from one's neighbor that can be economically harmful (stealing) and also dishonorable and inhumane (false witness). In 24:8–25:4 the particular concern of the instruction is proper treatment of the poor and marginal relative to property.

The interaction of these two sets of statutes is further indicated by the frequency of the key word *nepeš*, the word for "person" or "life" in the statute in 24:7 forbidding stealing a person (*nepeš*), that is, kidnapping. In an associative process effected by catchword, this statute is connected to the immediately preceding one in 24:6 by the reference there also to *nepeš* or "life": "No one shall take a mill or an upper millstone in pledge, for that would be taking a life [*nepeš*] in pledge." A close association is made between the *theft* of a person's life and the *economic deprivation* of a person's life by confiscating the primary means of providing bread on the table: a millstone for grinding the grain on which one may subsist. Here, the statute is not talking about stealing but about legitimate financial dealings: loans and collateral. Alongside a basic statute that deals directly with stealing a life (24:7) is set a corollary of the

327

protection of life: protection of the means of subsistence for life from *legal* deprivation (24:6). And the Eighth Commandment is seen to be open to a situation in which the neighbor may be in economic need and the neighbor's property vulnerable to loss in socially legitimated but not moral ways.

Deuteronomy 24:8–25:4

The opening of the statutes to the matter of loans and pledges as well as the protection of the means of subsistence as a sphere of moral space in which the commandment against stealing is worked out connects then with other verses in this section, a group of statutes that belong to the trajectory of meaning and implications effected by both the Eighth and Ninth Commandments. Except for one other passage (Deut. 15), all the treatment of loans and pledges is found in these two sections of Deuteronomy. After prohibiting taking interest on any loan to a neighbor in 23:19–20, the Deuteronomic law, recognizing that loans to the economically deprived are a part of the system and indeed expected, now guards against oppressive ways on the part of the creditor (24:10–13). The economic advantage a member of the community has over another one by holding a pledge may not be used to encroach on the property of another (v. 10) or to deprive another of the basic needs for life, such as clothing (vv. 12–13), a concern articulated in similar fashion in the Book of the Covenant (Exod. 22:25–27). Now it becomes clear why the coat or garment is included in the list of things that may be lost and must be returned if found (Exod. 22:9; Deut. 22:3). (For an actual case where returning a garment taken by a superior, possibly in pledge, is the subject matter, see the next chapter.)

The statute about the *pledge* of the *poor* in Deuteronomy 24:12–13 then leads into further statutes having to do with the protection of the weaker members of the society and their material goods or means of life. So the poor also have their wages covered in the statutes and with a similar motivation (24:14–15). Verse 15 reads: "You shall pay them their wages daily before sunset, because they are poor and their livelihood [life, *nepeš*] depends on them." Concern for the *nepeš*, the life, which is at the heart of the basic Deuteronomic formulation of the Eighth Commandment ("If a stealer of a *nepeš* is found . . ."; 24:7, my trans.), once again is the ground for further directive, this time about protection of wages.

328

The connection between stealing and withholding wages is even more explicit in Leviticus 19:13:

> You shall not defraud your neighbor; you shall not steal; and you shall not keep for yourself the wages of a laborer until morning.

All of these actions are forms of stealing. Two of them are stated more generally, but lest there be any uncertainty about the modes of defrauding and stealing, the specific example of withholding wages is given. In fact, the Hebrew word lying behind "defraud" in Leviticus 19:13 is translated more specifically in the NRSV of Deuteronomy 24:14 as "You shall not withhold the wages. . . ." The repetition of the matter of withholding wages from the poor in both Leviticus and Deuteronomy surely means that the example is more than that. It is paradigmatic, a basic form of theft to be avoided at all times. Lest there be any doubt about the ubiquity of this kind of theft, note its presence in the early Christian community (Jas. 5:1–6).

The instruction about how to act vis-à-vis pledges continues, then, with reference to the pledge of a widow in Deuteronomy 24:17 and thereby opens up the whole matter of appropriate justice for widow, orphan and stranger or alien—appropriate justice being economic support rather than economic deprivation. Thus the final laws in Deuteronomy 24 have to do with leaving grain, olives, and grapes in the fields rather than scavenging every last one, so that the widow, orphan, and alien may have access to the productivity of the allotment of land given by God for the sustenance of the community as a whole and thus for each clan, and within each clan, for each individual (24:17–22). That the poor are also in view is confirmed by Leviticus 23:22, which specifically sets this requirement as a means of providing support for "the poor and the alien." As time and circumstance have altered people's situation and pressed some into poverty, without goods and the fundamental possession of land on which to support themselves, the Eighth Commandment uncovers a process for accessing the land and its productivity. "You shall not steal," like all the prohibitions of the Decalogue, has its positive side. In these statutes the positive implication of the commandment is a process of sharing one's possessions with those who need the basic provisions for living and may not have access to them, repre- 329 sented most specifically in widows, orphans, and immigrants. The "good work" implicit in this commandment is, according to Luther, "selflessness, a willingness to help and serve all men with one's own means" (*Good Works*, 106). In one of his catechism hymns on the Ten Commandments, he succinctly states the positive and the prohibitive dimensions of the commandment (Leaver, "Luther's Catechism Hymns," 412):

Steal not thy neighbor's goods or gold,
   nor profit by his sweat and blood;
but open wide thy loving hand
   to all the poor in the land.
     Kyrieleis

One should not leave these statutes without some specific recognition of the presence of strong motivational sentences, designed to urge, encourage, and motivate obedience to the instructions given: promises of blessing and righteousness (Deut. 24:13, 19), warnings of guilt before God (24:15), indications of God's compassionate intervention when the poor and needy are mistreated (24:15; cf. Exod. 22:27 [26 Heb.]; Jas. 5:4), and reminders of the people's own experience of being needy and mistreated in Egypt (Deut. 24:18, 22). These motivational elements are discussed in more detail in the treatment of Deuteronomy 24:8–25:4 in the next chapter, and the reader is referred to that discussion. Such motivational aspects of these statutes are not surprising in that they already occur in several of the Commandments themselves. They are important reminders that living by the Commandments makes sense and has benefits. Such conduct coheres with the experience of the people. To go another way is to risk endangerment in the future. Obedience is assumed, but it is also given rational justification and encouraged.

What is to be noted in all of these statutes having to do with the commandment against stealing is that there continues to be the kind of negative or prohibitive formulation that we know from the Commandments—you shall not steal, you shall not watch your neighbor's ox straying, and the like—but around such formulations are other things that belong to the dynamic of the commandment against stealing: positive formulation of what you should do and what is needful; explanations of the situation and reasons for the statute that serve to motivate and support its function as policy for communal life; references to the deity whose word and way

330

is embodied in these statutes, who places sanctions on disobedience of them, and who undergirds their protection of the weak; and associations of the experience of the weak and poor with the memory of the community as a whole: Remember that you were slaves. This is how the commandment draws into a complex whole personal and situational dimensions, varying economic standings and interdependencies, and God's undergirding of communal and personal life. All of this is in behalf of routinizing communal welfare and well-being when they are threatened by the vicissitudes (theft), contingencies (loss), and changes (economics) that inevitably but unpredictably happen. The sense of coherence and wholeness in this complexity is here, as in the statutes generally, embodied in and embedded in the constitutional directive of the Commandments.

The First Commandment

The way the First Commandment grounds all the rest means that its connection to the whole is complex and rich. It is the First Commandment that pushes beyond all the matters discussed thus far to raise questions about human love of property and the acquisitive instinct *in principle*. What human beings possess and the desire to possess more—whether in material goods, influence (a form of possession of persons), sex (the possession of persons), or other matters—have the potential to become the primary center of meaning and value in life, the ultimate value and thus the claim that has the force of another god. The danger here, against which the First Commandment speaks, is set forth sharply in Jesus' injunction: "You cannot serve God and mammon" (Matt. 6:24//Luke 16:13 RSV); that is, you cannot serve God and property, a claim so basic to the commandment against stealing that one interpreter makes it the whole focus of his treatment of the commandment (Reno, "God and Mammon"). The language of Jesus' succinct statement is explicitly the language of the First and Second Commandments ("serve"). The saying functions both to relativize any form of property so that it cannot ever be of ultimate value and to warn that the instinct to make it so is ever with us. Making and worshiping other gods begins with what one has and desires.

331

The Story of the Commandment

Jacob and Laban (Gen. 30–31)

It is hardly a surprise that one encounters numerous stories of theft in Scripture. We have already looked at the Joseph story as a cardinal example of stealing a life for profit. Prior to that incident, the account of the Abrahamic descendants presents another story of theft, one that is complicated and carried by a number of acts of lying and stealing on the part of all the parties involved. It is the story of Jacob and Laban in Genesis 30–31. Their interaction with each other, however, cannot be taken out of its context. The whole story of Jacob is characterized by deceit, tricks, and theft. Nearly all the central characters are involved. Esau is the victim of Jacob's maneuvers twice, losing his birthright and his blessing. But that happens in no small part because, according to the text "Esau despised his birthright" (25:34). Rebekah is the brains behind Jacob's deception of Isaac to take away the firstborn blessing from Esau, but the impetus for her action is not only her preference for Jacob (25:28) but also because of the way that Esau's Hittite wives treated her and Isaac (26:35; 27:46). Jacob's deception of Laban in using sympathetic magic to make the strongest goats breed striped, speckled, and spotted offspring, according to the agreement he had with Laban, is a response to Laban's taking off all the existing striped, speckled, and spotted male and female goats immediately after they reach their agreement about distribution of the animals (30:35–36). By means of his magic schemes with the goats, Jacob becomes exceedingly rich (30:43), and Laban's sons complain that Jacob has taken all their father's wealth (31:1). Jacob, however, regards his wealth as justified because "[Laban] cheated me and changed my wages ten times" (31:7, 41). Rachel steals her father's household gods (31:19, 30), and Jacob "steals" Laban's mind, that is, does not tell him he is leaving (31:20, 27). Both Leah and Rachel feel that their father has dealt harshly with them, selling them and using up all the money.

It is in many ways a sad story of family maneuvers against one another, cheating, lying, and tricking each other. No one is outside or above the machinations. And machinations they truly are. Reciprocal theft and cheating set the members of the family at odds with one another, and only formal covenantal acts at the end can restore some relationship among them. This is not a typical instance of theft of property, but one notes that property is at the heart of the matter. Acquisition of wealth through flocks and dowries and inheritance is the main concern in the whole. The closest connection to the concerns reflected in the legal codes is Jacob's complaint that Laban cheated him and changed his wages ten times, a point underscored by being mentioned twice (31:7, 41). It is in direct connection with this complaint that Jacob claims God's help and support, first reporting that "he changed my wages ten times, but God did not permit him to harm me" (31:7). Then, after he makes the same charge directly to Laban, he confesses: "If the God of my father, the God of Abraham and the Fear of Isaac, had not been on my side, surely now you would have sent me away empty-handed. God saw my affliction and the labor of my hands, and rebuked you last night" (31:42). Claus Westermann has drawn attention to this as at the heart of the conflict between Jacob and Laban and the reason for God's blessing Jacob:

> It should be noted that the accusation that Jacob makes against Laban is concerned with the unjust exploitation of the labor of a subordinate by one in power. This is so important for the narrator that he puts it into the center of the conflict and uses it to show God's intervention on behalf of the weak. The link with two traditions is clear: on the one hand with the laments of the "poor" in the Psalms, on the other with the social accusations of the prophets. It is surprising that already in the patriarchal stories the God of the fathers is the one who stands by the weak and the one to whom the weak can have recourse when oppressed by the powerful. (*Genesis 12–36*, 501)

One may add that along with the Psalms and the Prophets, the legal traditions place the matter of proper wages and treatment of those one has hired as a central concern of the commandment against stealing.

Achan's Theft of the Devoted Things (Josh. 6:18–7:26)

The account of Achan's theft of some of the material goods of Jericho that were to be devoted to destruction and not allowed to become booty for the Israelites is a story that seems clearly to have the Commandments in its background, at least implicitly if not explicitly. It

333

is also a quite particular instance of theft, different from what is usually involved in violation of the Eighth Commandment. Theft in the customary sense is meant, as indicated by the divine word to Joshua when he cries out in lament after his men have been routed by the men of Ai, a city that Joshua had thought would be easy to take. In response to Joshua's complaint, the Lord says:

> Israel has sinned; they have transgressed my covenant that I imposed on them. They have taken some of the devoted things; they have stolen, they have acted deceitfully, and they have put them among their own belongings. (7:11)

Taking the devoted things has involved both stealing and lying. Furthermore, when Achan confesses to the crime, he says:

> [20]It is true; I am the one who sinned against the LORD God of Israel. This is what I did: [21]when I saw among the spoil a beautiful mantle from Shinar, and two hundred shekels of silver, and a bar of gold weighing fifty shekels, then I coveted them and took them. They now lie hidden in the ground inside my tent, with the silver underneath. (7:20–21)

The theft arises out of Achan's coveting the articles because of their beauty and value. So the interplay of actions addressed and prohibited in the Commandments happens once again, and economic factors are clearly at work.

What this story presents that is in tension with what we have said about the Eighth Commandment up to this point is that the punishment for the crime is execution, although the statutes discussed earlier make clear that such is not to be the outcome of stealing material goods. In this case, however, the theft is a sin against God, and the punishment involves the destruction of Achan, the devoted things, and "all that he has" (7:15, 24–25): all his property and his sons and daughters. Achan's sin has tainted the whole community, and only as everything having to do with Achan is eliminated from the community does the burning anger of God go away. The punishment is *karet*, literally, "cutting off," removal from the covenant community either by banishment or execution (cf. *kārat* in Lev. 20:3, 5, 6). Such a drastic penalty is "God's prerogative, to be used only in special cases such as Achan's" (Freedman, *The Nine Commandments*, 107). The story places the human act as much

334

in the realm of the first table of the Decalogue as in the second. The theft from God thus is at the same level as apostasy, idolatry, blasphemy, and breaking the Sabbath, all of which are sins that are subject to the punishment of death. That this story must be seen as a particular and unique example of the violation of the commandment against stealing is evident when we read that execution of a child for the parent's sin or a parent for the child's sin is forbidden by Deuteronomic law (24:16), a statute that is underscored by its being cited in 2 Kings 14:6, where, in the report of King Amaziah's execution of his father's murderers, it is reported that he did not execute their children and the Deuteronomic statute is quoted as the basis for this decision (cf. Jer. 31:29–30; Ezek. 18:2–4, 20).

Naboth's Vineyard (1 Kgs. 21)

Once again the story of the Commandments takes us to Naboth's vineyard and the multiple violations of the Commandments in the machinations of Jezebel and Ahab in their successful effort to appropriate from Naboth the vineyard he will not release. For more extended discussion of the story, see the treatments of it in the chapters on the commandments against murder, false witness, and coveting. It is not necessary to take up the text further here, but simply to call attention to the fact that what the whole story is about is an act of theft. In this case, however, we do not have anything like the kinds of incidents described, for example, in the Book of the Covenant. Rather, the theft is an act of political power, a series of actions accomplished by the power of the king, all of them to gain property by manipulation of the legal or judicial machinery. There is no human framework within which to bring the king and queen to justice, so that is accomplished through prophetic word (21:19) and divine action (22:37–38; cf. 2 Kgs. 9:30–37).

The Postexilic Community (Neh. 5:1–13)

Safeguarding the property and thus the well-being of members of the community, the goal of the Eighth Commandment, is an enduring concern in Scripture, a fact reflected in Nehemiah 5, where an "outcry," the cry of the oppressed (see Exod. 22:22–23; Deut. 24:15), is raised by some members of the postexilic community—the common folk and their wives—against other citizens, "most probably the more affluent of those who had returned from the Babylonian diaspora with their leaders" (Blenkinsopp, *Ezra-Nehemiah*; Neh. 5:1, 6). In verse 7, these leaders are identified as "nobles and officials." Several complaints are made against them in verses 3–5, centering in having to pledge either their children (v. 3; so Brockington, *Ezra, Nehemiah, and Esther*, 150; and others) or their fields and vineyards (v. 4) in order to get food to eat. Pledges are being seized and presumably held on to (vv. 7, 11). Some of those complaining are property owners, but their circumstances are forcing them into poverty, into making pledges and indenturing their children. The concern of the commandment against theft to protect the property, especially of the impoverished and needy, is being ignored, as Nehemiah obviously recognizes. So he calls for the restoration of all the property taken in pledge (v. 11). Unlike other stories, this one has a happy ending as the nobles and wealthy agree to Nehemiah's demand and promise to restore everything (v. 12). The narrative is important, not simply as an illustration of the problem against which the commandment is directed, but also because it indicates that the community can be called to account and make amends for its mistreatment of the poor in depriving them of the material goods needed to live.

Other Voices

The Prophets' Judgments

In continuity with Elijah (cf. 1 Kings 21), the later prophets sound a strong word against the rich and powerful who oppress and rob the poor. In the prophecy of Isaiah, the Lord brings the leaders into court because "that which was robbed from the poor is in your houses" (my trans.); they are "grinding the face of the poor" (3:14–15), and judgment is announced against

> ¹you who make iniquitous decrees,
>   who write oppressive statutes,
> ²to turn aside the needy from justice
>   and to rob the poor of my people of their right,
> that widows may be your spoil,
>   and that you may make the orphans your prey!
>   (10:1–2)

In the background of this indictment, one hears echoes of the statutes of the legal codes that protect the poor, now being undone by new statutes that do just the opposite. The legal-judicial system is used by the leaders and the rich to oppress the poor and rob them. "Through directives and decrees, red tape and delay, they rob the widows and orphans of their rights, and through trickery render the judicial system into a heartless exercise for defrauding the vulnerable" (Childs, *Isaiah*, 87). In the same era, the prophet Micah denounces the powerful who lie awake at night devising schemes because "they covet fields, and steal them; houses, and take them away" (2:2). Once again the reader is reminded of the intimate connection between inordinate desire for what others have and the impetus it provides for violation of the Eighth Commandment, especially when, like Ahab, the power is in one's hands—by reason of political or economic standing—to get away with robbing the weak and poor, by definition the powerless and vulnerable.

At the same time as Micah and Isaiah point to the robbery of the poor in Judah, Amos sees it rampant in the northern kingdom of Israel.

> ⁶Thus says the LORD:
> For three transgressions of Israel,
>   and for four, I will not revoke the punishment;
> because they sell the righteous for silver,
>   and the needy for a pair of sandals—
> ⁷they who trample the head of the poor into the dust of the earth,
>   and push the afflicted out of the way;
> father and son go in to the same girl,
>   so that my holy name is profaned;
> ⁸they lay themselves down beside every altar
>   on garments taken in pledge;
> and in the house of their God they drink
>   wine bought with fines they imposed.
>
> (2:6–8)

"The perversion of the court by the rich and influential is a constant theme of Amos (5.10, 12, 15). Legal process was being used to exploit the poor and enslave them" (Mays, *Amos*, 46). The "righteous," those who are legally innocent, are sold into slavery, creditors forcing debtors to sell themselves into servitude without sufficient grounds or selling indentured servants to a third party,

337

into slavery—like Joseph (Jeremias, *Amos*, 35). The second clause in verse 7 above should probably be translated "they pervert/turn aside the way of the afflicted." The verb (*nāṭâ*) is the same as one finds in Exodus 23:6, which is in the background of Amos's accusation: "You shall not pervert the justice due to your poor in their lawsuits" (cf. Exod. 23:2; Deut. 24:17). The line between legality and illegality is fuzzy in the indictment of Amos 2:8, but the requirement to give garments taken in pledge back to the debtor before sundown is surely what is in view (Exod. 22:26; Deut. 24:13). "At the least, the portrayal shows that these worshippers felt no incongruity between what they did in the legal economic realm and the God worshipped with feasting and sacrifice" (Mays, *Amos*, 47).

As the account from Nehemiah 5 indicates (see above), violation of the Eighth Commandment was not confined to the preexilic history of Israel. The prophet Malachi also indicts members of the later community in a list that clearly reflects the prohibitions of the Decalogue. Along with his witness against those who commit adultery and swear falsely, the prophet bears testimony "against those who oppress the hired workers in their wages, the widow and the orphan, against those who thrust aside [or 'pervert'; see above on Amos 2:6–8] the alien" (Mal. 3:5). Clearly, the prophet has in mind just those kinds of negative actions toward the poor against which the statutes of the Book of the Covenant and the Deuteronomic Code seek to guard under the directive of the Eighth Commandment. All of these actions are drawn under the aegis of the First Commandment as the verse ends: "and [they] do not fear me." Lack of obedience and fear of the Lord are reflected in the violation of the guidelines of the second table of the Commandments.

The Sages' Wisdom

As is often the case, the book of Proverbs takes a pragmatic approach to the commandment as it cautions against oppressing the poor and giving to the rich because that will surely end up costing one rather than enriching (22:16). Similarly, the way of wisdom follows the Commandments as it warns against stealing from the poor and crushing the weak in the gate, that is, the court (22:22). Here as elsewhere, one may hear in the background the Ninth Commandment and its warning against false testimony and the use of bribes or other means to pervert the administration of justice. The warning is undergirded

338

by the reason that the Lord will plead their cause and despoil those who would despoil the poor (22:23). This is followed closely by a different kind of warning, a caution against giving pledges as surety for debts because if you are poor, you risk losing your bed (22:26–27)! Such counsel to the poor is a part of the function of wisdom, and one finds it again with regard to the poor person's obedience—or disobedience—of the commandment. According to the instruction of Proverbs, a thief is not despised who steals only to satisfy his appetite when hungry (6:30); such an attention to the motivation and context is what one would expect from wise and careful treatment of ethical issues. That same proverb, however, goes on to say that if caught, such a thief will still have to pay significant restitution, even more than one finds in the legal codes (v. 31). The ambiguity of disobedience, whatever the circumstance, is uncovered in the somewhat contradictory way in which theft by the poor is treated.

A different way of expressing the vantage point of the poor is found in Proverbs 30:7–9:

> [7] Two things I ask of you;
>   do not deny them to me before I die:
> [8] Remove far from me falsehood and lying;
>   give me neither poverty nor riches;
>   feed me with the food that I need, .
> [9] or I shall be full, and deny you,
>   and say, "Who is the LORD?"
> or I shall be poor, and steal,
>   and profane the name of my God.

In a genre not otherwise found in Proverbs, that is, prayer, the close association of lying and stealing is articulated (see chapter on the Ninth Commandment) as the wise person prays *"against* two great dangers to fidelity [to God]: unjust conduct in the law court (*šāwᵓ*, 'falsehood' can refer to false oaths sworn before Yahweh) and extremes of wealth or poverty that could lead to infidelity" (Clifford, *Proverbs*, 262–63). The false oath or witness in the courtroom is one of the ways the rich steal from the poor; theft is what the poor may resort to in their poverty. While that is understandable, it is not finally acceptable, so the wise one prays for help to keep that from happening. As a violation of the commandment, theft by the needy becomes in some sense, not explicit in the text, a profanation of the name of God.

339

As one would expect, we have a different picture in the book of Job, but not with regard to the seriousness of the commandment as a criterion of covenantal obedience and righteousness. In this case, however, the matter—defined once more by attention to the issues and concerns inherent in the negative and positive dimensions of the commandment against stealing (see above)—has to do with *God's* covenantal obedience. In chapter 24, Job's third response to Eliphaz, who has accused him of violation of the commandment (22:6–9), one finds a catalog of violations of the statutes and moral concerns inherent in or implicit in the concern for the property of the neighbor:

removing landmarks (Job 24:2a; cf. Deut. 19:14)
stealing the flocks of others and pasturing them with one's own flock (v. 2b; cf. Gen. 31:18)
driving off the donkey of the orphan (v. 3a)
taking the ox of a widow as a pledge (v. 3b; cf. Deut. 24:17; Exod. 22:22; see the discussion of ox and donkey above)
perverting the justice of the poor (v. 4a; cf. Exod. 23:2, 6; see the discussion of Amos 2:7 above)
taking the child of a poor person as a pledge (v. 9)

The plight of the poor is also described in ways that echo the statutes of the Book of the Covenant and the Deuteronomic Code as they elaborate the implications of the Eighth Commandment (Job 24:5–8, 10–12): reaping and gleaning in someone else's field because they do not have such and lying naked in the cold and rain at night, presumably because the garment taken in pledge has not been returned (Exod. 22:26–27; Deut. 24:12–13).

This does not exhaust the list of sins/crimes in Job's response that violate the Commandments, but these are particularly associated with the question of protection of the poor, their property, and their right to property. Job's complaint is that God does not set times for judgment (24:1) of persons who violate the covenant (= the Ten Words, Exod. 34:27; Deut. 4:13) and does not pay attention to the wrong that is done to the poor (Job 24:12) or listen to their cries. If the Commandments define the covenant from the side of the people, they do so also from God's side. That is Job's point. God's inattention to those who are victims of violation of the Commandments is an abdication of God's covenantal responsibility

340

and in fact totally counter to the very way in which God laid claim to Israel's loyalty and obedience. Before his speeches are over, Job will himself, in a series of self-imprecations shaped by the Commandments, claim innocence of any violation (Job 31). The ball is in God's court. Is Israel's way also God's way?

What about the New Testament?

With regard to the Eighth Commandment, what is most noticeable about the New Testament is the absence of the commandment per se from the Sermon on the Mount, even though other commandment concerns—such as murder, adultery, swearing falsely, and talion—are taken up by Jesus. This seems to be because Jesus' attention to the matter of property and possessions centers in teaching about the poor on the one hand and riches and wealth on the other more than specifically on theft in its various forms. The poor are much to the fore in the Beatitudes, especially the Lukan presentation, where those poor and hungry and weeping are extolled and promised blessing (the kingdom of God, sufficient food, and laughter), and those already rich, satiated, and laughing are pitied (Luke 6:20–26). Matthew (5:3) makes it clear that the poor and hungry may be religious as well as sociological categories: "Blessed are the poor in spirit." Whether poverty is economic or spiritual in nature, throughout the Gospels, Jesus speaks to the poor and announces good news to the poor. That is the heart of his ministry (Luke 4:18).

The dangers of riches capturing the soul of persons is underscored in such texts as the parable of the rich man and Lazarus (Luke 16:19–31); the parable of the rich fool, where Jesus is rather explicit in warning about greed and the assumption that the purpose of life is to accumulate riches (12:13–21); and the encounter with the rich young ruler who did everything right (obeying the Commandments) but could not let go (Luke 18:18–30//Matt. 19:16–30//Mark 10:17–31). The latter is especially relevant in this context because the young man professes to have kept the Commandments, including the one prohibiting theft, and Jesus does not challenge this. Rather, he says there is another dimension to the property matter and that is (1) letting it go, and (2) providing from your riches for the poor. The dismay of the young man at this word evokes Jesus' remark about how difficult it is for the wealthy to enter the kingdom of God: remember that the poor [in spirit] are the ones who

341

will inherit the kingdom, according to the Beatitudes. That remark has its counterpart in another teaching of Jesus' that, as we have noted earlier, places the matter of wealth and its use as an issue in the Christian's obedience of the First Commandment more than the Eighth: "You cannot serve God and mammon" (see above).

(For further discussion of the New Testament trajectory of this commandment, particularly in conjunction with the prohibition of false witness, see the next chapter and the discussion there of the relation between lying and stealing, property and honor.)

CHAPTER 8

Telling the Truth

You shall not bear false witness against your neighbor.
Exodus 20:16

Neither shall you bear false witness against your neighbor.
Deuteronomy 5:20

With the commandment against false witness, the covenantal requirements for living with one's neighbor move from dominant concern for *actions* to an explicit focus on *words and speaking*. It would be a mistake, however, to see this movement as one from more serious matters to lesser concerns. Quite the contrary. The prohibition against bearing false witness is not so much a general rule against lying as it is a guard against the capacity of words and speaking to endanger one's neighbor in various ways, or indeed, to bring about violation of the commandments that precede this one. Telling the truth is thus a neighbor matter. It is a form of the love of neighbor and a significant aspect of upholding communal relations. Safeguarding the neighbor by safeguarding truth is an inevitable sequence to the protection of the neighbor's marriage, life, and property, for lying against a neighbor creates a domino effect undoing the other safeguards. Truth or consequences is indeed the choice in speaking about one's neighbor.

The Meaning of the Commandment

The commandment against false witness does not pose the kind of translation issues that arise in some of the other commandments. Its meaning and force are clear. The customary translation, "You

343

shall not bear false witness against your neighbor," is accurate and found in most translations. Literally, the text could be read as "You shall not answer/testify against your neighbor as a false witness." The one aspect of translation that merits some attention is the fact that two different terms for "false" are used in the two forms of the Decalogue. In Exodus 20:16, the noun *šeqer* occurs, meaning "falsehood, deception," the phrase *ʿēd šeqer* literally meaning "a witness of falsehood." In the Deuteronomic form of the commandment, however, the word *šāwʾ* appears in the place of *šeqer*. *Šāwʾ* is the term used in the Third Commandment to describe the misuse of the name of God. The word is somewhat more complex in its usage than is *šeqer*. As the discussion of the term in our treatment of the Third Commandment (chap. 2) indicates, it often refers to swearing falsely. Exodus 23:1 refers to a "*šāwʾ* report" in a juridical context where there are other references to court testimony.

Other uses of this term, however, suggest the notion of something empty and without substance. As we have already suggested, the range of difference is narrow in this case. There is not much distinction between words that are false and words that are empty or worthless. Other words signifying something empty or worthless may also be used in parallel with *šeqer*, "falsehood." And several times one encounters references to prophecy that use the term *šāwʾ* to indicate false prophecy, often in parallel with "lying divination" (Lam. 2:14; Ezek. 12:24; 13:6, 7, 9, 23). But even as the range of meaning in the commandment protecting the name of God is open to the specific use of the name in false oaths, so the Deuteronomic form of the commandment against false witness is open to an understanding that is not exhausted by the notion of lying testimony. As the more general word of the commandment against misuse of the name of God has an important specification without losing its more general range of meaning, so also the more specific word of the commandment against false testimony incorporates a broader reference without losing its primary force in generality.

The prohibitive form of the commandment is crucial because it points quite directly to the critical issue of truth and lies: how the well-being of others is affected by what one says about them. Like all the commandments, this one opens up to a wider frame of reference as it is explicated and illustrated, but its primary direction against lying that is harmful and destructive is clear from its negative formulation. Whatever needs to be said about telling the truth in general, the commandment's concern, as always, is with the good of the neighbor. As one person has put it, the commandment has one eye on the truth and one eye on the neighbor.

The resonance of this commandment with the one protecting use of the divine name serves to create a particular emphasis on speaking the truth as a critical responsibility deeply affecting one's relation to God and the well-being of community life. Truth-telling is thus not a general virtue so much as it is a necessity for maintaining harmonious relationships. It is one of the clearest manifestations of love of God and love of neighbor.

The Violence of Words

When former heavyweight boxing champion Floyd Patterson died, the *New York Times* published a long obituary, noting what a sensitive person Patterson had been, easily embarrassed, quiet, not at all the blustering, bragging boxer that is our stereotypical, and usually accurate, image of a boxing champion. He was quoted as saying once: "You can hit me and I won't think much of it, but you can say something to me and hurt me very much" (May 12, 2006). It was his personal variation on the bit of folk wisdom: "Sticks and stones may break my bones, but words can never hurt me." While Patterson did not necessarily have false witness in mind, his sensitivity to the power of words as much as acts to do violence or to precipitate violent deeds is a central concern of the prohibition against false witness.

In her book on lying, Sissela Bok begins one of her key chapters with these words: "Deceit and violence—these are the two forms of deliberate assault on human beings" (*Lying*, 18). They are often, however, one and the same thing, as the Scriptures make explicit. Twice in the statutes of the Torah that have to do with judicial procedure and the role of witnesses (see below), there is a warning against what is called in many translations "a malicious witness," or more literally, "a witness of violence." In the first of the statutes explicating the danger of false witness, Exodus 23:1, one reads: "You shall not join hands with the wicked [or guilty] to act as a witness of violence (*ḥāmās*)." And in Deuteronomy 19:15–21, procedures are instituted for occasions when a "witness of violence rises up against another person to testify against him falsely" (v. 16, my trans.). Thus two of the main legal elaborations of the problem of false testimony

345

are explicit in speaking of it as an act of violence. In the Psalms also, where deceit and lies are probably the primary vehicle of oppression by one's neighbors, one encounters the violent witness:

> Malicious witnesses rise up;
>> they ask me about things I do not know.
>>> (35:11)

And in Psalm 27:12 the adversaries who rise up against the psalmist are described as "false witnesses," and "violent witnesses" (my trans.). The violence evoked by false testimony is presented in a more imaginative way but just as clearly in Proverbs 25:18, when the one who bears false witness against his neighbor is said to be like "a war club, a sword, or a sharp arrow," using words as weapons of personal destruction.

There are two other contexts in which we may well have reference to the violence of words that happens in false testimony, though in neither case is that the customary interpretation of the text. From chapter 9 on to chapter 27, much of the discourse of Job is legal rather than prayerlike, and the large issue is Job's need for a witness in his behalf (Newsom, *Job*). In chapter 18, Bildad says to Job: "How long will you hunt for words?" Job responds in chapter 19: "How long will you all torment me, and break me in pieces with words?" Then after accusing the friends of having reproached and humiliated him "ten times," he says, "Even when I cry out, 'Violence!' (*ḥāmās*) I am not answered; I call aloud, but there is no justice" (v. 19:7). The verses that follow, and other parts of the dialogue, suggest that the violence is at God's hands. May there not also be, however, a double meaning in light of the verses that precede? The violence Job experiences is also the violence of words, words that have broken him in pieces. The friends, as Gerald Janzen has put it with reference to an earlier speech, "should have served as witnesses to the crime against him and sought redress on his behalf"; they have instead testified against him, effecting violence without redress (Janzen, *Job*, 123).

The other instance is even less explicit but seems to be a case where the equation of lying and violence is operative. In the Servant Song in Isaiah 53, it is reported of the servant that he was buried with the wicked and the rich, "although he had done no violence, and there was no deceit [*mirmâ*; cf. Prov. 12:17] in his mouth" (v. 9 RSV). The text is quite open here with regard to meaning and reference, as it is throughout the poem, but in light of the parallel-

346

ism, it is difficult to avoid the conclusion that the innocence of the servant is specifically and primarily reflected in his adherence to the commandment against false testimony and its inevitable outcome in violence, the specifics of which are quite clear when one turns to the primary context in which the concern for true and false witness operates, the judicial system.

The Starting Point and Continuing Context of the Commandment

We may take our cues in this regard from the perceptive comment of Martin Luther in his Large Catechism:

> In its first and simplest meaning, as the words stand ("You shall not bear false witness"), this commandment pertains to public courts of justice, where one may accuse and malign a poor, innocent man and crush him by means of false witnesses, so that consequently he may suffer punishment in body, property, or honor. (in Kolb and Wengert, *Book of Concord*, 420)

The Courts and the System of Justice

As Luther recognized and as is obvious from the elaboration of this commandment in the statutes and ordinances of the legal codes, the main setting in life of the prohibition against false witness is the judicial system. Indeed, it is this commandment that is the starting point for the development of a careful system for administering justice in the human community.

The Book of the Covenant (Exod. 23:1–9)

In the Book of the Covenant, the various cases having to do with property theft and protection elaborate and specify what is at stake in the commandment against stealing (see chap. 7) and lead into matters having to do with testimony in the court, statutes that spell out what is at stake in telling the truth where it most matters, in the place of last resort for righteous and just dealing among human beings: the court. Exodus 23:1–3 and 6–9 take up the issues about truthful testimony, with a piece of instruction about property issues in verses 4–5 that carries over from the preceding chapter.

347

The opening verse clearly has the Ninth Commandment behind it or implicit in its formulation: "You shall not lift up an empty/false (*šāwʾ*) report" (Exod. 23:1a, my trans.). In this brief sentence various things come together. The unusual expression "lift up an empty/false (*šāwʾ*) report" echoes both the Third Commandment prohibiting the "lifting up" of the name of God emptily (*šāwʾ*) and the Deuteronomic form of the Ninth Commandment forbidding testifying against one's neighbor as a "false/empty (*šāwʾ*) witness." It is a general statement in which the community hears echoes of both of these commandments having to do with truthfulness and the seriousness of one's word. Yet as it leads directly into the more specific instructions about conduct in the court, the opening sentence connects any kind of misleading, empty, or clearly false report about another member of the community with truthfulness in the court, articulating "the responsibility to guard against dissimulating uncontrolled rumours which destroy [one's] reputation and prejudice a case without evidence" (Childs, *Exodus*, 481).

The primary context of the commandment against false testimony is from the beginning and in virtually all its references the administration of justice, but the starting point is a false or empty word, harmful or potentially so, uttered about a neighbor in the community even outside the court but most definitely inside the court. At issue ultimately is slander that leads to a court case (e.g., Deut. 22:13–19). That is indicated in the second part of verse 1 with its call to avoid joining with the wicked as a "witness of violence." The whole of the verse is then reiterated in verse 7, with its general word about keeping far away from any false report or charge and the follow-up word that spells out the implication of such action, the potential of a false report to bring about someone's death unjustly, thus the testimony of violence. The language of verse 7 is emphatic in various ways, underscoring "false report/charge" by its placement at the beginning of the sentence, the imagery of getting as far away as possible from false charges, and the double reference to the innocent: "innocent and those in the right." What sort of conduct is involved in the false charge or report is open. It may be giving false testimony, enlisting false witnesses, or handing down an indictment on the basis of evidently false testimony (Houtman, *Exodus*, 247–48).

348

A similar elaboration of the commandment is to be discerned in Leviticus 19:16:

> You shall not go around as a slanderer among your people, and you
> shall not profit by the blood of your neighbor: I am the LORD.

It is likely that the reference to the blood of the neighbor has to do
with a conviction in court, presumably a capital offense, arising from
slander or malicious gossip. Thus again we see the potential violence
of lies and empty words said against another member of the community (Milgrom, *Leviticus 17–22*, 1645). One thing is clear: the false
charge or report and the slander may lead to judicial murder, a central concern of the commandment against false witness, as we see
when we turn to Deuteronomy's explication of the commandment
before returning to Exodus 23 to uncover the other primary context
in which the commandment is especially operative.

The Deuteronomic Code (Deut. 17:2–7; 19:15–20)

The interpreters of Deuteronomy who have rightly seen the Deuteronomic Code as a development and elaboration of the particulars of the Commandments in concrete cases tend to agree that the
section of the Code that does this for the commandment against
false witness is 24:8–25:4 (Olson, *Death of Moses*, 108–12; Braulik,
"Sequence," 322; Kaufman, "Structure," 141). But before turning
to that section, one cannot help but notice that in earlier sections of
the Deuteronomic Code there are explicit instructions about witnesses in the court and the processes in which they are involved.
The importance of testimony and, more specifically, truthful testimony is underscored, not surprisingly, in sections of the Code that
elaborate the Fifth Commandment, having to do with parents and
authorities, and the Sixth Commandment, prohibiting killing. Deuteronomy 16:18–17:13 consists of detailed directions for proper
carrying out of justice by judges and other officials.

Deuteronomy 17:2–7 gives a special focus to the critical matter
of handling cases involving violation of the First Commandment,
the worship of other gods. Precisely because the punishment for
this crime is death, the instruction is very explicit about witnesses
and their role in the matter:

> [6]On the evidence of two or three witnesses the death sentence
> shall be executed; a person must not be put to death on the evi-
> dence of only one witness. [7]The hands of the witnesses shall be

the first raised against the person to execute the death penalty, and afterward the hands of all the people. So you shall purge the evil from your midst.

The critical point is the requirement of multiple witnesses before there can be conviction of a capital crime. The point is underscored and emphasized in verse 6, and further weight is given to the significance of testimony by the requirement that the witnesses in the case be the agents of execution, a symbolic acknowledgment of their role in deciding the fate of the person on trial. In each place where the legal codes take up the matter of killing and its punishment by killing, the issue of witnesses, their behavior, and their number is critical. In Numbers 35, where the commandment against killing is elaborated in detail (see chap. 5, "Protecting Life") and where capital punishment is stipulated for someone who kills another, the basis for that is the testimony of witnesses, but the point is made that execution cannot happen on the basis of the testimony of a single witness (v. 30). As in Deuteronomy 17:2–7, where the requirement is for "two or three witnesses," meaning two or more, the testimony must be fulsome and not minimal before one may put another to death legally.

Once more the danger in the whole process is judicial murder, killing a person legally but wrongfully. The centrality of the truthful witness to the proper administration of justice is the point. And because the place where the action of the malicious witness occurs or can lead to violence against the neighbor is the courtroom, there is an inevitable strong tie between false or empty witness and capital punishment. This tie is age-old. Its importance is evident in the Laws of Hammurabi, where the first three statutes have to do with crimes punishable by death, but the focus of the statutes is making sure that the testimony is truthful. If it is not truthful or is not substantiated, the false witness shall suffer the execution that would have been the fate of the falsely accused, as is also the case in the legal instruction of Deuteronomy 19:15–20, the passage that completes the Deuteronomic focus on the role of witnesses in the judicial process (cf. Sus. 61). There the insistence on adequate and multiple witnesses in the court when someone is under trial is extended to cover any offense (vv. 15–16; cf. Matt. 18:16; 1 Tim. 5:19). The witness of violence, the "malicious witness," can injure another at a lower but no less real level than killing. Further, the

350

prohibition against false witness is reinforced by setting into the trajectory of the commandment a requirement for just retribution, presumably a form of deterrence, with the principle of talion (v. 21; see chap. 5, "Protecting Life").

There is one other crucial part of the judicial process specified in both the Deuteronomic texts having to do with witnesses as well as in one other important text having to do with capital punishment: *the necessity for thorough inquiry into the case* (Deut. 17:4; 19:18; cf. 13:14), what one interpreter has properly described as "judicial initiative to gather empirical evidence" (McBride, "Annotations," 290). Implicit in that requirement is awareness that the presence of witnesses does not settle matters. Often there will be counter-testimony and one voice against another. Detailed investigation into all facets of the case is necessary before a decision is made. This requirement is couched in emphatic language in every instance and in doubly emphatic expression in Deuteronomy 13:14 (15 Heb.), well represented in the NJPS translation: "You shall investigate and inquire and interrogate thoroughly." With regard to this text in Deuteronomy 13, which has to do with cases of idolatry or apostasy, Jeffrey Tigay reports:

> To ensure such care and certainty in all capital cases, halakhic exegesis required that witnesses answer seven questions about time and place in order to prove their presence at the scene of the crime, and that they all agree about other details, such as the identity of the deity worshiped and the rite that was performed or, in the case of a murder, the weapon used and the clothing worn by both victim and killer.

He continues: "Such procedures made a sentence of capital punishment virtually impossible" (*Deuteronomy*, 134).

Evidence of all sorts may be brought to the case, but there will always be the question of truth-telling about what one has seen, heard, or found, whether on the part of witnesses or other persons responsible for handling the case. One should remember that the Deuteronomic form of the Ninth Commandment uses the term *šāwʾ* for the prohibited testimony, what is not only false but also careless, empty testimony. The judicial process is all about testimony and truth. Then and now, everything comes into the court's process by way of testimony. The trajectory of this commandment, therefore, in effect serves to create and preserve a complex and

351

workable system for the administration of justice, one that identifies dangers, holes, and problems and works to overcome them.
Particular attention is given to the cases when the life of a member
of the community is at stake and the illegal killing prohibited by
the Sixth Commandment can be transformed into a legal killing
without attention to the concerns explicit and implicit in the commandment against false witness.

There is probably no place in the legal system or systems of
ancient Israel where the concerns and statutes of the Bible have
their contemporary analogues and relevance more than in this
sphere. The contemporary judicial and legal arena is marked by the
issue of imprisonment or execution of the innocent and the manipulation of the legal system by the work of false witnesses, incorporating false or careless charges, evidence, and testimony. Hardly
a week goes by that the news does not tell of another such case,
behind which all too often is prosecutorial misconduct or manipulation of the legal system by false, biased, or manipulated testimony
or evidence to bring about convictions.

Though this book is not the context for extended illustration,
one example may show the pertinence of the biblical commandment and its development in the legal codes. Several years ago
George Ryan, then governor of Illinois, noting that a number of
innocent persons on death row had been exonerated and released
before they could be executed—one only forty-eight hours before
execution—commuted the sentences of all death-row prisoners
because, he said, "Our capital system is haunted by the demon
of error: error in determining guilt and error in determining who
among the guilty deserves to die" (Wilgoren, "Death Row"). The
outcome of a commission he had established to examine the practice of capital punishment in the state is very revealing. The two
matters signaled in the news accounts of their report were (1) a
recommendation of eighty-five ways to prevent unwarranted executions, the equivalent of Deuteronomy's call "to investigate and
inquire and interrogate thoroughly" (Deut. 13:15 JPS [14E]; cf.
17:4; 19:18), rightly understood as "extreme care in the investigation and absolute certainty in the verdict" (Tigay, *Deuteronomy*,
134); and (2) a ban on executing "those whose convictions had
been based solely on the testimony of a single eyewitness, prison
informer, or accomplice," the other large matter in the Deuteronomic trajectory of the commandment against false witness in

352

behalf of protecting innocent life (Wilgoren, "Death Sentence"). The conclusion of the Illinois commission's report is worth citing for its pertinence to the injunction of Exodus 23:7, not to kill the innocent: "No system, given human nature and frailties, could ever be devised or constructed that would work perfectly and guarantee absolutely that no innocent person is ever again sentenced to death" (Wilgoren, "Death Sentence"). That sounds very much as if the trajectory of this commandment leads finally to the practical end of capital punishment. Meanwhile, one may observe that the Ninth Commandment has served to create a complex and workable system for administration of justice, one from which many modern systems represent a step backward.

The Life of the Poor: Deuteronomy 24:8–25:4

Once again Martin Luther is our teacher as he places this commandment not only in the processes of the "public courts of justice" but also in the life of the poor (see above). Such a context is not immediately obvious in the commandment itself but clearly indicated in the way the legal codes spell out its implications and already identified in part in the discussion of the commandment against stealing. It is particularly the poor who are vulnerable and whose protection is a large aspect of the Ninth Commandment. While the poor of the community are not the only objects of the commandment's care— see, for example, the case of Naboth in 1 Kings 21—they are so thoroughly in view in the statutes or pieces of legal/ethical instruction in the Codes that one has to recognize the pertinence of the commandment to their well-being. While we have been dealing with the heart of the matter—the judicial process as the primary context in which the commandment operated in ancient Israel (and still today), we are only now getting to the section of the Deuteronomic Code where, according to most interpreters, the commandment against false witness is developed or spelled out in statute and ordinance: Deuteronomy 24:8–25:4. Because there is such consensus on the association of this section with the commandment, we shall let that be our focus while drawing in other related texts

One should begin by indicating the rationale for associating this passage with the Ninth Commandment when, on the surface, it seems to have nothing to do with the commandment against false witness. There are four reasons for doing so:

353

1. The immediately preceding verse, Deuteronomy 24:7, is the closest parallel to the commandment against stealing in the book of Deuteronomy. It serves to provide a transition from instruction about the implications of the Eighth Commandment to those concerning the commandment against false witness and thus concludes the section of statutes in the Deuteronomic Code having to do with stealing (see chap. 7, "Property and Possessions").

2. The unit after this section, 25:5–12, has to do with marital relations and clearly belongs with the commandment against coveting, reflecting the Deuteronomic form of the Decalogue, which places the neighbor's wife before his property (25:13–16) as things not to be coveted (see chap, 9, on coveting).

3. The concluding verses of the section, Deuteronomy 25:1–3, take us back into the court and its procedures for ensuring justice, a context that we have identified with the purposes of the Ninth Commandment (on 25:4, see below).

4. The first statute in this section, 24:8–9, seems to have nothing to do with the subject under consideration. Yet it makes clear that the Ninth Commandment is in view and that it has implications beyond the court to include any kind of lies against the neighbor. The case is indirect but clearly paradigmatic. While verse 8 is caution against the danger of leprosy—though the precise character of the disease in view is not clear—it is verse 9 that moves into the subject matter of the commandment against false witness: "Remember what the LORD your God did to Miriam on your journey out of Egypt." That reference takes one back to Numbers 12 and the divine judgment against Miriam, when she became "leprous." She (and Aaron) "spoke against" Moses because he had married a Cushite woman, though the real issue was their claim that the Lord had spoken through them as well as through Moses. There is no false witness in the court, but there is some kind of speaking violently, some kind of slander or verbal attack on Moses, an act that was illegitimate if not illegal.

The memory of that event is an implicit warning not to libel or speak against the leadership of the people. That carries over from the original leader to his successors, the Levitical priests. So the first case we have in the Deuteronomic explication of this commandment is not a case of judicial false witness—that is dealt with in earlier sections having to do with honoring parents and authorities and with killing—but more generally of slander or libel of the community's leader. So the range of truth-telling in view in this commandment, as has been suggested earlier, is actually broad and, while centered on the formal witness chair in the court, is not confined to it. There are all sorts of ways to use speech violently against another. Slander and libel against the neighbor of any sort, as exemplified in the primal case of Miriam and Aaron against Moses, violate the prohibition of false testimony.

The large impression one takes from the various pieces of instruction found in this part of the Deuteronomic Code is that, if these statutes are meant to spell out and illustrate what the Ninth Commandment is after, the primary focus is upon the poor and marginal members of society and the various ways in which their needs and rights are to be protected. Or as Dennis Olson has put it, this section of laws, as it develops the trajectory of the commandment against false witness, "seeks to preserve the reputation, dignity, and respect of people within the community, whatever their status or condition within the society" (*Death of Moses*, 108). The positive formulation becomes a requirement to secure and maintain the welfare and dignity of the poor, and its negative formulation issues a prohibition against using the judicial and economic system for illegal gain by oppressing the poor and the weak and the marginal. Several features of this teaching focus on the poor and needy or the unprotected and vulnerable members of the community.

Before looking at each unit in this section, we note that the explication of the false witness commandment in the Book of the Covenant (Exod. 23:1–9) has already focused on the poor and the marginal. The poor are mentioned twice. The most explicit reference is in verse 6, where the injunction not to kill the innocent by bringing false charges is introduced by the command: "You shall not pervert the justice due to your poor in their lawsuits." In other words, the primary victim of the false charges and false testimony is likely to be the poor. That is surely why this section includes a command against taking a bribe (v. 8), a perversion of justice only possible for those with the means to do so. The concern for the poor and marginal is then carried further with the injunction not to oppress a resident alien, an immigrant, temporary or permanent, who is another member of the community more vulnerable to judicial impropriety, the heart of which is false or corrupt testimony and evidence, along with bribes.   355

The other reference to the poor in Exodus 23:1–9 occurs in verse 3. The extended warning against acting as a malicious witness and siding with the wicked and the majority to pervert justice concludes with, if the text is correct, a caution against the danger of reverse prejudice in court: "nor shall you be partial to the poor in a lawsuit." It is highly likely, however, that a letter has been dropped from the Hebrew word for "poor" (*dāl*), which would have made the original word "the great" (*gādōl*), as Walter Houston and others before him have argued (Houston, *Contending for Justice*, 114–15; Van Seters, *Law Book*, 137). While Leviticus 19:15 warns against either being partial to the poor or honoring the great, a clear and legitimate concern in ensuring justice in the courts, the usual danger to justice is favoritism toward the rich and powerful. In Exodus 23:6 the most obvious sign of a corruption of the original text is the fact that the verb for showing partiality to the poor in that instance is not the common expression, which one finds in Leviticus 19:15, "lift up the face," but the word "honor," which is used for deferring to the great in Leviticus 19:15. The term "honor" is "invariably applied to people who are regarded as socially worthy of honour" (Houston, *Contending for Justice*, 114). So it is likely that the poor are very much in view in Exodus 23:3, but precisely in its intention to warn against excessive honoring and favoring of the rich and the powerful (= the great) in the judicial process.

As in Exodus 23:1–9, the two groups that are the primary focus of the relevant statutes in Deuteronomy are the poor and needy and the members of the community without status or power, specifically the widow, the orphan, and the resident alien. These are groups especially in need of protection from injustice because of their circumstances. Their vulnerability is always economic, but it also has to do with giving them humane and dignified treatment, even when they are subject to imposition by the rich and "the great." John Calvin, who saw the economic implications of this commandment when he pointed to the danger of depriving our neighbors of their goods by lying and even by defamation, also saw the positive demand of the commandment in its teaching that we should "sincerely keep their honor safe in our judgment, our ears, and our tongue" (Calvin, *Institutes* 2.8.47–48). These statutes develop those dimensions of the commandment, even as they recognize that honor and economic status are closely related and not entirely tied to matters of the tongue (cf. the discussion of these same statutes in chap. 7, on the Eighth Commandment).

356

Deuteronomy 24:10–15

The first protection, Deuteronomy 24:10–11, is an inhibition against barging into the home of a person—and this point is applicable to rich and poor alike, though it is more likely to happen to the poor—to extract a pledge for a loan. The vulnerability of especially the poor is then indicated in verse 11, with a caution against taking a pledge that may be an article of necessity for the poor person. The formulation is significant because it is not simply a prohibition against taking such an article, for example, the poor person's coat. Rather, taking the pledge is allowed, but for very practical reasons, *it must be returned each evening.* The reason is obvious. As a poor person, the borrower does not have many coats to use and needs it for protection from the elements at nighttime. One should not miss the implicit way in which such a practice serves regularly to confront the creditor with the reality of the poor person's plight and to require him to alleviate that plight each day, quite self-consciously. The poor may not ever depart from the earth (15:11), but they are not to be mistreated, humiliated, or ignored. One has only to encounter a beggar or homeless person on the street to know the potential for the poor to find themselves in such a plight.

The second statute in this section, Deuteronomy 24:14–15, parallels the first, this time to cover another crucial need of the poor: a daily wage. The needy do not have rich savings or investments and depend upon regular payment of wages. So even as the garment taken in pledge must be returned before sunset, the wage of the poor laborer must be paid before sunset each day. And as a reason is explicitly given in the previous statute, even though the rationale is probably self-evident in both cases, a reason is given here also: "for he is poor and urgently depends on it" (NJPS). As the poor person needs a coat to sleep in each night, so this one needs the daily wage for work done to put food on the table. Once again both economic need and human dignity are at stake. There is also a direct connection to the matter of true and false witness, but we find that outside of Scripture (see below).

The first of these two Deuteronomic statutes has its close parallel in the Book of the Covenant in Exodus 22:26–27. In both instances there is a further note that, in effect, *brings God into the picture.* In Exodus that happens as the community is told that this issue of

357

proper treatment of the poor and needy is a matter of such concern to the Lord that "if your neighbor cries out to me, I will listen, for I am compassionate." The poor and needy are protected by the legal structure of the community, set forth in these various statutes. If that structure breaks down, however, there is a "higher court" that will come into the picture: the compassion of God (cf. Jas. 5:4).

It is not that common for the statutes of either the Book of the Covenant or the Deuteronomic Code in chapters 12–26 to include some reference to God, but that is a fairly consistent feature of the statutes having to do with the poor and needy and the widow, orphan, and stranger. In the second of the statutes in this section, 24:14–15, one hears again a warning that failure to follow the instruction imbedded within it may evoke the cry of the unpaid laborer to the Lord. This time the further word is not one of God's compassion, already heard as a dimension of the situation in Exodus 22:27. Now the community is told of a further outcome of the cry of the needy: the guilt of the one who has withheld the wage and oppressed the poor laborer. A similar ascription of guilt, not surprisingly, is given in the statutes of Exodus 23:1–9, discussed above and having to do specifically with false charges and false witness against the poor and the innocent. In this instance, the divine first-person address occurs (as in Exodus 22:27): "for I will not acquit the guilty." The cry of the poor person in the face of economic oppression and inhumane treatment not only arouses the response of a compassionate God; it also has consequences for the one who acts in such a way.

That consequence is expressed both ways, however. Injustice is a sin and incurs guilt; but being careful to attend to the rights of the poor person leads to blessing and righteousness (Deut. 24:13, 19). The positive outcome of such action is as important as the negative. It is Deuteronomy's way of saying that living by these statutes works. All of the motivational aspects of these statutes serve not only to arouse obedience but also to underscore their importance for the life of the community. These are matters that arouse God's attention in a special way and also have consequences for those who live—or do not live—by the instruction set before them for the care and dignity of the poor and needy. Such care is not an end in itself, nor is it simply beneficial for those who are upheld. There is a reciprocity here, but it is not between the one obeying the statute and the beneficiary of that obedience. The one who obeys is enhanced, but that enhancement is a divine response to the keeping of the statute. While it is customary to think about the consequences of law in terms of the consequences of disobedience, these statutes focus upon the positive benefits of obedience and see the enhancement of the needy and the property-endangered as effecting an enhancement of the one who so acts.

Deuteronomy 24:16–22

The next sequence of statutes in this explication of the concern for truthful witness and the protection of the rights of others, especially the poor, focuses on the persons in the community who are outside the power structures and thus vulnerable because of not having persons to protect them: widows, orphans, and the resident aliens or immigrants in the community. These are in continuity with the preceding statutes with the following particularities:

1. Verse 16, prohibiting executing a member of the family for the crime of another member of the family, an important modification of tendencies toward corporate punishment, seems to stand outside the concerns of the Ninth Commandment and this section of its elaboration. That, however, is not really the case. As the verses that follow indicate, the particular focus on the needy and the powerless does not let go of the concern for proper administration of justice, which is at the heart of the commandment against false witness, as we have already seen. Further, the particular concern reflected in the Deuteronomic elaboration of the role of this commandment in preserving justice is the protection of life (see above). Finally, the concern for humaneness and dignity that is evident in the surrounding statutes is implicit also in the protection of members of the family of a criminal. In the Deuteronomic statutes developing and illustrating the force of the Ninth Commandment, Kaufman sees a single motif: "fairness to one's fellow as regards both his substance and his dignity"; he regards this verse as the "climax of the whole" and an introduction to the concerns for justice that follow in the rest of the verses (Kaufman, "Structure," 141–42).

2. The dual concerns of Exodus 23:1–9 and Deuteronomy 24:10–15, maintenance of justice for the poor and marginal and concern for their economic protection and dignity, are signaled in verse 17, which calls for justice for the orphan and resident alien and deals with the matter of a widow's pledge.

359

3. Economic need is still very much at the center, as evidenced by the intensification of the points made in the first section of statutes. In the case of a widow, one may not even take her garment in pledge (v. 17b). Further, economic provision for these categories of persons in the community is required. The statutes move beyond the earlier ones to require the community to provide food for widow, orphan, and resident alien by leaving some of the wheat, olives, and grapes in the field when time comes for reaping and gleaning (vv. 19–22; cf. Lev. 23:22).

4. An additional motivation is given and underscored by standing near the beginning of this section (Deut. 24:18) and at the end (v. 22). It is the memory of the exodus deliverance. The concern for the economic well-being and honor of these members of the community is accentuated and encouraged as the community remembers its own existence in a time and situation of injustice and economic oppression. As they were redeemed from their plight by the grace and mercy of God, so now they are called to act in ways that will ensure the well-being of the most vulnerable of the community. It is worth noting that the memory of the exodus experience and of God's redemption, the memory of slavery and of liberation, appears as a motivation in the Deuteronomic statutes only three times. In each instance, twice here and in 15:15, it is the impetus for the community's treatment of those in economic need. In effect, the Lord says through Moses, "You have been there and know what it is like to live under such conditions and to be released from them. So let the memory of that guide you now in your actions with your neighbor."

Deuteronomy 25:1–4

Deuteronomy 25:1–3 has been discussed already in the treatment of lex talionis in chap. 5, "Protecting Life," to which the reader is referred. Here one need only recognize that the statute takes us back into the administration of justice and the concern not only for fairness, but also for the courts to provide proper and humane treatment of members of the community, in this case avoiding of actions that degrade and shame a neighbor. Economic factors are not involved, at least not explicitly, but the neighbor or brother's dignity and honor are at the heart of the matter, even when that brother or sister has engaged in criminal activity.

Finally, even the animals in the community merit proper treatment (25:4). As Dennis Olson has put it: "The progression of the laws on false witness affirms the dignity and honor of all people, from leaders to criminals. Deuteronomy extends that dignity and honor even to oxen and the sphere of all creation" (*Death of Moses*, 110). The concern for animals as well as people is not a new thing in the Commandments. It is central to the Deuteronomic form of the Sabbath Commandment, where rest is provided not only for slaves or indentured servants but also for ox and ass (cf. Exod. 23:10–12 and chap. 3, "Keeping the Sabbath").

A Case from Real Life

Although the Deuteronomic Code does not tie these statutes in an explicit way to the matter of true and false witness, that does happen in a well-known Hebrew inscription of the seventh century BCE from the small fortress site Meṣad Ḥashavyahu. There a laborer, a worker in the fields, petitions a commander or officer (*śar*), presumably of the fortress, to have his garment, which had been taken from him by someone named Hoshaiah, restored to him. The inscription reads as follows:

> May my lord, the officer, hear the word of his servant. As for your servant, your servant was harvesting at Ḥazar-asam. And your servant harvested and measured and stored, according to the schedule, before quitting. Even as your [se]rvant measured the harvest and stored—according to schedule—Hoshaiah son of Shobai came and took the garment of your servant. When I had measured my harvest for some time, he took the garment of your servant. Now all my colleagues will testify for me—those who harvested with me in the heat of [the sun. All] my colleagues will testify for me (that) truly I am innocent of gu[ilt. Therefore, let him return] my garment, and if not, it is possible for the officer to ret[urn the garment of your] serva[nt and may you gran]t to him mer[cy.] . . . your [ser]vant and do not dismiss him. (Dobbs-Allsopp et al., *Hebrew Inscriptions*, 359)

The text is vague about the reason for the garment being taken, but the peasant petitioning clearly seeks to make his case for having worked hard for days reaping and measuring and in the heat of the sun. As one interpreter notes, the desperation of the petitioner is obvious, and his conclusion and climax are rather personal

361

and emotional (Parker, *Stories*, 16). Finally, he pleads for the commander to show mercy or compassion (*rḥmm*) upon him. While the reason for taking the garment is unstated, Frank Cross is probably correct in arguing: "The letter makes clear that the writer was a peasant under accusation of failing to render to his lord all that was his due, and as a result had his garment taken as a pledge against his rendering up his full obligation" (Cross, "Epigraphic Notes," 124).

What is significant in this context is the coalescence of several features. The central figure is a peasant laborer who makes a plea for justice involving a garment taken from him that should have been, according to his understanding, returned to him by this point. To that extent, one hears direct resonances with the statutes discussed above having to do with taking a poor person's garment in pledge and not returning it. That connection goes further in that the laborer's petition closes with a *plea to be dealt with with compassion* (*rḥmm*), an echo of the relevant statute in the Book of the Covenant (Exod. 22:26–27 [25–26 Heb.]), where the Lord promises to listen to the cry of the poor person whose garment was not returned, "because I am compassionate" (*ḥannûn*).

The petition adds to the picture the peasant's avowal that his colleagues, his coworkers (lit., "my brothers") "will testify for me. . . . All my brothers will testify for me that truly I am innocent of guilt." The petition is grounded in and totally dependent upon witnesses for the petitioner. That is all he has to put forth in the plea for justice. The heart of the judicial (or extrajudicial) process is always the matter of truthful evidence or testimony, and as in this instance, it often is maintenance of justice and fairness for the poor and needy. And when the process breaks down, the appeal is always to the one who can deal in mercy and compassion. The appeal for justice becomes a cry for compassion.

Lying and Stealing—Honor and Property

In one of his crime novels, Seymour Shubin ascribes to one of his characters an expression: "A liar and a thief are the same thing, they steal something from you" (*Witness to Myself*, 20). That is a succinct way of showing the connections between false witness and stealing. In the Bible, those connections are extensive, both formal and material. Stealing and lying against the neighbor are *formally* associated in that the two issues of theft and false witness are brought together in several instances within the Old Testament, in legal (e.g., Lev. 6:1–5; 19:11–13; and the Deuteronomic Code), prophetic (Hos. 7:1; Zech. 5:3–4; Mal. 3:5), and psalmic/cultic (Ps. 50:16–20) literature. In some instances, stealing and false witness are present as part of a longer series, for example, Hosea 4:2 and Jeremiah 7:9. In other cases, however, there is sufficient closeness of the two and focus on the two that a clear connection seems intended. That is evident, for example, in Hosea 7:1, where the prophet recounts the wicked deeds of Samaria: "they deal falsely, the thief breaks in, and the bandits raid outside." Lying and stealing are preeminently the sins of the northern kingdom. Even more direct in this regard is Zechariah 5:3–4, where a curse is directed against "everyone who steals" and "everyone who swears falsely," and the curse enters "the house of the thief" and "the house of anyone who swears falsely by my name," as a violator of both the commandment against false witness and the commandment against misusing the name of God. And in Jeremiah 6:13 (as well as, in similar words, 8:10) one reads:

> For from the least to the greatest of them,
>   everyone is greedy for unjust gain;
> and from prophet to priest,
>   everyone deals falsely.

The significance of the connection is best seen, however, in some groupings in Leviticus 6 and 19. In the first instance, a list of sins is given, all of which have to do with property and economic matters and for which a guilt or reparation offering is prescribed to make atonement and secure forgiveness:

> [2]When a person sins and commits an offense against the Lord by deceiving (*kāḥaš*) his neighbor in a matter of a deposit or a pledge, or by robbery [*gāzal*], or if he has defrauded (*ʿāšaq*) his neighbor, [3]or has found something lost and has lied about it—if you swear falsely regarding any of the various things that one may do and sin hereby—[4]when he has sinned and realized his guilt and would restore what he has defrauded or the deposit that was committed to him, or the lost thing that he found, [5]or anything else about which he swore falsely, he shall repay the principal amount and shall add one-fifth to it. (Lev. 6:2–5 [5:20–24 Heb.], my trans.)

363

Two things are significant in this text. First, *lying or deceiving* in ways that do detriment to the neighbor's good, specifically to the neighbor's property and possessions, and *theft* are bound up with one another in this formulation. There are clear connections to the theft statutes of the Book of the Covenant (discussed in chap. 7) in the references to possessions that had been left with or deposited with a neighbor and to a neighbor's lost property that someone had found and kept. The theft can take place in various ways, and the deception can be in regard to various kinds of property. The language of swearing falsely is only partially the language of the Ninth Commandment. In the reference to the neighbor and speaking falsely, one hears the language of that commandment, but the more formal "bear witness against" or "answer as a witness against" of the commandment, which points to a court setting, is missing. The heart of the commandment's intent is evident, however, in the passage, and one sees within it the complexity of the commandment against false witness.

False words toward a neighbor that harm that person may take place in the formal testimony of a court and may indeed lie behind these injunctions, as intimated by the reference to swearing falsely, which suggests a more formal process of lying: perjury. But the deception against the neighbor to get at the neighbor's property is not confined to that formal setting. The Leviticus formulation lays open a variety of ways in which deception in behalf of the appropriation of a neighbor's property may take place, in or out of court. In so doing, the text realistically identifies the complexity of the violation of the neighbor's property and the inherent connection between lying and theft, the fact that appropriation of what belongs to another often, if not most often, involves fundamental deceptions.

The second thing one discerns from the passage in Leviticus 6 is the connection to the cluster of legal formulations in Deuteronomy 24 discussed above and in the preceding chapter and also those in Exodus 21–23 that grow out of the Eighth Commandment: stealing, pledges, deposits entrusted to a neighbor, and withheld wages. The term for "defraud" in Leviticus 6 has to do specifically with withholding the wages of a neighbor, as one discerns from the use of the same Hebrew word (ʿāšaq) in Deuteronomy 24:14. In a list of violations of covenant obligations in Malachi 3:5, somewhat reflective of the Decalogue but not including stealing, the sequence of sins is sorcery, adultery, swearing falsely, oppression of hired workers in their wages (specifically the widow and orphan), thrusting aside the alien, and not fearing God. It appears, in this instance, as if stealing (or coveting?) is reflected in a specific and concrete instance—withholding wages of the poor—as well as in the varied ways of oppressing widow, orphan, and alien, all of which may be assumed to be manifestations of economic oppression.

That association is reinforced further in Leviticus 19:11–14:

> ¹¹You shall not steal [*gānab*]; you shall not deal falsely; and you shall not lie to one another [lit., each one to his neighbor]. ¹²And you shall not swear falsely by my name, profaning the name of your God: I am the LORD.
>
> ¹³You shall not defraud (*ʿāšaq*) your neighbor; you shall not steal (*gāzal*); and you shall not keep for yourself the wages of a laborer until morning. ¹⁴You shall not revile the deaf or put a stumbling block before the blind; you shall fear your God: I am the LORD.

To "deal falsely" is to use deception in gaining a neighbor's property—for example, denying that one had taken or possessed a neighbor's property. Swearing falsely again probably envisions more formal oaths, and the formulation here draws the Third Commandment, protecting the right invocation of the divine name, directly into view to undergird the proper handling of a neighbor's property. In the second complex, fraud, stealing, and withholding wages are to be seen as variants of the same thing (see above).

The interplay of the Eighth and Ninth Commandments thus identifies the close connection between theft of property and the legal and social structures, the role of lies in illegal and immoral appropriation of the goods of others. Truth-telling in the large and complex interassociation of regulative agencies, courts, corporations, and individuals is a primary safeguard against the misappropriation of property. Distortion, slanting of facts, misrepresentation of issues—all these and other maneuvers are forms of deception that are prohibited because they do not effect the good neighborhood where the protection of a neighbor's property is part of the associative relationship.

As the juxtaposition of stealing with falsehood and deceit appears in Psalm 50:16–20, it becomes clear that the Commandments' attention to the interplay of lies and property involves changing and shifting categories of goods:

365

[16]But to the wicked God says:
  "What right have you to recite my statutes,
    or take my covenant on your lips?
[17]For you hate discipline,
    and you cast my words behind you.
[18]You make friends with a thief when you see one,
    and you keep company with adulterers.
[19]You give your mouth free rein for evil,
    and your tongue frames deceit.
[20]You sit and speak against your kin;
    you slander your own mother's child."

The Commandments are clearly in view in this accusation of the wicked for rejection of "my statutes," "my covenant," "discipline," and "my words." The references to stealing and adultery in verse 18 suggest that the commandment prohibiting false witness against one's neighbor is in view here. But the indictment is for the way the mouth and tongue have become instruments of deceit used for evil purposes against one's brother and sister, against one's own kin. Slander, ascription of faults, gossip, and deceitful words used to hurt the neighbor are all in view. The deceit may involve material goods and economic values, as other texts have indicated, but the endangerment is also manifest with regard to one's name and reputation and dignity. What one "possesses" that is endangered by deceit is not only material property and personal goods but also the standing of a person in the community. Against the assumption that "You cannot take away my good name," the Commandments recognize that it is quite possible to do so, and they seek a community devoted to truth in the recognition that its opposite often endangers the "goods" of the neighbor, material and nonmaterial.

In light of the above, it is not surprising that John Calvin saw in the Ninth Commandment a protection of both honor and property: "To this prohibition the command is linked that we should faithfully help everyone as much as we can in affirming the truth, in order to protect the integrity of his name and possessions" (*Institutes* 2.8.47). One might put it as both *material good* and *good name*. The interaction of these two commandments thus invites further reflection on the interaction of the two kinds of property, material and name, and the way in which one supports the other, the good name being essential to the acquisition and protection of property, the presence of property and possessions accruing to one's reputation and honor.

Two New Testament texts carry forward the interaction of stealing and false witness. One is from the Letter to the Ephesians:

> [25]So then, putting away falsehood, let all of us speak the truth to our neighbors, for we are members of one another. [26]Be angry but do not sin; do not let the sun go down on your anger, [27]and do not make room for the devil. [28]Thieves must give up stealing; rather let them labor and work honestly with their own hands, so as to have something to share with the needy. [29]Let no evil talk come out of your mouths, but only what is useful for building up, as there is need, so that your words may give grace to those who hear. [30]And do not grieve the Holy Spirit of God, with which you were marked with a seal for the day of redemption. [31]Put away from you all bitterness and wrath and anger and wrangling and slander, together with all malice, [32]and be kind to one another, tenderhearted, forgiving one another as God in Christ has forgiven you. [1]Therefore be imitators of God, as beloved children, [2]and live in love, as Christ loved us and gave himself up for us, a fragrant offering and sacrifice to God. (4:25–5:2)

The admonition to the Ephesians has to do with maintaining and enhancing the way in which a community lives together, its language, its interactions, its values, its aims, its economy. What is most noticeable about the text is that it deals almost entirely with truth-telling and what Stephen Fowl has called "word-care," how Christians speak to and with one another, which includes truth to and about neighbors, words of anger and bitterness, and evil talk generally (Fowl, "Making Stealing Possible," 168). In the midst of all this, however, there is an injunction that those who steal must stop stealing and learn to do honest work with their hands, so as to share with those in need. The trajectory of the Eighth Commandment thus opens up from a narrow reading of the commandment as a guard of private property to a positive inducement to generosity. The concern about stealing is focused not so much on the property stolen as on the act of stealing to obtain things as a way to avoid working for what one gets. The latter, "work[ing] honestly . . . so as to have something to share," creates possibilities of sharing for the good of others. In this way, the injunction to the Ephesian community follows out of and builds upon the various Old Testament regulations growing out of the Eighth and Ninth Commandments,

367

which serve not only to protect the neighbor's economic well-being but also to enhance it, and especially those statutes protecting the poor from inhumane treatment and providing for their well-being. The Scripture thus argues implicitly for a countercultural assumption that our aim is not the acquisition and protection (by legal and illegal means, by work and by stealing, by truth-telling and by false witness) of our property and possessions but instead sharing the wealth that God provides.

Like Jesus' teaching, the Letter of James shares sense of the dangers of wealth as it arises out of or encourages favoritism and partiality in human dealings (2:1–13). Though there is no reference specifically to the commandments prohibiting stealing and false witness, both the commandments are in the background. Following his words about dishonoring the poor by showing favoritism toward the rich and about the rich oppressing the poor and dragging them into court (v. 6), James specifically cites the Sixth and Seventh Commandments—against murder and adultery (v. 11)—and warns about the need to keep the whole law and not just some of the commandments. The particular violation of the law that elicits the references to not committing adultery or murder is showing partiality to the rich (v. 9), something that is a part of the trajectory of the commandments against stealing and false witness as far back as the Book of the Covenant (Exod. 23:1–9) and the Holiness Code (Lev. 19:15–16). Being dragged into court by the rich is a mode of oppressing the poor and has to do with wages, debts, pledges, and the like. The close connection between stealing and lying is intimated by Frances Taylor Gench, who comments on persons being taken to court by the rich: "As a result, they may also have found themselves the objects of slander and popular gossip on the part of the rich—disparaged as bad citizens or unreliable debtors" (*Hebrews and James*, 102). As James says rather bluntly, "you have dishonored the poor" (2:6).

All of this is made even more explicit in James's emotional outburst in chapter 5, where he addresses the rich:

⁴Listen! The wages of the laborers who mowed your fields, which you kept back by fraud, cry out, and the cries of the harvesters have reached the ears of the Lord of hosts. ⁵You have lived on the earth in luxury and in pleasure; you have fattened your hearts

in a day of slaughter. [6]You have condemned and murdered the righteous one, who does not resist you.

Two things are particularly noticeable about this charge. First is its rootage in the Old Testament statutes that develop the commandments against stealing and lying. The Deuteronomic statute warning against withholding "the wages of poor and needy laborers" and requiring daily payment of wages before the sun goes down (24:14–15) goes on to say that if this is not done, "they might cry to the LORD against you." And in Exodus 22:24 and 27, we hear that when the oppressed poor whose pledged coat is not returned and the widow, orphan, and resident alien who are abused cry out to the Lord, the Lord will, as James reiterates, listen to their cries. Second, oppressing and dishonoring the poor is seen by James to be ultimately an attack on their very lives, in effect a form of murder (v. 6; the same term appears in the Greek version of the Decalogue: Exod. 20:15//Deut. 5:18) and thus a further violation of the Commandments, whose purpose is to safeguard and protect life, property, and personal honor.

The Story of the Commandment

Joseph and Potiphar's Wife (Gen. 39)

The episode in which the wife of Joseph's master seeks to seduce him has already been noted in connection with the commandment against adultery. It is also an instance of lying testimony that leads to oppression of another. Like all the stories involving false witness, the act usually is in behalf of the violation of another commandment. Lies against a neighbor are not simply for the fun of lying but in order to violate the right and well-being of the neighbor. When Joseph refuses to betray the trust of his master and commit adultery with his master's wife and runs from her, she promptly accuses him falsely of having initiated the whole thing, telling first the members of the household and then her husband that Joseph came in to rape her—the opposite of what actually happened.

The terrible outcome of false witness is immediately evident. The enraged master turns against Joseph and throws him into prison. Coveting the handsome young man, Potiphar's wife seeks to

369

seduce him and, when that fails, brings about his imprisonment by false accusations. One gathers no impression of formal court matters. Potiphar has the power over Joseph to jail him simply on the testimony of his wife. Once again injustice is the outcome of the testimony of a person against the neighbor

Naboth's Vineyard (1 Kgs. 21)

The story of Jezebel's plot to fulfill the desire of her husband, King Ahab, for the vineyard of one of his subjects, Naboth, has to do with most of the commandments on the second table of the Decalogue. It is the best narrative illustration of the interplay of false witness and stealing, and that is the focus in this context. But it also reminds the reader of the capacity of lies to kill and the danger of desire being so strong it leads to acts of false witness, murder, and theft. The impetus for all that happens is King Ahab's desire for the vineyard of Naboth the Jezreelite for a royal vegetable garden because the vineyard is so close to the royal palace. The king's approach is a proper one in that he offers to give a better vineyard or to pay money for it if Naboth prefers. The story seems to presume that Ahab does not expect any resistance to his seemingly fair proposal. What he does not take into account is Naboth's commitment to the land allotted by the Lord to his family. Naboth quickly and strongly refuses the king's offer. It is only after this refusal that the extent of Ahab's desire for the land is revealed to be at the level of covetousness (vv. 4–6), enough so that when his wife suggests the use of royal power to bring off a scheme that will allow Ahab to appropriate the vineyard, he lets her carry out the plan without resistance.

To appropriate the vineyard illegally, to steal it, Jezebel manipulates the legal process to have Naboth accused falsely of having cursed God and the king. The result is his conviction and execution, with a resultant appropriation of Naboth's vineyard by Ahab. The object is theft, and the process whereby the theft is accomplished is a combination of false witness and murder under the guise of capital punishment. Various things come together here. Among the most obvious and relevant to this context are the following:

370

- the major role that false witness or lying plays in stealing a neighbor's property,

- the centrality of false witness in the corruption of the legal system,
- the guise of legality achieved through the use of two witnesses, in accordance with the Deuteronomic law (Deut. 17:6; 19:15),
- the close connection between the testimony of witnesses and capital punishment (Deut. 17:6),
- as in the case of David and Uriah (1 Sam. 11), the ease with which ruling power is led to (or can) use that power to turn its greed into corruption, manifest in the violation of the basic guidelines of the community's life together, the Commandments. Lord Acton's saying about absolute power corrupting absolutely is not far off the mark as far as the biblical stories are concerned.

The final matter of importance is the realization that on the surface, all that happens here is according to Hoyle, as best as one can reconstruct the situation of the story. A formal court procedure thus convicts a person on the basis of multiple witnesses, sentences him to death, and has him executed. The Deuteronomic statutes are to be presumed to lie in the background of the story. Nevertheless, a terrible injustice is done, and an innocent person is executed. With the possibility of false testimony, there is no guarantee that someone who is innocent will not be convicted. To all outward appearances, everything that is legally proper has been done. The outcome, however, is judicial murder. The tie between testimony and capital punishment that has been noted above is seen to be, literally, a life-and-death matter. The statutes of Deuteronomy seek to guard against such an injustice as has happened here. But there is no guarantee that it will work. The story of Naboth's trial and execution is a central illustration of what is at stake in the Ninth Commandment and is an early precursor of the many executions that have taken place as a result of false and improper testimony. Bernard Levinson has suggested that the story before us is a kind of metanarrative:

> The real story is the vulnerability of the law to political abuse. It shows that even the laws most concerned to ensure the integrity of the legal system itself (laws concerned with due process and the integrity of evidence) are insufficient without appropriate attention to how they are implemented and the integrity of the authorities responsible for implementing the law. (personal communication)

371

Already in the stories of Scripture, the commandment against false witness is a window into the danger of capital punishment effecting terrible and irretrievable injustice. The statutes may permit such a court action, but the stories show us why it cannot work (cf. Sus. 44–59).

The Execution of Jesus
(Matt. 26:57–67//Mark 14:53–65)

The account of Jesus' trial demonstrates the widespread propensity to use false witness as a tool for destroying those with whom one is at odds, in this case bringing literal destruction. And once more capital punishment is the intended outcome of efforts of the powerful to suborn persons to be their agents of destruction by giving false testimony against a victim. In this case also, however, the function of the various statutes and ordinances about false witness to build a barrier against such things happening is manifest and significantly, if not finally, effective. The point of the narrative is clear in the leading sentence: "Now the chief priests and the whole council were looking for false testimony against Jesus so that they might put him to death" (Matt. 26:59//Mark 14:55a). The move is an attempt at legal murder and the usual tool is false testimony. Yet here the interesting thing, in contrast to what we are told about Naboth's trial, is that they do not succeed. The text goes on to say, "But they found none" (Matt. 26:60//Mark 14:55b). Many came forward and spoke lies, but the necessary agreement of two or more witnesses, as required in Israelite law (Deut. 17:6–7; 19:15; cf. Matt. 18:16; 1 Tim. 5:19) could not be found, though the Gospels are not entirely the same in their depiction of what happens when the leaders seek to arouse false testimony.

Both Matthew and Mark indicate that there is much disagreement, that the leaders had difficulty conforming to the requirement for multiple witnesses agreeing on their testimony in order to bring about conviction. In Matthew's case, the story reports that two witnesses agreed in their claim that Jesus had said, "I am able to destroy the temple of God and to build it in three days" (Matt. 25:61), while Mark's witnesses do not even agree about this (Mark 14:59). The ultimate tool of the leaders is Jesus' refusal to deny any charges and his answer to their query whether he is the Messiah, the Son of God. His words, which do not deny the charges or make a clear messianic claim, are sufficient for the high priest to accuse him of blasphemy, and it is clear that any response from Jesus would have been so interpreted. The story thus is a vivid testimony to the common use of false witnesses to bring about a person's death while also demonstrating that the development of legal procedures to block such an event were effective, at least to some degree. Even so, violation of the commandment against false witness was one of the judicial instruments used against Jesus. Execution as the outcome of false witness is at the center of the Christian story and casts a shadow over every instance of capital punishment that has followed.

Ananias and Sapphira (Acts 5)

The account of this couple's selling some land and Peter's confrontation with them resonates with both the laws and the narratives that have been discussed to this point. The text is clearly to be read in relation to the preceding verses (Acts 4:32–37). The thematic thread is found in the references to members of the community selling property and laying the proceeds at the feet of the apostles (4:35, 37; 5:2). The context is the practice in the community of turning over the proceeds of property that was sold to the apostles for use in the community, to meet its needs, with the result that there were no needy persons among them (4:34–35). Though the practices are different, one can hear echoes of the statutes in Leviticus and Deuteronomy (cf. Exod. 23:11) requiring persons to leave some of the harvested grain and olives and grapes in the fields after the harvest so that those without the provisions of life could have access to them. The community lived by rules ensuring that those who had much would share with those who did not so that there might be none in need.

The story of Ananias and Sapphira is once again a report of the interplay of lying and theft. The property belonged to the couple, but once it was sold and given to the community by presenting it to the apostles, proceeds were expected to be given over wholly for use in the community to provide for everyone. In this case the lie is to God. One may presume a false oath of dedication, at least implicit if not explicit. The purpose is in order to hold on to some of the proceeds. That may not be the usual kind of theft, but according to the expectations of the community, it clearly was. We are once

373

more confronted with a subtle case of the wealthy lying in order to steal from the poor, even if, in this instance, the property actually belonged to the couple. That was no longer the case once it was sold and the proceeds offered. The proceeds belonged to the whole group specifically to support the poor and the needy. Once more the plight of the poor is the context for truth-telling and lying, and once more the key to the theft is a lie.

The Arrest of Stephen (Acts 6:8–15)

The claim that Jesus would destroy the temple, which is the false accusation brought by witnesses against Jesus in Matthew and Mark, is ascribed to Stephen in Acts and becomes the heart of the false testimony conjured up by synagogue members against him. The passage requires little comment except to observe that it somewhat replays the trial of Jesus and that once again the root cause of Stephen's execution/murder is the manipulation of testimony—indeed the creation of false testimony. Though issues are involved in the details of the testimony, for our purposes it is only necessary to add the narrative to the list of stories showing violation of the Ninth Commandment and especially its violation as a vehicle for the destruction of other human beings. Bearing false witness seems to be almost a natural resort. One is no longer surprised that Deuteronomy creates statutes that deal particularly with false testimony that may lead to execution. It was then and is now a common path. Words really can hurt. They often kill.

Other Voices

The Prophets' Judgments

The prophets ring the changes on the judicial and economic abuses of the poor by the rich, abuses that center especially in the maladministration of justice in the court and the resistance to truth-telling therein. Since we have already called attention to a number of their indictments against false witness, especially as a vehicle for theft of the neighbor's property, only a few additional texts need to be cited here as indicative of the prophetic concern for the use of lies as a weapon.

Jeremiah, like Diogenes with his lantern searching for one honest person, decries the absence of any in the community who really care about the truth:

> ¹Run to and fro through the streets of Jerusalem,
>   look around and take note!
> Search its squares and see
>   if you can find one person
> who acts justly
>   and seeks truth—
> so that I may pardon Jerusalem.
> ²Although they say, "As the LORD lives,"
>   yet they swear falsely.
>
> (5:1–2)

The equation of justice and truth is at the heart of the matter. Without the latter, the former disappears. The capital city is dominated by false oaths as instruments of destruction. In the process both the Third and Ninth Commandments are thrown to the earth. The name of God is taken up in oaths to legitimate actions, but there is no truth in those oaths. Claims, evidence, witness—all of this is to no avail for no one cares about the truth.

A similar picture may be seen as the context for Amos's strong judgment oracles. He speaks, for example, of those who "turn justice to wormwood, and bring righteousness to the ground!" (5:7). Then he becomes specific about what he means: "They hate [are in strong opposition to] the one who reproves in the gate [the court]" and "abhor the one who speaks the truth [does not bear false witness]" (5:10). They cannot stand the one who will speak the truth or the one who umpires, who adjudicates the issues, weighs the evidence, insists on sufficient witness, and insists on truth over partiality. In the next verse, it becomes clear that the allusion is to the use of the court to extract the goods of the poor: "You trample on the poor and take from them levies of grain." As James Mays puts it:

> The judicial process had been corrupted by the powerful and rich, and was used as instrument of oppression (5.12; 2.7). Courts were no more than markets to enslave the needy and wring the last bit of land and produce from him. His rights were violated with impunity. The source of the little man's right had been turned into a spring of injustice. (*Amos*, 11)

375

The commandment against false witness is in view as it serves to see that the community living by these signs and values does not let the court become a vehicle for misappropriation of the property of a neighbor and especially that of the poor. Truth and integrity in the courts is justice's last resort on the human plane.

The connection between lies and illegal appropriation of the property of others is attested in Micah 6:12:

> Your [or, "Whose"] wealthy are full of violence;
>> your [or, "whose"] inhabitants speak lies,
>> with tongues of deceit in their mouths.

The reference is to the city of Jerusalem, and the parallelism equates the violence of the rich with the speaking of lies. The capacity of lies to inflict injury is underscored again. The inference is that the wealthy have gained their wealth by various modes of lying, one of which may have been, and probably was, false testimony in the court (Wolff, *Micha*, 169). "Tongues of deceit" suggests false oaths and spoken lies. In the text that follows, the specific cited is falsifying of weights and measures. All of this is a form of stealing the property of others by modes of deceit. The prophet's concerns are those reflected in the statutes of the Deuteronomic Code discussed above, not only market transactions but presumably also "repayment of loans to creditors or payments of rents and tithes to landlords" (Hillers, *Micah*, 82). "The injury is more than economic; it damages the lives and status of persons in the fabric of society and destroys that fabric" (Mays, *Micah*, 147).

Isaiah 32 is a much–debated text but one that seems to characterize the future reign of justice and righteousness under God's chosen ruler. Within that description is a series of negative formulations about what will not happen under the ideal king, one of which is as follows:

> The villainies of villains are evil;
>> they devise wicked devices
> to ruin the poor with lying words,
>> even when the plea of the needy is right.
>>> (v. 7)

The last line, translated by NJPS as "and the needy when they plead their cause," likely has in mind the appearance of the poor in court.

So the lying words are once again presumably the false witness of the wicked against the poor in order, one way or another, to steal from them.

Finally we may call attention to Isaiah 59:1–4, a searing indictment of the iniquities of the postexilic community in Judah:

> ¹See, the LORD's hand is not too short to save,
>   nor his ear too dull to hear.
> ²Rather, your iniquities have been barriers
>   between you and your God,
> and your sins have hidden his face from you
>   so that he does not hear.
> ³For your hands are defiled with blood,
>   and your fingers with iniquity;
> your lips have spoken lies,
>   your tongue mutters wickedness.
> ⁴No one brings suit justly,
>   no one goes to law honestly;
> they rely on empty pleas, they speak lies,
>   conceiving mischief and begetting iniquity.

The implied charge against the Lord in verse 1 (cf. 58:3) is answered by the prophet's word that the problem is not God's inability to help but the community's oppressive acts. The accusation is strong and initially general: iniquities, sin, blood. In verses 3b–4, however, it becomes clear that once more the rampant sin of the community is lying in the courtroom. Both terms for "false" witness in the Commandments appear here: "Your lips have spoken lies [*šeqer*]," and "They speak lies [*šāwʾ*]." The accusation is extreme: "No one" brings suit justly or goes to court honestly, that is, telling the truth (cf. Jer. 5:1–5). While such indictments are familiar from the pre-exilic prophets, the pervasiveness of mendacity as an instrument of injustice was not confined to one period in Israel's history. It seems to have been—and remains—a perduring form of human sin.

The Cries of the Psalmists

References to false witness in an explicit way are not frequent in the Psalms, the clearest examples being Psalms 27 and 35, discussed above. In the former a song of trust leads into a prayer for God's help. In both parts are references to the psalmist's enemies and adversaries. The only specific crime mentioned as having been committed against the one praying is that false witnesses//witnesses of violence have risen up against him or her (v. 12). No more detail is given as to how the one praying has been injured, but the originating cause is false testimony, with its power to wreak havoc in the lives of the one falsely accused.

Psalm 35 also speaks about persons who are devising evil against the psalmist, and here too the central feature of that evil is false accusations being made against the petitioner (v. 11). More specifically, the psalmist goes on to say (vv. 19–21):

> [19]Do not let my treacherous enemies
>> [enemies of falsehood; cf. 69:5 (4E)] rejoice over me,
>> or those who hate me without cause wink the eye.
> [20]For they do not speak peace,
>> but they conceive deceitful words
>> against those who are quiet in the land.
> [21]They open wide their mouths against me;
>> they say, "Aha, Aha,
>> our eyes have seen it [or 'him']."

The reference to the speech of the enemies as deceitful words and especially their claim to "have seen it/him," something that the psalmist did, suggests false accusations in the court. The reference to the "quiet in the land," translated by NJPS as "harmless folk," points to a widespread pattern of false accusations or schemes to do in the innocent. Since the court system of justice has broken down, the falsely accused has no other source of redress than the justice of God, to which he now appeals. Furthermore, the speaker clearly identifies himself or herself with the poor and needy who are robbed by the lying actions of the strong:

> All my bones shall say,
>> "O LORD, who is like you?
> You deliver the weak
>> from those too strong for them,
>> the weak and needy from those who rob them."
>>>> (v. 10, my trans.)

378   These words are then followed by the reference to the witnesses of violence, and the connection between false witness and theft of

the poor is given poignant articulation, this time not in formal legal language but in the voice of one who is just such a victim.

Since, as has already been recognized in chapter 2, lying and deceit are probably the most common complaints in the prayers for help and petitions of the psalmists, many more texts could be cited than can be taken up in this context. Four psalms that take up the matter of lies against the neighbor in a different context merit a specific look. One of these is Psalm 12. The problem of the psalmist is the actions of the wicked, specifically in regard to what they speak. For three verses (2–4 [3–5 Heb.]) the psalmist decries the lies, deceit, and boasting that go on all around. The initial colon, "They utter lies to each other," uses the word *šāwʾ*, the term for false witness in the Deuteronomic Decalogue. The turning point comes at verse 5, as it announces the Lord's decision to intervene in the situation:

> "Because of the oppression of the poor, because of the groaning
> of the needy,
> Now I will arise," says the LORD.
> "I will place in safety the witness in his behalf."

> (my trans.)

It is possible to read the last line as "I will provide as salvation a witness for him" (Janzen, "Another Look"). In either reading, it is God's intention to provide a witness in behalf of the one who has suffered from lies and deceit. Furthermore, the connection of true and false witness with the fate especially of the poor and needy is underscored. In verses 2–4 the detailed description of that violence in terms of what and how the wicked or ungodly speak leads quite naturally to the divine promise (v. 5) to provide a truth-speaker or to protect the one who speaks truly and with integrity for the poor and the afflicted, the one who is a witness in their behalf over against any *ʿēd šāw*, any false or empty witness. Such testimony in behalf of the poor may have been in juridical proceedings, or it may have been as a witness to transactions or contracts, as in Jeremiah 32 (Miller, "*Yāpîaḥ*"). That testimony in the courts in behalf of the poor could endanger the witness is evident from Amos's description of those who hate the ones who speak the truth in the court (5:10).

Two psalms, belonging to quite different genres, serve to identify criteria and standards for human behavior and put heavy weight on the importance of speaking the truth and the evil of lies. One is the royal Psalm 101, wherein the king expresses a strong commitment to a just rule of the people and opposition to all forms of wickedness. The latter is articulated in various ways but at least twice with reference to slander and deceit: "Whoever slanders his neighbor in secret I will destroy" (v. 5, my trans.); and "No one who practices deceit shall remain in my house" (v. 7). Ruling justice is thus defined in terms of truthfulness, not just on the part of the ruler but also as a characteristic for the whole community. The king commits himself to making the Ninth Commandment, with all its ramifications, a major piece of the implicit charter for his reign. In so doing, the psalm uncovers the significance of truth and trust for the maintenance of society. Or to put the matter more sharply: "Life together is not possible without a minimal trust in the veracity of words. Unless checks are placed on the proclivity to evade truthfulness, corporate existence flounders and is altogether nasty and brutish" (Swezey, "Exodus 20:16," 407).

Psalm 15, like Psalm 24, has been characterized as an entrance liturgy describing the requirements for entering the presence of God in the sanctuary. Among those requirements is speaking truth from one's heart and not slandering with one's tongue (vv. 2b–3a). Verses 4–5 say that the behavior appropriate for one coming before God includes standing by one's oath, not lending money at interest, and not taking a bribe against the innocent, all of which are actions related to the commandment against false witness as it is elaborated in the legal codes discussed above. Psalm 24 is more succinct in its characterization of appropriate behavior, but the weight is again on truthfulness. When the question is asked as to who may stand in the Lord's holy place, the answer is as follows: "[Whoever] has clean hands and a pure heart, who has not taken a false oath by My life or sworn deceitfully" (v. 4 NJPS). The translation of the second half is uncertain, but it is likely that the reference is to obeying the Third and Ninth Commandments, telling the truth under oath and not lying. In short, telling the truth to and about the neighbor is a fundamental requirement for life under God's rule (Psalm 101) and in God's presence (Psalms 15 and 24).

The Wisdom of Proverbs

380

Wisdom, as well as stupidity and foolishness, is manifest very much. in the realm of speech, in what people say as much as in what they do. Proverbs reflects that concern for proper speaking over and over, as in the following examples, which can be multiplied greatly:

> A scoundrel and a villain goes around with crooked speech.
> (6:12)

> The words of the wicked are a deadly ambush,
>> but the speech of the upright delivers them.
>> (12:6)

> Rash words are like sword thrusts,
>> but the tongue of the wise brings healing.
>> (12:18)

> Truthful lips endure forever,
>> but a lying tongue lasts only a moment.
>> (12:19)

> Fine speech is not becoming to a fool;
>> still less is false speech to a ruler.
>> (17:7)

Thus the concern for truth and the repudiation of lies and false witness is addressed again and again. In Proverbs 25:18 the one who bears false witness against a neighbor is said to be "like a war club, a sword, or a sharp arrow." Words become weapons of personal destruction! In Proverbs 6:16–19, among the seven things that the Lord hates are "a lying tongue" and then, more specifically, "a lying witness who testifies falsely," a rather strong expression that uses two different expressions for false witness. In some instances the saying instructs simply by defining clearly, as, in the following:

> Whoever speaks the truth gives honest evidence,
>> but a false witness speaks deceitfully.
>> (12:17)

> A faithful witness does not lie,
>> but a false witness breathes out lies.
>> (14:5)

In other cases, the proverb identifies consequences and implications of telling the truth and of lying for the person in the court:

> A truthful witness saves lives,
>> but one who utters lies is a betrayer.
>> (14:25)

381

The first line has in mind the same issue reflected in the legal codes, that truth in the court is a matter of life and death. Elsewhere the instruction will point to consequences for the one who bears false witness:

> A false witness will not go unpunished,
>   and a liar will not escape.
>   (19:5; cf. v. 9)

Proverbs 21:28 combines both kinds of consequences:

> A false witness is doomed,
>   but one who really heard will testify with success.
>   (21:28 NJPS)

In all of these instances, the commandment against false witness is made a part of the wisdom of living properly, enjoying the good life, and thus conforming to the reality of life in this world. What is commanded is right and makes sense. Here, the "word" of the commandment is seen to incorporate both obedience and good sense. It is what one *must* do but also what one *would* do to live in this world. The divine command is echoed in the parents' teaching.

The Continuing Trajectory of the Commandment

Throughout our discussion of the commandment against false witness, its starting point, its contexts, its reverberations throughout Scripture, we have taken our cues from Martin Luther. It is appropriate, therefore, to listen to him once more in order to underscore an important dimension of the wider ramifications of the commandment. For Luther saw not only the importance of the courts of justice and the dangers for the poor and the needy when people bear false witness. He also went on to say that the commandment "forbids all sins of the tongue by which we may injure or offend our neighbor" (Large Catechism, in Kolb and Wengert, *Book of Concord*, 421). The Ninth Commandment centers in the operation of the court to achieve justice by honest testimony, yet it moves outside the strict confines of the court to speak about all things we say about our neighbor and their potential for harm. As we have noted,

382

this broader framework is present at various points in the Old Testament. Slander, gossip, and false rumor against the neighbor are all in mind when this commandment stands before us and calls us to a way of living in behalf of the well-being of our neighbor.

Thus the prohibition against a malicious or violent witness in Exodus 23:1 is preceded with the prohibition, "You shall not spread [or 'lift up'] a false report." And in Leviticus 19:11 and 16, alongside the prohibition of swearing falsely in the name of God, one hears a prohibition against dealing falsely or lying to one another and then the words: "You shall not go around as a slanderer among your people." Although here the term for "slanderer" is debated, the most likely conclusion is that it refers to "the kind of malicious gossip that might lead to the accusation and condemnation of a 'member of the congregation'" (Gerstenberger, *Leviticus*, 270; cf. Milgrom, *Leviticus 17–22*, 1644–45). When Psalm 50 follows up its condemnation of the wicked as making friends with a thief and keeping company with adulterers, its reference to the next commandment, against false witness, speaks broadly of giving one's mouth free rein for evil, speaking deceit and, as NJPS puts it, "maligning your brother, defaming the son of your mother" (v. 20).

Recalling the prophets' condemnation of the tendency of the false prophets to cry peace when there was no peace and so to lie to the community and against its well-being, Walter Brueggemann has properly brought into the sphere of falsity embodied in this prohibition the dangers of euphemism, propaganda, and spin, all of which are ways of corporate lying to the detriment of the common good and the possible harm of many people. With reference to such passages as Jeremiah 6:13; 8:11; and Ezekiel 13:10, he writes:

> These recognized voices of established reality [the religious leadership] deliberately misrepresent the true state of the economy and of foreign policy. Society has broken down and is not working, and they legitimate the dysfunction and give false assurance. The voices of accepted legitimacy present a fake reality, with failed fact disguised as workable fantasy. The prophetic traditions accepted as canonical are agreed that such fantasy will bring devastation upon a deceived community. (Brueggemann, "Truth-Telling," 91)

So the prohibition of this commandment moves out into the broader sphere of lying generally and especially any form of lying about the neighbor. The positive dimension of the commandment (always implicit in the negative, as Calvin has reminded us) is therefore the requirement always to speak the truth. That is not the primary word of this commandment, but it grows out of it. The danger of the false word against the neighbor puts a premium on truth. Three important caveats may be stated at this point:

1. The truth, when it is half-truth, when it is corrupted truth or spin, as noted above, can be used to deceive. Then it is lying. Much rumor, much undoing begins with partial truths. Thus reporters and writers, political leaders and their representatives need to keep this in mind. Half-truths about our neighbor can be as violent in their effects as the intended false witness.

2. The second caveat arises out of the apostle's words in the Letter to the Ephesians: "Speaking the truth in love, we must grow up in every way into him who is the head, into Christ" (4:15). There are some forms of speaking the truth that are incompatible with Christian faith. Speaking the truth is done in love in the Christian community. It is indeed an act of loving God—see the Third Commandment—and loving neighbor. If it is truth that hurts, then it needs to be rethought. How does the truth spoken truly become an act of love lovingly enacted? There may be many occasions in which that issue confronts a pastor.

3. The third caveat about speaking the truth is found in what a colleague has formulated succinctly as the freedom to lie (Rolf Jacobson, oral presentation). Truth-telling is the norm, but it may not always be the moral choice. Two stories involving the freedom to lie, both involving women, come immediately to mind. One is the story of the Hebrew midwives, Shiphrah and Puah, who are told by Pharaoh to kill any boy babies they help bring to birth (Exod. 1:15–22). When they do not and are confronted by Pharaoh as to why they have let the boys live, they give a deliberate lie: "Because the Hebrew women are not like the Egyptian women; for they are vigorous and give birth before the midwife comes to them" (v. 19). The text twice speaks of this act as fearing God. A similar lie for the good is Rahab's response to the king's men in Jericho when they come to her home looking for the Hebrew spies (Josh. 2). She tells the men that the spies have gone off in one direction when in fact they are hidden right there in her home. In both cases we encounter the freedom to lie for the glory of God, the evangelical freedom to lie for the good. Sin boldly that grace may abound.

384

The primary spheres in which this commandment charts out a space for life, therefore, are the realms of justice and honor and dignity, justice for the neighbor and honor and dignity for the neighbor. Yet in both cases, as we have seen, we are reaching for larger horizons than a simple reading involves. For the commandment charts the moral topography not just for perjury as an aspect of the administration of justice but also for the whole system of justice, which depended primarily on eyewitness report and careful investigation—and still does. Truth-telling is at the heart of the system of justice from top to bottom. Integrity and fair dealing are the grounds of justice and humane treatment of one's neighbor(s). They begin with the truth of witnesses, but they flow out into every other sphere of life, so that truth-telling is seen to be a social virtue in every sense of the term, one without which the community cannot function. Communal trust begins with truth, and the common good is not possible without a foundation of trust that is built on truth.

Truth-Telling as a Theological Issue

Truth-telling is a fundamental *theological* issue. Nobody said it any better than Job. It is to his theological friends that he addresses these words:

> ⁴As for you, you whitewash with lies;
>   all of you are worthless physicians.
> ⁵If you would only keep silent,
>   that would be your wisdom!
> ⁶Hear now my reasoning,
>   and listen to the pleadings of my lips.
> ⁷Will you speak falsely for God,
>   and speak deceitfully for him?
> ⁸Will you show partiality toward him,
>   will you plead the case for God?
>   (13:4–8)

So the minister of the Word—and all others who would speak for God—hears a directive about bearing false witness against God, about speaking the truth and not telling lies in God's behalf. There is also an implicit word here, signaled by Luther's claim that the

385

commandment calls us to "put the best construction on all we may hear about our neighbors" (Large Catechism, in Kolb and Wengert, *Book of Concord*, 424). That includes their theological views, especially the views of those with whom we disagree theologically. One of the primary dangers in the church today is the danger of not telling the truth about what one's theological opponent says. When that happens, communal trust and the good neighborhood of the church will crumble, not in the face of differing views on moral and theological issues but on an underlying and profound mendacity.

CHAPTER 9

Desire and Its Repercussions

You shall not covet your neighbor's house; you shall not covet your neighbor's wife, or male or female slave, or ox, or donkey, or anything that belongs to your neighbor.
Exodus 20:17

Neither shall you covet your neighbor's wife.
  Neither shall you desire your neighbor's house, or field, or male or female slave, or ox, or donkey, or anything that belongs to your neighbor.
Deuteronomy 5:21

Here at the end the Ten Words given to guide the life of the community of faith take us into what seems to be, and in various ways is, new territory. At their close, the Commandments open up the large matter of desire and its repercussions, suggesting that it is not only exterior acts that need guidance and direction but also interior feelings, attitudes, and desires. There is some debate as to how much the commandment actually has in mind only feelings and not actions, but there can be no doubt that the realm of the heart and mind—how one feels and thinks about the neighbor and what is the neighbor's—is much in view. Indeed, by its place at the end, the concern for desire and its control provides a climactic conclusion to the Commandments, a climax suggested in the very way the commandment is set up. To see how that is so, one needs to look at how the concern for coveting is constructed and particularly the place of this commandment in the numeration of the Commandments.

The Unresolved Problem of Numbering the Commandments

Variation in numbering the Ten Commandments is rooted in their beginning and their end. While the rationale for there being *ten* commandments is not altogether clear, the tradition of Scripture that there were "ten words" spoken by the Lord to the people on Sinai (Exod. 34:28; Deut. 4:13; 10:4) requires a numbering that ends up with ten units, no more and no less. As we have seen, however, it is possible to find more than ten "words" or commandments or, since that is not permitted, to read them in ways that connect commandments differently to produce the number ten. If the commandments having to do with other gods and images are read as two separate commandments, the first two in the sequence (Reformed numbering), or if the prologue is read as the first "word" or commandment or is joined with the commandment against other gods as a single commandment (Jewish numbering), then it is clear that the sentences about desire or coveting will have to be understood as a single commandment. If, however, the commandments against other gods and against images are read as a single commandment, then the commandment against false witness ends up as the Eighth Commandment and it is necessary to find two commandments in the sentences about coveting rather than one (Lutheran and Catholic numbering).

The rationale for seeing only one commandment in the prohibitions having to do with coveting is clear and obvious. The sentences in Exodus 20:17 and Deuteronomy 5:21 are focused entirely on the matter of coveting. That is evident in the Exodus version, where the verb *ḥāmad*, "desire," is repeated in the two sentences, the only difference being the objects of the verb. Deuteronomy uses two different verbs (see below), but both have to do with desire. The subject matter indicates a single concern—desiring or coveting what belongs to one's neighbor—with the verb repeated in Exodus 20 and changed in Deuteronomy 5.

There are aspects of the sentences about desire or coveting, however, that can easily lead one to see two commandments rather than one. The most explicit is the presence of two prohibitions: "You shall not covet" occurs twice, and in Deuteronomy the verb changes in the second prohibition. The distinction, then, would reside either in different modes of desire—but only in the case of Deuteronomy, with its two verbs; or in different objects of the two prohibitions, the first prohibiting a single object—house (Exod. 20:17) or wife (Deut. 5:21), and the second more comprehensively itemizing all that is covered by "house" in the one instance (Exodus), and in the other (Deuteronomy) separating the wife from the property or chattel of the Israelite male (Levinson, "Deuteronomy," 378–79, 417).

Further, in the Deuteronomic form of the Decalogue, the two prohibitions are separated into two paragraphs in the Masoretic Text,
and there is a conjunction between the two coveting prohibitions
analogous to the conjunction between each of the preceding four
commandments. These conjunctions are reflected in the NRSV's
translation: "*Neither* shall you commit adultery. *Neither* shall you
steal. *Neither* shall you bear false witness against your neighbor."
The presence of this conjunction twice in the verse having to do
with coveting is further indication of the possibility of reading two
commandments instead of one.

However one resolves the numeration, there is no escaping
the emphasis placed on this commandment. That is evident in the
repeated prohibition, the extended list of things not to be coveted,
and the comprehensive concluding clause "or anything that is your
neighbor's" (NJPS). The Commandments do not taper off at the
end. Rather, they come to a conclusion and underscore it, so much
so that it is possible to see two commandments on the same topic.
Even if one does not so number the Decalogue, it is impossible to
avoid the stress placed on this prohibition. So what is it about?

The Meaning of the Tenth Commandment

The specific point of this commandment is a matter of some consid-
erable debate. Before opening that debate, however, it is important
to stress that it has to do with understanding the range of action and
feeling within what is clearly and importantly an emphasis on desire
and its control as a part of neighborly living and, as we shall see,
one's relationship to God. The large topic of the commandment is
clear. Discussion about the particular meaning and force of verbs
and of the order of objects is a reflection of the complexity of the
commandment in the proper sense of that term, not an indication
that it is unclear or incoherent.

What Is Implied in the Verbs?

The primary verb of the commandment is *ḥāmad*, whose basic
meaning is "to desire." This verb is used in both sentences of the
Exodus version and in the first prohibition of the Deuteronomic
version: "You shall not *ḥāmad* your neighbor's wife." Both verbs are

used to speak of proper and improper desire, much as is the case with the English term "desire." In the case of *ḥāmad*, the meaning "covet" comes to the fore only when there is an object, and even then there are legitimate objects of desire, for example, the commandments or law of the Lord in Psalm 19:10 [11 Heb.]. In a number of instances, the verb signals an inordinate or ungoverned desire that leads to an act of taking what is desired. The following examples make this point:

> For I will cast out nations before you, and enlarge your borders; no one shall covet your land when you go up to appear before the LORD your God three times in the year. (Exod. 34:24)

> The images of their gods you shall burn with fire. Do not covet the silver or the gold that is on them and take it for yourself, because you could be ensnared by it; for it is abhorrent to the LORD your God. (Deut. 7:25)

> When I saw among the spoil a beautiful mantle from Shinar, and two hundred shekels of silver, and a bar of gold weighing fifty shekels, then I coveted them and took them. They now lie hidden in the ground inside my tent, with the silver underneath. (Josh. 7:21)

> [1]Alas for those who devise wickedness
>   and evil deeds on their beds!
> When the morning dawns, they perform it,
>   because it is in their power.
> [2]They covet fields, and seize them;
>   houses, and take them away;
> they oppress householder and house,
>   people and their inheritance.
>   (Mic. 2:1–2)

In Exodus 34:24, taking what belongs to someone else is implicit in the verb "desire." The verse does not mean that no one will want the people's land but that no one will want it and be able to appropriate it. Here, therefore, *ḥāmad,* or desire, involves both the improper desire and the action to get what one has coveted. In the other instances quoted above, the desire is followed by an act to take what is desired. As in the case of Joshua 7:21, it is money 390 as gold and silver or valuable property that is desired and taken. In Micah 2:1–2 the same objects that appear in the Deuteronomic second sentence—house and field—are coveted.

So what is in view is a combination of feeling and action in pursuit of what one is greedy for but may not have. While it would be wrong to describe every *ḥāmad* as involving actions against another's property, that seems to be where the weight of the verb's force falls. The commandment serves to protect another's property from the kind of desire that often leads someone to take an action commensurate with that desire (Childs, *Exodus*, 427). Coveting is not just ardent desire. Coveting is desire strong enough that it leads to acts to take away what belongs to a neighbor. At this point the commandment overlaps with other commandments, prohibitions against stealing and against adultery, but the further and important point of the last one(s) is to inhibit the avarice that leads one to appropriate wrongly what belongs to another. One can see the further important step of this commandment in the movement of the Decalogue as a whole toward what happens in the heart and mind on the way to a person's oppressive acts. In this regard the effect of the commandment is to forestall what other commandments prohibit.

In the second part of the Deuteronomic commandment a different verb, *hitʾawweh*, is used. It also connotes desire and longing and often involves bodily appetites: craving rich food or delicacies (Num. 11:4, 34//Ps. 106:14; Prov. 23:3, 6; 31:4); extreme thirst (2 Sam. 23:15); and longing for a beautiful woman (Ps. 45:11). Both the verb and the derivative noun often have the word *nepeš*, which speaks of the inner person, the soul or self, as the subject of the verb. The emphasis here clearly is on craving. It may involve an action arising out of the inordinate lust for something or someone, but often is not. The focus is much more on the emotion within the person (Childs, *Exodus*, 427) than on the act precipitated by the emotion.

The two verbs of Deuteronomy 5:21 clearly overlap in meaning and both have to do with strong desire. Brevard Childs is correct in concluding:

> The original command was directed to that desire which included, of course, those intrigues which led to acquiring the coveted object. The Deuteronomic substitution of the verb *hitʾawweh* did not mark a qualitative difference of approach which had the effect of internalizing a previously action oriented commandment.... Rather, the Deuteronomic recension simply made more explicit the subjective side of the prohibition which was already contained in the original command. (Childs, *Exodus*, 427)

391

This complexity is crucial for the force and meaning of the commandment. The initial and primary focus is on the greed that results in avarice and cupidity, in actions to take away what belongs to another. Use of the second verb *hitʾawweh* underscores the point by warning against a craving of the things of another even if one has not acted on that desire. Longing for what someone else has is a dangerous direction. The commandment reminds the community of the role of desire in negative acts against the neighbor. Protection of what belongs to the neighbor—and the commandment makes it clear that *everything* is included with its final words "or anything that is your neighbor's"—begins in the mind and heart, and the wrongful act is inhibited at its starting point when the neighborhood puts up a coveting watch over its life.

Legal and Illegal Avarice

It is likely that the commandment means to include both legal and illegal modes of appropriation of what belongs to another. That at least is how Maimonides saw the commandment when he wrote about its force:

> This Commandment admonishes us not to contrive schemes for acquiring what belongs to someone else. That is what the Exalted One means by saying "You shall not covet your neighbor's house." ... Thus it is made clear that this injunction warns against developing stratagems for getting hold of what belongs to someone else, even if we are prepared to buy it at a high price. Any action of this sort is a violation of "You shall not covet."

And then, when he moves to discuss craving in distinction from coveting, Maimonides goes on to say:

> One's desire for the object may grow stronger, to the point of devising a scheme to obtain it, and one will not stop begging and pressing the owner to sell it, or give it in exchange for something better or more valuable. If a person has his way, he breaks not only this prohibition (of craving) but "You shall not covet" as well, since by his persistence and scheming he has acquired a thing with which the owner did not want to part. (Rofe, "The Tenth Commandment," 46)

392

In the texts of Scripture are also indications that intrigue to get at someone else's goods may involve legal as well as illegal moves, for example, King Ahab's effort first to bargain with Naboth to get his vineyard before resorting to criminal modes in violation of several commandments when Naboth refuses to negotiate away his allotted property. The wicked referred to in Micah 2:1–2 (see above) "plan" or "devise" wicked schemes "on their beds" and then execute those plans to rob (*gāzal*) others. Here one may assume, as in any period and especially in the contemporary world, that the line between the legal and illegal is often very shady. One has only to think of the schemes to suck persons into mortgages designed to entrap them in debt or cause them to lose the mortgaged property, or of the nefarious but legal credit card plans that also entice persons into actions that end up costing them large amounts of money and possibly placing them in permanent debt. The commandment seeks to inhibit all stratagems, legal or illegal, that arise from craving what belongs to someone else.

The Goods Coveted

Although one may recognize the inclusiveness of the neighbor's goods being protected by the commandment, the fact that things are indeed listed and spelled out rather than simply saying "Do not covet anything that is your neighbor's" suggests that one should pay some attention to the details of the listing. Erhard Gerstenberger has observed that the commandment against coveting divides the property over which a "man" has authority into three categories: real estate, people under him, and animals (*Leviticus*, 441). This is evident in both forms of the commandment, although the Deuteronomic version mixes these categories and does not follow the Exodus order. The threefold categorization is confirmed in Leviticus 27:1–25 and also in summary fashion in verses 28–29. The distinctions are important because of the way they help to provide an understanding of the categories of goods that belong to the realm of "property," the "goods" that one has some claim over and that merit protection in the common life.

These include animals, particularly animals whose value and signification is their place in the culture's economy, with their potential for providing the "good" of livelihood and sustenance. This is one large category of goods in the common culture.

393

A second category of property in the Tenth Commandment is persons. The complex understanding of personal goods, of property, is thereby further indicated because in very basic senses the two types of persons mentioned in the commandment do not stand as property and possession in the same way; nor are they that in quite the same sense as either of the other two categories (real estate and animals). Assuming that the male and female slave are bonded slaves—and that seems to be the category the statutes are most concerned about—these are persons who exist as the property and possession of another in only a temporary fashion. As such, their valuation is economic in that, like the ox and donkey, they contribute to the productivity and economic value of the master. But they can also make claims on the one under whose authority they come. The possession exists in a kind of reciprocal relationship with the possessor so that at the end of the period of servitude, according to the Deuteronomic Code, the male or female slave becomes a possessor of some of the possessions of the slave master (Deut. 15:14–17).

The other person whom one is prohibited from coveting in the Tenth Commandment is the wife of a neighbor. This commandment has been one of the grounds for interpreting the social system portrayed within the Old Testament as reflecting an understanding of women as property of their husbands. One response to such a commandment is to see it as indicating a devaluing of women and wives. Another response is to hear in the commandment an understanding of possession that incorporates *personal relationships* as well as economic goods. The biblical stories and legislation reveal the complex relationships that husbands and wives have with one another. Rarely would one judge those stories as indicating that the wife was primarily an economic good, though it is clear that the provision of sons was an important good for the economic well-being of the family. What was possessed or could be taken away from one therefore incorporated the family relationships and specifically the nurtured relationship between husband and wife that produced children and created a family (or "house," household). At this point the commandment against adultery comes into play in the same relation to the commandment against coveting as does the commandment against stealing. The prohibition of adultery as a safeguard against taking a neighbor's wife—or as came to be the case, also a husband—is a pointer to the way in which human pos-

394

sessions incorporate significant human relationships. The definition of property as inferred from the Commandments is too narrowly conceived when it focuses simply upon economic goods or material goods. If the latter contribute to the self-understanding and self-worth of the individual member of the community, how much more is that the case for the familial relationships?

It is difficult to read anything about the age of the Deuteronomic version or the status of women out of Deuteronomy's sequence of verbal objects—putting the neighbor's wife ahead of his house (Moran, "Conclusion of the Decalogue"). The Deuteronomic family laws that give more detail on the place of women in Israelite society help to provide protection for vulnerable women, but they do not indicate a different family structure than the hierarchical, male-defined structure one sees in Exodus and elsewhere (Pressler, *View of Women*). What does happen in the Deuteronomic form of the Decalogue is to focus attention on the woman and her protection by this commandment and to separate the wife from the more typical property categories. "By removing her altogether from the list of other chattels, they establish that the law does not regard the woman as merely one commodity among others comprising a house" (Levinson, "Deuteronomy," 378).

The third category of "goods" envisioned in the coveting commandment and Leviticus 27 is a house. As Marvin Chaney has shown, the "house" does not simply return one to a purely material and economic value. In the agricultural and peasant culture of early Israel, wherein each family unit was given an allotment of land upon which and by which to live,

> the *bayit* [house] referred variously to the extended family, their dwelling, the family plot which provided their common livelihood, and the whole gestalt of meaning and value which inhered in these technoenvironmental and socioeconomic realities. . . . [It] signaled both an extended family's means of sustenance and shelter and the network of human nurture which could grow only once these survival needs had been met securely. (Chaney, "You Shall Not Covet," 8)

Here again, therefore, the commandment envisions a large understanding of what belongs to a person, incorporating various goods and categories of goods and possessions that together make up the ingredients of the common life.

The fullness of this notion of property is further indicated by the last clause of the commandment, "anything that belongs to your neighbor." René Girard has imaginatively reconstructed how the commandment comes to an end:

> In reading the Tenth Commandment one has the impression of being present at the intellectual process of its elaboration. To prevent people from fighting, the lawgiver seeks at first to forbid all the objects about which they ceaselessly fight, and he decides to make a list of these. However, he quickly perceives that the objects are too numerous: he cannot enumerate all of them. So he interrupts himself in the process, gives up focusing on the objects that keep changing anyway, and he turns to what never changes. Or rather, he turns to that one who is always present, the neighbor. One always desires *whatever belongs to that one*, the neighbor. (Girard, *I See Satan*, 9)

Who Covets?

The universality of the Commandments is to be assumed. Though their particular formulation has the individual free male in view, that stands in tension with their presentation as address to the whole assembly of Israel and their being taught to and learned by all members of the community. Furthermore, they function in contemporary societies where women are on equal status with men, wives with husbands, and servants with those they serve. As such, the Commandments are seen to lay out modes of acting and feeling that are not to be restricted to any set or category of individuals but are to be policy for all members of the community.

In this case, however, the question of address arises in another way. It is often suggested that the commandment against coveting arose out of a propertied class protecting its material goods from the encroachment of the poor. That is not necessarily the case, however. Where one encounters instances of coveting in the Old Testament, they are largely *acts of royalty and the wealthy*. Coveting is not a problem of the poor, insofar as the biblical story gives us a clue. It is the king and the wealthy who lust after and take from others, often from the powerless or the lesser members of the community. David's lust for the wife of one of his soldiers comes immediately to mind. Physical desire for a beautiful woman, coveting a neighbor's wife, leads to adultery and murder in order to

396

make the object of desire one's own (2 Sam. 11). No less central to the story is the power of the king to do whatever he wants or needs to do to take what he craves: his neighbor's wife. David is a prime example of the wicked person scheming on his bed at night, developing intricate stratagems to appropriate the wife of another, whatever it takes (Mic. 2:1–2).

The same is true of King Ahab in his coveting the vineyard of his subject Naboth (1 Kgs. 21). The desire is reasonable at first glance. Naboth's land is right next to the king's garden, so it would make a good royal vegetable garden. Ahab makes a practical case, on the surface, for wanting the land. He tries to make a good deal for Naboth to make it worth his while to sell. He offers Naboth more than the land is technically worth. As Ellen Davis has pointed out, however, all of this is probably part of a scheme to break up the "covenantal economics" of Israel's land system in favor of royal economics to expand royal wealth. She suggests that Ahab "means to break the traditional land tenure system at its base" (*Scripture, Culture, and Agriculture*, 113). Naboth refuses to sell, however, and for good reason. This is clearly the "house and field" about which the coveting commandment speaks. This is Naboth's ancestral allotment, the land given to his family for perpetual use to provide the necessities of life for his family forever. Whatever Ahab's motive or intent, his desire is an instance of coveting. The narrative is explicit about the emotional reaction of Ahab to Naboth's refusal:

> Ahab went home resentful and sullen because of what Naboth the Jezreelite had said to him; for he had said, "I will not give you my ancestral inheritance." He lay down on his bed, turned away his face, and would not eat. (1 Kgs. 21:4)

No reference is made to "coveting" in the story, but here is a classic example, perhaps the classic scriptural example, of consuming desire combined with political power that will not stop short of doing whatever is necessary to get what is coveted. And once again a stratagem by the powerful and wealthy accomplishes what the Tenth Commandment prohibits. Jezebel proposes a scheme to steal the coveted property by means of false witness against Naboth, leading to his execution. The story is an obvious instance of inordinate desire and acting on that desire. The action, however, is only possible because of the power of the king. The violator of

397

the commandment is one who already has much and craves more. When legal approaches fail, the king and queen resort to multiple crimes and, like David, violate several commandments.

When the prophets inveigh against those who violate this commandment, as does Micah in the oracle quoted above, they have in mind the wealthy who want to acquire more. We encounter prophetic indictment again in Micah's contemporary, Isaiah:

> Ah, you who join house to house, who add field to field, until there is room for no one but you, and you are left to live alone in the midst of the land! (5:8)

The prophet decries the unrelenting craving of the property owners to accumulate more and more, precisely those things that provide the means and goods of life—house and field—for the neighbor, who needs this foundation to sustain the life of the family. This does not mean that the poor do not steal (Prov. 30:7–9). But the large problem in the way this commandment plays out in the biblical texts is the acquisitiveness of the rich and powerful and the development of means, legal and illegal, to appropriate the property of others.

What More Do the Stories Tell Us?

From narratives and prophetic sayings, we learn something of who violates this commandment and under what circumstances. We also learn some other things about coveting and its destructive role in the good neighborhood:

1. *The subjects/objects protected* by the commandment are indeed what the stories reveal to be endangered. One form of the Decalogue places to the fore house (and implicitly, field); the other places the wife. We learn from the stories why these are out front. The two large stories mentioned above offer a narrative example of each. Ahab and Jezebel steal, plot false witness, truly in this instance a "witness of violence," and commit judicial murder in order to confiscate the field of Naboth. This is his *naḥălâ*, his inheritance or his family portion allotted by God, that same inheritance of house and field that Micah sees being taken away by the schemes of the powerful (2:1–2). David commits adultery and murder because he covets his neighbor's wife.

2. *The lure of silver and gold* is large in the biblical stories of coveting and taking. Sometimes it is the gold and silver of another,

398

as in the account of Ben-Hadad's siege of Samaria and his ulti-
matum to King Ahab: "Your silver and gold are mine; your fairest
wives and children also are mine" (1 Kgs. 20:3). Wealth and beauty
evoke avarice; the property and the wives of one king are coveted
by another who is confident he has the power to take them. Finally
the threat of the Aramean king is to take "everything you prize [find
desirable]" (v. 6 NJPS).

Silver and gold also arouse a craving on the part of Achan, who
covets the silver and gold of Jericho and takes it, hiding it among
his own belongings rather than devoting it to the Lord (Josh. 7).
Here we do not have an act against the neighbor, but we do see
an inordinate desire for money or its equivalent that leads an otherwise loyal citizen to act in a way that violates the commandment
and sets the community in danger. As in other stories of coveting,
Achan's avarice leads to violation of other commandments: "They
have stolen; they have acted deceitfully" (v. 11). The incident is an
unusual one, involving the *ḥērem*, or ban, which required the goods
of a conquered Canaanite city to be devoted to the Lord and not
coveted and taken as spoils by the Israelites (6:18). Whatever valuation one makes of the biblical account of the conquest of Canaan,
its purpose was to provide land for the people as a place to live and
sustain themselves. It was not to be a source of appropriated wealth
for the people. On the contrary, Israel was to separate itself from
the predatory economy of Canaan.

The background for this event may be seen in another text,
cited above. It is Moses' instruction to the people in Deuteronomy,
telling them to burn the images of the gods of the Canaanite nations
when they have been conquered: "Do not covet the silver or the
gold that is on them and take it for yourself, because you could be
ensnared by it; for it is abhorrent to the LORD your God. Do not
bring an abhorrent thing into your house, or you will be set apart
for destruction like it" (7:25–26). Several things need to be noted.
For one, the danger is once again the irresistibility of silver and gold
and the ease with which one may be drawn to taking it. Further,
one learns of a danger in fooling with idols and images of gods,
which might not have been expected. They are often if not usually made of precious metals or jewels (e.g., Exod. 32:2–4, 24, 31;
Judg. 8:24–27; 17:1–5) and so become enticing in a different way, as
access to wealth. No wonder the prophets often inveighed against
idols made of silver and gold (e.g., Isa. 2:20; 30:22; 31:7; 40:19; Jer.

10: 4, 8–9; Ezek. 16:17) or that the Letter to the Colossians equates covetousness with idolatry (3:5). The two are intimately intertwined in the biblical story. In some respects we have here another angle on the God or mammon choice familiar from the New Testament. Although it is not altogether clear how the one who covets and takes the silver and gold on the idols will be "ensnared," as Deuteronomy 7:25 puts it, the text suggests that making such a move will lead to fateful consequences, as indeed it does in Achan's case.

The texts referred to here are diverse. They make no single point. What they share, however, is the danger of entrapment, of being snared by things of silver and gold, or their equivalents. Desire must be controlled, and people are most in danger of losing control when the desired objects are things of wealth and great value. In his helpful essay on greed, William Schweiker quotes Bernard Mandeville at a much later time in a way that bridges between these texts and the modern world: "Great Wealth and Foreign Treasure will ever scorn to come among Men, unless you'll admit their inseparable companions, Avarice and Luxury" ("Reconsidering Greed," 251).

3. In the biblical story *the human predicament begins with desire let loose* and uncontrolled. The beginnings of dangerous desire are in Eden; because of that, Eden is lost forever, and the human story becomes filled with pain and toil. The effecting moment in Genesis 3 is not simply the words of the wily serpent to the woman. The serpent's words prompt a further look on the part of the woman whom God created. As the narrative spells out in some detail, however, it is the desirability of the fruit of the tree in the middle of the garden that leads to the couple's disobedience of the divine command: "So when the woman saw that the tree was good for food, and that it was a delight (*ta ʾăwâ*) to the eyes, and that the tree was to be desired (*neḥmad*) to make one wise, she took of its fruit and ate; and she also gave some to her husband, who was with her, and he ate" (v. 6). Only here are words from the two roots for desire in Deuteronomy 5:21 also found together. The elaboration underscores the power of desire. It is what the eyes see and the body wants: "good for food," "a delight to the eyes," and "to be desired to make one wise." All of this seems quite natural: beautiful fruit that is good for one.

The desirability of the fruit is so evident and in so many ways that the serpent's contribution seems relatively minor in the whole

400

story and the original prohibition forgotten. Except that God created *all* of the trees "good for food" and "pleasing to the sight" (Gen. 2:9 NJPS). There is plenty in the garden, all that one can desire. Sufficiency, enjoyment, and delight are part of the life that God has provided for the man and woman. But when the serpent points out another characteristic of the tree in the middle, the woman "takes" its fruit (cf. covet and take in Deut. 7:25; Josh. 7:21; Mic. 2:2; etc.). There is no neighbor here. Only a violation of the constraints of life in the garden, a violation due wholly to desire and its power to make one forget and ignore, in this case forget the divine command and ignore its consequences. The first act of disobedience is the couple's unrestrained craving. Desire out of control changes the human way in the world.

4. *The chaotic and destructive outcome of unrestrained sexual desire,* what has been known classically as concupiscence, is evident in several stories. In all instances, someone sees an attractive person and desire takes over. So Potiphar's wife sees the "handsome and good-looking" Joseph and desires him uncontrollably. Joseph's refusal to lie with her leads to her "lying" and ultimately to Joseph's imprisonment by her husband (Gen. 39). David sees the "very beautiful" Bathsheba, and his lust for Uriah's wife leads not only to his taking her and committing adultery and later murder but begins the downfall of his house by the judgment of God and the acts of others growing out of David's disobedience (2 Sam. 11–12). A piece of that is the account of Amnon's rape of his sister Tamar (2 Sam. 13), already discussed in chapter 6.

Here we simply note several dimensions of the Amnon story appropriate to thinking about desire: One is that the rape is explicitly an outcome of Amnon's uncontrolled desire for his "beautiful" half sister. Once again what the eye sees arouses excessive desire, leading to Amnon's seizing Tamar and forcing her to have sex with him (13:14). Second, as is so often the case (see above), Amnon pursues the object of his desire by a secret scheme, whose goal is to get what he cannot get and should not have. His "friend" Jonadab, described as "a very crafty man" (v. 3), dreams up a plan to get Tamar off by herself in Amnon's chamber. Third, while the neighbor's wife is not in view, as the story makes clear, Tamar is Absalom's sister. So the family relationship has been terribly violated, and we see, as we noted earlier, that personal relationships can be injured when craving is not controlled. The outcome is further chaos and

401

disintegration of the family of David, brother against brother, son against father, and the like.

One other story adds to the terrible picture of what happens when sexual desire runs wild. It is the story of Shechem's rape of Dinah (Gen. 34). She is not the wife of a neighbor. But here is what the prohibition of coveting is after. "When Shechem . . . saw her, he seized her and lay with her by force" (v. 2). What the eye sees it desires. That is a part of being human. It is also a point of great vulnerability, when desire is not restrained. Here is a classic case of craving and taking. The outcome is one of the terrible stories of Scripture, as Shechem tries to marry the woman he raped but ends up having his whole tribe slaughtered by Dinah's brothers, not unlike Absalom's response to Amnon after he has raped Tamar. Personal relationships are violated, and social chaos erupts. The revenge of Dinah's brothers against Shechem's clan is at first hidden from their father, Jacob; when he finds out about their acts, he says "You have brought trouble on me, making me stink among the inhabitants of the land" (v. 30). The common good is once more torn apart by desire run wild, and violence is the final outcome.

Elaborating the Commandment in the Laws

The force of the command not to covet may be reflected in any number of statutes in the legal codes, as others have noted. One thinks of statutes in the Book of the Covenant warning against abuse of widows, orphans, and the poor (Exod. 22:21–24), against exacting interest from the poor (22:25), requiring the return of the garment taken in pledge before nighttime (22:26–27), and returning the ox or donkey of one's enemy when it has wandered astray (23:4–5). Similarly, in the Deuteronomic Code one encounters inhibitions or barriers against coveting what belongs to one's neighbors in the statutes requiring that garments taken in pledge be restored quickly (24:10–13) and wages be paid promptly (24:14–15). Leaving the gleanings in the fields and vineyards for the widow and the orphan is also a counter to excessive desire (24:19–22), as is the whole sabbatical program for release of debts and debt servitude (Deut. 15). Even as the commandment against coveting interacts with and helps to safeguard and undergird the commandments leading up to it, so its statutory manifestations overlap with those that are associ-

402

ated with other commandments. They serve to set guards against excessive craving and taking, setting limits on the possibilities of the powerful to develop ways of taking the goods of the weak.

Still, near the end of the Deuteronomic Code is a section that may well be associated particularly with the commandment against coveting. It is found in 25:5–16 (so Braulik, "Sequence"; Olson, *Death of Moses*, 111–14; Kaufman, "Structure," 142–44). The statute in verses 11–12 is not particularly relevant to the coveting prohibition. The other two statutes in this legal block, verses 5–10 and 13–16, are aspects of the trajectory of the Tenth Commandment as the community developed its implications.

Levirate Marriage (Deut. 25:5–10)

In accordance with the order of clauses in the Deuteronomic form of the Tenth Commandment and in distinction from the order in Exodus 20, the first of these statutes, Deuteronomy 25:5–10, deals with the wife rather than house or property. It is what has come to be known as the law of levirate marriage (Latin *levir* = "husband's brother"). The statute preserves the name and lineage of an Israelite man who dies without an heir by prescribing that his brother shall take the dead man's wife as his own and provide an heir to carry on the name of the deceased (vv. 5–6). A further provision is added for what to do if the brother is unwilling to take the widow as wife (vv. 7–10). A formal process is created that includes appeal to the elders by the widow, the brother's stated rejection of his sister-in-law, and her symbolic act to shame the brother for refusing to marry her.

It is possible to read this statute as a "sanctioned exception to the basic prohibition of the Tenth Commandment" (Kaufman, "Structure," 143; cf. Olson, *Death of Moses*, 111). The law would thus provide an instance in which it was acceptable for a man to desire and take the wife of his brother/neighbor. Indeed, the situation would create an obligation for the brother to take his sister-in-law as his wife. There is much that is unclear about the circumstances here and the significance of the various acts, but it is equally, if not more likely, that the statute is a way of safeguarding the intention of the Tenth Commandment by preserving the integrity, both personal and economic, of the household. It does so by obligating the brother to marry his dead brother's wife and so carry on the line and keep the economic goods of the deceased husband available

403

to his widow and his posterity. The statute addresses the treatment of both the neighbor's/brother's wife and his goods, but with the accent on the latter. So a brother may take the wife of his neighbor (who in this instance is actually his brother)—notice there is nothing about desire in the statute—and is actually obligated to do so in order to avoid coveting and taking the property of his brother.

The statute thus sets the whole area of *family relations*, including both personal relationships and property, as a sphere in which one needs to think about desire and its effects as well as responsibility to take care of the goods of the neighbor/brother/sister. In other words, we have here not so much an exception to the coveting commandment as a form of its positive manifestation. Taking the wife of the brother is not in this instance a form of desire. On the contrary, it is a manifestation of controlled desire in order to protect the family and the economic goods of the brother/neighbor. The statute itself is unusual and seems antiquarian in the modern world. Its intention, however, does not fade with time. It is an illustration of one of the social structures most vulnerable to uncontrolled desire. There is probably no place where desire for what someone else has operates as constantly as within family relationships. This Deuteronomic law seeks to show how it is possible to control such desire and provide for one's brother/sister rather than take from the sibling. The very unique and ancient case points in a direction that is perduring, whatever may be the ways one now seeks to follow it.

Possessing Only Honest Weights and Measures (Deut. 25:13–16)

This brief statute, with its straightforward stipulation against having different kinds of weights and measures in one's pouch or house, is more "weighty" in regard to the commandment against coveting than might seem to be the case at first glance. Having different-sized weights and measures is, as the prophet Amos says, in order to "practice deceit with false balances" (8:5). "The heavier weight would be used to weigh the silver received when selling, and the lighter one to weigh what one would pay out when buying" (Nelson, *Deuteronomy*, 301). With syntactical emphasis the Deuteronomic statute says, "You shall have" only "perfect" and "right/accurate" weights and measures (25:15, my trans.).

Clearly, the community must be careful about honest transactions. That concern is safeguarded by the commandment against stealing. Here, however, the critical point is not simply the *use* of false weights and measures. It also is having such *in one's possession*. Owning weights and measures of different scales, thus some that are not true, is an obvious sign of the desire to use them to take what belongs to another. Avarice is the only basis for possessing different scales. Having them in the house or in one's possession when one goes to bargain with another indicates an already-existing desire to take more than one should. They are in effect tokens of greed, reflections of the clear intention to rob from another. Again the Tenth Commandment in its particularity via this illustrative statute points one toward the state of mind before the act of robbing or defrauding and the securing ahead of time of the technical means to do so. Such prior planning may be as likely a commercial device as a personal or individual one.

The "weight" of this statute, already indicated by its formulation in both commandmentlike prohibition and its positive counterpart, is further underscored by the presence of two motivation clauses. These are typical of Deuteronomy but not to be ignored because of their familiarity. One reason for keeping this statute is "that your days may be long in the land that the LORD your God is giving you" (25:15b; cf. Deut. 5:16). The assumption is that having such false weights and measures in one's possession creates a persistent and systemic possibility of fraudulent and oppressive practices. If that is widespread, the common good is undermined, and an economy of greed will lead to chaos and the undoing of the social structures that guide and uphold the community. Either that, or the people's days may be shortened by the judgment of God. Perhaps they are one and the same thing.

The latter possibility is further suggested by the word that everyone who does this, who acts dishonestly—for possession of false weights is in order to act—is "abhorrent to the LORD" (v. 16b). It is possible that this final word is here as "a fitting conclusion to the civil and criminal laws of Deuteronomy" (Tigay, *Deuteronomy*, 235). For the Deuteronomic Code, an elaboration of the Ten Commandments, comes to its end at this point. Two things are to be noted, however. One is that having or using false weights and measures is not only regularly condemned in the wisdom of Proverbs, but it is also regularly described as "an abomination to the LORD"

405

(16:11; 20:10, 23). Thus, dishonesty in economic matters is one of the practices that is marked as particularly repulsive to Israel's God. Further, the expression "abhorrent to the LORD" in Deuteronomy is especially associated with the worship of other gods and the practices associated with them. This leads Olson to suggest that intending to take from another involves not only wrong desire or coveting but also idolatry. "The worship of the false god of materialism has replaced the true worship of Yahweh alone" (Olson, *Death of Moses*, 114).

The First and the Last Commandments

At various points, we have noted the interaction among the Commandments and the way they resonate with one another. That is probably most evident in regard to this last commandment, as it warns against the kind of desire for what another has that leads to violation of other commandments, specifically the prohibitions against killing, adultery, theft, and false witness. The connections of the Tenth Commandment, however, are not only with the neighbor commandments of the second table. The command not to covet goods belonging to one's neighbor points back to the beginning of the Decalogue and as such rounds off the whole. The Decalogue begins with "I am the LORD your God" and ends with "your neighbor," or more specifically, "anything that is your neighbor's" (NJPS). Between those two subjects lies all the moral space of the Commandments.

It is especially the First Commandment, however, to which we are pointed by the substance and intention of the prohibition against coveting. Martin Luther made the connection in a specific and positive way as he associated the obedience of not coveting with generosity. In his *Treatise on Good Works* (109), he wrote: "A man [*sic*] is generous because he trusts God and never doubts but that he will always have enough. In contrast a man is covetous and anxious because he does not trust God. Now faith is the master workman and the motivating force behind the good work of generosity." His point is already anticipated in Proverbs 21:26: "All day long the wicked covet, but the righteous give and do not hold back."

406   Coveting and taking arise out of lack of trust in the God who has made and provided for the human creature. That turns the possession of goods and the accumulation of wealth into a god in sharp

distinction from the generosity that lets go because of gratitude and trust that God will provide (Gen. 22:8, 14). Trust that one will have enough and does not need to covet or act to take from others what they have is a positive manifestation of the First Commandment, articulated as the love and fear of God (Deut. 6:4, 13). The prohibition against coveting is thus a safeguard of the worship of the Lord alone as much as it is a safeguard of the goods of the neighbor.

In his final defense and articulation of his righteousness before God, Job sets out both a number of ways that he has not violated the Commandments and how he has acted as one who fears God, a primary characterization of Job in the Prologue to the book (1:1; 2:3). In the course of his "negative confessions" of innocence, Job contends:

> ²⁴If I have made gold my trust,
>   or called fine gold my confidence;
> ²⁵if I have rejoiced because my wealth was great,
>   or because my hand had gotten much;
> . . . .
> ²⁸this also would be an iniquity to be punished by the judges,
>   for I should have been false to God above.
>
> (31:24–28)

This claim on the part of one who is righteous but oppressed does two things: it makes the enjoyment of excessive riches a violation of the First Commandment, and it indicates that what is at issue in that commandment is whom and what you trust. The acquisition of excessive wealth as it arises out of coveting and taking is indeed a neighbor issue, but it is fundamentally a matter of the fear of God and the sole reliance on the Lord for the provision of life. In that regard, it is clear that inordinate desire is sufficient to entice one away from the full devotion, even if one does not take from the neighbor.

One of the more helpful ways of framing the relation between desire and the love of God is offered by Reinhard Hütter:

> [The Commandments] stubbornly keep our desires directed toward God. To be clear: Desire as such is not the problem; it is not "bad." Indeed we are created as creatures with desires; to be human is to be desiring. All of our desires, however, are created to come to a rest in their one ultimate good, communion with God. Augustine's famous sentence from the *Confessions*—"You

have made us and drawn us to yourself, and our heart is unquiet until it rests in you"—expresses how our desires find rest and fulfillment only in God. If other created things are elevated to the position of the ultimate good in ceaseless exchange, coveting is the unavoidable result, since none of these created things will ultimately bring our desiring to a rest. Without desire we would cease to be human; without God as desire's ultimate end, we become inhumane. ("Twofold Center of Lutheran Ethics," 47)

A classic instance of this inability to let go so that one may truly worship and fear God is found in the New Testament, to which we now turn.

From the Old Testament to the New

Jesus in the Gospels

The story of the rich man and Jesus is found in all three Synoptic Gospels (Matt. 19:16–30//Mark 10:17–31//Luke 18:18–30). We shall focus on the Markan account as the basis of interpretation. It is, as Lamar Williamson remarks, a call story, one whose negative outcome strikes "a note of realism" and also "attests the special power of possessions to hinder Christian discipleship" (Williamson, *Mark*, 183).

> [17]As he [Jesus] was setting out on a journey, a man ran up and knelt before him, and asked him, "Good Teacher, what must I do to inherit eternal life?" [18]Jesus said to him, "Why do you call me good? No one is good but God alone. [19]You know the commandments: 'You shall not murder; You shall not commit adultery; You shall not steal; You shall not bear false witness; You shall not defraud; Honor your father and mother.'" [20]He said to him, "Teacher, I have kept all these since my youth." [21]Jesus, looking at him, loved him and said, "You lack one thing; go, sell what you own, and give the money to the poor, and you will have treasure in heaven; then come, follow me." [22]When he heard this, he was shocked and went away grieving, for he had many possessions.

The importance of the text for the trajectory of the commandment against coveting is evident in several ways:

1. In the Markan account, and only there, Jesus includes the Tenth Commandment in his recitation of the second table of

408

the Decalogue but in an initially surprising form: *"You shall not defraud."* This formulation represents the commandment in its external force, which is central to its meaning from the beginning, since it pertains to coveting what belongs to one's neighbor and making legal, commercial, or other moves to take it. Jesus recites the commandments as they were understood in the Judaism of his day and certainly by the young man who asks him what must be done to "inherit" eternal life. The reference to fraud, a common way by which the rich would take what they covet from others, makes it clear that "the law is measurable and its keeping observable" (Bruckner, "On the One Hand," 112).

2. The young man has indeed kept all these Commandments and receives a sign of approval from Jesus, reflected in the report that Jesus, "looking at him, loved him." This is a good man, who has labored to keep the Commandments, loving God and neighbor. It is, however, the last Commandment that uncovers the deeper problem: *desire*. The more subjective dimension of the commandment against coveting is brought to the fore as the commandment is

> radicalized in that the object of his desire is his own property. . . .
> What the ruler lacks is that he covets, in the radical sense of the
> word, so he cannot follow Jesus. He is captivated by his desire for
> his own wealth. This stands as the insurmountable obstacle to his
> discipleship. (Bruckner, "On the One Hand," 112)

3. Jesus' word to the young man, to *go and sell all* he has and give the money to the poor and then come and "Follow me," joins together release from the grip of desire to have and the true object of uncontrolled, extravagant desire. At the end, the love of God and the love of neighbor are melded into one. The neighbor is preeminently there in the poor, as is evident throughout the Commandments; faith and trust in God are found now in devotion to Jesus and his way. It is the way of the Lord.

4. This text should not be read apart from its context, at least in the Gospel of Mark. In the preceding text, Mark 10:13–16, Jesus welcomes the little children, saying that it is "to such as these that the *kingdom of God* belongs" (emphasis added). By contrast, in the text that follows Jesus' conversation with the young man, he expounds on "how hard it will be for those who have wealth to enter the kingdom of God!" and then repeats it (Mark 10:23–24)! The impact of these words is strong on his audience of disciples, who

409

do not see how anyone can be saved (i.e., receive eternal life, the desire of the young man with riches) if this be true. To which Jesus replies: "For mortals it is impossible, but not for God; for God all things are possible."

> These last words transform the contrast from a contradiction to a paradox. Entrance to the Kingdom of God, or eternal life, or salvation, so far from being easy, demands our best obedience and all we have. Yet all we can do is not enough to achieve the life we seek. Such life and wholeness is possible only for God, and we can receive it only as gift. Jesus' blessing of children (10:13–16) can be read as cheap grace. Jesus' call to the rich man (10:17–22) can be read as works salvation. Jesus' teaching to disciples (10:23–27) draws gift and demand together in a paradox that is astonishing but true. (Williamson, *Mark*, 185)

Paul on Coveting

The bridge between this conversation of Jesus with the rich young man and Paul's own experience and theological discernment is quite direct. For as it is the commandment against coveting that exposes what is missing from the obedient life of the rich man, so it is with Paul. Romans 7 is a rich and complex text, very much at the heart of Paul's view of both sin and the law. The immediately relevant portion of his argument is verses 7–12:

> [7]What then should we say? That the law is sin? By no means! Yet, if it had not been for the law, I would not have known sin. I would not have known what it is to covet if the law had not said, "You shall not covet." [8]But sin, seizing an opportunity in the commandment, produced in me all kinds of covetousness. Apart from the law sin lies dead. [9]I was once alive apart from the law, but when the commandment came, sin revived [10]and I died, and the very commandment that promised life proved to be death to me. [11]For sin, seizing an opportunity in the commandment, deceived me and through it killed me. [12]So the law is holy, and the commandment is holy and just and good.

As Paul Meyer has shown, the issue here is not the effect of the law per se (Meyer, "Worm," 71). Nor is it a description of the situation of "the pious Jew," as Käsemann sees it (*Romans*, 195). "The transcendentally . . . demonic nature of sin is its power to pervert

410

the highest and best in *all* human piety, typified by the best in Paul's world, his own commitment to God's holy commandment, in such a way as to produce death in place of the promised life" (Meyer, "Worm," 71). What the law does is identify sin and make it known. It is no accident that Paul's specific illustration of the power of sin to turn the law into a way to death is the commandment "You shall not covet." For it is precisely in the power of inordinate desire to take over one's being that sin finds its way into the human condition. None of the other commandments could uncover what sin does as clearly as the last one.

The subjective dimension of the commandment, the dimension of thought and feeling, is clearly what is in Paul's mind as evidenced by the absence of any specifying word or phrase with the noun "covetousness" (*epithymia*), which he uses twice (vv. 7, 8), and the absence of any object for the verb *epithymeō*, which he uses in quoting the first words of the commandment (v. 7). Once again there is no reason to assume that Paul has in mind natural desires and feelings but rather inordinate desire, though his formulation is quite strong: "Sin . . . produced in me *all kinds of covetousness*" (lit., "all desire"), suggesting the many possibilities for sin to use desire. Sin's "opportunity in the commandment" is precisely in the fact that the commandment uncovers or identifies covetousness as sin and leads one to see how thoroughly desire takes hold of heart, will, and mind and leads to death (v. 10). The danger and sin that Paul sees operating so powerfully in coveting is underscored in the Letter to the Colossians as Paul calls on his audience to "set your minds on things that are above" (3:2) and "put to death, therefore, whatever in you is earthly" (v. 5). He proceeds to list earthly things that need to be put to death because they are manifestations of the power of sin: "fornication, impurity, passion, evil desire [*epithymia*], and greed [or avarice, *pleonexia*]" (v. 5). The list is clearly climaxed by and weighted toward wrong desire. But Paul goes further here, adding the explanatory note about greed, "which is idolatry," an equation underscored by its repetition in Ephesians 5:5. Here one sees once more how the Tenth Commandment represents a kind of inclusion, returning to the most fundamental issue of all, what one finds in the first two commandments, the proper relation to God. What Paul discerned is the power of greed to turn the heart away from true devotion to God and create objects of great desire, the kind of desire that belongs rightly only to the heart's love of God.

411

James on Coveting

James 3:13–4:10 has been called "the heart of James's writing and the key to its understanding" (Johnson, "James," 1275). In these verses his moral instruction is oriented around a contrast between two ways, characterized at one point as wisdom that is "earthly, unspiritual, devilish" versus "wisdom from above," which is "pure, then peaceable, gentle, willing to yield" (3:15–17); and then identifies a contrast between friendship with the world and friendship with God (4:4). The problem with earthly wisdom and friendship with the world centers around "envy" (*zēlos*), a term that appears three times in this piece of instruction. It is the heart of the matter, envy for what others have. For James, this is the root of human conflict, and he makes this point in strong fashion:

> ¹Those conflicts and disputes among you, where do they come from? Do they not come from your cravings that are at war within you? ²You want something and do not have it; so you commit murder. And you covet something and cannot obtain it; so you engage in disputes and conflicts. (4:1–2)

Translated more literally, the second verse reads: "You desire [*epithymeō*] and do not have; you commit murder. You envy [*zēloō*] and are not able to obtain." The root of human conflict is found in the desire for what one does not have. As we have seen in the Old Testament texts, the desire for something that belongs to another leads to murder, war, and other kinds of conflict. The language here for "conflict and dispute" is literally "war and fighting." Whether the language is symbolic or not, one cannot say, for conflict can manifest itself at all levels and at all extremes, including war and murder. Whatever be the case, it is unwarranted, jealous desire that seems, in James's understanding, to precipitate the conflict.

Wrapping It Up

So we have come to the end. No single commandment embodies the love of neighbor more than the commandment against coveting, for it is the prohibition that from the start inhibits whatever inclinations we may have to do in our neighbor's life, property, mar-

412

riage, honor, and all that is our neighbor's. It also takes us back to the beginning in two ways, the beginning of the Commandments and the beginning of the human story. As Paul discerned, avarice and desire when uncontrolled take over our lives and turn us away from the ultimate object of devotion by placing penultimate goods as the objects of our affections rather than the Lord of heaven and earth, who has made us and redeemed us. At the same time, we are reminded that when God created human beings (Gen. 2:7), then "the Lord God planted a garden" and made the world a "desirable" place for human existence (2:8–9). And the openness of this created world to human desire and enjoyment is reinforced in the context of the covenant as well as in the creation.

In Deuteronomy 14:26, Moses concludes the long set of instructions developing the meaning and implications of the first table of the Commandments with this permission: "Spend the money for whatever your heart desires—oxen, sheep, wine, strong drink, or whatever your heart asks for. And you shall eat there before the Lord your God and rejoice, you and your household" (my trans.). As James Bruckner observes: "This open permission is given at the end of three chapters of laws concerning what is within and what is outside the clean/unclean boundary (Deuteronomy 12–14). 'Whatever you desire' in this context means 'whatever you desire that I have given for the purpose of desiring'" (Bruckner, "On the One Hand," 100). The same is true of the gifts in the garden. The world is full of things pleasant and desirable that the Lord God has provided for our enjoyment. In the context of what God has provided for our desire and in the context of the specific rules God gives for our daily life, desire is to be enjoyed. There is some restriction both by God's ordering of creation and by the commands of God. From the beginning, desire for the things of this world for our enjoyment is both part of what it means to be human and part of what it means to be a member of the covenant community.

This world God has given is a desirable place, and that is our glory and our damnation. Sexual desire is part of our created humanity. Sexual lust for another's partner is our disobedience. We live in both possibilities, and the Commandments serve to remind us of the reality of desire, which is where we find joy, and to hold and restrain us from excessive desire that leads to our downfall, the oppression of our neighbor, and the dissolution of the common

413

good. Satisfaction and contentment with what God provides is the positive form of the Tenth Commandment. Like its negative form, that is both act and feeling.

We live in an increasingly consumer-oriented culture that clearly presumes the importance of desire in the human experience and also shows us the possibility of human desire run wild. The first and primary restraint of the commandment is on the desire that leads to violation of the well-being of our neighbor. The second restraint is a reminder of the subjective dimension of desire: even when not directed toward the neighbor, it may take us over and become our "consuming" passion, if not our god.

The Ethics of
the Commandments

The Ten Commandments have a simplicity that, upon closer examination, opens up into a greater and richer complexity than is immediately apparent. We are looking at that all along the way with individual commandments. That deeper complexity beneath a surface simplicity is reflected also in any effort to think about the *ethics* of the Commandments, about the way in which the Commandments are grounded and function as a guide to the moral life or life with God and neighbor. As commandments, they belong within the framework of a divine command theory of ethics: obedience is an obligation arising out of the command of God. Such an assumption, however, is a *starting point* for thinking about the ethics of the Decalogue and merits a fuller development with regard to this particular text, these particular commands. Further, one should not assume that the Decalogue is to be consigned simply to a divine command theory in a narrow sense without reference to other modes of ethical discourse and other grounds for the moral life. Or to put it another way, if the initial or primary category for thinking about the Decalogue is divine command—and that is how many people begin—that category is a rich and complex one touching base with other forms of thinking about how human beings live in relation to God and to the world. Viewing the Commandments as functioning within a divine command theory should not be a reductionistic enterprise. On the contrary, reflection on that functioning indicates a wider rather than a narrower framework for comprehending the way the Commandments work as guides for human living and flourishing.

The Givenness of the Commands

While divine command ethics has suffered under substantial critique in the modern period, it has experienced a substantial amount of staying power. Some of that lies in the fact that within certain religious traditions—and in this case we are concerned with the Judaic and Christian traditions—divine command plays a significant part in the foundational story that shapes faith and action. Most practitioners of Judaism and of Christianity probably think of divine commands first with reference to the commands of God given to the community at Sinai, the Ten Commandments.

It is not my intention or a necessity to argue for a divine command theory of ethics as *the* framework for dealing with and reflecting upon the moral life. That might fall into the reductionistic tendency I am resisting. In this case, the starting point is not a *theory* of divine command but the *givenness* of the divine commands in the Decalogue. There may well be other ethical approaches to understanding the moral life in relation to God of equal validity and usefulness. Indeed, there are other approaches and Scripture contributes to an articulation and interpretation of such other approaches. What is needed with regard to the Commandments is to think through what sort of ethics is uncovered in their form and content, which seems clearly to begin in divine command—"And God said, . . . You shall have no other gods before me"—and to place some weight on that starting point. But one must then move deeper into the range of ethical grounding so that the divine command functions for the ethics of the Commandments in the same way as the Commandments function for the ethics of Scripture and the Christian life, as the starting point and framework, from which and in which further discernment takes place.

The *givenness* of the divine command is evident in the *identification* of the one commanding—the *Lord*—and in the *form* of moral direction—*command*, both positive and negative. The givenness of the text does not allow one to begin with or necessarily to extrapolate comprehensive theories, to make claims about the wholeness

416

of moral virtue being found entirely in obedience to the commands of God. Those commands are what we have in the text. If one turns, for example, to Wisdom literature, one may find something rather different by way of implicit and explicit moral grounding.

Yet one cannot be too casual at this point. This is not any text; it is not pulled out of the hat; it is not an obscure text. Rather, by context, tradition, and content the Ten Commandments are a *foundational* text, if there are such things. This is the only place in the Scriptures where God speaks directly to the whole assembly of the people of God. One can hardly say that the character of God's speaking the Ten Words as largely command is a matter of little moment or simply one option among others that could have provided a moral grounding and framework for the community of faith that began in the Israelite people. No, the divine command is the character of the divine word at a critical point. When God speaks to the community, it is in the form of command, and that form assumes fundamental obligation. Thus a significant and climactic milestone in the experience of the believing community, one that seems from various directions to provide lasting and shaping influence upon their lives and their future, comes in the form of divine command.

If the *textual character of this instance* seems to make the divine command ad hoc and so tends to inhibit any large conclusions about a comprehensive theory of divine command, arising out of the Decalogue, the *particular character of this text* suggests that divine command—or at least *these* divine commands—are a more foundational and normative way of connecting between the human and the divine vis-à-vis the moral life. The fact that the divine commands of this moment and place (Exod. 20, Sinai) are then recalled at a much later time and place (Deut. 5, Moab) lends weight to the *formative* character of the *form* of the text. It is divine discourse, and it is in the form of command. Indeed, the experience of hearing and receiving these divine commands directly from the Lord is so overwhelming and terrifying that the people resist letting it ever happen again (Exod. 20:18–21; Deut. 5:23–33). Out of that form and that spoken voice arises a charter for the moral life. The community of Israel learns to listen at Sinai; it hears many kinds of words, but the divine speech it hears is command that places obligations upon the community and its members.

There is a sense, therefore, in which the divine command is the primary and primal form of speech for the community's life.

417

It is also the case that while other commands come, either to individuals or mediated to the community through an individual, and God speaks in other ways, the other commands are ad hoc and the other ways are derivative of the divine commands to a large degree. The Commandments give priority to the command of God without excluding other forms of revelation and without claiming that through the Commandments the total will of God is revealed. These represent a necessary, sufficient, and comprehensive formulation of the divine will as to what is obligatory for human existence. There is more to be said, but it is relativized, specifying, illustrative, and/or ad hoc. That does not mean that the rest of the divine discourse as a representation of God's will for the life and action of the people is unimportant. But that discourse is separated off in a rather dramatic way from the primal command speech, the Commandments (see "Introduction"). If "divine command ethics cannot encompass the whole of theological ethical reflection" (Schweiker, "Divine Command Ethics," 169), it is also true that the divine command does not encompass the whole of divine discourse and the revelation of the divine will. The divine command, however, provides a starting point and framework for further moral reflection, discourse, and action. That is the meaning of the givenness of the Commandments and the mode of their givenness in the story.

The Context of the Divine Commands:
The Covenant and the Prologue

The centrality of the Commandments for the Sinai/Horeb covenant and, vice versa, the determinative character of the covenant as the context for the Commandments—both are evident in a variety of ways from the text (e.g., Exod. 31:18; 34:28; Deut. 4:13). The heart of the covenant is the deity's claim: "I will be your God, and you shall be my people" (e.g., Exod. 6:7; Lev. 26:12; Deut. 26:17, 19). This sets a *social relation* immediately at the core of the covenant (Adams, *Finite and Infinite Goods*, 197). That is evident in the I–you formulation of the covenantal formula, the recognition of two parties in formal relationship with each other. The stipulations of the covenant then lay out *how* the relationship is to work and what the requirements of the relationship are. The mutuality implicit in

418

the formula "I will be your God, and you shall be my people" is deceptive, however, because it conceals the character of this covenant as not a covenant of equals, but a relationship between a greater party and a lesser party. It also conceals the fact that one part of the covenant precedes the other: first come the decision of the deity to be the God of this people and the act of liberation that has accomplished that fact.

Two implications grow out of that relational reality. One is that the stipulations include requirements of the people vis-à-vis *the deity*: thus the first table of the Commandments, the commands that have directly to do with honoring and worshiping the Lord. The second is the characterization of the relationship from the *people's* end as *obligation* and the *divine* speech as *command*. The covenantal relationship assumes, at least in this form of the treaty-covenant model, both a *relationship* that *places obligation* and a prior *establisher* of the relationship who can place obligation upon the community.

The presence of directives or regulations parallel to the second table of the Decalogue in *other societies* has often been recognized. But the covenantal context of the obligations found in the Decalogue assumes a relationship that begins with the I-you of the deity and the people and so includes stipulations that have to do directly with that relationship. The presence of the first table of the Decalogue along with the second table causes problems in contemporary life when the presence and power of the Commandments in the larger civic community is at issue. For many individuals, what is to be kept before the community is only the second table of the Decalogue, a move that takes the Commandments out of the covenantal context and turns the stipulations into a kind of natural law. They may have that character also; indeed, I suggest that here one sees the rationality of the divine commands, their rootage in a more universal sense of value and obligation (see Jenson, *Systematic Theology*, 2:86). But the obligatory, command character of the Decalogue comes out of the covenantal relationship and assumes the first table as a required starting point.

The complexity of this covenantal relationship is further indicated by the *social* character of the "*you*," the "people." The "you" is a *community*, and while covenantal relationships did not and do not have to be only communal, this particular one between God and people was so constituted. The covenant, therefore, assumes a complex and intimate relationship, and the Commandments stand at the center precisely to identify and spell out the character of that relationship, how it works, what holds it together, what creates an intimacy. If they are to be "my people," then their peoplehood is an issue; their functioning as a people whose defining characteristic is found in the pronoun "my" is determinative of the relationship. The social nature of the relationship is discerned and identified not only in the two parties to the covenant but also in the complex "you" of the community.

The covenantal context of the Commandments has further implications for an understanding of the ethics of the Commandments. One is the principle of *reciprocity* that is inherent in the covenant and in the particular character of these stipulations. That reciprocity is first of all indicated in the responsibility of *both* partners in the relationship to "keep the covenant" (see Deut. 5:10//Exod. 20:6 and Deut. 10:12–13; 11:1; Exod. 19:4–5 and Deut. 7:9). The specifics of keeping covenant on the part of the Lord are less clear than are the specifics of the people's responsibility. But the assumption is clear that the people can count on the Lord's preserving the covenantal relationship with them, that the *obedience* of the people, their faithfulness, is reciprocated in the *faithfulness* of God. Keeping the Commandments is not an activity that stands by itself. It is part of a relational dynamic, a reciprocity of faithfulness on the part of the partners in the covenant. Here is where Paul Lehmann's sense of the descriptive character of the Commandments is on target in the sense that the covenant and the reciprocity inherent in it lay out the future between the partners and describe their life together (*The Decalogue*, 22). The descriptive dimension is there in that the future cannot work if the two partners do not "keep/obey" the covenant. What is often lost in assessing this relationship is the reciprocity of the obligation so that the Lord is also under obligation to keep covenant.

The further implication is the fact that obedience is a *consensual* matter. And the consensual dimension is related to the reciprocity. The giving of the Commandments is preceded by the divine speech to Moses in Exodus 19:3–6, in which the Lord promises to make this people the Lord's treasured possession and also a priestly kingdom and a holy nation. The last two promises may well be the content of the first: Israel becomes God's treasured possession in and as they function as a priestly kingdom and a holy nation. But these promises are premised on obedience to the voice and keeping the covenant: "If you obey my voice and keep my covenant, you shall be my treasured possession" (v. 5). When these words were reported to the people, they all "answered as one: 'Everything that the LORD has spoken we will do'" (19:8; cf. 24:3, 7). It is to be assumed that "everything that the LORD has spoken" anticipates the words to be spoken in the next chapter, the Commandments. So the divine commands are not imposed. They are *assented to*, in light of the past deliverance and in anticipation of the future promise. The *descriptive* character of the Commandments is further indicated in this process of reciprocity and consent in that the Commandments describe the way that the community will become and exist as a *holy nation*.

The covenantal context of the Commandments is embodied in the *Prologue*, the deity's self-presentation to the people. While its content might be presumed in any event because it is in one sense simply an encapsulation of the story of the preceding chapters, the formulation of the Prologue before any of the divine commands plays a crucial role in the ethics of the Commandments.

First of all, some Jewish numbering of the Commandments and the technical definition of them in the books of Exodus and Deuteronomy as "the ten words" (Exod. 34:28; Deut. 4:13; 10:4) mean that the "first" commandment, or "word," is not a commandment at all (see chap. 1, above). The opening word is something quite different, beginning the covenantal stipulations in a definition of the divine, so that whatever is said about the divine command has to be understood and qualified by what is first said about God . There is not some prior or assumed definition of God, some general theory of the divine or of the good or the right but a self-revelation of a God who reveals self as *this* God, defined *this* way, and commands only in light of this understanding, this self-definition.

Second, the Prologue can thus be understood to say something about the *character* of the commander and to particularize what matters in the *identity of the one who commands*. It is "YHWH," "Adonai," "the LORD." Again one does not have to think theoretically about what belongs to deity or theoretically about the character of the God who commands in order to ground or justify obedience to particular commands. The character is known in the name and the way this deity speaks and acts in the story. The importance of this identifying name is further seen when one recognizes how often the declaration "I am the LORD" occurs in relation to instruction and laws that are set before the people. That is especially evident

421

in the Holiness Code: thus Leviticus 18, with its collections of laws on sexual conduct, begins and ends with the sentence "I am the LORD your God" (vv. 2, 30) and reiterates it twice more in relation to keeping the ordinances and statutes (vv. 4 and 5). In Leviticus 19, "I am the LORD" or "I am the LORD your God" becomes almost a refrain at the end of every piece of instruction or legislation, and it recurs periodically throughout the rest of the Code (e.g., 21:15, 23; 22:2, 16, 31, 32, 33; 23:22; etc.). Obedience to the Commandments and to the rest of the laws is rooted in who this God is.

This deity is specified further in the covenantal formula "*your God.*" Obligation arises out of a *relationship* between the one commanding and those commanded, a relationship that is wrought out in their history. That is made concrete in the final identifying characterization of the one who commands: "who brought you out of the land of Egypt, the house of bondage." The rest of the legislation reiterates this relationship, with its almost monotonous repetition of the appellation "your God" after the name of the deity: "the LORD *your God.*" Obedience to these commands is never allowed to lose its rootage in the character of the one who commands and the relationship of that God to those who are placed under divine command.

Another dimension of this divine identification is that questions about the *goodness* of the God who commands or the *appropriateness* of what is commanded—both important ethical issues—are answered in the clause "who brought you out of the land of Egypt." This identification must be judged to be fundamental. Its meaning is spelled out in the whole Exodus story: the account of a compassionate God who remembers "his" people and the covenant with their ancestors, who hears the cries of oppressed slaves, and who moves against the forces of oppressive tyranny to set this oppressed people free. In such a manner, the *value* and *power* lying behind these commands is made known.

The Prologue, therefore, can be understood from the side of the divine covenantal partner to *lay a claim* and from the side of the human partner(s) to *evoke a response*. Obedience, acceptance of the obligation, is to be understood in part as *recognition* of the *claim* that the prior divine act makes and in part as *grateful response* to the *activity* of the commander. The point is not just that the character of the divine commander is generally good and right and worthy of obedience; it is rather that the commander has acted in a way of benefit to those upon whom obligation is being

422

placed. There is a *prior reality* and a *prior act*, and that reality-act is determinative for the divine commands. The command does not presuppose some *theoretical* understanding of the commander, of God, but it provides an *actual* understanding.

The grounding of the commands is found in the attributes of the deity, but those are not logically inferred (omnipotence, first cause, love, etc.). They are a given in the Prologue. The point is similar to that of Karl Barth, who says: "God calls us and orders us and claims us by being gracious to us in Jesus Christ" (*Church Dogmatics*, II/2:560). Furthermore, in this way one discerns the force of Barth's claim that ethics is a task of the doctrine of God (509).

Understood as *one of the (ten) words* and in some fashion not different from the commands, the Prologue is inextricably joined with the commands so that one cannot take the commands apart from the character, the history, the response, and the complex relationship. The form of the Prologue is clearly different from what follows, but as one of the words, the Prologue locks in the interrelationship of character and command, of relation and command, of gratitude, response, and command.

The intimate connection of the Prologue to the First Commandment, "You shall have no other gods besides me," is a feature of the ethics of the Commandments and the shape of the divine command ethics they presume. The First Commandment gives further impetus to the divine command framework by asserting the religious requirement that God shall be the supreme focus of one's loyalties, a fundamental dimension of divine command ethics. The *first* of the divine commands lays the groundwork for the giving of the *rest* of the divine commands. There is a kind of circular force at work here as the "requirement" that God be the supreme focus is discerned by divine command, but that requirement, when accepted, tends then to validate the obligation to obey the divine commands that are given. (For further discussion of the Prologue, see chap. 1.)

Responsibility, Character, and the Narrative of the Commandments

423

Although the above discussion has characterized the people's end in this covenantal relationship as obligation and thus the divine speech as command, one may equally well describe the relationship embodied in the Commandments and their covenantal context as *response* on the part of the people to the divine deliverance (Exod. 19:3–8; 20:2) and the divine speech as describing the *content of response* and thus spelling out the *content of responsibility* in the context of an ethic of responsible relationship. William Schweiker's identification of the threefold character of the imperative of responsibility finds a resonance in the way in which the Commandments open up a trajectory of responsible living within covenantal and communal existence:

> In all actions and relations we are to respect and enhance *persons* before God; in all actions and relations we are to respect and enhance the *common good* before God. In light of the new global reality of increased human power, we can further specify the imperative as follows: in all actions and relations we are to respect and enhance the *community of life*. (*Responsibility and Christian Ethics*, 209)

The Commandments describe an integration of the respect and enhancement of *persons* and of the *common good* before God via the mode of the Commandments.

As one probes more deeply into the trajectory of the Commandments, one finds that Schweiker's third responsibility—respect and enhancement of the *community of life*—begins to emerge even in a world where the ecological imperative is not yet crystallized as a particularly large concern, where the larger community of life is not yet seen as under threat and challenge. For in the specifying of the Commandments that goes on in the legislation of the statutes and ordinances, there are serious concerns for animals of various kinds (ox, and donkey, as in Exod. 23:4–5; cf. v. 12; Deut. 22:4) and for the continued possibility of the land to produce what was needed for existence (Exod. 23:11; Lev. 25:1–7). The animals mentioned come into play largely as property of a neighbor, but their well-being is seen as a part of the neighbor relation. And in some instances, there is legislation that is less specifically tied to the neighbor, such as the protection of mother birds (Deut. 22:6–7) and the preservation of trees in the wood from being indiscriminately cut down without purpose (20:19–20).

424   Even more apt is the way in which the Commandments play their part in the understanding of the responsible self, which was at the heart of H. Richard Niebuhr's ethics. Specifically, the Com-

mandments are the way in which moral action is human action in response to the redeeming action of God, the response of those set free, literally, from the burdens of the past. The ethics of responsibility for Niebuhr centered in the *fitting* action, "the one that fits into a total interaction as response and as anticipation of further response" (*The Responsible Self*, 61). What is going on is God's redemptive work and the creation of a people to live as God's people. That is always the situation in which the Commandments function. They define the character of the fitting response. The significance of the Commandments is precisely in their perduring insight into what is going on and how human life responds to that. With Niebuhr, the Commandments involve acts of interpretation that seek to discern the way things are and how one acts/responds to that reality. The trajectory of the Commandments—through narrative and law, through Scripture and tradition, through reason and experience— provides an interpretive avenue for responsible discernment of the appropriate action in relation to what is going on.

This is by way of illustrating that the Commandments function within more than one mode of ethical theory or more than one mode of ethical description. Modes of ethical grounding other than divine command may be seen as operative in the function of the Commandments in the Christian life. Especially important, for example, is the connection of the Commandments to the understanding of the ethical role of narrative and the concern for the development of character and virtue that flows out of the personal and communal stories of individuals within the larger community. I would identify three ways in which narrative comes to play in the functioning of the Commandments, suggesting that they are not finally and fully comprehended only as manifestations of individual divine commands that are to be obeyed simply because they are expressions of the divine will (though one may argue that case):

1. As the Prologue illustrates well, the Commandments grow out of *a shaping narrative*, out of the story of the people's deliverance. The Commandments are placed at a climactic point in a narrative that is understood to be definitive for the community's life, the context in which the commands make sense and are to be understood and appropriated. They serve to shape the moral life of later members of the community in an ongoing narrative of the community's life and individuals' lives, a story that is still going on. Thus Moses reiterates the Commandments to the Israelites poised

425

on the boundary of the promised land, long past Sinai. He says with much emphasis: "Not with our ancestors did the LORD make this covenant, but with us, who are all of us here alive today" (Deut. 5:3). As the story goes on, the Commandments carry the next generation forward.

2. *The interpretation and specifying* of the Commandments thus involves *narrative* as well as law. When later generations ask about the Commandments and the statutes and the ordinances and their meaning, they are not given legal interpretations; they are told the basic story that is in the Prologue to the Commandments (Deut. 6: 20–25). At critical points in the moral life, that story can provide significant motivation for obedience to the commands (e.g., 5:15; 15:15; 24:22). Thus one comes to understand the meaning of the Commandments and be motivated to keep them by the telling of the master narrative out of which the Commandments themselves arise and also by telling particular stories in which the Commandments come to have their play. Narrative carries the Commandments. It is not that they are without obligation apart from narrative, but that the story, particularly the story of disobedience, encourages obedience by teaching about the consequences of disobedience. The story also serves to describe the playing field, the human circumstances, the social context, and the personal and communal dynamics in which this relationship and this way of living function. The attractiveness of obedience or of the way of life set forth in the Commandments is worked out not only positively, by the motivation clauses, which we shall come to next; but also negatively, by the stories of what happens when the Commandments are not obeyed.

3. *The trajectory* of the Commandments is itself a *narrative* mode. Trajectory is an image that implies an ongoing movement of the commandment, worked out in the ongoing story of the community and its dealing with moral issues, with the relationship between human life and God and the relationship with the neighbor.

Thinking about the different modes of ethical grounding and description in relation to the Commandments should not fail to identify the way in which they prominently set forth a *love ethic*, understanding the moral life to be a love of God and neighbor that is in response to and imitation of the love that has been manifested or demonstrated toward us. William Moran ("The Love of God") has demonstrated the rootage of the love of God in the character of covenant and the identification of the responsibility of the

426

covenantal partner to love the ruler who has delivered and cared for the community. When Deuteronomy seeks to encapsulate the Commandments in a single claim, it is in terms of the love of God: "Hear, O Israel: The LORD is our God, the LORD alone. You shall love the LORD your God with all your heart, and with all your soul, and with all your might" (6:4–5). But that language of loving God keeps popping up throughout the book and specifically in parallel with and thus in identification with "keeping the commandments" (e.g., 10:12–13; 11:1, 13, 22; 30:15–16; etc.). The command to love your neighbor as yourself, which is a part of the sequence of commands in Leviticus 19 that is probably closest to the Decalogue's formulations, is made to be the definitive way of speaking about what is involved in the second table of the Decalogue, spelling out and giving guidance about the various ways in which the love of neighbor is manifest. What does it mean to love God and neighbor? As Paul says in Romans 13:8–10: Listen to what God says in the Commandments (cf. 1 John 5:2–3).

Finally, one may recognize, specifically within the Sabbath Commandment, that there is some sense also of an ethic of *correlation* or *correspondence* at work as a fundamental ground for living by this commandment. That happens in two ways. In the Deuteronomic form of the commandment, the rest to be provided for servants, which is the primary motivation for the sabbath rest, is because "they are like you" (5:14, my trans.). The correspondence between your situation and theirs is the ground for providing the rest. The text does not say how they are "like you." But it is in their similarity to "you" that "you" find the rationale for giving the male and female servants a regular time of rest.

More clearly indicative of an ethic of correlation, however, are the dual motivation clauses that conclude the Sabbath Commandment in Exodus and Deuteronomy. In Exodus 20 the sabbatical practice of each family in the community, interrupting its work with a day of rest, is a self-conscious reflection and imitation of the work of God, who also interrupted the divine creative activity with a day of rest (v. 11). The work of God sets a kind of model for human work, and the cycle of human work and rest is a reflection of God's way. Thus an *imitatio Dei* is set as an element of the ethical grounding of the Commandments.

427

A similar move is then made in Deuteronomy 5:15, but here the human moral act corresponds not to the creative activity of God but to the Lord's redemption of the people from Egyptian slavery. The "like yourself" dimension carries over into this verse, but now it is placed specifically in the context of the Lord's liberating work, and the similarity between the recipient of the command and the servants is made explicit. As you were set free from slavery by the power of God, so now in your power you provide freedom for slaves, the cessation of labor and a rest for your servants.

Motivation and Rationality:
The Reasonableness of the Commandments

One of the primary features of Israelite law and one that appears first in the Commandments is the presence of *motivation* clauses: "For I am a jealous God . . . ," "for the Lord will not hold guiltless the one . . . ," "so that your slave who is like you may rest . . . ," "that you may live long . . ." These clauses or sentences serve as a mode of *divine persuasion* on the one hand and a manifestation of the *rationality* of the Commandments on the other. Both dimensions of the motivation clauses are important for comprehending the ethics of the Commandments. The presence of divine persuasion indicates that the Commandments cannot be reduced to blind obedience. They are not arbitrary or capricious. Nor does God simply set them out to be obeyed. The one who commands also encourages obedience and seeks to draw forth a positive response from those before whom the commands are set. From the side of God, on God's part, it is not assumed that the rightness of the commands is self-evident or to be imposed from above. The consent of the commanded people is a true consent of the mind and heart. It arises not only because of the act of divine deliverance or the word of divine command but also because of the word or act of divine persuasion. The deity who *commands* seeks to *lure* the people to a way of living that is appealing.

The commandments, therefore, and the statutes and ordinances that flow from them, not only lay upon the hearers a *claim*; they also *invite its reception*. Consent is not only a formal and communal agreement (Exod. 19:7–8); it is also a movement of the mind and heart persuaded by the Lord of the value, desirability, and reasonableness of living this way. Such motivation clauses mean that in the face of rules, statutes, laws, and regulations in the moral life, one does not abandon the question of whether we are attracted to this way of living. The reasons may be positive or negative, but they assume the *sensibility* and *attractiveness* of following the way that is set forth in the Commandments. In this way, teleological and consequentialist elements come into the ethical functioning of the Commandments. The moral life that is rooted in an effort to achieve a particular goal, to bring about a vision of the human community, or to maintain and enhance a particular value—such a moral life does so because one is drawn to that goal, that vision, that value. The more deontological approach of command and obligation may seem to set aside the issue of disposition and attitude toward a particular mode of action or moral life and simply impose upon us a duty, whether we like it or not. The presence of the motivation clauses suggests, however, that one may be drawn to obedience, that one may be attracted to the will of God, that one may be genuinely persuaded that following the Lord's way as reflected in the Commandments and in the statutes and ordinances is not only good and right but also good and valuable. It is both appropriate and *attractive* so to do.

The law is at one and the same time *rationalized* and *encouraged*. It is not simply a matter of sheer willpower to obey, as Seneca once put it: "Tell me what I have to do. . . . I do not want to learn. I want to obey." Rather, we are told why such acts and ways are desirable, and in hearing why, one is drawn to obey. The motivation clauses of the Commandments and the laws of the Old Testament are, therefore, one of the clearest indications of the sensibility and attractiveness of the moral life in the biblical perspective.

The quotation from Seneca provides another foil as it reminds us that the Commandments are a form of torah: instruction and teaching. While Deuteronomy is explicit about Moses' responsibility to teach the statutes and ordinances (4:5; 5:31; 6:1; etc.), in the context of the whole—as the verses cited indicate—this teaching is about the Commandments and relating them to particular situations, about the implications of the Commandments in specific instances. So what is *commanded* is also what is *taught*. The community is expected to learn how to obey and what that means in specific instances. The teaching of the Commandments is a continuing responsibility. They are not promulgated; they are said and taught. The reasonableness of the Commandments is implicit in the assumption of their teachability. The need to interpret and understand is also implicit in the

429

character of the law as instruction. There is no assumption here that the Commandments can be posted and that is sufficient. That apparently would suffice for Seneca, but not for the covenant people, who are constantly being taught by Moses what their duty is and how to live as free people on God's way.

The divine commands of the Decalogue, therefore, do not free one from responsibility for interpretation and application, from moral competence that is learned and developed. On the contrary, it is expected that such interpretation and careful thought are necessary, and so the Commandments and the other statutes are taught to the young and their questions are answered (Deut. 6:20–25), so that they may be drawn in and become competent to live as neighbors in the good neighborhood that is delimited or laid out by the Commandments.

Sin and Guilt

The motivation clauses within the Ten Commandments point us to the way in which obligation to obey the divine commands confronts the individual and the community with the possibility of sin and guilt as outcomes of moral action, more specifically of disobedience to the divine commands. That sin and guilt may be a part of the relationship between members of the community. The sin may be against the neighbor and the guilt a result of an action or inaction with regard to the neighbor. But within the framework of the Commandments, sin and guilt are first and foremost outcomes of the breach in the relationship between the human being and the Lord. Disobedience is a violation of the covenantal relationship between the divine and human partners and only incidentally—if also really—a violation of the intercommunal relationship (see below on David's sin). The value of moral behavior insofar as that is defined by the Commandments is, therefore, defined in the relationship. There may be all sorts of good reasons for acting according to the Commandments, as the other motivation clauses indicate; but the determination of moral worth is a feature of the relationship and not of some other calculus or determinative.

430 In relation to the obligation of the Commandments, the possibility of sin and sanction, of guilt and accountability, is explicit in the commandments having to do with idolatry and the divine name. In

the Second Commandment, making and worshiping images of the divine is placed under direct sanction. The jealous God will brook no competitors, and disobedience means punishment (Exod. 20:5// Deut. 5:9; cf. 4:22). The sanction, however, is not confined to this commandment per se; it is there for those who "reject me," an act that is manifest in any manifest disobedience of the Commandments. At least, that inference may be made on the basis of the explicit corollary, the *ḥesed* of the Lord to those who "love me and keep my commandments [plural]" (Exod. 20:6//Deut. 5:10). Similarly, misuse of the name of God incurs guilt (Exod. 20:7//Deut. 5:11).

One might be inclined to think that when one moves to the second table of the Commandments, the sin there is against the neighbor and the reality of guilt is with regard to the relationship with the neighbor. That seems, however, to be only secondarily the case. When David disobeys the commandments having to do with coveting, adultery, and murder, his confession of sin is noticeable specifically by its identification of the sinned against as neither Bathsheba nor Uriah but the Lord. The denunciation of David's sin by the prophet Nathan makes it clear that killing Uriah and taking his wife are specifications of a larger reality:

> Why have you despised the word of the LORD, to do what is evil in his sight? You have struck down Uriah the Hittite with the sword, and have taken his wife to be your wife, and have killed him with the sword of the Ammonites. (2 Sam. 12:9)

David confirms this perception by his immediate response: "I have sinned against the LORD" (v. 13). Nathan's word about the death of the child of this sinful union further seals the understanding of the violation of the divine command as a sin against the one commanding: "Because by this deed you have utterly scorned the LORD, the child that is born to you shall die" (v. 14). David's response is the catchword that leads to the association of Psalm 51 with David's confession. In this paradigmatic penitential psalm, the psalmist says:

> Against you, *you alone*, have I sinned,
>   and done what is evil in your sight,
> so that you are justified in your sentence
>   and blameless when you pass judgment.
>   (v. 4; emphasis added)

431

The corollary of this understanding of obedience as a violation or breach in the relationship between the human being and the Lord who commands is found in the fact that forgiveness is always a divine act, an amelioration, a release from the weight of guilt that God brings about. If therefore one follows the definition of guilt suggested by Robert Adams, "alienation from those who have (appropriately) required of us what we did not do," the first line of the requirement and the one that is critical in the framework of the Commandments is the (appropriate) requirement of the Lord who speaks and commands in the covenantal relationship (*Finite and Infinite Goods*, 240).

The reciprocity of the sanctions is, however, a complete one. Obedience has its blessings as much as disobedience has its sanctions. Thus the divine *ḥesed* is manifest through the generations for those who are obedient (Exod. 20:6//Deut. 5:10), and the promise of a long and good life in the good land provided by the Lord is the outcome of obedience to the commandment to honor parents. It is possible to connect that outcome directly to the specific command and perceive it as an outworking of the human activity, such that honoring *your* parents may bring about your own being honored and cared for in old age. But like the other sanctions, this blessing is not to be confined to the one command but is applicable to the wholeness of the Commandments, and it occurs in the sphere of divine blessing: "the land that the LORD your God is giving you" (Exod. 20:12//Deut. 5:16).

BIBLIOGRAPHY

For Further Study

Ben-Zion Segal, and Gershon Levi, eds. *The Ten Commandments in History and Tradition*. Hebrew version, 1985. Jerusalem: Magnes Press, 1990.

Braaten, Carl E., and Christopher R. Seitz. *I Am the Lord Your God: Christian Reflections on the Ten Commandments*. Grand Rapids: Wm. B. Eerdmans Publishing Co., 2005.

Harrelson, Walter. *The Ten Commandments and Human Rights*. Overtures to Biblical Theology. Macon, GA: Mercer University Press, 1997.

Hauerwas, Stanley, and William Willimon. *The Truth about God: The Ten Commandments in Christian Life*. Nashville: Abingdon Press, 1999.

Kuntz, Paul Grimley. *The Ten Commandments in History: Mosaic Paradigms for a Well-Ordered Society*. Edited by Thomas D'Evelyn. Grand Rapids: Wm. B. Eerdmans Publishing Co., 2004.

Lehmann, Paul L. *The Decalogue and a Human Future: The Meaning of the Commandments for Making and Keeping Human Life Human*. Eugene, OR: Wipf & Stock, 2002.

Lochmann, Jan. *Signs of Freedom: The Ten Commandments and Christian Ethics*. Minneapolis: Augsburg Press, 1982.

Miller, Patrick D. *The God You Have: Politics and the First Commandment*. Facet Books. Minneapolis: Fortress Press, 2004.

———. *The Way of the Lord: Essays in Old Testament Theology*. Grand Rapids: Wm. B. Eerdmans Publishing Co., 2007.

Olson, Dennis. *Deuteronomy and the Death of Moses: A Theological Reading*. Overtures to Biblical Theology. Minneapolis: Fortress Press, 1994.

Literature Cited

Achtemeier, Paul. *Romans*. Interpretation: A Bible Commentary for Teaching and Preaching. Atlanta: John Knox Press, 1985.

433

Adams, Robert M. *Finite and Infinite Goods: A Framework for Ethics*. Oxford: Oxford University Press, 1999.

Amir, Yehoshua. "The Decalogue according to Philo." In *The Ten Commandments in History and Tradition*, edited by Ben-Zion Segal, 131–160. Jerusalem: Magnes Press, 1985.

Appiah, Kwame Anthony. *Thinking It Through: An Introduction to Contemporary Philosophy*. New York: Oxford University Press, 2003.

Balentine, Samuel. *Leviticus*. Interpretation: A Bible Commentary for Teaching and Preaching. Louisville, KY: John Knox Press, 2002.

Barmash, Pamela. *Homicide in the Biblical World*. Cambridge: Cambridge University Press, 2005.

Barth, Karl. *Church Dogmatics*. Vol. II/2. Translated by G. W. Bromiley. Edinburgh: T&T Clark, 1957.

———. *Church Dogmatics*. Vol. III/4. Translated by G. W. Bromiley. Edinburgh: T&T Clark, 1961.

Betz, Hans-Dieter. *The Sermon on the Mount: A Commentary on the Sermon on the Mount, including the Sermon on the Plain (Matthew 5:3–7:27 and Luke 6:20–49)*. Hermeneia. Minneapolis: Fortress Press, 1995.

Blenkinsopp, Joseph. *Ezra-Nehemiah*. The Old Testament Library. Philadelphia: Westminster Press, 1988.

Blidstein, Gerald. *Honor Thy Father and Mother: Filial Responsibility in Jewish Law and Ethics*. New York: KTAV Publishing House, 1975.

Bockmuehl, Markus. "'Keeping It Holy': Old Testament Commandment and New Testament Faith." In *I Am the Lord Your God: Christian Reflections on the Ten Commandments*, edited by Carl E. Braaten and Christopher R. Seitz, 95–124. Grand Rapids: Wm. B. Eerdmans Publishing Co., 2005.

Bok, Sissela. *Lying: Moral Choice in Public and Private Life*. New York: Vintage Books, 1999.

Braulik, Georg. *Die deuteronomischen Gesetze und der Dekalog: Studien zum Aufbau von Deuteronomium 12–26*. Stuttgarter Bibel-Studien 145. Stuttgart: Verlag Katholisches Bibelwerk, 1991.

———. "The Sequence of the Laws in Deuteronomy 12–26 and in the Decalogue." In *A Song of Power and the Power of Song: Essays on the Book of Deuteronomy*, edited by Duane L. Christensen, 313–35. Sources for Biblical and Theological Study 3. Winona Lake, IN: Eisenbrauns, 1993.

Brichto, Herbert. *The Problem of "Curse" in the Hebrew Bible.* Philadelphia: Society of Biblical Literature, 1963.

Brockington, L. H. *Ezra, Nehemiah, and Esther.* The Century Bible. London: Thomas Nelson, 1969.

Bruckner, James K. "On the One Hand . . . On the Other Hand: The Twofold Meaning of the Law against Covetousness." In *To Hear and Obey: Essays in Honor of Fredrick Carlson Holmgren,* edited by Bradley J. Bergfalk and Paul E. Koptak, 97–118. Chicago: Covenant Publications, 1997.

Brueggemann, Walter. "Foreword." *Journal for Preachers* 26 (Easter 2003): 1–2.

———. "Of the Same Flesh and Bone (Genesis 2:23a)." *Catholic Biblical Quarterly* 32 (1970): 532–42.

———. "Truth-Telling as Subversive Obedience." In Walter Brueggemann, *The Covenanted Self: Explorations in Law and Covenant,* edited by Patrick D. Miller, 91–98. Minneapolis: Fortress Press, 1999.

Buber, Martin. *Moses: The Revelation and the Covenant.* New York: Harper & Brothers, 1958.

Calloway, P. R. "Deut 21:18–21: Proverbial Wisdom and Law." *Journal of Biblical Literature* 103 (1984): 341–52.

Calvin, John. *Institutes of the Christian Religion.* Edited by John T. McNeill. Translated by Ford Lewis Battles. 2 vols. Library of Christian Classics 20–21. Philadelphia: Westminster Press, 1960. Reprint, Louisville, KY: Westminster John Knox Press, 2001.

———. *John Calvin's Sermons on the Ten Commandments.* Edited and translated by Ben W. Farley. Grand Rapids: Baker Book House, 1980.

———. *The Sermons of John Calvin Upon the Fifth Book of Moses Called Deuteronomy.* London: Henry Middleton, 1583.

Carter, Stephen L. *The Culture of Disbelief.* New York: Basic Books, 1993.

Chaney, Marvin L. "'You Shall Not Covet Your Neighbor's House.'" *Pacific Theological Review* 15 (Winter 1982): 3–13.

Childs, Brevard. *The Book of Exodus.* The Old Testament Library. Philadelphia: Westminster Press, 1974.

———. *Isaiah.* The Old Testament Library. Louisville, KY: Westminster John Knox Press, 2001.

————. *Old Testament Theology in a Canonical Context*. Philadelphia: Fortress Press, 1985.

Chirigno, G. *Debt Slavery in Israel and the Ancient Near East*. Journal for the Study of the Old Testament: Supplement Series 141. Sheffield: JSOT Press, 1993.

Clifford, Richard. *Proverbs*. The Old Testament Library. Louisville, KY: Westminster John Knox Press, 1999.

Cochrane, Arthur C. *The Church's Confession under Hitler*. Philadelphia: Westminster Press, 1962.

Craigie, Peter. *The Book of Deuteronomy*. The New International Commentary on the Old Testament. Grand Rapids: Wm. B. Eerdmans Publishing Co., 1976.

Cross, Frank Moore. "Epigraphic Notes on Hebrew Documents of the Eighth–Sixth Centuries B.C.: II. The Muraba'ât Papyrus and the Letter Found near Yavneh-Yam." In Frank Moore Cross, *Leaves from an Epigrapher's Notebook: Collected Papers in Hebrew and West Semitic Palaeography and Epigraphy*, 116–24. Harvard Semitic Studies 51. Winona Lake, IN: Eisenbrauns, 2003.

Crüsemann, Frank. *The Torah: Theology and Social History of Old Testament Law*. Minneapolis: Fortress Press, 1996.

Davidman, Joy. *Smoke on the Mountain*. Philadelphia: Westminster Press, 1954.

Davis, Ellen. *Proverbs, Ecclesiastes, and the Song of Songs*. Westminster Bible Companion. Louisville, KY: Westminster John Knox Press, 2000.

————. *Scripture, Culture, and Agriculture: An Agrarian Reading of the Bible*. New York: Cambridge University Press, 2009.

Dobbs-Allsopp, F. W., J. J. M. Roberts, C.-L. Seow, and R. E. Whitaker. *Hebrew Inscriptions: Texts from the Biblical Period of the Monarchy with Concordance*. New Haven: Yale University Press, 2005.

Dowey, Edward. "Law in Luther and Calvin." *Theology Today* 41 (1984):146–53.

Elssner, Thomas R. *Das Namensmissbrauch-Verbot (Ex 20,7/Dtn 5/11): Bedeutung, Entstehung und früh Wirkungsgeschichte*. Erfurter Theologische Studien 75. Leipzig: Benno-Verlag, 1999.

Finkelstein, J. J. *The Ox That Gored*. Transactions of the American Philosophical Society 71/2. Philadelphia: The American Philosophical Society, 1981.

436

Fishbane, Michael. *Biblical Interpretation in Ancient Israel*. Oxford: Clarendon Press, 1985.

Fowl, Stephen E. "Making Stealing Possible: Criminal Thoughts on Building an Ecclesial Common Life." In *Engaging Scripture: A Model for Theological Interpretation*, 161–77. Oxford: Blackwell, 1998.

Freedman, David Noel. *The Nine Commandments: Uncovering the Hidden Pattern of Crime and Punishment in the Hebrew Bible*. New York: Doubleday, 2000.

Freund, Richard A. "Murder, Adultery, and Theft." *Scandinavian Journal of the Old Testament* 2 (1989): 72–80.

Gench, Frances Taylor. *Hebrews and James*. Westminster Bible Companion. Louisville, KY.: Westminster John Knox Press, 1996.

Gerstenberger, Erhard. *Leviticus*. The Old Testament Library. Louisville, KY: Westminster John Knox Press, 1996.

Girard, René. *I See Satan Fall Like Lightning*. Translated by James G. Williams. Maryknoll, NY: Orbis Books, 2001.

Green, Steven K. "The Fount of Everything Just and Right? The Ten Commandments as a Source of American Law." *Journal of Law and Religion* 14 (1999–2000): 525–58.

Gundry, Robert H. *Matthew: A Commentary on His Handbook for a Mixed Church under Persecution*. Grand Rapids: Wm. B. Eerdmans Publishing Co., 1994.

Halpern, Baruch. *Leviticus*. The JPS Torah Commentary. Philadelphia: The Jewish Publication Society, 1989.

Hamilton, Jeffries M. *Social Justice in Deuteronomy: The Case of Deuteronomy 15*. Society of Biblical Literature Dissertation Series 136. Atlanta: Scholars Press, 1992.

Hammer, Reuven, trans. *Sifre: A Tannaitic Commentary on the Book of Deuteronomy*. New Haven: Yale University Press, 1986.

Hamp, Vincenz. "ganabh." *Theological Dictionary of the Old Testament*, edited by G. Botterweck and H. Ringgren, 3:37–45. Grand Rapids: Wm. B. Eerdmans Publishing Co., 1978.

Hays, Richard B. *First Corinthians*. Interpretation: A Bible Commentary for Teaching and Preaching. Louisville, KY: John Knox Press, 1997.

———. *The Moral Vision of the New Testament: Community, Cross, New Creation; A Contemporary Introduction to New Testament Ethics*. San Francisco: HarperCollins, 1996.

The Heidelberg Catechism. *The Constitution of the Presbyterian Church (U.S.A.)*, Part I, *Book of Confessions*. New York. Office of the General Assembly, 1983.

Hendel, Ronald S. "The Social Origins of the Aniconic Tradition in Early Israel." *Catholic Biblical Quarterly* 50 (1988): 365–82.

Heschel, Abraham J. *The Sabbath: Its Meaning for Modern Man*. New York: Farrar, Straus & Giroux, 1951.

Hillers, Delbert R. *Micah*. Hermeneia. Philadelphia: Fortress Press, 1984.

Hossfeld, Frank-Lothar. *"Du sollst nicht töten!" Das fünfte Dekaloggebot im Kontext alttestamentlicher Ethik*. Beiträge zur Friedensethik 26. Stuttgart: W. Kohlhammer, 2003.

Houston, Walter J. *Contending for Justice: Ideologies and Theologies of Social Justice in the Old Testament*. Library of Hebrew Bible/Old Testament Studies 428. London: T&T Clark, 2006.

Houtman, Cornelis. *Exodus*. Historical Commentary on the Old Testament. Leuven: Peeters, 2000.

Hütter, Reinhard. "The Ten Commandments as a Mirror of Sin(s): Anglican Decline—Lutheran Eclipse." *Pro Ecclesia* 14 (2004): 46–57.

———. "The Twofold Center of Lutheran Ethics: Christian Freedom and God's Commandments." In *The Promise of Lutheran Ethics*, edited by Karen L. Bloomquist and John R. Stumme, 31–54. Minneapolis: Fortress Press, 1998.

Janzen, J. Gerald. "Another Look at Psalm xii 6." *Vetus Testamentum* 54 (2004): 157–64.

———. *Job*. Interpretation: A Bible Commentary for Teaching and Preaching. Atlanta: John Knox Press, 1985.

———. "On the Most Important Word in the Shema." *Vetus Testamentum* 37 (1987): 280–300.

Jenson, Robert W. *Systematic Theology*. 2 vols. New York: Oxford University Press, 1997.

Jeremias, Jörg. *The Book of Amos*. The Old Testament Library. Louisville, KY: Westminster John Knox Press, 1998.

Johnson, Luke. "James." *Harper's Bible Commentary*, edited by James L. Mays, 1272–78. San Francisco: Harper & Row, 1988.

Jungbauer, Harry. *"Ehre Vater und Mutter": Der Weg des Elterngebots in der biblischen Tradition*. Tübingen: Mohr Siebeck, 2002.

Käsemann, Ernst. *Commentary on Romans*. Grand Rapids: Wm. B. Eerdmans Publishing Co., 1980.

438

Kaufman, Stephen. "The Second Table of the Decalogue and the Implicit Categories of Ancient Near Eastern Law." In *Love and Death in the Ancient Near East: Essays in Honor of Marvin H. Pope,* edited by John H. Marks and Robert M. Good, 111–16. Guilford, CN: Four Quarters Publishing Co., 1987.

———. "The Structure of the Deuteronomic Law." *Maarav* 1, no. 2 (1978–79): 105–58.

Kolb, Robert, and Timothy J. Wengert, eds. *The Book of Concord: The Confessions of the Evangelical Lutheran Church.* Minneapolis: Fortress Press, 2000.

Leaver, Robin. "Luther's Catechism Hymns: 2. Ten Commandments." *Lutheran Quarterly* 11 (1997): 410–21.

Lehmann, Paul L. *The Decalogue and a Human Future: The Meaning of the Commandments for Making and Keeping Human Life Human.* Grand Rapids: Wm. B. Eerdmans Publishing Co., 1995.

———. *Ethics in a Christian Context.* New York: Harper & Row, 1963.

Levenson, Jon. "The Theologies of Commandment in Biblical Israel." *Harvard Theological Review* 73 (1980): 17–33.

Levinson, Bernard. "Deuteronomy: Introduction and Annotations." *The Jewish Study Bible,* edited by Adele Berlin and Marc Zvi Brettler, 356–450. New York: Oxford University Press, 2004.

Lochmann, Jan. *Signs of Freedom: The Ten Commandments and Christian Ethics.* Minneapolis: Augsburg, 1982.

Lohfink, Norbert, SJ. "The Decalogue in Deuteronomy 5." In Norbert Lohfink, *Theology of the Pentateuch: Themes of the Priestly Narrative and Deuteronomy,* 248–64. Minneapolis: Fortress Press, 1994.

———. *Great Themes from the Old Testament.* Edinburgh: T&T Clark, 1982.

———. "ḥāram." *Theological Dictionary of the Old Testament,* edited by G. Botterweck and H. Ringgren, 5:180–203. Grand Rapids: Wm. B. Eerdmans Publishing Co., 1986.

———. "Poverty in the Laws of the Ancient Near East and of the Bible." *Theological Studies* 52 (1991): 34–50.

Long, Thomas G. *Matthew.* Westminster Bible Companion. Louisville, KY: Westminster John Knox Press, 1997.

Luther, Martin. *Treatise on Good Works.* In *Luther's Works: The Christian in Society I,* edited by James Atkinson, 21–114. Philadelphia: Fortress Press, 1966.

Marcus, Joel. "Idolatry in the New Testament." *Interpretation* 60 (2006): 152–64.

Mays, James L. *Amos.* Old Testament Library. Philadelphia: Westminster Press, 1969.

———. *Hosea.* Old Testament Library. Philadelphia: Westminster Press, 1969.

———. *Micah.* Old Testament Library. Philadelphia: Westminster Press, 1976.

———. *Psalms.* Interpretation: A Bible Commentary for Teaching and Preaching. Louisville, KY: John Knox Press, 1994.

McBride, S. Dean. "The Deuteronomic Name Theology." Unpublished Ph.D. diss., Harvard University, 1969.

———. "The Essence of Orthodoxy: Deuteronomy 5:6–10 and Exodus 20:2–6." *Interpretation* 60 (2006): 133–51.

———. "Introduction and Annotations to the Book of Deuteronomy." In *The Harper Collins Study Bible,* edited by Wayne Meeks et al. New York: HarperCollins, 1993.

McCarter, Kyle. *II Samuel.* Anchor Bible. Garden City, NY: Doubleday, 1984.

McCloskey, Deirdre. "Avarice, Prudence, and the Bourgeois Virtues." In *Having: Property and Possession in Religion and Social Life,* edited by William Schweiker and Charles Mathewes, 312–36. Grand Rapids: Wm. B. Eerdmans Publishing Co., 2004.

Meyer, Paul. "The Worm at the Core of the Apple." In *The Word in This World: Essays in New Testament Exegesis and Theology,* edited by John P. Carroll, 57–77. New Testament Library. Louisville, KY: Westminster John Knox Press, 2004.

Milgrom, Jacob. *Leviticus 17–22.* Anchor Bible. New York: Doubleday, 2000.

———. *Leviticus 23–27.* Anchor Bible. New York: Doubleday, 2000.

———. *"Lex Talionis* and the Rabbis." *Bible Review* 12, no. 2 (April 1996): 16, 48.

Miller, Patrick D. "The Book of Jeremiah." In *The New Interpreter's Bible,* vol. 6: 555–926. Nashville: Abingdon Press, 2001.

———. "Commandments in Reformed Perspective." *See* "Old Testament Exegesis."

———. *Deuteronomy.* Interpretation: A Bible Commentary for Teaching and Preaching. Louisville, KY: John Knox Press, 1990.

———. "Divine Command and Beyond: The Ethics of the Commandments." In *The Ten Commandments: The Reciprocity of*

Faithfulness, edited by William P. Brown, 12–29. Library of Theological Ethics. Louisville, KY: Westminster John Knox Press, 2004.

———. "Faith and Ideology in the Old Testament." In *Magnalia Dei: The Mighty Acts of God; Essays on the Bible and Archaeology in Memory of G. Ernest Wright,* edited by Frank Moore Cross, Werner E. Lemke, and Patrick D. Miller Jr., 464–79. New York: Doubleday, 1976. Reprinted in Patrick D. Miller, *Israelite Religion and Biblical Theology: Collected Essays,* 629–47. Journal for the Study of the Old Testament: Supplement Series 267. Sheffield: Sheffield Academic Press, 2000.

———. *Genesis 1–11: Studies in Structure and Theme.* Journal for the Study of the Old Testament Supplement Series 8. Sheffield: JSOT, 1978.

———. "God the Warrior: A Problem in Biblical Interpretation and Apologetics." *Interpretation* 19 (1965): 39–46. Reprinted in Patrick D. Miller, *Israelite Religion and Biblical Theology: Collected Essays,* 356–64. Journal for the Study of the Old Testament: Supplement Series 267. Sheffield: Sheffield Academic Press, 2000.

———. *The God You Have: Politics and the First Commandment.* Minneapolis: Fortress Press, 1994.

———. "The Good Neighborhood: Identity and Community through the Commandments." In *Character and Scripture: Moral Formation, Community, and Biblical Interpretation,* edited by William P. Brown, 55–72. Grand Rapids: Wm. B. Eerdmans Publishing Co., 2002. Reprinted in Patrick D. Miller, *The Way of the Lord: Essays in Old Testament Theology,* 51–67. Grand Rapids: Wm. B. Eerdmans Publishing Co., 2007.

———. "In Praise and Thanksgiving." *Theology Today* 45 (1988): 180–88. Reprinted in Patrick D. Miller, *Theology Today: Reflections on the Bible and Contemporary Life,* 114–23. Louisville, KY: Westminster John Knox Press, 2006.

———. *Interpreting the Psalms.* Philadelphia: Fortress Press, 1986.

———. "Is There a Place for the Ten Commandments?" *Theology Today* 60 (2004): 1–5. Reprinted in Patrick D. Miller, *Theology Today: Reflections on the Bible and Contemporary Life,* 103–8. Louisville, KY: Westminster John Knox Press, 2006.

———. "Metaphors for the Moral." Reprinted in Patrick D. Miller, *The Way of the Lord: Essays in Old Testament Theology*, 37–50. Tübingen: Mohr Siebeck, 2004; Grand Rapids: Eerdmans, 2007.

———. "Old Testament Exegesis in the Reformed Perspective: The Case of the Commandments." In *Reformed Theology: Identity and Ecumenicity II; Biblical Interpretation in the Reformed Tradition*, edited by Wallace M. Alston, Jr. and Michael Welker, 217–29. Grand Rapids: Wm. B. Eerdmans Publishing Co., 2004. Reprinted as "The Commandments in Reformed Perspective." In Patrick D. Miller, *The Way of the Lord*, 123–35. Grand Rapids: Wm. B. Eerdmans Publishing Co., 2007.

———. "Prayer and Divine Action." In *God in the Fray: A Tribute to Walter Brueggemann*, edited by Timothy Beal and Tod Linafelt, 211–32. Minneapolis: Fortress Press, 1998. Reprinted in Patrick D. Miller, *Israelite Religion and Biblical Theology: Collected Essays*, 445–69. Journal for the Study of the Old Testament: Supplement Series 267. Sheffield: Sheffield Academic Press, 2000.

———. "The Psalms as a Meditation on the First Commandment." Reprinted in Patrick D. Miller, *The Way of the Lord: Essays in Old Testament Theology*, 91–122. Grand Rapids: Wm. B. Eerdmans Publishing Co., 2007.

———. *The Religion of Ancient Israel*. The Library of Ancient Israel. Louisville, KY: Westminster John Knox Press, 2000.

———. "The Story of the First Commandment: Joshua." In *Covenant or Context: Essays in Honour of E. W. Nicholson*, edited by A. D. H. Mayes and R. B. Salter. Oxford: Oxford University Press, 2003. Reprinted in Patrick D. Miller. *The Way of the Lord: Essays in Old Testament Theology*, 80–90. Grand Rapids: Wm. B. Eerdmans Publishing Co., 2007.

———. "The Sufficiency and Insufficiency of the Commandments." In Patrick D. Miller, *The Way of the Lord: Essays in Old Testament Theology*, 17–36. Grand Rapids: Wm. B. Eerdmans Publishing Co., 2007.

———. "'That It May Go Well with You': The Commandments and the Common Good," In *In Search of the Common Good*, edited by Patrick D. Miller and Dennis McCann, 14–40. Theology for the Twenty-First Century. New York: T&T Clark, 2005. Reprinted in Patrick D. Miller, *The Way of the Lord: Essays in*

Old Testament Theology, 103–24. Grand Rapids: Wm. B. Eerdmans Publishing Co., 2007.

———. *They Cried to the Lord: The Form and Theology of Biblical Prayer*. Minneapolis: Fortress Press, 1994.

———. "What the Scriptures Principally Teach." In *Homosexuality and Christian Community*, edited by Choon-Leong Seow, 53–63. Louisville, KY: Westminster John Knox Press, 1996. Reprinted in Patrick D. Miller, *The Way of the Lord: Essays in Old Testament Theology*, 286–96. Grand Rapids: Wm. B. Eerdmans Publishing Co., 2007.

———. "*Yāpîaḥ* in Psalm xii 6." *Vetus Testamentum*, 29 (1979): 495–500.

Moran, William L. "The Ancient Near Eastern Background of the Love of God in Deuteronomy." *Catholic Biblical Quarterly* 27 (1963): 77–87.

———. "The Conclusion of the Decalogue (Ex 20, 17 = Dt 5, 21)." *Catholic Biblical Quarterly* 29(1967): 543–54.

Nelson, Richard. *Deuteronomy*. Old Testament Library. Louisville, KY: Westminster John Knox Press, 2002.

Newsom, Carol. *The Book of Job: A Contest of Moral Imagination*. New York: Oxford University Press, 2003.

Niebuhr, H. Richard. *The Responsible Self: An Essay in Christian Moral Philosophy*. New York: Harper & Row, 1963.

Niebuhr, Reinhold. *The Nature and Destiny of Man: A Christian Interpretation*. Vol. 1, *Human Nature*. New York: Charles Scribner's Sons, 1949.

Olson, Dennis. *Deuteronomy and the Death of Moses: A Theological Reading*. Overtures to Biblical Theology. Minneapolis: Fortress Press, 1994.

Parker, Simon. *Stories in Scripture and Inscriptions: Comparative Studies on Narratives in Northwest Semitic Inscriptions and the Hebrew Bible*. New York: Oxford University Press, 1997.

Patrick, Dale. *Old Testament Law*. Atlanta: John Knox Press, 1985.

Philo. *On the Decalogue*. In *Philo*, vol. 7. Loeb Classical Library. Cambridge, MA: Harvard University Press, 1937.

Pressler, Carolyn. *Joshua, Judges, and Ruth*. Westminster Bible Commentary. Louisville, KY: Westminster John Knox Press, 2002.

———. *The View of Women Found in the Deuteronomic Family Laws*. Beihefte zur Zeitschrift für die alttestamentliche Wissenschaft 216. Berlin: Walter de Gruyter, 1993.

Reno, R. R. "God and Mammon." In *I Am the Lord Your God: Christian Reflections on the Ten Commandments,* edited by Carl E. Braaten and Christopher R. Seitz, 218–36. Grand Rapids: Wm. B. Eerdmans Publishing Co., 2005.

Riemann, Paul. "Am I My Brother's Keeper?" *Interpretation* 24 (1970): 482–91.

Ringe, Sharon. "Holy as the Lord Your God Commanded You: Sabbath in the New Testament." *Interpretation* 59 (2006): 17–24.

Rofe, Alexander. "The Tenth Commandment in the Light of Four Deuteronomic Laws." In *The Ten Commandments in History and Tradition,* edited by Ben-Zion Segal and Gershon Levi, 45–65. Jerusalem: Magnes Press, 1990.

Rordorf, Willy. *Sunday: The History of the Day of Rest and Worship in the Earliest Centuries of the Christian Church.* Philadelphia: Westminster Press, 1968.

Rösel, Martin. *Adonaj—warum Gott "Herr" genannt wird.* Forschungen zum Alten Testament 29. Tübingen: Mohr Siebeck, 2000.

Sakenfeld, Katharine D. *Ruth.* Interpretation: A Bible Commentary for Teaching and Preaching. Louisville, KY: John Knox Press, 1999.

Scharbert, J. "ʾālâ." In *Theological Dictionary of the Old Testament,* 1: 261–66. Grand Rapids: Wm. B. Eerdmans Publishing Co., 1974.

Schechter, S. *Facsimiles of the Fragments Hitherto Recovered of the Book of Ecclesiasticus in Hebrew.* London: Oxford University Press, 1901.

Schmidt, Werner, with Holger Delkurt and Axel Graupner. *Die zehn Gebote im Rahmen alttestamentlicher Ethik.* Erträge der Forschung 281. Darmstadt: Wissenschiftliche Buchgesellschaft, 1993.

Schweiker, William. "Divine Command Ethics and the Otherness of God." In *Power, Value, and Conviction: Theological Ethics in the Postmodern Age,* 155–70. Cleveland: Pilgrim Press, 1998.

———. "Reconsidering Greed." In *Having: Property and Possession in Religious and Social Life,* edited by William Schweiker and Charles Mathewes, 249–71. Grand Rapids: Wm. B. Eerdmans Publishing Co., 2004.

———. *Responsibility and Christian Ethics.* New Studies in Christian Ethics. Cambridge: Cambridge University Press, 1995.

Seow, Choon-Leong. "A Heterotextual Perspective." In *Homosexuality and Christian Community*, edited by Choon-Leong Seow, 14–27. Louisville, KY: Westminster John Knox Press, 1996.

Sheahen, Laura. "Beliefwatch Thou Shalt." *Newsweek*, September 4, 2006.

Shubin, Seymour. *Witness to Myself*. New York. Dorchester Publishing Co., 2006.

Soulen, R. Kendall. "The Name of the Holy Trinity: A Triune Name." *Theology Today* 59 (2002): 244–61.

Swezey, Charles. "Exodus 20:16—'Thou shalt not bear false witness against thy neighbor.'" *Interpretation* 34 (1980): 405–10.

Thomas Aquinas. *Summa theologiae*. Vol. 29, *The Old Law*. New York: McGraw-Hill, 1969.

Tigay, Jeffrey H. *Deuteronomy*. The JPS Torah Commentary. Philadelphia: The Jewish Publication Society, 1996.

Tillich, Paul. *The Protestant Era*. Chicago: University of Chicago Press, 1948.

Van Seters, John. *A Law Book for the Diaspora: Revision in the Study of the Covenant Code*. New York: Oxford University Press, 2003.

Walsh, Jerome T. "Leviticus 18:22 and 20:13: Who Is Doing What to Whom?" *Journal of Biblical Literature* 120 (2001): 201–9.

Weinfeld, Moshe. *Social Justice in Ancient Israel and the Ancient Near East*. Minneapolis: Fortress Press, 1995.

Welker, Michael. "Recht in den biblischen Überlieferungen in systematisch-theologischer Sicht." *Das Recht der Kirche*, vol. 1, *Zur Theorie des Kirchenrechts*, edited by Gerhard Rau, Hans-Richard Reuter, and Klaus Schlaich, 390–414. Gütersloh: Gütersloher Verlagshaus, 1997.

———. "Security of Expectations: Reformulating the Theology of Law and Gospel." *Journal of Religion* 66 (1986): 237–60.

Westbrook, Raymond. "The Prohibition on Restoration of Marriage in Deuteronomy 24:1–4." In *Studies in Bible 1986*, edited by Sara Japhet, 387–405. Scripta Hierosolymitana 31. Jerusalem: Magnus Press, 1986.

Westermann, Claus. *Genesis 1–11: A Commentary*. Minneapolis: Augsburg Press, 1984.

———. *Genesis 12–36: A Commentary*. Minneapolis: Augsburg Press, 1985.

445

Wilgoren, Jodi. "Citing Issue of Fairness, Governor Clears Out Death Row in Illinois." *New York Times*, January 12, 2003.

———. "Panel in Illinois Seeks to Reform Death Sentence." *New York Times*, April 14, 2002.

Williamson, Lamar. *Mark*. Interpretation: A Bible Commentary for Preaching and Teaching. Atlanta: John Knox Press, 1983.

Willis-Watkins, David. *The Second Commandment and Church Reform: The Colloquy of St. Germain-en-Laye, 1562*. Studies in Reformed Theology and History 2/2. Princeton: Princeton Theological Seminary, 1994.

Wolff, Hans Walter. "The Day of Rest in the Old Testament." *Lexington Theological Quarterly* 7 (1972): 65–92.

———. *Dodekapropheten*. Vol. 4, *Micha*. Biblischer Kommentar 14. Neukirchen: Neukirchener Verlag, 1982.

Wright, N. T. *The Climax of the Covenant: Christ and Law in Pauline Theology*. Minneapolis: Fortress Press, 1992.

Yoder, John H. "Exodus 20:13—'Thou shalt not kill.'" *Interpretation* 34 (1980): 394–99.

SCRIPTURE INDEX

447

451

452

453

457

459

SUBJECT INDEX

461